Oracle Press™

Oracle Database 11*g*: Building Oracle XML DB Applications

Jinyu Wang

New York Chicago San Francisco
Lisbon London Madrid Mexico City Milan
New Delhi San Juan Seoul Singapore Sydney Toronto

The McGraw-Hill Companies

Cataloging-in-Publication Data is on file with the Library of Congress

Oracle Database 11*g*: Building Oracle XML DB Applications

1 2 3 4 5 6 7 8 9 0 DOC DOC 1 0 9 8 7 6 5 4 3 2 1

ISBN 978-0-07-175129-2
MHID 0-07-175129-7

Sponsoring Editor
Wendy Rinaldi

Editorial Supervisor
Janet Walden

Project Manager
Tania Andrabi, Cenveo Publisher Services

Acquisitions Coordinator
Stephanie Evans

Technical Editors
Coby D. Adams Jr., Vikas Arora, Kongyi Zhou

Copy Editor
Paul Tyler

Proofreader
Carol Shields

Indexer
Karin Arrigoni

Production Supervisor
James Kussow

Composition
Cenveo Publisher Services

Illustration
Cenveo Publisher Services

Art Director, Cover
Jeff Weeks

Cover Designer
Pattie Lee

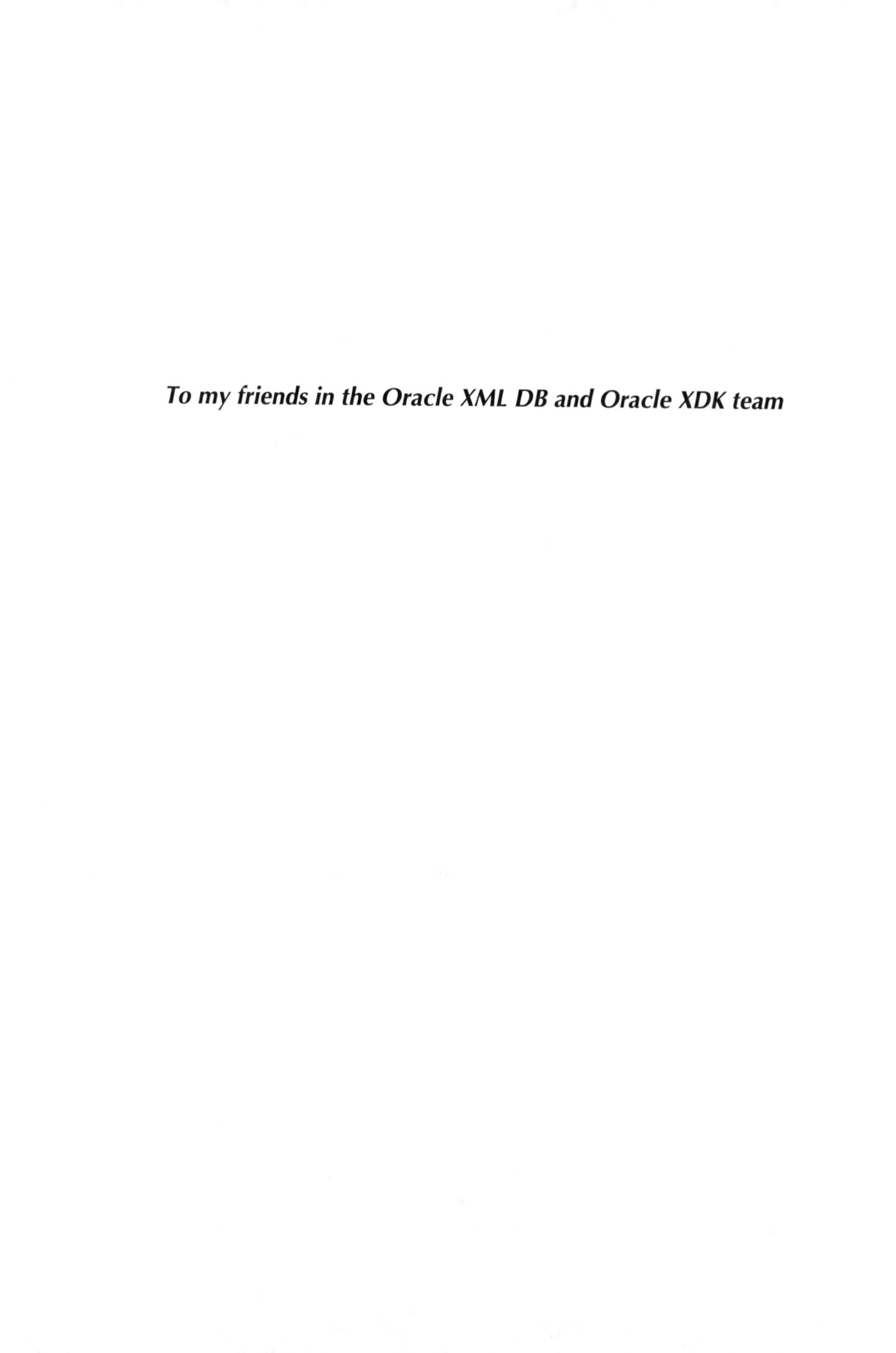

To my friends in the Oracle XML DB and Oracle XDK team

About the Author

Jinyu Wang is a principal product manager in the Oracle Server Technology product management team. She has managed several Oracle products over the last 10 years in Oracle, including Oracle XDK, Oracle XML DB, Oracle Secure Enterprise Search (SES), and Oracle Text. Jinyu's current interests are in database, XML, and search. Jinyu frequently speaks at conferences, publishes papers in journals, and holds U.S. patents. She is a coauthor of *Oracle Database 10g XML & SQL: Design, Build, & Manage XML Applications in Java, C, C++, & PL/SQL* (McGraw-Hill/Oracle Press, 2004).

About the Technical Editors

Coby D. Adams Jr. is a United States Navy veteran and 16-year IT professional specializing in Oracle Database Technologies. He is certified as an Oracle Certified Professional, Microsoft Certified Database Administrator, and Microsoft Certified Systems Engineer. He worked as a network administrator and database administrator for five years before joining Oracle Corporation. As a member of Oracle Global Customer Support he has risen to the level of Senior Principal Support engineer and has held the responsibility of Global Technical Lead for XML Database for the last five years.

Vikas Arora is director of the XML development team at Oracle Corporation, overseeing the development of XML Objects and Extensibility support in the Oracle database, as well as XML Development Kit (XDK) libraries for Java and C. Prior to his management role, Vikas worked as technical staff in the SQL Query, Data Dictionary, Objects, and Language interoperability areas. Vikas holds a B.Tech from Indian Institute of Technology, Kharagpur, and an M.S. from University of California, Santa Barbara.

Kongyi Zhou has been a senior developer in the Oracle XDK group for more than 10 years. He is the lead developer in Java XML parser, DOM, XML Schema processor, and XST/XPath processors. His recent work is in streaming processing, Scalable DOM, and Binary XML. He also represents Oracle in the W3C XML Schema working group.

Contents at a Glance

PART III
Building XML Applications

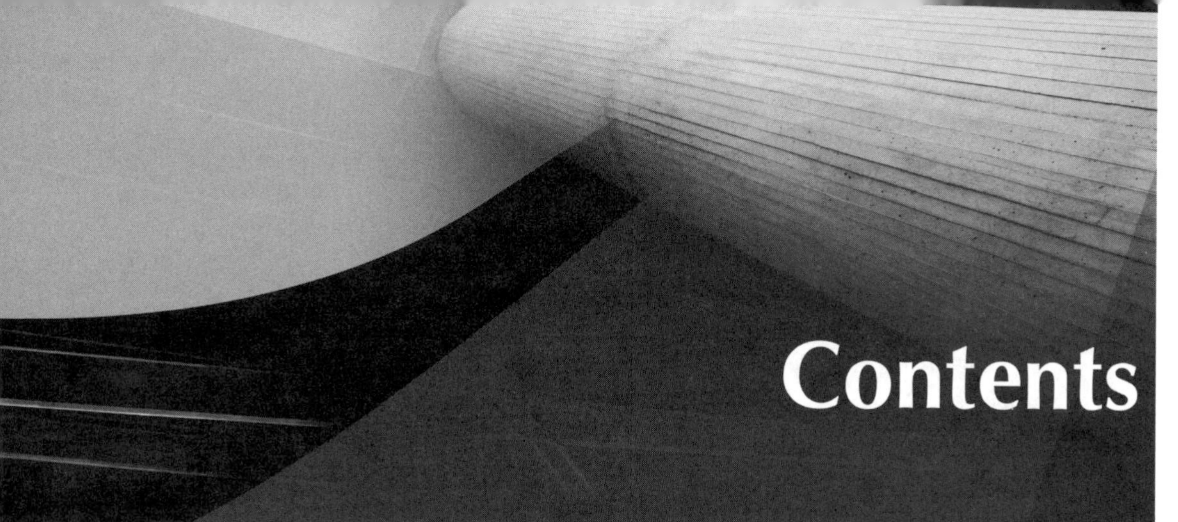

Contents

PART II
MANAGING ORACLE XML DATABASE

Acknowledgments

I appreciate my Oracle colleagues, customers, and partners. With their help and talent, I am able to enjoy exploring incredible technologies and solutions.

I also thank my acquisitions team at McGraw-Hill, Stephanie Evans and Wendy Rinaldi, for making this book possible.

Many thanks to the technical reviewers: Coby Adams, Vikas Arora, and Kongyi Zhou. Many thanks to other reviewers and those who helped me with the technical problems, including Shijun Cheng, Susan Duncan, Geoff Lee, Tim Yu, Hui Zhang, Vadiraj Hosur, Mark Dake, Nipun Agarwal, Ravi Palakodet, Rohan Anguish, Sam Idicula, Thomas Baby, Timothy Chien, and Vinay Agarwal. Thanks for your patience in explaining the product features, and for the valuable discussions on the technology and products.

Thanks to my managers, Vishu Krishnamurthy and Andrew Mendelsohn. Your support makes my journey at Oracle challenging but enjoyable.

Introduction

Since first published in 1998, XML has become one of the core Internet technologies. XML now has spawned an entire family of standards that form the foundation of electronic publishing, information sharing, and application integrations.

If you are an Oracle database developer, choosing to use XML can simplify your tasks and bring efficiency to data access and operations. XML and its processing are also flexible enough to allow you to complete tasks in different ways. However, XML's strength is also its weakness: XML's format and processing are infinitely flexible and extensible. Therefore, quite often, there are a myriad of ways that you can use XML technologies to achieve the same goal. You may have difficulty choosing the best approach. This book provides you with the means to put Oracle XML technology to work by exploring the product features with examples, and by demonstrating best practices when using the XML technologies to build Oracle database applications.

If you are an Oracle DBA, your decisions involve where and how to store the XML documents, what to allow access to the XML data, and how to optimize Oracle database performance for XML storage and operations. This book explains XML storage options, backup and recovery strategies, and the basic techniques to manage XML storage and security.

In general, this book is written so that you can work through examples to update your knowledge of Oracle XML technologies in Oracle Database 11*g*.

Content Structure

The book is divided into three parts.

Part I: Basic Concepts and Technologies

Part I discusses the basic XML concepts and Oracle XML DB product features. The content is presented via short examples highlighting best practices and potential pitfalls.

Chapter 1 provides a high-level overview of Oracle's XML technologies. The discussion walks you through Oracle's XML support and explains several key concepts for XML processing and management. You will learn how to create your first XML programs.

Chapter 2 introduces *XMLType*, the native XML object type in the Oracle database. You will learn how to create, store, query, and update XMLTypes in Oracle Database 11*g*.

Chapter 3 continues the XMLType discussion to explain a file-based XML storage in the Oracle database called Oracle XML DB Repository. You will learn what it is, how to enable it, and when to use it.

Chapter 4 explains how to parse XML in Java and SQL. The discussion gives examples for both DOM and SAX parsing, and introduces the new *Scalable DOM* and *binary XML* parsing techniques in Oracle Database 11*g*.

Chapter 5 explains XML Schema/DTD and the XML validation processing inside and outside the Oracle database.

Chapter 6 discusses XPath and its processing and builds the foundation for understanding XSLT and XQuery.

Chapter 7 explains XSLT and how to use it in Java and SQL.

Chapter 8 explains XQuery and how to use it to process XML in Oracle XML DB.

Chapter 9 discusses XML support on relational tables, including how to load XML documents into relational tables, how to create XML documents from relational tables, and how to create SQL view from XMLTypes.

Chapter 10 discusses XML full-text search using XMLType queries, Oracle Text, and Oracle Secure Enterprise Search (SES). The chapter provides step-by-step instructions to create an enterprise search application for searching XML documents.

Part II: Managing Oracle XML Database

Part II discusses Oracle XML DB management techniques including installation, storage management, backup and recovery, security, and performance tuning.

Chapter 11 explains the Oracle XML DB installation steps.

Chapter 12 discusses XMLType storage options and explains how you can review XML storage in Oracle Database 11*g*.

Chapter 13 provides the steps needed for XML DB backup and recovery.

Chapter 14 describes the security for XML DB and discusses various performance tuning techniques.

Part III: Building XML Applications

Part III discusses how to build XML applications using Oracle Database 11*g* and Oracle XML technologies.

Chapter 15 explains how to build a Web Service application using XMLType and the Oracle XML DB Web Services feature.

Chapter 16 explains how to use Oracle JDeveloper 11*g* XML features to create XML documents and deploy/debug XML applications. The discussion includes an example creating a Java Stored Procedure in the Oracle database to run XSLT 2.0 (a subset of XSLT 2.0 features).

Chapter 17 builds a Web-based database application using Oracle Database 11*g* to manage contacts stored in XML files. The XML documents are stored in Oracle XML DB Repository. Web publishing and management is set up with Oracle Application Express (APEX). In this application, you learn how to create, update, and transform XML documents in APEX applications. You will find examples on integrating APEX applications with search applications, and sending personalized emails using Oracle XML DB.

Finally, the Appendix provides the APEX installation steps for Oracle Database 11*g*.

If you have questions or suggestions regarding the book, please send an email to jinyu.wang@oraclexmlbook.com. I welcome your feedback.

About the Examples

All of the examples provided in this book are organized in Oracle JDeveloper applications. You can download the examples and find additional material and updates for the book at www.oraclexmlbook.com and www.mhprofessional.com. All of the examples have been tested with the following products:

- Oracle Database 11*g*R2 (11.2.0.2) including Oracle XML DB, Oracle XDK, Oracle APEX, and Oracle Text
- Oracle JDeveloper 11*g* (11.1.1.4.0)
- Oracle Secure Enterprise Search 11*g* (11.1.2)

To run the examples, please first refer to Chapter 11 to make sure Oracle XML DB is installed. Then, there are a few additional setup steps needed:

1. Create a demo user in your Oracle Database 11*g*R2 instance (by default we use XMLDEMO) to run database examples. For example, you can log in to SYS user (as SYSDBA) and run the following commands (*create_xmldemo_user.sql*):

```
create user xmldemo identified by xmldemo;
grant resources, connect to xmldemo;
grant create any directory to xmldemo;
grant alter session to xmldemo;
grant create view to xmldemo;
-- Needed to run Dynamic SQL
grant create any table to xmldemo;
-- Needed to create materialized views
grant create materialized view to xmldemo;
-- Needed to run Oracle Text
grant ctxapp to xmldemo;
```

2. Create a database directory (*xml_dir*) pointing to the sample data directory (*$EXAMPLE_HOME/data,* where $EXAMPLE_HOME is the folder in which you extract the downloaded example zip file for the book). This folder contains the sample XML documents. You need to connect to the XMLDEMO user to run the following command (*create_directory.sql*):

   ```
   create directory xml_dir as 'D:\xmlbook\data';
   grant read on directory xml_dir to xmldemo;
   ```

   In this example, the $EXAMPLE_HOME/data folder is *D:\xmlbook\data.*

3. To optimize the SQL query output, run the following commands in SQL*Plus after logging in to the XMLDEMO user:

   ```
   set serveroutput on
   set long 100000
   set pagesize 80
   ```

4. Upload the subdirectories (the subfolders) under the *$EXAMPLE_HOME/data* folder to the */public* folder in Oracle XML DB Repository before running the examples. Any path changes require code changes in the examples.

5. If this is the first time you have run Java examples in Oracle JDeveloper 11*g*, please refer to Chapter 16 for more information.

PART I

Basic Concepts and Technologies

CHAPTER 1

Introducing Oracle XML DB

ML (W3C XML Standard 1.0) stands for *eXtensible Markup Language*. XML defines a standard to encode documents with data (content) and metadata. Over the past 10 years, XML has been widely used for electronic publishing, data transmission, and application integrations.

Oracle XML Database (XML DB) refers to the database technology in the Oracle database designed to store, manage, and retrieve XML. In the enterprise database applications, Oracle XML DB plays a key role in offering large-scale XML data storage, simplified XML data management, and high-performance XML retrieval and processing.

This chapter introduces XML and Oracle XML DB through a discussion of key XML DB components, its native XMLType storage, and the basic XML processing capabilities.

EXAMPLE SETUP
If this is the first time you run XML DB SQL commands, please refer to Chapter 11 for instructions on how to set up Oracle XML DB. You also need to complete the example setup described in the "About the Examples" section in the Introduction to this book.

What Is Oracle XML DB?

Oracle introduced Oracle XML DB as part of Oracle9*i*R2. Oracle XML DB is a built-in component inside the Oracle database, which extends the Oracle database's relational storage by adding *XMLType*, a new native XML storage type. XMLType becomes the fundamental component in Oracle XML DB for XML storage, retrieval, and processing.

XMLType simplifies the XML storage, retrieval, and processing in the Oracle database. Without native XML storage, XML documents have to be either "shredded" to store in multiple relational tables and then render XML as the output, or store XML intact as large text/binary objects in CLOBs or BLOBs. XML's *hierarchical* data structure normally doesn't work well with the relational *table-row* format. Storing XML in relational tables can easily lose the XML document fidelity. Re-creating XML with table joins can also result in long-running queries. Storing XML in text/binary objects well-preserves the XML document; however, because it lacks efficient XML data retrieval, the storage can't be used by mission-critical applications demanding high performance on XML data access. The native XML storage not only eliminates the processing burden to "shred" and re-creates XML from tables, but it also enables built-in performance optimizations for XML-based queries and updates.

Oracle XML DB is different from "pure" XML databases. Because it is seamlessly integrated within the Oracle database, it effectively bridges the gaps between relational and native XML storage. Using Oracle XML DB, you can easily leverage the power of both in a single database.

What Is Provided by Oracle XML DB?

Figure 1-1 summarizes Oracle XML DB architecture and its XML storage and processing capabilities.

Inside Oracle XML DB, XML documents are stored in XMLTypes. XMLTypes preserve XML documents and provide XML-based APIs, such as XPath query and *XQuery*, to access the XML data.

In Oracle Database 11*g*, XMLTypes can reside in *relational tables* as a *column*, in an XMLType *object table*, or can be stored in XML DB repository, which is a file system inside the Oracle database.

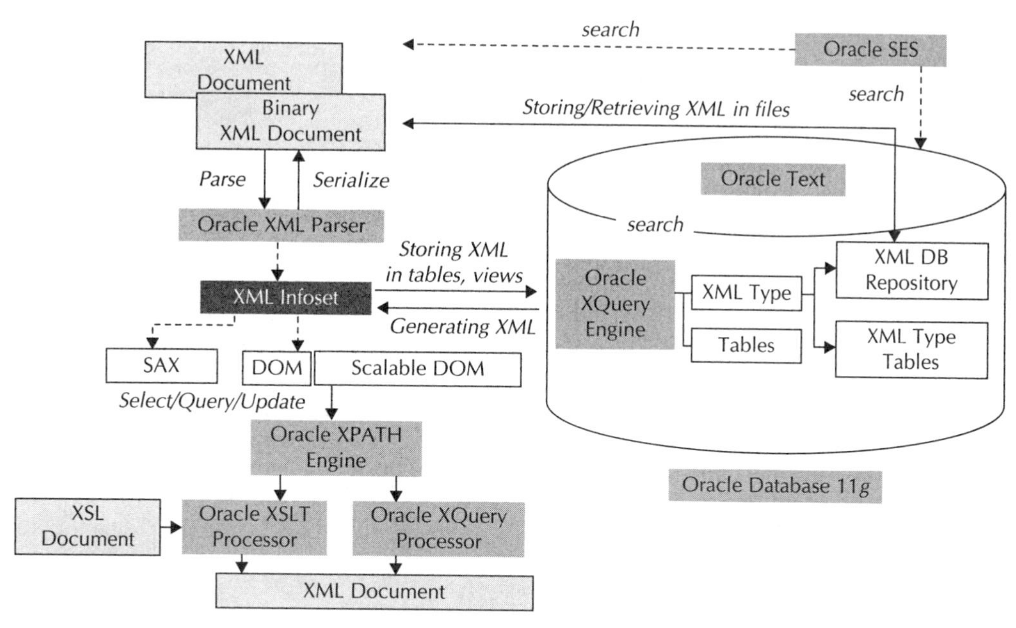

FIGURE 1-1. *Oracle XML DB and its XML features*

XMLType can be stored in different formats. XMLType can be stored in CLOBs, called *CLOB* XMLType. XMLType can also be stored in object-relational tables, called *Object-Relational* (*O-R*) XMLType, in which XML data is internally mapped to a set of object relational tables. In Oracle Database 11*g*, XMLType has a new format called *Binary* XMLType. Binary XMLType stores XML in a pre-parsed binary format with compressed storage and optimized query access. The binary XML format is defined as an Oracle standard, which can be used across Oracle applications.

XMLType can have assigned XML Schema(s), which is then differentiated to be either an XML Schema-based or non-XML-Schema-based XMLType.

XMLType can be searched. Oracle full-text search tools, including both Oracle Text and Oracle Secure Enterprise Search (SES), can create full-text indexes on XML documents stored in XMLType and enable content search.

Outside Oracle Database 11*g*, you can process XML and XMLType objects using the Oracle XML processing tools. The processing tools are mainly offered by Oracle XML Developer's Kit (XDK), Oracle XML DB Java library, and Oracle JDeveloper. Using these XML processing tools, you can perform basic XML processing such as XML parsing, Document Type Definition (DTD) and XML Schema validations, XSL transformations, and XMLType operations.

In summary, Oracle XML DB enhances the Oracle database by adding the native XML storage and processing capabilities to develop XML capabilities.

What Is Native XML Storage?

Native XMLType storage is essential to XML DB operations. Let's start by learning a few key details about it.

Well-Formedness Rules

As a native XML object, XMLType only stores well-formed XML documents or XML fragments. The following is an example XML document (*john_smith.xml*):

```
<?xml version="1.0" encoding="UTF-8"?>
<contact xmlns="http://xmlbook.com/sample/contact.xsd" id="1">
  <category>customer</category>
  <first_name Chinese="约翰">John</first_name>
  <last_name>Smith</last_name>
  <email>john.smith@hfarm.com</email>
</contact>
```

In the XML document, there are a set of tags (or markups), such as *<contact>*, *<first_name>*, and *<last_name>*. Each *tag* explains the content and constructs an XML element. For example, *<contact>* creates a contact XML element; *<first_name>* creates a first name element; and *<last_name>* creates a last name element. The nested XML elements structure represents the elements' parent and child relationship; for example, the *<first_name>* within the *<contact>* element means the first name of the specified contact. XML elements can have *attributes* defined in *name-value* pairs. For example, `id="1"` and `Chinese="约翰"` are both XML attributes.

XML Tip: Are XML names case sensitive?
Yes. Unlike SQL names, all XML names, including element tag names and attribute names are case sensitive. For example, *<Contact>* and *<CONTACT>* are two different XML elements.

XML documents can have *namespaces*. An XML namespace provides a method to avoid the name conflicts. XML namespaces can be defined in two formats: the *default* namespace and the *prefixed* namespace. A *default* XML namespace is defined using `xmlns:="..."` with no namespace prefix. This means the current XML element and its child elements without namespace prefixes will have the default namespace. The default namespace can be specified at any level of the XML document and has the effect of overriding previous namespace declarations. In the example XML document, the default namespace is set to be `xmlns="http://xmlbook.com/sample/contact.xsd"`. A *prefixed* namespace is defined with a namespace prefix, in the format `xmlns:namespace_prefix="..."`. Any element or attribute with the namespace prefix will be part of the defined namespace.

XML Tip: What is the meaning of `xmlns="..."`?
A special case for default namespaces is `xmlns="..."`. This namespace definition removes the default namespace declaration from the document's sub-tree.

Elements or attributes with a namespace are referred to by their qualified names, which include both their names and namespace.

XML Tip: Does the default namespace apply to XML attributes?
No. If you want the XML attributes to have the namespace, you have to define them with the namespace prefix. If you don't do this, the attributes will have no namespace.

XML *well-formedness* rules include a set of rules for the XML elements, attributes, and XML contents, which are summarized as follows:

- All XML elements have to be enclosed within a start tag and a matching end tag. Text can be added between XML tags as the XML element's content. In the given example, the *<first_name>* element's content is `John`.
- All XML attributes are represented as `name="value"` pairs and defined within an XML element's start tag. In the example, `id="1"` is an attribute of the *<contact>* element.
- All XML elements have to be well nested without missing or overlapping. This means the "child" element has to be well nested inside its "parent" element, with both its start tag and end tag within its "parent."
- There is one and only one root XML element per XML document.
- XML can only contain properly encoded legal Unicode characters. Certain characters such as "<" or "&" must be escaped. We will discuss XML special characters later in this chapter.

Content stored in XMLType has to be compliant with the rules. The well-formedness rule-checking is performed when creating XMLTypes. Any error is shown as an XML parsing error.

The following example creates an XMLType from a well-formed XML document and checks the namespace of the XML document element with the XMLType.getnamespace() function (*get_namespace.sql*).

Listing 1-1 *Getting the Namespaces of XMLType*

```
select XMLType( '<?xml version="1.0" encoding="UTF-8"?>
<contact xmlns="http://xmlbook.com/sample/contact.xsd" id="1">
  <category>customer</category>
  <first_name Chinese="约翰">John</first_name>
  <last_name>Smith</last_name>
  <email>john.smith@hfarm.com</email>
</contact>').getnamespace() AS result
from dual;

RESULT
----------------------------------------------------------------------------
http://xmlbook.com/sample/contact.xsd
```

XML Encoding

XMLType stores XML documents in the database character encoding. To create XMLTypes, you need to understand the XML document's encoding and its conversion to the database character encoding. In XML documents, the encoding is specified in the *encoding* attribute of the XML prologue as follows:

```
<?xml version="1.0" encoding="UTF-8">
```

The *encoding* attribute should be consistent with the document's actual encoding. Otherwise, the XML parsing will raise errors.

When an XML document contains multi-byte characters, you need to make sure that both the XML encoding and the database character set can handle multi-byte characters. It is recommended that you use *AL32UTF8*. In the Oracle database, you can check the database character set with the following command:

Listing 1-2 *Checking Database Character Set*

```
select value$ from props$ where name='NLS_CHARACTERSET';
```

When creating XMLTypes from documents stored outside of the Oracle database, you need to properly set up the NLS_LANG environment variable to ensure a correct encoding conversion from the XML document's encoding to the database encoding. The NLS_LANG is in the following format:

```
NLS_LANG=<language>_<territory>.<character set>
```

An example to check the user client's environment language setting is shown here:

```
select userenv('language') from dual;

USERENV('LANGUAGE')
----------------------------------------------------
AMERICAN_AMERICA.AL32UTF8
```

NLS_LANG tells the Oracle database what character encoding is used on the client side. For example, to load the example XML document (*john_smith.xml*) containing Chinese characters to Oracle XML DB, you can set the NLS_LANG environment variable as follows (we use Windows platform as an example):

```
set NLS_LANG= SIMPLIFIED CHINESE_CHINA.ZHS16GBK
```

Oracle Database Tip: Why do I get unrecognized characters in SQL*Plus prompted messages after setting NLS_LANG?

You also need to set up the operating system to properly display non-Unicode characters. For example, on Windows, you need to select Start | Control Panel | Regional and Language Options | Advanced | Language and set Non-Unicode Programs to Chinese (PRC) in the example. The `NLS_LANG` needs be set to ZHS16GBK.

Then, connect to a database user (i.e., XMLDEMO) and run the following SQL command (*create_xmltype.sql*):

Listing 1-3 *Loading XML with Multi-byte Characters to Oracle Database*

```
select XMLType(bfilename('XML_DIR', 'chp01/john_smith.xml'),
       nls_charset_id ('AL32UTF8')) result from dual;
```

This example uses the database directory (XML_DIR) created in the example set up and the bfilename() function to read the XML file stored outside of the Oracle database. Note that the database directory name has to be capitalized. Otherwise, you will get the following error:

```
ORA-22285: non-existent directory or file for FILEOPEN operation
ORA-06512: at "SYS.XMLTYPE", line 296
ORA-06512: at line 1
```

The XML document returned is shown in SQL*Plus:

```
RESULT
-----------------------------------------------------------
<?xml version="1.0" encoding="GBK"?>
<contact xmlns="http://xmlbook.com/sample/contact.xsd" id="1">
  <first_name Chinese="约翰">John</first_name>
  <last_name>Smith</last_name>
</contact>
```

The automatic conversion from the local client encoding to database encoding has taken place.

Oracle XML DB Tip: Why do I get the OCI-31011: *XML parsing failed* error when creating an XMLType object?

If you can parse the XML document outside the Oracle database, but you get this error when creating an XMLType object, it is normally because `NLS_LANG` either is not set up or its setup is incorrect. For example, if `NLS_LANG` is not set up, the following SQL command returns an XML parsing error:

```
SQL> select XMLType(bfilename('XML_DIR', 'chp01/john_smith.xml'), NLS_
CHARSET_ID ('AL32UTF8')) from dual;
ERROR:
OCI-31011: XML parsing failed
```

Special Characters

To store XML in XMLTypes, several special characters have an effect on the XMLType creation.

XML Special Characters

First, you need to properly include XML special characters. Table 1-1 lists some XML special characters and their escaped formats. You can find more information on the XML special characters in the W3C XML specification (www.w3.org/TR/REC-xml/).

In an XML document, two special characters, the ampersand character (&) and the left angle bracket (<), have to be escaped or included in a CDATA `(<![CDATA[ ...]]>)` section. Violation of this will result in violating the well-formedness rule and reporting XML parsing errors. For example, you will get an XML parsing error without escaping XML characters in the following example (*escape_char_xmltype.sql*):

Listing 1-4 *Escaping Ampersand (&) in XMLType() Functions*

```
set define off
select XMLType('<?xml version="1.0" encoding="UTF-8"?>
<contact xmlns="http://xmlbook.com/sample/contact.xsd" id="1">
  <category>customer</category>
  <first_name Chinese="约翰">John</first_name>
  <last_name>Smith</last_name>
  <email>john.smith@hfarm.com</email>
  <web url="http://localhost:7777/people.jsp?id=307387&ilocation_id=221-1"/></
contact>') as result
from dual;

 ERROR:
 ORA-31011: XML parsing failed
 ORA-19202: Error occurred in XML processing
 LPX-00241: entity reference is not well formed
 Error at line 1
```

The error is caused by the unescaped ampersand (&). XML parser treats the ampersand (&) as the start of an entity reference. Without the entity reference defined, the error will appear. The correct SQL command to create the XMLType is as follows:

```
set define off
select XMLType('<?xml version="1.0" encoding="UTF-8"?>
<contact xmlns="http://xmlbook.com/sample/contact.xsd" id="1">
  <category>customer</category>
  <first_name Chinese="约翰">John</first_name>
  <last_name>Smith</last_name>
  <email>john.smith@hfarm.com</email>
  <web url="http://localhost:7777/people.jsp?id=307387&amp;ilocation_
id=221-1"/></contact>') as result
from dual;
```

Characters	References	Notes
< (less than) > (greater than)	`<` (`<`) `>` (`>`)	The less-than character (<) starts *element markup* (the first character of a start tag or an end tag). The greater-than character (>) ends a start tag or an end tag.
& (ampersand)	`&` (`&`)	The ampersand character (&) starts *entity markup* (the first character of an entity reference).
" (double quote)	`"` (`"`)	The double-quote character (") can be symbolized with this character entity reference when you need to embed a double quote inside a string that is already double quoted. You don't have to escape this if the string is not already double quoted.
' (single quote)	`'` (`'`)	The apostrophe or single-quote character (') can be symbolized with this character entity reference when you need to embed a single quote or apostrophe inside a string that is already single quoted. You don't have to use this if the character is not embedded in a single quote.

TABLE 1-1. *XML Special Characters*

XML Tip: Can I define XML entities using XML Schema?

No, you can't. You can define entities using DTD. For example, you can define a copyright entity as follows:

```
<!ENTITY copyright "#xA69;"> or <!ENTITY copyright "#169;">
```

With XML Schema, you can only use special characters in Unicode format. For example, the copyright entity's Unicode format is &xA69; and the ampersand (&) is &.

Another approach to include XML special characters is to use a `<![CDATA ...]]>` section. An example is shown as follows (*cdata_xmltype.sql*):

Listing 1-5 *Including CDATA in XMLType() function*

```
set define off
select XMLType('<?xml version="1.0" encoding="UTF-8"?>
<contact xmlns="http://xmlbook.com/sample/contact.xsd" id="1">
  <category>customer</category>
  <first_name Chinese="约翰">John</first_name>
  <last_name>Smith</last_name>
  <email>john.smith@hfarm.com</email>
  <web><![CDATA[http://localhost:7777/people.jsp?id=307387&ilocation_
id=221-1"]]></web></contact>') as result
from dual;
```

You can also create a CDATA section using SQL/XML and append the updates to the XMLType as follows (*escape_char_sqlxml.sql*):

Listing 1-6 *Creating a CDATA Section in SQL/XML*

```
select XMLType('<?xml version="1.0" encoding="UTF-8"?>
<contact xmlns="http://xmlbook.com/sample/contact.xsd" id="1">
  <category>customer</category>
  <first_name Chinese="约翰">John</first_name>
  <last_name>Smith</last_name>
  <email>john.smith@hfarm.com</email></contact>').appendchildxml('/contact',
  XMLElement("web",
   XMLCDATA('http://localhost:7777/people.jsp?id=307387&ilocation_id=221-1')),
'xmlns="http://xmlbook.com/sample/contact.xsd"')
from dual
```

Another example is to escape a less-than character in a comparison condition in an XSL stylesheet, as shown here:

Listing 1-7 *Escaping Less-Than (<) Character in XSL Stylesheet*

```
<xsl:if test="position() &lt; 5">
```

In XSL Stylesheet, you normally escape the less-than (<) and greater-than (>) characters in the XPath condition statements so that the XSL stylesheet is a well-formed XML document.

SQL and SQL*Plus Special Characters

Second, you need to properly handle the special characters in SQL and SQL*Plus. Table 1-2 lists the special characters.

Special Character	Notes
& (ampersand)	This needs to be escaped when using SQL*Plus because SQL*Plus uses *¶meter_name* to allow prompted inputs. In SQL*Plus, the SET DEFINE OFF setting can be changed to allow & (ampersand) to be used in text.
' (single quote)	Single quote is used to quote string variables in SQL. Therefore, if the content has the single quote, you have to add another ' (single quote) to escape it. The double quote is actually represented by four single quotes ('''').

TABLE 1-2. *SQL and SQL*Plus Special Characters*

The ampersand (&) in SQL*Plus is used for the prompt inputs. When processing XML documents containing & or *&*, you can use the *SET DEFINE OFF* command. The single quote is used in SQL to quote string variables. When processing XML documents containing single quote (') in SQL, we need to use another single quote to escape the character. Let's look at an example that creates an XMLType from an XML document containing single quotes (*escape_char_sql.sql*):

Listing 1-8 *Escaping SQL Characters in XML Functions*

```
set define off
select XMLTransform(XMLTYPE('<?xml version="1.0" encoding="UTF-8"?>
<session url="http://www.xmlbook.com/session_details.jsp?isid=307387&amp;
ilocation_id=221-1"></session>'),
XMLType('<?xml version="1.0" encoding="UTF-8"?>
<xsl:stylesheet version="1.0" xmlns:xsl="http://www.w3.org/1999/XSL/Transform">
 <xsl:output indent="yes" media-type="text/xml"
             cdata-section-elements="session_link"/>
 <xsl:template match="session">
  <xsl:if test="@url !=''''">
  <result>
   <session_link>
    <xsl:attribute name="url">
     <xsl:value-of select="@url" disable-output-escaping="yes"/>
    </xsl:attribute>
    <![CDATA[<notes>The ampersand (&) in the session link url needs to be
escaped.</notes>]]>
   </session_link>
   <copyright>&#169; XMLBook.com</copyright>
  </result>
  </xsl:if>
  <xsl:apply-templates/>
 </xsl:template>
</xsl:stylesheet>')) from dual;
```

In this example, in addition to the *SET DEFINE OFF* command, we escape the single quote in the SQL statement by adding another single quote as the escaping character. Otherwise, we will get the following error:

```
ERROR:
ORA-01756: quoted string not properly terminated
```

Summary

This chapter introduces XML and Oracle XML DB. The highlights include the XML well-formedness rules, XML encoding, and special characters, which are involved in creating XMLTypes in the Oracle database. In general, you should create XMLTypes with well-formed XML documents, specify the correct XML document encodings, and escape all special characters as necessary.

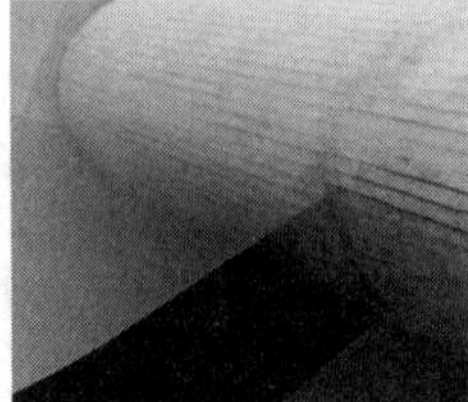

CHAPTER 2

Native XML Storage: XMLType

In Oracle XML DB, XMLType stores XML documents and is used to naively process XML data. This chapter extends the XMLType discussion in Chapter 1 by exploring the techniques for creating XMLTypes in various formats, updating XMLTypes, querying XMLTypes, and processing XMLTypes.

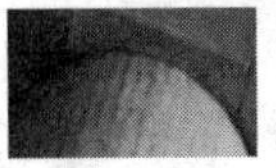

EXAMPLE SETUP

To run the Java examples in this chapter, you need to open the Oracle JDeveloper project using Oracle JDeveloper 11g. Please refer to Chapter 16 for more information on running applications in Oracle JDeveloper.

Creating XMLTypes

An XMLType can be a relational table *column*, an XMLType *object table*, a PL/SQL parameter, or a document resource in XML DB Repository. Let's learn about each of them through examples. A detailed discussion of creating XML DB Repository resources will be provided in Chapter 3.

The following example creates a relational table with an XMLType column (*create_xmltype_col.sql*):

Listing 2-1 *Creating an XMLType Column*

```
CREATE TABLE contact_tbl (id NUMBER, content XMLType)
XMLTYPE COLUMN "CONTENT" STORE AS BINARY XML;
```

The `XMLTYPE COLUMN "CONTENT" STORE AS BINARY XML` option specifies the binary XMLType format. We can check the table definition using the following command:

```
SQL> desc contact_tbl;
Name                                      Null?    Type
----------------------------------------- -------- ----------------------------
ID                                                 NUMBER
CONTENT                                            SYS.XMLTYPE STORAGE BINARY
```

You can also store XMLTypes in an XMLType object table as follows (*create_xmltype_xtbl.sql*):

Listing 2-2 *Creating an XMLType Table*

```
CREATE TABLE contact_xtbl of XMLType
XMLType STORE AS BINARY XML;

SQL> desc contact_xtbl;
 Name                                      Null?    Type
 ----------------------------------------- -------- ------------------
 TABLE of SYS.XMLTYPE STORAGE BINARY
```

To refer to the XMLType objects in the XMLType object table, we can use object_value (*insert_xmltype_col.sql*):

Listing 2-3 *Creating and Inserting XMLTypes*

```
INSERT INTO contact_xtbl(object_value) VALUES(' <?xml version = "1.0" encoding
= "UTF-8"?>
<!DOCTYPE contact SYSTEM "/public/chp02/contact.dtd">
<contact id="1">
 <first_name>John</first_name>
 <last_name>Smith</last_name>
</contact> ');
```

Note that you need to make sure that the DTD file has a valid file path in the XML DB Repository. Otherwise, you will get the following error:

```
ORA-31001: Invalid resource handle or path name "/public/chp02/contact.dtd"
```

This is due to parsing of the included DTD file. The *alter session set events='31156 trace name context forever, level 2'* command can be used to turn off the DTD parsing and validation in the current database session.

Then, we can retrieve the XML document from the XMLType table as follows (*print_xmltype_xtbl.sql*):

Listing 2-4 *Serializing XMLTypes*

```
SELECT XMLSerialize(CONTENT x.object_value AS CLOB) FROM contact_xtbl x;

XMLSERIALIZE(CONTENTX.OBJECT_VALUEASCLOB)
-----------------------------------------------
<?xml version="1.0" encoding="UTF-8"?>
<!DOCTYPE contact SYSTEM "/public/chp02/contact.dtd" [
<!ELEMENT contact (first_name, last_name)>
<!ATTLIST contact id CDATA #REQUIRED>
<!ELEMENT last_name (#PCDATA)>
<!ELEMENT first_name (#PCDATA)>
]>
<contact id="1">
  <first_name>John</first_name>
  <last_name>Smith</last_name>
</contact>
```

When using XMLSerialize(), the CONTENT keyword means that the data is an XML fragment. The DOCUMENT keyword means that the data are an XML document.

Oracle XML DB Tip: How do I refer to the object value in XMLType tables?
For O-R (Object-Relational) XMLType tables, you can use *xmldata*. For all XMLType tables, including binary and O-R XMLType tables, you can use *object_value*.

In a PL/SQL program, XMLType can be a PL/SQL variable. The following PL/SQL function specifies one function input as an XMLType (*create_xmltype_plsql.sql*):

Listing 2-5 *Printing XMLTypes*

```
CREATE OR REPLACE FUNCTION printxml(p_xml in XMLType, p_is_pretty in VARCHAR2
:= 'TRUE') RETURN CLOB AS
 v_output_xml CLOB;
BEGIN
 IF (p_is_pretty = 'TRUE') THEN
   SELECT XMLSerialize(DOCUMENT p_xml AS CLOB INDENT size=2) INTO v_output_xml
   FROM DUAL;
 ELSE
   SELECT XMLSerialize(DOCUMENT p_xml AS CLOB) INTO v_output_xml FROM DUAL;
 END IF;
 RETURN v_output_xml;
END;
```

The *p_xml* variable is the XMLType input. The function's default XML output is a "pretty" print XMLType. When the *p_is_pretty* variable is set to *FALSE*, the XML content is printed in a "compact" format shown as follows (*run_xmltype_plsql.sql*):

```
SELECT printxml(XMLType('<contact><first_name>john</first_name><last_
name>smith</last_name></contact>'), 'FALSE') output FROM dual;
OUTPUT
----------------------------------------
<contact><first_name>john</first_name><last_name>smith</last_name></contact>
```

When storing XML, we don't store it in a "pretty" print format. Using XMLSerialize(), however, can provide such "pretty" output. (Insignificant whitespaces are removed in XMLType storage, except in CLOB XMLType.)

In addition to creating XMLType from text, you can use BFILE or DBUri. We will discuss DBUri in Chapter 3. Refer to Listing 1-3 in Chapter 1 to learn how to use BFILE to read XML files from file systems.

XML Schema–based XMLType

By default, without specifying XML schemas, XMLTypes are non-XML-Schema-based XMLTypes. However, in some applications, you may wish to create an XML Schema–based XMLType to optimize the XMLType storage and enable XML Schema–aware operations. To create an XML

Schema–based XMLType, you first need to register an XML schema (*contact.xsd*). The SQL command is shown as follows (*register_xsd_bfile.sql*):

Listing 2-6 *Registering an XML Schema from BFILE*

```
BEGIN
DBMS_XMLSCHEMA.registerSchema('http://xmlbook.com/sample/contact.xsd',
XMLType(bfilename('XML_DIR','contact/contact.xsd'),nls_charset_id('AL32UTF8')),
genTypes => FALSE,
genTables => FALSE,
options => DBMS_XMLSCHEMA.REGISTER_BINARYXML);
END;
/
```

This command registers an XML schema as `http://xmlbook.com/sample/contact.xsd`. The `DBMS_XMLSCHEMA.REGISTER_BINARYXML` option enables the XML schema to be used for binary XMLTypes.

To delete a registered XML schema, use the following command (*delete_xsd.sql*):

Listing 2-7 *Deleting an XML Schema*

```
BEGIN
DBMS_XMLSCHEMA.deleteSchema('http://xmlbook.com/sample/contact.xsd', DBMS_
XMLSCHEMA.DELETE_CASCADE_FORCE);
END;
/
```

The *DBMS_XMLSCHEMA.DELETE_CASCADE_FORCE* means to remove all the objects created by the XML schema registration.

The XML Schema registration process can retrieve XML schemas from the XML DB Repository, shown as follows (*register_xsd_xdburi.sql*):

Listing 2-8 *Registering an XML Schema from XML DB Repository*

```
BEGIN
DBMS_XMLSCHEMA.registerSchema('http://xmlbook.com/sample/contact.xsd',
xdburitype('/public/contact/contact.xsd'),
genTypes => FALSE,
genTables => FALSE,
options => DBMS_XMLSCHEMA.REGISTER_BINARYXML);
END;
/
```

In Oracle Database 11g, an XML Schema–based binary XMLType table can be created as follows (*create_xmltype_xsd.sql*):

Listing 2-9 *Creating a Binary XMLType with Secure File Storage*

```
Drop table contact_xsxtbl;
CREATE TABLE contact_xsxtbl OF XMLTYPE
XMLTYPE STORE AS SECUREFILE BINARY XML
XMLSCHEMA "http://xmlbook.com/sample/contact.xsd" ELEMENT "contact";
```

You can insert XML into this table as usual (*insert_xmltype_xsd.sql*):

```
INSERT INTO contact_xsxtbl VALUES(XMLType('<?xml version="1.0" encoding="UTF-8"?>
<contact xmlns="http://xmlbook.com/sample/contact.xsd" id="1">
  <category>customer</category>
  <first_name>John</first_name>
  <last_name>Smith</last_name>
  <email>john.smith@hfarm.com</email>
</contact>'));
```

You can do a batch insertion by inserting all of the files from an XML DB Repository folder to the binary XMLType table. The following is an example PL/SQL command (*insert_xmltype_xsxtbl_batch.sql*):

Listing 2-10 *Batch Uploading XML Documents into an XMLType Table*

```
declare
   cursor contact_files_cur is
   SELECT path
   FROM PATH_VIEW
   WHERE under_path(res, '/public/contact/xml')=1;
begin
 for contact_rec in contact_files_cur loop
     insert into contact_xsxtbl values(xdburitype(contact_rec.path).getxml());
  end loop;
end;
/
```

The XML will be validated against the registered XML schema before insertion. For non-XML-Schema-based XMLTypes, you can validate the inserted data with the following command (*read_xmltype_xsd.sql*):

Listing 2-11 *Validating Binary XMLTypes*

```
SELECT c.object_value.isSchemaValid('http://xmlbook.com/sample/contact.xsd')
FROM contact_xsxtbl c;
```

The input parameter of the isSchemaValid() function is the registered XML schema URL. The isSchemaValid() function returns 1 (one) if the inserted document is valid against the XML schema. If the XML document is invalid, the isSchemaValid() function will return 0 (zero).

Querying XMLTypes

The best way to query XMLTypes in Oracle Database 11*g* is to use XQuery. We will discuss XQuery further in Chapter 8. Here let's learn from a simple example on how to extract the first_name from a contact (*query_xmltype_xsxtbl.sql*):

Listing 2-12 *Query XMLType Using XQuery*

```
SELECT XMLQuery('declare namespace ns="http://xmlbook.com/sample/contact.xsd";
/ns:contact/ns:first_name'
PASSING c.object_value RETURNING CONTENT) result
from contact_xsxtbl c;

RESULT
--------------------------------------------------------------------------------
<first_name xmlns="http://xmlbook.com/sample/contact.xsd">John</first_name>
```

In this example, we first need to declare the namespace and then use the namespace to specify the qualified XML element name in XPath.

In Oracle XML DB 11*g*R2, the extract(), extractValue(), and existsNode() SQL functions are no longer recommended. You need to replace them with the XMLQuery(), XMLTable(), XMLCast(), and XMLExists() functions, as shown in Table 2-1. To help with this migration, let's try some examples that show how to use the new functions.

Table 2-2 shows how to replace the old extract(), extractValue(), and existsNode() functions with the now recommended XQuery and SQL/XML functions.

Function	Description
XMLQuery()	XMLQuery(<xquery_expression> passing by <value_expression> as <identifier>)
XMLTable()	XMLTable(<xmlnamespaces_clause>, xquery_string, xmltable_options)
XMLCast()	XMLCast(<xmltype_expression> as <sql_data_type>)
XMLExists()	XMLExists(<xquery_expression> passing by <value_expression> as <identifier>)

TABLE 2-1. *XMLQuery(), XMLTable(), XMLCast(), and XMLExists() Functions*

Old Function	New Function	Query Expression

extract()	XQuery()	**extract() Expression** (*replace_extract.sql*):
		`select extract(object_value,'/ns:contact/`
		`ns:first_name', 'xmlns:ns="http://xmlbook.com/`
		`sample/contact.xsd"') from contact_xsxtbl;`
		XMLQuery() Expression:
		`select XMLQuery('declare namespace ns="http://`
		`xmlbook.com/sample/contact.xsd"; /ns:contact/`
		`ns:first_name'`
		`PASSING c.object_value RETURNING CONTENT)`
		`from contact_xsxtbl c;`

extractValue()	XMLCast() and XQuery()	**extractValue() Expression** (*replace_extractvalue.sql*):
		`select extractValue(object_value,'/`
		`ns:contact/ns:first_name', 'xmlns:ns="http://`
		`xmlbook.com/sample/contact.xsd"') as first_`
		`name from contact_xsxtbl;`
		XMLQuery() Expression:
		`select XMLCast(XMLQuery('declare namespace`
		`ns="http://xmlbook.com/sample/contact.xsd"; /`
		`ns:contact/ns:first_name'`
		`PASSING c.object_value RETURNING CONTENT)`
		`as varchar2(300)) as first_name`
		`from contact_xsxtbl c;`

existsNode()	XMLExists()	**existsNode() Expression** (*replace_existsnode.sql*):
		`select extractValue(object_value,'/ns:contact/`
		`ns:first_name', 'xmlns:ns="http://xmlbook.com/`
		`sample/contact.xsd"') as first_name`
		`from contact_xsxtbl`
		`where existsNode(object_value,'/ns:contact/`
		`ns:email', 'xmlns:ns="http://xmlbook.com/`
		`sample/contact.xsd"')>0;`
		XMLQuery() Expression:
		`select XMLCast(XMLQuery('declare namespace`
		`ns="http://xmlbook.com/sample/contact.xsd"; /`
		`ns:contact/ns:first_name/text()'`
		`PASSING c.object_value RETURNING CONTENT)`
		`as varchar2(300)) as first_name`
		`from contact_xsxtbl c`
		`where XMLExists('declare namespace ns="http://`
		`xmlbook.com/sample/contact.xsd"; /ns:contact/`
		`ns:email' passing c.object_value);`

TABLE 2-2. *Replacing extract(), extractValue(), and existsNode() with XMLQuery(), XMLExists(), and XMLCast()*

Updating XMLTypes

The easiest way to update an XMLType is to use the updateXML() function. The following is an example of updateXML() (*update_xmltype_updatexml.sql*):

Listing 2-13 *Updating XMLTypes with UpdateXML()*

```
UPDATE contact_xsxtbl SET object_value =
updateXML()(object_value,
'/ns:contact/ns:first_name/text()','John Jr.', 'xmlns:ns="http://xmlbook.com/
sample/contact.xsd"')
WHERE XMLExists('declare default element namespace "http://xmlbook.com/sample/
contact.xsd"; $d/contact[first_name="John"]' passing object_value as "d");
```

Another way to update XMLType is to use the XMLPatch() function (*update_xmltype_xmlpatch.sql*):

Listing 2-14 *Using XMLPatch() to Update XMLTypes*

```
update contact_xsxtbl  set object_value=XMLPatch(object_value,
XMLType('<xd:xdiff xmlns:pfx="http://xmlbook.com/sample/contact.xsd"
xmlns:xd="http://xmlns.oracle.com/xdb/xdiff.xsd">
<?oracle-xmldiff operations-in-docorder="true" output-model="current"?>
<xd:update-node xd:xpath="/pfx:contact/pfx:first_name/text()" xd:node-
type="text">
<xd:content>John Jr.</xd:content></xd:update-node></xd:xdiff>'))
WHERE XMLExists('declare default element namespace "http://xmlbook.com/sample/
contact.xsd"; $d/contact[first_name="John"]' passing object_value as "d");;
```

The XMLPatch() function is used along with the XMLDiff() function as shown in Figure 2-1.

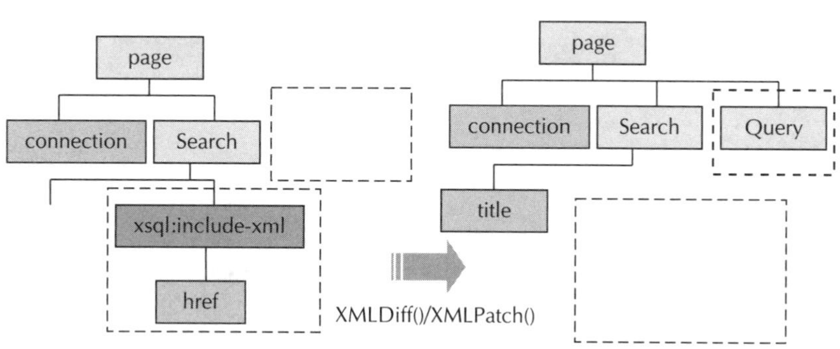

FIGURE 2-1. *XMLDiff() and XMLPatch()*

Function	Description
updateXML()	updateXML(<xmltype_instance>, <xpath_expression>, <new_content>, <namespaces_declarations>)
XMLPatch()	XMLPatch(<old_xmltype_doc>, <xmlpatch_instruction_in_xmltype>)
appendChildXML()	appendChildXML(<xmltype_instance>, <xpath_expression>, <new_xmltype_content>, <namespaces_declarations>)
insertChildXML()	insertChildXML(<xmltype_instance>, <xpath_expression>, <new_xmltype_content>, <namespaces_declarations>)
insertXMLBefore()	insertXMLBefore(<xmltype_instance>, <xpath_expression>, <new_xmltype_content>, <namespaces_declarations>)
deleteXML()	deleteXML(<xmltype_instance>, <xpath_expression>, <namespaces_declarations>)

TABLE 2-3. *XMLType Update Functions*

The following example uses XMLDiff() to generate the XML difference document (*xmldiff.sql*):

Listing 2-15 *Using XMLDiff() to Compare XMLTypes*

```
SELECT XMLDiff(XMLType(bfilename('XML_DIR','chp02/contact_1.xml'),
               nls_charset_id('AL32UTF8')),
               xmltype(bfilename('XML_DIR','chp02/contact_2.xml'),
               nls_charset_id('AL32UTF8'))) AS difference
FROM dual;

DIFFERENCE
--------------------------------------------------------------------------------
<xd:xdiff xsi:schemaLocation="http://xmlns.oracle.com/xdb/xdiff.xsd http://
xmlns.oracle.com/xdb/xdiff.xsd" xmlns:xd="http://xmlns.oracle.com/xdb/xdiff
.xsd" xmlns:xsi="http://www.w3.org/2001/XMLSchema-instance">
<?oracle-xmldiff operations-in-docorder="true" output-model="snapshot"
diff-algorithm="global"?>
</xd:xdiff>
```

In summary, Table 2-3 lists the major functions that can be used to update XMLTypes.

Transforming XMLTypes

The XMLType.transform() or XMLTransform() function can be used to transform XMLTypes. The XSL transformation conforms to the W3C XSLT 1.0 standard. The following example transforms an XMLType by removing data from reports. The XSL stylesheet is shown as follows (*public_view.xsl*):

```
<?xml version="1.0" encoding="windows-1252" ?>
<xsl:stylesheet version="2.0" xmlns:xsl="http://www.w3.org/1999/XSL/Transform"
xmlns="http://xmlbook.com/sample/contact.xsd">
```

```
    <xsl:template match="*" priority="2">
      <xsl:if test="local-name()!='category'">
      <xsl:element name="{local-name()}"   namespace="http://xmlbook.com/sample/
contact.xsd" >
        <xsl:apply-templates select="@*|node()" />
      </xsl:element>
      </xsl:if>
    </xsl:template>
    <xsl:template match="@*|node()">
    <xsl:copy>
     <xsl:apply-templates select="@*|node()"/>
    </xsl:copy>
  </xsl:template>
</xsl:stylesheet>
```

The two types of SQL commands to perform the XSL transformations are shown as follows (*transform_xmltype.sql*):

Listing 2-16 *Transforming XMLTypes*

```
SELECT XMLTransform(object_value, XMLType(bfilename('XML_DIR', 'public_view
.xsl'), nls_charset_id('AL32UTF8'))) result
FROM contact_xsxtbl;

SELECT c.object_value.transform(XMLType(bfilename('XML_DIR', 'public_view.xsl'),
nls_charset_id('AL32UTF8'))) result
FROM contact_xsxtbl c;
```

The XMLTransform() function is described in Table 2-4. An example result is

```
RESULT
----------------------------------------------------------------
<contact xmlns="http://xmlbook.com/sample/contact.xsd" id="1">
  <first_name>John</first_name>
  <last_name>Smith</last_name>
  <email>john.smith@hfarm.com</email>
</contact>
```

The <category> element is removed from the output after the XSL transformation. We will discuss XSL transformation further in Chapter 7.

Function	Description
XMLTransform()	XMLTransform(<XML_XMLType>, <XSL_XMLType>)

TABLE 2-4. *XMLTransform() Function*

You can create an XMLType view for users to access the transformed content as follows (*create_public_contact_xsxtbl_vw.sql*):

```
create or replace view contact_public_xsxtbl_vw of xmltype
as
SELECT XMLTransform(object_value,
XMLType(bfilename('XML_DIR', 'chp02/public_view.xsl'),
nls_charset_id('AL32UTF8')))
FROM contact_xsxtbl;
```

Reading Binary XMLTypes in Java

In Java applications, you can read XMLTypes from Oracle XML DB. The following example shows how to query binary XMLTypes in the Oracle database, and use them in a Java program.

To run the Java program, you need to make sure that the *xmlparserv2.jar*, *ojdbc5.jar*, and *xdb.jar* are included in the Java CLASSPATH. You can refer to Chapter 11 for the details of the Java libraries required by the Oracle XML DB applications. Chapter 16 explains how to add these libraries into Oracle JDeveloper projects.

Oracle XML DB Tip: Why do I get the "oracle.jdbc.driver.OracleSQLXML cannot be cast to oracle.xdb.XMLType" exception?

You have to use the correct JDBC driver. In Oracle Database 11.2.0.2, Oracle XML DB is compliant with JDK 1.5. Therefore, you have to choose ojdbc5.jar instead of the ojdbc6.jar. Otherwise, you will get this error message.

The Java program is listed as follows (*ReadBinaryXMLType.java*):

Listing 2-17 *Reading Binary XMLTypes in Java*

```
package xmlbook.chp02;

import java.io.File;
import java.io.FileOutputStream;
import java.io.OutputStream;
import java.sql.Connection;
import java.sql.DriverManager;
import java.sql.PreparedStatement;
import java.sql.ResultSet;

import oracle.jdbc.internal.OracleConnection;
import oracle.xdb.XMLType;
import oracle.xml.binxml.BinXMLDecoder;
import oracle.xml.binxml.BinXMLMetadataProviderFactory;
import oracle.xml.binxml.BinXMLProcessor;
```

```
import oracle.xml.binxml.BinXMLStream;
import oracle.xml.binxml.BinXMLStreamImpl;
import oracle.xml.binxml.DBBinXMLMetadataProvider;
import oracle.xml.parser.v2.DTDBuilder;
import oracle.xml.parser.v2.XMLSAXSerializer;

public class ReadBinaryXMLType {
    Connection conn = null;
    XMLType poxml = null;
    ResultSet rset = null;
    PreparedStatement stmt = null;

    public static void main(String[] args) {
        String host_name = "localhost";
        String port = "1522";
        String sid = "orcl11g";
        String user = "xmldemo";
        String password = "xmldemo";
        int counter = 1;

        //Create ReadBinaryXMLType instance
        ReadBinaryXMLType readBinXMLType = new ReadBinaryXMLType();
        //Initialize the database connection
        readBinXMLType.init_db(host_name, port, sid, user, password);
        //Retrieve the Binary XMLType from DB.
        readBinXMLType.getBinXMLStreamFromDB(counter, "contact");
        //Close the DB connection
        readBinXMLType.closeDB();
    }

    //Initialize the DB connection
    private void init_db(String hostname, String port, String sid, String user,
                         String passwd) {
        String ConnectionString =
            "jdbc:oracle:thin:@" + hostname + ":" + port + ":" + sid;
        try {
            DriverManager.registerDriver(new oracle.jdbc.OracleDriver());
            conn = DriverManager.getConnection(ConnectionString, user, passwd);
            conn.setAutoCommit(false);
        } catch (Exception e) {
            e.printStackTrace();
        }
    }
    // Decode Binary XML and print out to files.
    public void decode(BinXMLStream bstr, String filename) {
        try {
            DTDBuilder builder = new DTDBuilder();
            BinXMLDecoder dec = bstr.getDecoder();
            File outxml = new File(filename + ".out");
            FileOutputStream out = new FileOutputStream(outxml);
```

```
            XMLSAXSerializer saxser = new XMLSAXSerializer(out);
            dec.setDeclHandler(saxser);
            dec.setLexicalHandler(saxser);
            dec.setDTDHandler(saxser);
            dec.decode(saxser, saxser);
        } catch (Exception e) {
            e.printStackTrace();
        }
    }

    // Retrieve the Binary XMLTypes
    public void getBinXMLStreamFromDB(int column, String filename) {
        BinXMLProcessor binProc;
        BinXMLStream binstrm = null;
        int record_num = 0;
        try {
            //Create XML Metadata Provider
            DBBinXMLMetadataProvider dbmeta =
                BinXMLMetadataProviderFactory.createDBMetadataProvider();
            if ((conn != null) && (conn instanceof OracleConnection))
                dbmeta.setConnection((OracleConnection)conn);
            //Specify the SQL query
            stmt = conn.prepareStatement("select * from contact_xsxtbl e");

            rset = stmt.executeQuery();
            while (rset.next()) {
                //Retrieve the Binary XMLType column
                poxml = (XMLType)rset.getObject(column);
                binstrm = poxml.getBinXMLStream();
                //Decode the Binary XML stream
                decode(binstrm, filename + record_num);
                record_num++;
            }
            binProc = ((BinXMLStreamImpl)binstrm).getBinXMLProcessor();
            binProc.setMetadataRepository(dbmeta);
        } catch (Exception e) {
            e.printStackTrace();
        }
    }

    private void closeDB() {
        try {
            if (poxml != null)
                poxml.close();
            if (rset != null)
                rset.close();
            if (stmt != null)
                stmt.close();
```

```
            if (conn != null)
                conn.close();
        } catch (Exception e) {
            e.printStackTrace();
        }
    }
}
```

The program contains four steps, as explained next.

Step 1 connects to the Oracle database instance with the following function:

```
private void init_db(String hostname, String port, String sid, String user,
String passwd){...}
```

In this function, a JDBC thin connection is established.

Step 2 gets the binary XMLType from the Oracle database by calling the getBinXMLStreamFromDB() function:

```
ReadBinaryXMLType readBinXMLType = new ReadBinaryXMLType();
...
BinXMLStream bstr = readBinXMLType.getBinXMLStreamFromDB(counter, "contact");
```

The getBinXMLStreamFromDB() function is defined as follows:

```
public BinXMLStream getBinXMLStreamFromDB(int column){...}
```

Within in the getBinXMLStreamFromDB() function, we create *oracle.xml.binxml .DBBinXMLMetadataProvider* from *oracle.xml.binxml.BinXMLMetadataProviderFactory*:

```
DBBinXMLMetadataProvider dbmeta =
    BinXMLMetadataProviderFactory.createDBMetadataProvider();
```

Then read the *oracle.xdb.XMLType* object and use the XMLType.getBinXMLStream() function to retrieve the binary XML stream from the XMLType object:

```
poxml = (XMLType)rset.getObject(column);
binstrm = poxml.getBinXMLStream();
```

The returned binary XML is in oracle.xml.binxml.BinXMLStream. You can perform an operation on *BinXMLStream*. In this example, we simply decode the binary XML stream and print it out in a text file:

```
stmt = conn.prepareStatement("select * from contact_xsxtbl e");
rset = stmt.executeQuery();
while (rset.next()) {
    //Retrieve the Binary XMLType column
  poxml = (XMLType)rset.getObject(column);
  binstrm = poxml.getBinXMLStream();
  //Decode the Binary XML stream
  decode(binstrm, filename + record_num);
  record_num++;
}
```

The key functions are

```
BinXMLDecoder dec = bstr.getDecoder();
...
dec.decode(saxser, saxser);
```

Please also refer to Chapter 4 to learn how to create DOM from *BinXMLStream*. You can then perform DOM operations on the binary XML data from XMLTypes.

Summary

XMLType is the foundation of the Oracle XML DB platform. In this chapter, we learned the basic XMLType operations by using examples. In the later chapters we will use XMLType extensively and focus on using the new binary XMLType.

CHAPTER 3

XML Database Repository

racle XML Database (XML DB) Repository is a queryable, hierarchically organized file system in the Oracle database. This repository is ideal for storing unstructured content, including both XML and non-XML files.

In this chapter, we learn the basics of Oracle XML DB Repository. We first explore how to store files in XML DB Repository by creating, updating, and managing XML DB Repository resources (folder or files). Then, we discuss how to query and access XML DB Repository content through SQL, Java, and Internet protocols. We conclude by using XML DB Repository events.

EXAMPLE SETUP

If you haven't set up Oracle XML DB Repository for Oracle Database 11g, please refer to Chapter 11 for the XML DB Repository setup instructions. Make sure the sample data are loaded to the XML DB Repository as described in the "About the Examples" section in the Introduction of this book.

Creating Resources

When loading documents via FTP, HTTP, or WebDav to XML DB Repository, we are creating XML DB Repository resources. In addition to this approach, creating XML DB Repository resources in SQL.

In Oracle XML DB, the following PL/SQL functions/procedures can be used to create/delete XML DB Repository resources:

- **DBMS_XDB.createResource()** This function creates a new XML DB file.
- **DBMS_XDB.createFolder()** This function creates a new folder.
- **DBMS_XDB.existsResource()** This function checks whether a file exists in XML DB Repository. Normally, you need to check if a file exists before creating a new one.
- **DBMS_XDB.deleteResource()** This procedure deletes an existing XML DB Repository resource.

The following example creates a folder and a file in XML DB Repository (*create_resources.sql*):

Listing 3-1 *Creating a Folder and a Resource in XML DB Repository Using SQL*

```
DECLARE
  v_res BOOLEAN;
BEGIN
  IF (NOT DBMS_XDB.existsResource('/public/chp03')) then
     v_res:=DBMS_XDB.createFolder('/public/chp03');
  END IF;

  IF (NOT DBMS_XDB.existsResource('/public/chp03/john_smith.xml')) THEN
     v_res:=DBMS_XDB.createResource('/public/chp03/john_smith.xml',
   XMLType('<contact>
```

```
    <first_name>John</first_name><last_name>Smith</last_name></contact>'));
  end if;
END;
/
commit;
```

When neither the */public/chp03* folder nor the *john_smith.xml* file exists, this example creates the */public/chp03* folder and adds the *john_smith.xml* file to the */public/chp03*. Note that because the preceding SQL processing is a database transactional process, the created folder and file will not show up outside the current database session until we *commit* the operation.

Oracle XML DB Tip: Why do I get the PLS-00221: *'CREATEFOLDER' is not a procedure or is undefined* error?

dbms_xdb.createFolder() is a function, not a procedure. It returns a *boolean* value. Therefore, you need to declare a *boolean* variable—e.g., v_*res*—in PL/SQL when calling the function shown as follows:

```
v_res := dbms_xdb.createFolder('/home');
```

Otherwise, you will get this error.

Listing 3-1 is a simple example of creating XML DB Repository folders that require the */public* folder to exist before creating its subfolder */public/chp03*. If you create a folder like */public/chp03/event/xmlbook_ann* using DBMS_XDB.createFolder() without having the */public/chp03/event* folder in XML DB Repository, you will get the ORA-31001: *Invalid resource handle or path name "/public/chp03/event/xmlbook_ann"* error. This is because the DBMS_XDB.createFolder() function doesn't create the necessary folders recursively. To avoid this error and simplify folder creation, we create a PL/SQL function to allow recursive folder creation in XML DB Repository. This is used in Chapter 17 when discussing contact XML documents export. The code is shown as follows (*create_folder_recursively.sql*):

Listing 3-2 *Recursively Creating Folders in XML DB Repository Using SQL*

```
-- Create the tokenize_func() to extract path level
CREATE OR REPLACE FUNCTION splitter_count_func(p_str IN VARCHAR2, p_delim IN
CHAR) RETURN INT AS
  v_val INT;
BEGIN
  v_val := length(replace(p_str, p_delim, p_delim || ' '));
  RETURN v_val - length(p_str);
END splitter_count_func;
/
show errors;

CREATE OR REPLACE TYPE token_list_typ IS VARRAY(100) OF VARCHAR2(200);
/
CREATE OR REPLACE FUNCTION tokenize_func(p_str VARCHAR2, p_delim CHAR) RETURN
token_list_typ AS
```

```
  v_ret token_list_typ;
  v_target INT;
  v_i INT;
  v_j INT;
  v_this_delim INT;
  v_last_delim INT;
  v_current_token VARCHAR2(400);
BEGIN
  v_ret := token_list_typ();
  v_i := 1;
  v_j := 1;
  v_last_delim := 0;
  v_target := splitter_count_func(p_str, p_delim);
  WHILE v_i <= v_target
  LOOP
    v_this_delim := instr(p_str, p_delim, 1, v_i);
    v_current_token := substr(p_str, v_last_delim + 1, v_this_delim - v_last_
delim -1);
    IF v_current_token IS NOT NULL THEN
    v_ret.extend();
    v_ret(v_j):= substr(p_str, v_last_delim + 1, v_this_delim - v_last_delim -1);
    v_j := v_j+1;
   END IF;
    v_i := v_i + 1;
    v_last_delim := v_this_delim;
  END LOOP;
  v_ret.extend();
  v_ret(v_j):= substr(p_str, v_last_delim + 1);
  RETURN v_ret;
END tokenize_func;
/
show errors;

-- Create function get_paths_func() to get the path to create folder recursively
CREATE OR REPLACE FUNCTION get_paths_func(p_path IN VARCHAR2) RETURN token_
list_typ AS
  v_j VARCHAR2(300);
  v_i NUMBER;
  v_path_elements token_list_typ;
  v_current_path VARCHAR2(4000) :='';
BEGIN
  SELECT tokenize_func(p_path,'/') into v_path_elements FROM DUAL;
  v_j := v_path_elements.FIRST;
  v_i :=1;
  WHILE v_j IS NOT NULL LOOP
   IF v_path_elements(v_j) != '/' then
   v_current_path:= v_current_path ||'/'|| v_path_elements(v_j);
   v_path_elements(v_i):= v_current_path;
   v_i := v_i+1;
   END IF;
```

```
    v_j := v_path_elements.NEXT(v_j);
  END LOOP;
  RETURN v_path_elements;
END get_paths_func;
/
show errors;

-- Create function create_path_proc() to create the XML DB Repository folder
recursively
CREATE OR REPLACE PROCEDURE create_path_proc(p_path IN VARCHAR2, p_authorized_
level IN NUMBER) AS
 v_j VARCHAR2(300);
 v_path_elements token_list_typ;
 v_current_path VARCHAR2(4000) :='';
 v_res BOOLEAN;
BEGIN
  SELECT get_paths_func(p_path) INTO v_path_elements FROM DUAL;
  v_j := v_path_elements.FIRST;
  WHILE v_j IS NOT NULL LOOP
   IF (v_j >= p_authorized_level) THEN
     v_current_path:= v_path_elements(v_j);
     IF ( not DBMS_XDB.existsResource(v_current_path)) THEN
       v_res :=DBMS_XDB.createFolder(v_current_path);
       IF v_res THEN DBMS_OUTPUT.put_line(v_current_path||'created.'); END IF;
     END IF;
    END IF;
     v_j := v_path_elements.NEXT(v_j);
  END LOOP;
END create_path_proc;
/
show errors;
```

When creating this PL/SQL function, we first create a tokenize_func() function to parse the folder path string into a set of tokens. The tokens are stored in a VARRAY of VARCHAR2 datatype called *token_list_typ* (*run_create_folder_recursively.sql*):

```
SQL> SELECT tokenize_func('/public/chp03/event/xmlbook_ann', '/') result
     FROM DUAL;
RESULT
--------------------------------------------------------
TOKEN_LIST_TYP('public', 'chp03', 'event', 'xmlbook_ann')
```

Then the get_paths_func() function reads the tokens and returns a list of the folders that need to be created:

```
SQL> SELECT get_paths_func('/public/chp03/event/xmlbook_ann') result FROM
DUAL;
RESULT
--------------------------------------------------------------------------------
TOKEN_LIST_TYP('/public', '/public/chp03', '/public/chp03/event',
'/public/chp03/event/xmlbook_ann')
```

Then, we iterate the list of folders in order and create all of the folders in the create_path_proc() procedure. In the following example, we only have the */public/chp03* folder, but we create a folder called */public/chp03/event/xmlbook_ann* (*run_create_folder_recursively.sql*):

```
SQL> CALL create_path_proc('/public/chp03/xmlbook_ann/contacts', 2);
```

The second parameter in create_path_proc() is the top authorization level that the current user has. Because the XMLDEMO user has the privilege to create the folder under */public*, we then set the authorization level to 2. To check the created path, we run the following command (*check_folder_content.sql*):

```
SQL> SELECT path FROM path_view WHERE under_path(res, '/public/chp03')=1;
PATH
-------------------------------------------------------
/public/chp03/event
/public/chp03/event/xmlbook_ann
/public/chp03/john_smith.xml
```

You find that two new folders are created.

Deleting Resources

To delete the created files or folders, run the following commands (*delete_resources.sql*):

Listing 3-3 *Deleting Folders and Files in XML DB Repository Using SQL*

```
delete from RESOURCE_VIEW
where equals_path(res,'/public/chp03/john_smith.xml')=1;
ROLLBACK;

exec dbms_xdb.deleteresource('/public/chp03/john_smith.xml');
ROLLBACK;
```

Note that to continue our examples in the following sections, we roll back the file and folder deletions with the ROLLBACK command.

Querying XML DB Repository

To query XML DB Repository in SQL, we need to clarify the two key elements in XML DB Repository—*resource* and *path*:

- **Resource** Each document or folder in XML DB Repository is represented as a resource. A resource normally includes a resource name, a description, and the resource content. A file resource can be XML or non-XML documents, or even XML views. The XML resources are stored in XMLTypes. Non-XML resources are stored in BLOB. You can find a more detailed description of the XML DB resources in the */sys/schemas/PUBLIC/xmlns.oracle.com/xdb/XDBResource.xsd* file.
- **Path** A link which represents the location of a resource related to the repository storage root (*/*).

Using RESOURCE_VIEW and PATH_VIEW

There are two views provided by Oracle XML DB to access XML DB Repository: RESOURCE_VIEW and PATH_VIEW.

```
SQL> desc resource_view
 Name                      Null?    Type
 ---------------------- -------- ----------------------------
 RES                                SYS.XMLTYPE(XMLSchema "http://xmlns.oracle.com
                                    /xdb/XDBResource.xsd"
                                    Element "Resource")
 ANY_PATH                           VARCHAR2(4000)
 RESID                              RAW(16)

SQL> desc path_view
Name                       Null?    Type
----------------------- -------- ----------------------------
PATH                                VARCHAR2(1024)
RES                                 SYS.XMLTYPE(XMLSchema "http://xmlns.oracle.com
                                    /xdb/XDBResource.xsd"
                                    Element "Resource")
LINK                                SYS.XMLTYPE
RESID                               RAW(16)
```

RESOURCE_VIEW lists the resources in XML DB Repository. Each resource is represented as an XMLType column named *RES*. Each resource is associated with a path (*ANY_PATH*) and a resource ID (*RESID*). The path is no different from the path that you use in other file systems. PATH_VIEW provides all possible paths to access a resource. Different from the ANY_PATH column in RESOURCE_VIEW, the PATH in PATH_VIEW can be relative paths and even links to the resources.

To check if any XML DB Repository resource exists, you can run the following SQL command (*check_xdbRepository.sql*):

Listing 3-4 *Checking XML DB Repository Resources in SQL*

```
SELECT count(1) FROM resource_view;
```

An example output is

```
  COUNT(1)
----------
       312
```

To specify a particular resource, you can use two SQL functions, under_path() and equals_path(). Both functions use a path to locate the resources. The equals_path() function lists resources at the specified path. The under_path() function lists all files/folders in the specified folder and its subfolders. The following example calculates all resources under the */public/chp03* folder using under_path() (*check_xdbrepository.sql*).

Listing 3-5 *Counting the Resources Number Under an XML DB Repository Folder Using SQL*

```
SELECT count(1)
FROM resource_view
WHERE under_path(res,'/public/chp03',1)>0;
```

The example output is

```
  COUNT(1)
----------
         3
```

The following example lists all the paths under the */public/chp03* folder using the under_path() function (*check_xdbrepository.sql*):

Listing 3-6 *Setting the Depth of under_path()*

```
SELECT path
FROM path_view
WHERE under_path(res,1,'/public/chp03') >0;
PATH
-------------------------------
/public/chp03/event
/public/chp03/john_smith.xml
```

The second parameter in under_path()—the numeral `1`—indicates the number of levels for under_path() to traverse down from the specified path. In this example, we only list the files/folders directly under the */public/chp03* folder.

In both PATH_VIEW and RESOURCE_VIEW, the *RES* column includes the resource data and metadata description. The following example locates one resource in the repository and shows its resource description (*check_resource_desc.sql*):

Listing 3-7 *Querying the XML DB Resource Description and ID in SQL*

```
set long 1000000
select res
from resource_view
where equals_path(res,'/public/chp03/john_smith.xml',1)>0;
```

An example output is as follows:

```
RES
---------------------------------------------------------------------------------
<Resource xmlns="http://xmlns.oracle.com/xdb/XDBResource.xsd">
  <CreationDate>2010-09-02T19:18:47.007000</CreationDate>
  <ModificationDate>2010-09-02T19:18:47.007000</ModificationDate>
  <DisplayName>john_smith.xml</DisplayName>
  <Language>en-US</Language>
  <CharacterSet>UTF-8</CharacterSet>
  <ContentType>text/xml</ContentType>
  <RefCount>1</RefCount>
</Resource>
```

You can use XQuery functions to query and update data and metadata stored in XML DB Repository. In the following example, we create a relational view by querying XML DB Repository resources' data and metadata (*create_email_template_img_vw.sql*):

Listing 3-8 *Creating Resource Index View from RESOURCE_VIEW*

```
CREATE OR REPLACE VIEW email_template_img_vw
                                                AS
  SELECT xdburitype(a.any_path).getblob() AS photo,
    c.filename                            AS filename,
    c.mimetype                            AS mimetype,
    a.any_path
  FROM resource_view a,
    XMLTable(
    XMLNamespaces(DEFAULT 'http://xmlns.oracle.com/xdb/XDBResource.xsd'), '$r/
Resource'
    passing a.res AS "r"
    columns
      filename VARCHAR2(100) path 'DisplayName',
       mimetype VARCHAR2(4000) path 'ContentType') c
  WHERE under_path(a.res,'/public/chp17/email_template/images')=1;
```

Refer to Chapter 17 to find out how this view is used in APEX applications when we add images to emails.

Oracle XML DB Tip: Why do I get the ORA-00904: *"A"."RES": invalid identifier* error?

Make sure you put the RESOURCE_VIEW "a" before the XMLTable() function in the SQL *from* clause because XMLTable() relies on the *RES* content. Otherwise, you will get this error.

In Listing 3-8, a default namespace is defined using *DEFAULT* in the XMLNamespaces() function. You can also specify the namespace using a prefix as follows:

```
CREATE OR REPLACE VIEW email_template_img_vw AS
SELECT xdburitype(a.any_path).getblob() AS photo,
                    c.filename AS filename,
                    c.mimetype AS mimetype,
                     a.any_path
  FROM resource_view a,
    XMLTable( XMLNamespaces('http://xmlns.oracle.com/xdb/XDBResource.xsd' as
"r"),
    'for $i in . return $i/r:Resource'
     passing a.res COLUMNS
     filename VARCHAR2(100) path 'r:DisplayName',
     mimetype VARCHAR2(4000) path 'r:ContentType') c
WHERE under_path(a.res,'/public/email_template/images')=1;
```

You need to make sure you add " " (double quotes) when defining namespace prefixes in XMLNamespaces(). If you define a namespace prefix in XMLNamespaces() without double quotes, you get the ORA-19228: *XPST0008 – Undeclared identifier: prefix 'r' local-name 'r:contact'* error.

Using XDBUriType

XDBUriType can be used to retrieve resources from XML DB Repository. From XDBUriType, you can retrieve XMLType with getXML(), CLOB with getCLOB(), and BLOB with getBlob(). Table 3-1 lists some common LINUX file system commands and the corresponding XML DB queries that have similar functionality but work on XML DB Repository.

Oracle XML DB Tip: What are Oracle Database *UriTypes*?

In Oracle Database 11*g*, *UriTypes* are data types that can be used to store and query Uri-refs inside the database. There are three subtypes of the *UriType*: *HTTPUriType, DBUriType,* and *XDBUriType. HTTPUriType* represents a URL that begins with *http://.* It allows Oracle database users to create an object from an HTTP URL. *DBUriType* is in the format /oradb/<schema_name>/<table_name>, which refers to the relational table/rows with URIs. *XDBUriType* points to an XML document stored in XML DB Repository with the format of the file path in XML DB Repository.

File System Command	XML DB Repository Query

ls <path_name>	**Using RESOURCE_VIEW:**
	`SELECT XMLQuery('declare namespace ns="http://xmlns`
	`.oracle.com/xdb/XDBResource.xsd"; (: :)`
	`$r/ns:Resource/ns:DisplayName/text()'`
	`passing res as "r" returning content) as files`
	`FROM resource_view`
	`WHERE under_path(res,'<path_name>') =1;`

more <file_name>	**Using RESOURCE_VIEW:**
	`SELECT XMLQuery('declare namespace ns="http://xmlns`
	`.oracle.com/xdb/XDBResource.xsd"; (: :)`
	`$r/ns:Resource/ns:Contents/*'`
	`PASSING res as "r" returning content) as content`
	`FROM resource_view`
	`WHERE any_path='<file_name>';`
	Using XDBUriType:
	`SELECT XDBUriType('/public/chp03/john_smith.xml')`
	`.getXML()`
	`FROM dual;`

Note: The (: :) in SQL is used for line returns within quoted strings.

TABLE 3-1. *XML DB Repository Query Access*

XML DB Repository can include non-XML documents such as Microsoft Word, PDFs, images, and others. Though these unstructured documents are not in XML format, you can manage them via XMLTypes. For example, Listing 3-8 shows that after you have loaded image files into XML DB Repository, you can create a SQL view retrieving the image content using XDBUriType [xdburitype(a.any_path).getblob()].

Linking to Resources

Another useful operation in XML DB Repository is to create links. The following example creates a folder in XML DB Repository and adds resources to this folder by linking to the existing resources (*create_file_link.sql*):

Listing 3-9 *Creating Links in XML DB Repository*

```
CALL create_path_proc('/public/chp03/event/xmlbook_ann/contacts', 2);

DECLARE
  v_res BOOLEAN;
BEGIN
  DBMS_XDB.link('/public/contact/xml/john_smith.xml',
                '/public/chp03/event/xmlbook_ann/contacts', 'john_smith.xml');
END;
/
COMMIT;
```

We can check the created link using the following SQL query (*check_created_links.sql*):

Listing 3-10 *Listing Resources in an XML DB Repository Directory*

```
SELECT path FROM PATH_VIEW
WHERE under_path(res, '/public/chp03/event/xmlbook_ann/contacts')=1;
```

The newly created link is

```
PATH
--------------------------------------------------------------------------------
/public/chp03/event/xmlbook_ann/contacts/john_smith.xml
```

To delete a link, we need to use PATH_VIEW (*delete_file_link.sql*):

Listing 3-11 *Deleting Links from XML DB Repository*

```
DELETE FROM PATH_VIEW
WHERE equals_path(res,'/public/chp03/event/xmlbook_ann/contacts/john_smith
.xml')=1;
ROLLBACK;
```

Again, we ROLLBACK the deletion so the created file can be used for later examples. If there are multiple links to the same resource, the resource deletion will delete all of the links.

Updating Resources

You can update XML DB Repository resources using RESOURCE_VIEW. Refer to Table 2-3 in Chapter 2 for the list of XML update functions.

The most commonly used function is the updateXML() function. The following example uses updateXML() to update the XML DB Repository resources (*update_xdb_repository.sql*):

Listing 3-12 *Updating XML DB Repository Using RESOURCE_VIEW*

```
UPDATE RESOURCE_VIEW r
  SET r.res = updateXML(r.res,
     '/r:Resource/r:Contents/c:contact/c:first_name/text()','John Jr.',
    'xmlns:r="http://xmlns.oracle.com/xdb/XDBResource.xsd" xmlns:c="http://
xmlbook.com/sample/contact.xsd"')
where equals_path(res,'/public/chp03/event/xmlbook_ann/contacts/john_smith
.xml')=1;
```

In this process we update the linked resource `john_smith.xml` by changing the <first_name> element content to *"John Jr."*. From the result, you can see that after updating the linked resource, the original XML DB resource is also updated.

Version Control

The DBMS_XDB_VERSION and DBMS_XDB PL/SQL packages provide a way to create and manage a *Version Controlled Resource* (VCR) in XML DB Repository.

When an XML DB Repository resource is turned into a VCR, a flag is set to mark it as a VCR and the current resource becomes the initial version.

To make an XML DB Repository resource versioned, run the following command (*create_vcr.sql*):

Listing 3-13 *Creating a VCR from an XML DB Repository Resource*

```
declare
  v_resid  DBMS_XDB_VERSION.RESID_TYPE;
begin
  v_resid := dbms_xdb_version.makeversioned('/public/chp03/john_smith.xml');
end;
/
Commit;
```

You have to *commit* to complete the preceding operation.

Oracle XML DB Tip: Can I switch a VCR resource back to a non-VCR resource?
No, you can't.

You can access the VCR resources via the functions provided in the DBMS_XDB_VERSION package. For example, to update a VCR, you need to first check out the resource, make the updates, and then check in the updated resource back to XML DB Repository, as follows (*update_vcr.sql*):

Listing 3-14 *Updating a VCR Resource*

```
declare
 v_resid dbms_xdb_version.resid_type;
 v_res xmltype;
 v_out clob;
begin
   -- Print out the existing content
  select xdburitype('/public/chp03/john_smith.xml').getxml().getclobval()
    into v_out from dual;
  dbms_output.put_line('Existing content:');
  dbms_output.put_line(v_out);

  -- Check out the resource
  dbms_xdb_version.checkout('/public/chp03/john_smith.xml');

  -- Update the resource
  UPDATE RESOURCE_VIEW r
   SET r.res = updateXML(r.res,
     '/r:Resource/r:Contents/contact/first_name/text()','Johnson',
     'xmlns:r="http://xmlns.oracle.com/xdb/XDBResource.xsd"')
  WHERE equals_path(r.res,'/public/chp03/john_smith.xml')=1;

  -- Check in the resource
  v_resid := dbms_xdb_version.checkin('/public/chp03/john_smith.xml');

  -- Print out the updated content
  v_res := dbms_xdb_version.getresourcebyresid(v_resid);
  select v_res.extract('/r:Resource/r:Contents/contact',
         'xmlns:r="http://xmlns.oracle.com/xdb/XDBResource.xsd"').getclobval()
  into v_out from dual;
  dbms_output.put_line('Updated content:');
  dbms_output.put_line(v_out);
end;
/
```

Note that after a resource is checked out, it is not updatable by others until the file is checked in. If you want to cancel the updates after the checkout, you can "uncheck out" the resource (*uncheckout_vcr.sql*):

```
declare
 v_resid dbms_xdb_version.resid_type;
begin
  v_resid:=dbms_xdb_version.uncheckout('/public/chp03/john_smith.xml');
end;
/
```

Using XML DB Repository Events

Oracle XML DB Repository events are a set of events triggered by operations performed in XML DB Repository. Table 3-2 summarizes a subset of XML DB system-defined events, which are mostly used by XML applications. You can find the complete list in *Oracle XML DB Developer's Guide*.

In Oracle XML DB Repository, each repository operation is associated with one or more repository events. You can assign *repository event listeners* to the repository events by updating the XML DB Repository configuration file. The listener can be a Java class, a PL/SQL package, or an object type. A repository event listener can be configured for a particular resource or for the entire repository. The procedures in the repository event listeners are called the *repository event handlers*. Each event handler processes a single event.

The XML DB Repository event is not enabled by default. Therefore, the first step is to check whether the XML DB Repository event is enabled in the SYS user (as SYSDBA):

```
SQL> show parameters xml_db_events
NAME                                 TYPE        VALUE
------------------------------------ ----------- ------------------------------
xml_db_events                        string      enable
```

If the *xml_db_event* parameter has the *enable* value, then the XML DB Repository event is enabled. Otherwise, you need to run the following command:

```
alter system set xml_db_events = enable;
```

This enables the XML DB Repository event in the current database instance. You can also enable the XML DB Repository event within the current database session:

```
alter session set xml_db_events = enable;
```

Event	Description
Create	This event is fired when a resource is created.
Delete	This event is fired when the resource and its contents are removed.
Update	This event is fired when a resource is updated.
Lock	This event is fired during a lock resource operation.
Unlock	This event is fired during an unlock resource operation.
Render	This event is fired when the resource contents are accessed using the following interfaces: — Protocols — get{CLOB, BLOB, XML} methods on XDBUriType — getContent* methods in JNDI when invoked from a stored procedure The following interfaces do not trigger the *Render* event: — Select ... from RESOURCE_VIEW — getResource() method on XDBUriType

TABLE 3-2. *Commonly Used XML DB Repository Events*

After the event feature is enabled, we can then work on an example to understand how to set up the XML DB Repository event.

Creating Event Handlers

First, we need to decide which event to process. The following example chooses to perform the operation after the XML DB system-defined *Render* event. The *Render* event is fired when the XML DB Repository resource is accessed via a protocol interface, XDBUriType or JNDI.

Second, we need to decide on the operations to perform after the event is triggered. In this example, we decide to record the resource access in a database table, including which resource is accessed by which user. Listing 3-15 shows the PL/SQL package, which includes the XML DB Repository event handler (*create_event_handler.sql*):

Listing 3-15 *Create XML DB Repository Event Handlers*

```
CREATE TABLE event_records_tbl(res VARCHAR2(4000), usr VARCHAR2(400), event
VARCHAR2(4000), access_time DATE);

CREATE OR REPLACE PROCEDURE record_access_proc(
               p_ev DBMS_XEvent.XDBRepositoryEvent,
               p_res IN VARCHAR2, p_usr IN VARCHAR2, p_event IN VARCHAR2) AS
  PRAGMA AUTONOMOUS_TRANSACTION;
BEGIN
   INSERT INTO event_records_tbl values(p_res, p_usr, p_event, sysdate);
   COMMIT;
END;
/
show errors;

CREATE OR REPLACE PACKAGE events_pkg AS
  PROCEDURE handleRender(p_eventObject DBMS_XEvent.XDBRepositoryEvent);
END events_pkg;
/

CREATE OR REPLACE PACKAGE BODY events_pkg AS
  PROCEDURE handleRender (p_eventObject DBMS_XEvent.XDBRepositoryEvent) AS
    v_res_path VARCHAR2(4000);
    v_usr VARCHAR2(4000);
  BEGIN
    v_res_path := dbms_xevent.getname(dbms_xevent.getpath(p_eventObject));
    v_usr := dbms_xevent.getcurrentuser(dbms_xevent.getxdbevent
(p_eventObject));
    record_access_proc(p_eventObject, v_res_path, v_usr, 'render');
  END handleRender;
END events_pkg;
/
show errors;
```

In this example, we create an *event_records_tbl* table to keep records of the XML DB Repository events. Then, we create a PL/SQL procedure, record_access_proc(), to write the event record to the

Function	Description
DBMS_XEVENT.GETPATH(ev IN XDBRepositoryEvent) RETURN XDBPath;	Returns the path of the source from which the event was fired.
DBMS_XEVENT.GETNAME(path IN XDBPath) RETURN VARCHAR2;	Returns the string representation of the source path from the DBMS_XEVENT.XDBPath object.
DBMS_XEVENT.GETXDBEVENT(ev IN XDBRepositoryEvent) RETURN XDBEvent;	Returns the XDBEvent object.
DBMS_XEVENT.GETCURRENTUSER(ev IN XDBEvent) RETURN VARCHAR2;	Returns the name of user executing the operation that triggers the event.

TABLE 3-3. *DBMS_XEVENT Functions: getPath(), getName(), getXDBEvent(), and getCurrentUser()*

event_records_tbl table. In the *events_pkg* PL/SQL package, the handleRender() procedure calls the record_access_proc() function.

Let's look at the handler function in detail:

```
PROCEDURE handleRender (p_eventObject DBMS_XEvent.XDBRepositoryEvent) AS
  v_res_path VARCHAR2(4000);
  v_usr VARCHAR2(4000);
BEGIN
  v_res_path := DBMS_XEVENT.getname(dbms_xevent.getpath(p_eventObject));
  v_usr := DBMS_XEVENT.getcurrentuser(dbms_xevent.getxdbevent(p_eventOb
ject));
  record_access_proc(p_eventObject, v_res_path, v_usr, 'render');
END handleRender;
```

In each XML DB Repository event handler function, you get a *DBMS_XEVENT.XDBRepositoryEvent* object as a passed-in object. With this object, you can call functions in the DBMS_XEVENT package to get the event and resource-related information. Table 3-3 lists the functions used in the example.

In this example, we get the current user and the current resource name and path, and store them in the *event_records_tbl* table.

Registering Event Handlers

To enable the XML DB Repository event, we need to update the XML DB Repository resource configuration file (*register_event.sql*):

Listing 3-16 *Registering XML DB Repository Event Handler*

```
DECLARE
v_isCreatedBln BOOLEAN := false;
BEGIN
  v_isCreatedBln := DBMS_XDB.createfolder('/public/resconfig');
```

```
  v_isCreatedBln := DBMS_XDB.createresource('/public/resconfig/rc2.xml',
  '<ResConfig xmlns="http://xmlns.oracle.com/xdb/XDBResConfig.xsd"
xmlns:xsi="http://www.w3.org/2001/XMLSchema-instance"
xsi:schemaLocation="http://xmlns.oracle.com/xdb/XDBResConfig.xsd
http://xmlns.oracle.com/xdb/XDBResConfig.xsd">
<event-listeners>
<listener>
<description>Access Record Application</description>
<schema>XMLDEMO</schema>
<source>EVENTS_PKG</source>
<language>PL/SQL</language>
<events><Render/></events>
</listener>
</event-listeners>
</ResConfig>');
end;
/
Commit;
```

These PL/SQL commands create a new *rc2.xml* configuration file in the */public/resconfig* folder in XML DB Repository. In this configuration file, it defines one listener to process the *<Render/>* event. The PL/SQL package handling the event is EVENTS_PKG. After the configuration file is created, we need to assign the configuration file to XML DB Repository resources.

First, let's create two new XML DB Repository resources, *r1.xml* and *r2.xml* (*run_events.sql*):

```
DECLARE
v_res boolean;
BEGIN
  IF (NOT DBMS_XDB.existsResource('/public/chp03')) then
     v_res:=DBMS_XDB.createFolder('/public/chp03');
  END IF;
  v_res:=DBMS_XDB.createresource('/public/chp03/r1.xml',
'<Profile><Name>Sumit1</Name><Company>Oracle</Company></Profile>');
  v_res:= DBMS_XDB.createresource('/public/chp03/r2.xml',
'<Profile><Name>Sumit2</Name><Company>Oracle</Company></Profile>');
END;
/
COMMIT;
```

We then register the just-created *rc2.xml* configuration file to these two resources:

```
EXEC DBMS_RESCONFIG.addresconfig('/public/chp03/r1.xml', '/public/chp03/
resconfig/rc2.xml');
EXEC DBMS_RESCONFIG.addresconfig('/public/chp03/r2.xml', '/public/chp03/
resconfig/rc2.xml');
COMMIT;
```

Now, we have enabled the XML DB Repository event.

Next, let's try to access the files via the XDBUriType, which will trigger the *Render* event:

```
SELECT xdburitype('/public/chp03/r1.xml').getclob()
from resource_view
where any_path = '/public/chp03/r1.xml';
SELECT xdburitype('/public/chp03/r2.xml').getclob()
from resource_view
where any_path = '/public/chp03/r2.xml';
```

Then, we check the *event_record_tbl* to find out whether the registered event handler records the access:

```
column res format a25
column usr format a10
column event format a10
column access_time format a15
select * from event_records_tbl;
RES                       USR        EVENT      ACCESS_TIME
------------------------- ---------- ---------- ---------------
/public/chp03/r1.xml        XMLDEMO       render     20-JUN-10
/public/chp03/r2.xml        XMLDEMO       render     20-JUN-10
```

You will find that two new records are added. The event handler operated as expected.

To check the XML DB Repository event listeners registered to a specified resource, run the following command:

```
SELECT DBMS_RESCONFIG.GETLISTENERS('/public/chp03/r1.xml') from dual;
```

This command lists all of the listeners registered to the */public/chp03/r1.xml* resource. To delete the event handler, run the following command (*check_event_listener.sql*):

```
EXEC DBMS_ResConfig.deleteResConfig('/public/chp03', '/public/chp03/resconfig/
rc2.xml', DBMS_ResConfig.DELETE_RECURSIVE);
```

The preceding command deletes all of the listeners registered to */public/chp03/resconfig/rc2.xml* in the */public/chp03* folder.

Summary

Oracle XML DB Repository provides new access to database data. Using XML DB Repository, you can store both XML and non-XML files in the Oracle database just like using a file system and query and process documents with SQL and PL/SQL. With both SQL and Internet protocol access, Oracle XML DB Repository is very convenient to use, and is ideal for unstructured data management in Oracle database.

CHAPTER 4

Parsing XML

ML parsing is the fundamental step in processing XML. XML parsers read the XML document, identify each meaningful object in the document, and then pass the objects to XML applications. XML parsers also provide services such as DTD or XML schema validations.

This chapter explores the XML parsing techniques. Inside the Oracle database, we will discuss parsing XML documents using XMLType functions and the DBMS_XMLDOM PL/SQL package. Outside the Oracle database, the discussion focuses on the XML parsers in Oracle XDK Java. There are three such parsers: DOM (Document Object Model), SAX (Simple API for XML), and JAXP (Java XML Processing APIs). The DOM parser represents XML in an object tree (DOM tree) and provides APIs with which users can create, query, and update the DOM tree. The SAX parser creates a set of events and callback functions to process the reported XML data. The JAXP parser provides standard Java APIs for XML processing. The discussion in this chapter focuses on Oracle Database 11*g* new features including Oracle *Scalable DOM* and *binary XML* technology. Because these features are not supported by JAXP, we mainly use Oracle XDK native DOM/SAX parsing APIs.

DOM Parsing in Java

DOM parsing is the basis for XSLT/XQuery processing. It's very convenient to use DOM APIs to access and update XML documents.

Basic DOM Parsing

Let's get started with a simple DOM parsing example using Oracle XDK Java (*DOMSimple.java*):

Listing 4-1 *DOM Parsing in Oracle XDK*

```
package xmlbook.chp04;

import java.io.File;
import java.io.FileInputStream;
import oracle.xml.parser.v2.DOMParser;
import oracle.xml.parser.v2.XMLDocument;
import oracle.xml.parser.v2.XMLElement;
import oracle.xml.parser.v2.XMLNode;
import oracle.xml.parser.v2.XMLParser;

public class DOMSimple {
    public static void main(String[] argv) {
        DOMParser dp = new DOMParser();
        dp.setAttribute(XMLParser.STANDALONE, Boolean.TRUE);
        dp.setPreserveWhitespace(false);
         try {
            dp.parse(new FileInputStream(new File("src/xml/john_smith.xml")));
            XMLDocument doc = dp.getDocument();
            // Access DOM object
            XMLElement elem = (XMLElement)doc.getDocumentElement();
```

```
            XMLNode node = (XMLNode)elem.getFirstChild();
            System.out.println("First Child of " + elem.getNodeName() +
                               " is: " + node.getNodeName());
            System.out.println("The First Child Node is:");
            node.print(System.out);
            //Print out the XML document
            System.out.println("Document:");
            XMLPrintDriver pd = new XMLPrintDriver(System.out);
            pd.setEncoding("UTF-8");
            pd.setFormatPrettyPrint(false);
            doc.print(pd);
        } catch (Exception ex) {
            ex.printStackTrace();
        }
    }
}
```

Parse the following XML document (*john_smith.xml*):

```
<?xml version = '1.0' encoding = 'UTF-8'?>
<!DOCTYPE contact_list SYSTEM "contact.dtd">
<contact id="1">
 <first_name>John</first_name>
 <last_name>Smith</last_name>
</contact>
```

The example output is as follows:

```
First Child of contact is: first_name
First Child Node:
<first_name>John</first_name>
Document:
<?xml version = '1.0' encoding = 'UTF-8'?><!DOCTYPE contact_list
SYSTEM "contact.dtd"><contact id="1"> <first_name>John</first_name>
<last_name>Smith</last_name></contact>
```

The first step of DOM parsing in Oracle XDK is to create an *oracle.xml.parser.v2.DOMParser* instance:

```
DOMParser dp = new DOMParser();
```

The next step is to parse the input XML document:

```
dp.parse(new FileInputStream(new File("src/xml/john_smith.xml")));
```

The DOM object (*oracle.xml.parser.v2.XMLDocument*) can be retrieved after the XML parsing:

```
XMLDocument doc = dp.getDocument();
```

You then can retrieve and update DOM nodes using DOM APIs. In this example, an example DOM access is given:

```
XMLElement elem = (XMLElement)doc.getDocumentElement();
XMLNode node = (XMLNode)elem.getFirstChild();
```

The XML document element is retrieved first and then its first child node. The DOM document is printed to an output stream:

```
XMLPrintDriver pd = new XMLPrintDriver(System.out);
pd.setEncoding("UTF-8");
pd.setFormatPrettyPrint(false);
doc.print(pd);
```

This example uses *oracle.xml.parser.v2.XMLPrintDriver* to remove formatting whitespaces by setting XMLPrintDriver.setFormatPrettyPrint(false).

In this example, we also turn off DTD parsing using the following setup:

```
dp.setAttribute(XMLParser.STANDALONE, Boolean.TRUE);
```

If you don't set this up, you get the following error:

```
java.net.MalformedURLException: no protocol: contact.dtd
```

DTD can be used in XML documents for two main purposes. One is to define the XML document content model for validation. The other is to define entities that can be referred to in the XML document. To resolve *entity references* in XML documents, you need to turn on the DTD parsing.

> **Oracle XDK Tip: How do I print out DOM element content?**
> Oracle XDK provides DOM classes with their name in the format of XML*(DOMObjectName), such as *XMLDocument* for Document, *XMLElement* for Element, *XMLNode* for Node, and so on. All of these Oracle XDK DOM document, element, or node classes have a print() member function that you can use to serialize out the content.

Next, let's review some frequently used DOM operations and highlight some Oracle XDK native APIs that can simplify the DOM-based XML processing.

Splitting XML Using DOM

Let's learn how to split a large XML document into a set of small documents using the Oracle XDK DOM parser. The following example splits a contact list document (*contact_list.xml*) into a set of contact documents (*DOMSplit.java*):

Listing 4-2 *Splitting an XML Document Using Oracle XDK DOM*

```
package xmlbook.chp04;

import java.io.File;
import java.io.FileWriter;
import java.io.PrintWriter;

import javax.xml.parsers.DocumentBuilder;
import javax.xml.parsers.DocumentBuilderFactory;
```

```
import oracle.xml.parser.v2.XMLDocument;
import oracle.xml.parser.v2.XMLDOMImplementation;
import oracle.xml.parser.v2.XMLNode;

import org.w3c.dom.Element;
import org.w3c.dom.Node;
import org.w3c.dom.NodeList;

public class DOMSplit {
    public static void main(String[] args) throws Exception {
        // Retrieve the XML Element from the input XML document and create documents
        createXMLDocuments("src/xml/contact_list.xml", "contact");
        return;
    }

    public static void createXMLDocuments(String fileName,
                                          String tag) throws Exception {
        DocumentBuilderFactory dbf = DocumentBuilderFactory.newInstance();

        try {
            DocumentBuilder db = dbf.newDocumentBuilder();
            XMLDocument doc = (XMLDocument)db.parse(new File(fileName));
            // You can get the document element
            Element el = doc.getDocumentElement();
            NodeList nl = doc.getElementsByTagName(tag);
            for (int i = 0; i < nl.getLength(); i++) {
                //XMLNode n = (XMLNode)nl.item(i);
                //n.print(new FileOutputStream(tag+"_"+i+".xml"));
                Node n = nl.item(i);
                //Create an XML document for the XMLElement
                XMLDocument sub_doc = createXMLDoc(n);
                if (sub_doc != null) {
                    sub_doc.print(new PrintWriter(
                      new FileWriter("output/" +tag + "_" +i + ".xml")));
                }
            }
        } catch (Exception ex) {
            ex.printStackTrace();
        }
    }

    public static XMLDocument createXMLDoc(Node node) {
        try {
            // Create New XML Document
            XMLDOMImplementation dimpl = new XMLDOMImplementation();
            XMLDocument xmldoc =
                (XMLDocument)dimpl.createDocument(node.getNamespaceURI(),
                                                  "copied_node", null);
```

```
            Node newNode = xmldoc.importNode(node, true);
            xmldoc.getDocumentElement().appendChild(newNode);
            return xmldoc;
        } catch (Exception e) {
            e.printStackTrace(System.out);
            return null;
        }
    }
}
```

In this example, we first parse *contact_list.xml* and then get all of the DOM elements with the tag name to be "contact" using the XMLDocument.getElementsByTagName() function. Then, we iterate all of the elements returned and pass the node of each "contact" element to the createXMLDoc() function. In the createXMLDoc() function, new XML documents are created using *oracle.xml.parser.v2.XMLDOMImplementation*:

```
XMLDOMImplementation dimpl = new XMLDOMImplementation();
```

Then, from *XMLDOMImplementation*, you can create a new DOM document with the namespace, node name, and an optional DTD:

```
XMLDocument xmldoc =
    (XMLDocument)dimpl.createDocument(node.getNamespaceURI(),
                                       "copied_node", null);
```

To append a DOM node from another DOM object, we first need to import the XML node to the current DOM document by calling the importNode() function:

```
Node newNode = xmldoc.importNode(node, true);
xmldoc.getDocumentElement().appendChild(newNode);
```

A new node is created after importNode() and then is used to append to the new DOM document.

With this program, you can split large XML documents by running the following command:

```
XMLNode n = (XMLNode)nl.item(i);
n.print(new FileOutputStream("output/"+tag+"_0"+i+".xml"));
```

Oracle XDK Tip: Why do I get an error when appending a DOM node?

When copying a DOM node from one document to another, you can't directly use the appendNode() function. You first have to change the DOM document owner of the node using adoptNode() or importNode(). Otherwise, you will get the "oracle.xml.parser.v2.XMLDOMException: cannot add a node belonging to a different document" error. The difference between adoptNode() or importNode() is that adoptNode() removes the original node from the source document while importNode() creates a copy.

Scalable DOM Parsing

DOM parser builds in-memory DOM objects. This requires a lot of memory to store the DOM objects. As XML documents get bigger, they can easily raise an "out-of-memory error."

To allow the Oracle XDK DOM parser to process large XML documents in Oracle Database 11*g*, Oracle (XDK) Java introduced a new DOM parser called Scalable DOM parser. Instead of keeping all the XML DOM objects in memory, Scalable DOM parser only creates DOM objects when needed. In addition, the in-memory DOM objects are stored in binary XML to reduce the memory space. Scalable DOM parsers can also set up the *Page Managers* so that it can dump binary XML to the disk or other storage when there is not enough memory space. In Oracle Database 11*g*, Scalable DOM parser is the basis for scalable XPath, XSLT, and XQuery operations and is provided via a set of new Oracle XDK native APIs.

Let's look at the following example using the Scalable DOM parser (*SDOMSimple.java*):

```
package xmlbook.chp04;

import oracle.xml.parser.v2.DOMParser;
import oracle.xml.parser.v2.XMLDocument;
import oracle.xml.scalable.BinaryStream;
import oracle.xml.util.XMLUtil;

public class SDOMSimple {
    public static void main(String[] args) throws Exception {
        DOMParser dp = new DOMParser();
        dp.setPreserveWhitespace(false);
        dp.setAttribute(dp.STANDALONE, true);
        dp.setAttribute(DOMParser.PARTIAL_DOM, true);
        dp.setAttribute(BinaryStream.BINARY_FORMAT,BinaryStream.XDB_BINXML);
        try {
            dp.parse(XMLUtil.createURL(args[0]));
        } catch (Exception ex) {
            ex.printStackTrace();
        }
        XMLDocument doc = dp.getDocument();
        doc.print(System.out);
    }
}
```

To use scalable DOM, you need to pass XML with the Oracle XDK DOM parser, which is the *oracle.xml.parser.v2.DOMParser*.

```
DOMParser dp= new DOMParser();
```

Then, enable Scalable DOM parsing by setting up the parser attributes:

```
dp.setAttribute(DOMParser.PARTIAL_DOM, true);
dp.setAttribute(BinaryStream.BINARY_FORMAT,BinaryStream.XDB_BINXML);
```

`DOMParser.PARTIAL_DOM` tells Oracle XDK parser to build a Scalable DOM. In Oracle Database 11gR2, you can set up the binary XML format using the `BinaryStream.BINARY_FORMAT` property. There are two binary XML formats:

- **BinaryStream.XDB_BINXML** Use for binary XML compliant with Oracle XML DB binary XML.
- **BinaryStream.XDK_CXML** Use the Oracle XDK binary XML format.

After the parser setup, you can parse the input XML documents:

```
try {
  dp.parse(XMLUtil.createURL(args[0]));
}
catch(Exception ex) {
ex.printStackTrace();    }
XMLDocument doc = parser.getDocument();
```

This is no different from using normal DOM parsing. All the rest of the Scalable DOM operations are transparent to the end users. However, with Scalable DOM, you can perform DOM operations on large XML documents.

The previous example doesn't set up a page manager; the binary XML is kept in memory, and disk paging will be used when the memory space is not enough. However, you have the option to provide your own page manager to perform memory management. The following example enables *oracle.xml.scalable.FilePageManager* (*SDOMFilePageManager.java*):

```
package xmlbook.chp04;

import oracle.xml.parser.v2.DOMParser;
import oracle.xml.parser.v2.XMLDocument;
import oracle.xml.parser.v2.XMLNode;
import oracle.xml.scalable.BinaryStream;
import oracle.xml.scalable.FilePageManager;
import oracle.xml.util.XMLUtil;

public class SDOMFilePageManager {

    public static void main(String[] args) throws Exception {
        DOMParser dp = new DOMParser();
        dp.setPreserveWhitespace(false);
        dp.setAttribute(DOMParser.PARTIAL_DOM, true);
        dp.setAttribute(BinaryStream.BINARY_FORMAT, BinaryStream.XDB_BINXML);
        FilePageManager pageFile = new FilePageManager("sDOMPageFile", "new");
        dp.setAttribute(DOMParser.PAGE_MANAGER, pageFile);
        try {
            dp.parse(XMLUtil.createURL("src/xml/3mInput.xml"));

        } catch (Exception ex) {
            ex.printStackTrace();
        }
```

```
        XMLDocument doc = dp.getDocument();
        MyNSResolver nsr= new MyNSResolver();
        XMLNode nd = (XMLNode) doc.selectSingleNode("/po:PurchaseOrder/po:ShipTo",
nsr);
        nd.print(System.out);
}
```

When creating *oracle.xml.scalable.FilePageManager,* the first parameter is the paging file name, and the second parameter tells how to use the paging file. There are two options:

- **new** Create a new paging file.
- **rw** Open an existing paging file and create a new file only when the file doesn't exist.

With the *PageManagers,* Scalable DOM only creates a DOM node in memory as needed. It's good practice to set up a page manager when using Oracle XDK Scalable DOM.

Cutting and Pasting Across Documents

For many people, DOM-based XML content navigation is complicated. To simplify the process, Oracle XDK offers two functions, XMLDocument.selectSingleNodes(XPath) and XMLDocument .selectNodes(XPath). The XMLDocument.selectSingleNode() function returns a single DOM node from the XPath input. The XMLDocument.selectNodes() function selects a set of DOM nodes from the XPath input. The following example copies a DOM node from one XML document and inserts the copied node into a new XML document using one of these functions (*SDOMCopy.java*):

```
package xmlbook.chp04;

import oracle.xml.parser.v2.DOMParser;
import oracle.xml.parser.v2.XMLDocument;
import oracle.xml.parser.v2.XMLParser;
import oracle.xml.scalable.BinaryStream;
import oracle.xml.util.XMLUtil;
import org.w3c.dom.Node;

public class SDOMCopy{
    public static void main(String[] args) throws Exception {
        DOMParser dp1 = new DOMParser();
        dp1.setAttribute(XMLParser.STANDALONE, Boolean.TRUE);
        dp1.setAttribute(DOMParser.PARTIAL_DOM, true);
        dp1.setAttribute(BinaryStream.BINARY_FORMAT,BinaryStream.XDB_BINXML);
        DOMParser dp2 = new DOMParser();
        dp2.setAttribute(DOMParser.PARTIAL_DOM, true);
        dp2.setAttribute(BinaryStream.BINARY_FORMAT,BinaryStream.XDB_BINXML);
        try {
            dp1.parse(XMLUtil.createURL(args[0]));
            XMLDocument doc1 = dp1.getDocument();
            dp2.parse(XMLUtil.createURL(args[1]));
            XMLDocument doc2 = dp2.getDocument();
            MyNSResolver nr = new MyNSResolver();
```

```
            Node node1= doc1.selectSingleNode("/book:contact", nr);
            Node node2 = doc2.selectSingleNode("/resume");
            Node node3 = doc1.importNode(node2, true);
            node1.appendChild(node3);
            doc1.print(System.out);
        } catch (Exception ex) {
            ex.printStackTrace();
        }
    }
}
```

In this example, XPath is used to select the *<contact>* and *<resume>* elements. To resolve the namespace, we create the following namespace resolver (*MyNSResolver.java*):

```
package xmlbook.chp04;

import java.util.Hashtable;
import oracle.xml.parser.v2.NSResolver;

public class MyNSResolver implements NSResolver {
    Hashtable m_htNS = new Hashtable();
    MyNSResolver() {
        m_htNS.put("book", "http://xmlbook.com/sample/contact.xsd");
        m_htNS.put("po", "http://www.globalcompany.com/ns/sales");
    }
    public String resolveNamespacePrefix(String prefix) {
        return (String)m_htNS.get(prefix);
    }
}
```

In this example, a hash table *m_htNS* is created for the namespace lookup. When resolveNamespacePrefix() is given a namespace prefix, the namespace URI is returned from the hash table. Running this program on the *john_smith.xml* document and its resume document is shown as follows (*resume/john_smith.xml*):

```
<?xml version="1.0" encoding="WINDOWS-1252"?>
<resume>
  <header>
    <firstname>John</firstname>
    <surname>Smith</surname>
    <phone>650-506-4000</phone>
    <fax>650-633-5405</fax>
    <email>randerson@gmail.com</email>
  </header>
  <objective>
    <emphasize>Leading software projects from conception through implementation
and maintenance.</emphasize>
  </objective>
  ...
</resume>
```

You will get a document with the resume merged into the contact:

```
<?xml version = '1.0' encoding = 'UTF-8'?>
<!DOCTYPE contact SYSTEM "contact.dtd" []>
<contact xmlns="http://xmlbook.com/sample/contact.xsd" id="1">
 <first_name chinese="约翰"">John</first_name>
 <last_name>Smith</last_name>
<resume xmlns="">
  <header>
    <firstname>John</firstname>
    <surname>Smith</surname>
    <phone>650-506-4000</phone>
    <fax>650-633-5405</fax>
    <email>randerson@gmail.com</email>
  </header>
  <objective>
    <emphasize>Leading software projects from conception through implementation
and maintenance.</emphasize>
  </objective>
...
</resume></contact>
```

Note that there is no namespace for the *<resume>* element. If you'd like to add a namespace to *<resume>* and its child XML elements, don't use DOM but rather use XSLT (refer to Listing 7-4 for more info).

Oracle XDK Tip: How can I differentiate between the element node and the text node in DOM?

When performing DOM update operations, you sometimes find nothing is changed after the operations. For example, here we want to update the <first_name> to be *Richard* instead of *John*:

```
<contact><first_name>John</first_name><last_name>Smith</last_name>
</contact>
```

After getting the *<first_name>* element using

```
Node node= doc.selectSingleNode("/contact/first_name");
```

you update the *<first_name>* element using the following code:

```
node.setNodeValue("Richard");
```

This will not result in any change in the document! What you need to update is not the *<first_name> element* node but its child *text* node. Therefore, you need to get the text node from *<first_name>* and update it using the setNodeValue() function:

```
Node node= doc.selectSingleNode("/contact/first_name/text()");
node.setNodeValue("Richard");
```

DOM Parsing in SQL

You don't really need to perform many DOM operations in Oracle Database 11*g*—when you create an XMLType object, you can process it using XMLType and XQuery functions. However, there are some operations where you might need to use DOM processing. Let's take a look at a few examples.

Retrieving and Creating a CDATA Section

This first example uses DBMS_XMLDOM (with alias XMLDOM) and DBMS_XMLPARSER (with alias XMLPARSER) to retrieve and create a new CDATA node (*create_cdata.sql*):

Listing 4-3 *Creating a CDATA Section in SQL*

```
declare
l_xml                clob;
l_parser             xmlparser.parser;
l_domdocument        xmldom.domdocument;
l_domnode            xmldom.domnode;
l_domtnode           xmldom.domnode;
l_domfnode           xmldom.domnode;
l_domcnode           xmldom.domnode;
l_domnodelist        xmldom.domnodelist;
l_domcharactersection xmldom.DOMCDataSection;
l_data               varchar2(200);
length               NUMBER;
begin
l_xml := '<?xml version="1.0"?>
<Test>
<Data>
<Height>1</Height>
<Width>1</Width>
<Length>1</Length>
<Note><![CDATA[
One cubic unit of measure...
]]></Note>
</Data>
</Test>';

l_parser := xmlparser.newparser;
xmlparser.parseclob(l_parser, l_xml);
l_domdocument := xmlparser.getdocument(l_parser);
xmlparser.freeparser(l_parser);

l_domnode := xmldom.makenode(l_domdocument);

l_domtnode := xslprocessor.selectsinglenode(l_domnode,'/Test/Data/Note');
xmldom.writetobuffer(l_domtnode,l_data);
dbms_output.put_line('CDATA Node:');
dbms_output.put_line(l_data);
-- Get CDATA Node
```

```
l_domnodelist := xmldom.getChildNodes(l_domtnode);
length := xmldom.getLength(l_domnodelist);

FOR i IN 1..length-1 LOOP
dbms_output.put_line('CDATA Node Value:');
dbms_output.put_line(xmldom.getNodeValue(xmldom.item(l_domnodelist, i)));
END LOOP;

-- Create a new CDATA section
l_domcharactersection := xmldom.createCDataSection(l_domdocument,'This is a
<[CDATA[..]]> section);
l_domcnode := xmldom.makenode(l_domcharactersection);
if not xmldom.isnull(l_domcnode) then
l_domfnode :=xmldom.appendChild(l_domtnode, l_domcnode);
end if;
xmldom.writetobuffer(l_domnode,l_data);
dbms_output.put_line('After appending created CDATA section:');
dbms_output.put_line(l_data);

xmldom.freedocument(l_domdocument);
exception
when others then
xmldom.freedocument(l_domdocument);
dbms_output.put_line('Exception! ('||sqlcode||') '||sqlerrm);
end;
/
```

In this DOM process, the DOM parser is created and then parses an XML document stored in a CLOB with the following code:

```
l_parser := xmlparser.newparser;
xmlparser.parseclob(l_parser, l_xml);
l_domdocument := xmlparser.getdocument(l_parser);
```

You have to initialize the parser object and then use it to parse the XML inputs. The DOM object is returned as an *xmldom.domdocument* object. After the DOM process, you can free the *xmlparser.parser* object:

```
xmlparser.freeparser(l_parser);
```

To retrieve a CDATA section content, we call the xmldom.getNodeValue() function:

```
l_domtnode := xslprocessor.selectsinglenode(l_domnode,'/Test/Data/Node');
...
-- Get CDATA Node
l_domnodelist := xmldom.getChildNodes(l_domtnode);
length := xmldom.getLength(l_domnodelist);
FOR i IN 1..length-1 LOOP
dbms_output.put_line('CDATA Node Value:');
dbms_output.put_line(xmldom.getNodeValue(xmldom.item(l_domnodelist, i)));
END LOOP;
```

To create a CDATA section, we call the following functions:

```
 l_domcharactersection := xmldom.createcdatasection(l_domdocument,'This is a
<[CDATA[..]]> sectioin');
l_domcnode := xmldom.makenode(l_domcharactersection);
if not xmldom.isnull(l_domcnode) then
l_domfnode :=xmldom.appendChild(l_domtnode, l_domcnode);
end if;
```

Importing a DOM Node

The second example creates a DOM node from CLOB content and imports the new DOM node to a DOM document (*import_dom_node.sql*).

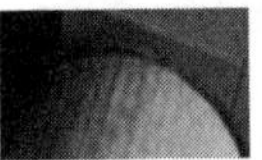

EXAMPLE SETUP

You need to run the create_hr_schema.sql *before running this example.*

Listing 4-4 *Importing a DOM Node in SQL*

```
set echo on
set serveroutput on
declare
v_tdoc xmltype;
v_clob clob;
v_result clob;
v_doc dbms_xmldom.DOMDocument;
v_subdoc dbms_xmldom.DOMDocument;
v_doc_elem dbms_xmldom.DOMElement;
v_subdoc_elem dbms_xmldom.DOMElement;
v_node dbms_xmldom.DOMNode;
v_impnode dbms_xmldom.DOMNode;
v_cdata dbms_xmldom.DOMCDataSection;
begin
-- Create the Main XML document
select XMLType(dbms_xmlgen.getXML('select * from departments where department_
id = 20'))
into v_tdoc from dual;

-- Create the Sub XML document
select dbms_xmlgen.getXML('select * from employees where department_id = 20')
into v_clob from dual;

-- Merge the document together by using importNode() and appendChild()
v_doc := dbms_xmldom.newDOMDocument(v_tdoc);
-- Escape the content
v_subdoc :=dbms_xmldom.newDOMDocument(v_clob);
v_doc_elem := dbms_xmldom.getDocumentElement(v_doc);
v_subdoc_elem := dbms_xmldom.getDocumentElement(v_subdoc);
```

```
v_impnode := dbms_xmldom.importNode(v_doc,dbms_xmldom.makeNode(v_subdoc_elem),
true) ;
v_node := dbms_xmldom.appendChild(dbms_xmldom.makeNode(v_doc_elem),
v_impnode);

dbms_lob.createtemporary(v_result,true,dbms_lob.session);
dbms_xmldom.writetoclob(v_doc,v_result);
dbms_output.put_line(v_result);
dbms_lob.freetemporary(v_result);
end;
/
```

In this example, we first create an XML document in CLOB using the following SQL query:

```
select dbms_xmlgen.getXML('select * from employees where department_id = 20')
into v_clob from dual;
```

Then we create a new document from this CLOB XML input:

```
v_subdoc :=dbms_xmldom.newDOMDocument(v_clob);
......
v_subdoc_elem := dbms_xmldom.getDocumentElement(v_subdoc);
```

The target document to merge the CLOB content is created from an XMLType object:

```
select XMLType(dbms_xmlgen.getXML('select * from departments where department_
id = 20')) into v_tdoc from dual;
......
v_doc := dbms_xmldom.newDOMDocument(v_tdoc);
v_doc_elem := dbms_xmldom.getDocumentElement(v_doc);
```

We can't directly append the CLOB content element to the target document. Instead, we need to import the DOM node first and then perform the append operation:

```
v_impnode := dbms_xmldom.importNode(v_doc,dbms_xmldom.makeNode(v_subdoc_elem),
true) ;
v_node := dbms_xmldom.appendChild(dbms_xmldom.makeNode(v_doc_elem),
v_impnode);
```

SAX Parsing

The SAX parser won't build objects in memory as the DOM parser does. When XML is parsed by SAX parsers, SAX events are generated to report the parsed XML infosets. To receive the SAX events, you need to register a document handler to the SAX parser. The following are the major Oracle XDK SAX parsing handlers:

- **Document Handler** Provides functions receiving SAX parsing events. There are several DocumentHandlers, including org.xml.sax.DefaultHandler and oracle.xml.parser.v2.XMLDocumentHandler.
- **Event Handler** Provides error handling, including handling errors, warnings, and exceptions.

- **DTD Handler** Provides functions receiving DTD parsing events.
- **EntityResolver** Provides functions receiving entity resolving events.
- **XMLSAXSerializer** Creates serialized XML output.

Basic SAX Parsing

The following is a SAX parsing example (*SAXSimple.java*):

```
package xmlbook.chp04;

import java.io.File;
import javax.xml.parsers.SAXParser;
import javax.xml.parsers.SAXParserFactory;

import org.xml.sax.Attributes;
import org.xml.sax.SAXException;
import org.xml.sax.SAXParseException;
import org.xml.sax.helpers.DefaultHandler;

public class SAXSimple {

public static void main(String[] argv) {
        SAXSimple ss = new SAXSimple();
        ss.parseXML("src/xml/contact_list.xml");
    }

public void parseXML (String inputXML){
SAXParserFactory spf = SAXParserFactory.newInstance();

try {
             SAXParser sp = spf.newSAXParser();
             MyDefaultHandler mdh= new MyDefaultHandler();
             sp.parse(new File(inputXML), mdh);
         } catch (SAXParseException ex) {
             System.out.println(ex.getMessage());
         } catch (Exception ex) {
             ex.printStackTrace();
             System.out.print("error");
         }
}

private class  MyDefaultHandler extends DefaultHandler {
MyDefaultHandler(){
             super();
         }
public void startDocument() throws SAXException {
             System.out.println("Event: startDocument");
         }
```

```
public void endDocument() throws SAXException {
            System.out.println("Event: endDocument");
        }
public void startElement(String uri, String localName, String qName,
Attributes attributes) {
System.out.println("Event: startElement - "+localName);
for (int i=0 ; i<attributes.getLength();i+\+ ) {
             System.out.println("Attribute:" +
                   attributes.getLocalName(i)+"="+attributes.getValue(i));
            }

}
public void endElement(String uri, String localName, String rawName){
            System.out.println("Event: endElement - "+localName);
        }
}
}
```

In this simple SAX parsing example, we first create a SAXSimple class with the parseXML() function, which involves the following steps to perform SAX parsing:

1. **Create SAXParser.**
   Using JAXP standard APIs, we first create SAXParserFactory:

   ```
   SAXParserFactory spf = SAXParserFactory.newInstance();
   ```

   Then, from the newly created SAXParserFactory we can initialize a SAX parser for XML processing:

   ```
   SAXParser sp = spf.newSAXParser();
   ```

2. **Create the Document Handler to respond to the SAX events.**
   In this example, we create a private class called *MyDocumentHandler* that extends the DefaultHandler and simply prints out the content parsed by the SAX parser.

   For example, in the startElement() events, we get the following response:

   ```
   public void startElement(String uri, String localName, String qName,
   Attributes attributes) {
   System.out.println("Event: startElement - "+localName);
   for (int i=0 ; i<attributes.getLength();i+\+ ) {
                System.out.println("Attribute:" + attributes
   .getLocalName(i)+"="+attributes.getValue(i));
              }
   }
   ```

3. **Parse the XML document.**
   The parser parses the input XML document giving the file input and the document handler.

   ```
   sp.parse(new File(inputXML, mdh);
   ```

Because DefaultHandler does not have an error handing process, we need to overwrite the error(), warning(), and fatalError() methods to report errors:

```
public void warning(SAXParseException e) throws SAXException {
          System.out.println("Warning: ");
          printInfo(e);
      }
public void error(SAXParseException e) throws SAXException {
          System.out.println("Error: ");
          printInfo(e);
      }
public void fatalError(SAXParseException e) throws SAXException {
          System.out.println("Fatal error: ");
          printInfo(e);
      }
private void printInfo(SAXParseException e) {
      System.out.println("   Public ID: "+e.getPublicId());
      System.out.println("   System ID: "+e.getSystemId());
      System.out.println("   Line number: "+e.getLineNumber());
      System.out.println("   Column number: "+e.getColumnNumber());
      System.out.println("   Message: "+e.getMessage());
      }
```

There are three types of errors in SAX parsing:

- **Fatal Error** Normally occurs when XML is not well-formed and can't be parsed. public void fatalError(SAXParseException e) throws SAXException { }
- **Error** Shown when there is an XML validation error. public void error(SAXParseException e) throws SAXException { }
- **Warning** Reports other minor errors in the process. public void warning(SAXParseException e) throws SAXException { }

Finally, we create an instance of the SAXSimple class and invoke the parseXML() function.

```
public static void main(String[] argv) {
 SAXSimple ss = new SAXSimple();
 ss.parseXML("src/xml/contact_list.xml");
}
```

In the example JDeveloper project, right-click *SAXSimple.java* in the Application Navigator and select Run. You will get the following output, reporting four SAX events: start/end Document, start/end Element, and the names of XML elements and attributes parsed as follows:

```
Event: startDocument
Event: startElement - contact_list
Event: startElement - contact
Attribute:id=1
Event: startElement - first_name
Event: endElement - first_name
```

```
Event: startElement - last_name
Event: endElement - last_name
Event: endElement - contact
Event: startElement - contact
Attribute:id=2
Event: startElement - first_name
Event: endElement - first_name
Event: startElement - last_name
Event: endElement - last_name
Event: endElement - contact
Event: endElement - contact_list
Event: endDocument
```

Table 4-1 summarizes the five most common events that you can use with the SAX parser.

There are other SAX events to handle notation declarations (notationDecl), processing instructions (processingInstruction), ignorable whitespaces (ignorableWhitespace), entities (unparsedEntityDecl, skippedEntity), and namespace prefix URI mappings (start/endPrefixMapping). Because these events are not used very often, we won't discuss them here. You can check the Java documentation for these functions/events when needed.

Now, let's work on a few examples using the advanced SAX parsing features in Oracle XDK.

Event	Methods in DefaultHandler
startDocument	Invoked when starting to parse an XML document (before reading the declaration of XML <?XML...?>). `public void startDocument()`
endDocument	Invoked when completing the parsing of an XML document (after the closing tag of XML root element). `public void endDocument()`
startElement	Invoked when starting to parse a new XML element. `public void startElement(String uri, String localName, String qName, Attributes attributes)` When dealing with an XML element with namespace, — **uri** will be the namespace URI. — **qName** will be the XML element name with the namespace prefix.
endElement	Invoked when ending the parsing of an XML element. `public void endElement(String uri, String localName, String qName, Attributes attributes)` —The **uri** will be the namespace URI. —The **qName** will be the XML element name with the namespace prefix.
characters	Invoked when parsing the text content in XML elements. `public void characters(char[] ch, in start, int length)`

TABLE 4-1. *Main SAX Methods*

SAX Print

oracle.xml.parser.v2.XMLSAXSerializer is a SAX handler extended from *DefaultHandler* that provides the XML serialization support for the Oracle XDK SAX parser. In the following example, we use it to print out the XML parsing result (*SAXPrintSimple.java*):

```
package xmlbook.chp04;

import java.io.File;
import javax.xml.parsers.SAXParser;
import javax.xml.parsers.SAXParserFactory;
import oracle.xml.parser.v2.XMLSAXSerializer;

import org.xml.sax.SAXParseException;

public class SAXPrintSimple {

public static void main(String[] argv) {
        SAXPrintSimple sps = new SAXPrintSimple();
        sps.parseXMLandPrint("src/xml/contact_list.xml");
    }
public void parseXMLandPrint(String inputXML) {
SAXParserFactory spf = SAXParserFactory.newInstance();
try {
            XMLSAXSerializer ss = new XMLSAXSerializer(System.out);
            SAXParser sp = spf.newSAXParser();
            sp.parse(new File(inputXML), ss);
        } catch (SAXParseException ex) {
            System.out.println(ex.getMessage());
        } catch (Exception ex) {
            ex.printStackTrace();
            System.out.print("error");
        }
}
}
```

Oracle XDK *XMLSAXSerializer* provides a nicely formatted XML output by default. You also have several options to set up *XMLSAXSerializer* using oracle.xml.parser.v2.setProperty():

- Set up the XML encoding of the output. The default is UTF-8.

  ```
  oracle.xml.parser.v2.setProperty(XMLSAXSerializer.ENCODING, "UTF-8")
  ```

- Decide whether to omit the XML declaration:

  ```
  oracle.xml.parser.v2.setProperty(XMLSAXSerializer.OMIT_XML_DECL, false)
  to keep the XML declaration (default)
  oracle.xml.parser.v2.setProperty(XMLSAXSerializer.OMIT_XML_DECL,true)
  to omit the XML declaration <?XML ?>
  ```

Parsing Binary XML

Binary XML is an Oracle-defined XML format for storing and processing large XML documents. The following are some basic concepts of the binary XML format:

- **All XML element tags and attributes are tokenized in binary XML.**
  Binary XML has an index table storing all XML element and attribute names (tokens), and their reference IDs (token IDs). In the document, all of the XML elements and attributes are referred to by the reference IDs. This reduces the XML document size, especially when long (normally meaningful) tag names are used for the XML element and attribute names.
- **Binary is a pre-parsed format.**
  XML parsing information is stored within binary XML documents. The Oracle XML processor can quickly locate the XML objects. You can think of binary XML as serialized a DOM object, through which the XML processors know where to get the data.
- **Binary XML has two formats: XML DB binary XML and XDK binary XML.**
  The XML DB binary XML is used to store and process XML within Oracle XML DB. XDK binary XML is used to exchange binary XML documents outside the Oracle XML DB. Oracle XML DB maintains the binary XML token definition inside the Oracle database and the token definitions are not attached to each binary XML document. Oracle XDK instead includes the token definitions inline with the binary XML document so that other applications or databases receiving the XML document can interpret the encoded binary XML document. Oracle XDK can convert Oracle XML DB binary XML format to Oracle XDK binary XML format when needed.

The following are the main reasons to use binary XML:

- **Use binary XML in Oracle XML DB to store XMLTypes.**
  Binary XML's size is normally smaller than the actual XML in text, you can save the storage space.
- **Use binary XML in mid-tier when you need to deal with large XML data; for example, XML files larger than 1 megabyte.**
  The size of a DOM object is normally two times as large as the XML document in text. You need to consider memory space when the XML document size is large. You can use SAX parser, but DOM APIs are much easier to use and are the basis for XSL transformations and XQuery. Therefore, using binary XML and Scalable DOM in mid-tier is a good choice.

Writing XML to Binary XML

If you have a DOM object, you can save it to a binary XML document. Let's start with this example (*BinaryXMLWrite.java*):

```
package xmlbook.chp04;

import java.io.File;
import java.net.URL;
import oracle.xml.binxml.BinXMLEncoder;
import oracle.xml.binxml.BinXMLProcessor;
import oracle.xml.binxml.BinXMLProcessorFactory;
```

```
import oracle.xml.binxml.BinXMLStream;
import oracle.xml.parser.v2.DOMParser;
import oracle.xml.parser.v2.XMLDocument;
import oracle.xml.scalable.BinaryStream;
import oracle.xml.scalable.InfosetWriter;

public class BinaryXMLWrite {

    public static void main(String[] args) throws Exception {
        DOMParser dp = new DOMParser();
        dp.setPreserveWhitespace(false);
        try {
            dp.parse(fileToURL(args[0]));
            XMLDocument doc = dp.getDocument();
            writeToBinaryXML(doc,args[1]);
        } catch (Exception ex) {
            ex.printStackTrace();
        }
    }

    public static void writeToBinaryXML(XMLDocument doc, String fileName) throws
Exception{
        BinXMLProcessor proc = BinXMLProcessorFactory.createProcessor();
        BinXMLStream bstr =
            proc.createBinXMLStream(new File(fileName));
        BinXMLEncoder enc = bstr.getEncoder();
        enc.setProperty(BinXMLEncoder.ENC_INLINE_TOKEN_DEFS, true);
        enc.setProperty(BinXMLEncoder.ENC_SCHEMA_AWARE, false);
        InfosetWriter writer = enc.createInfosetWriter();
        doc.save(writer);
        writer.close();
    }
}
```

The writeToBinaryXML() function writes *XMLDocument* to binary XML files with the following steps.

The first step is to create a *BinXMLProcessor* from *BinXMLProcessorFactory* and then create *BinXMLStream* from *BinXMLProcessor*.

```
BinXMLProcessor proc = BinXMLProcessorFactory.createProcessor();
BinXMLStream bstr =  proc.createBinXMLStream(new File(fileName));
```

A new file is created to store in the binary XML. In the Java code, we create a new File object and pass it to *BinXMLStream*.

The second step is to set up *BinXMLEncoder* to encode the binary XML:

```
BinXMLEncoder enc = bstr.getEncoder();
enc.setProperty(BinXMLEncoder.ENC_INLINE_TOKEN_DEFS, true);
enc.setProperty(BinXMLEncoder.ENC_SCHEMA_AWARE, false);
```

XMLBinEncoder will write the binary XML output using the following code:

```
InfosetWriter writer = enc.createInfosetWriter();
doc.save(writer);
writer.close();
```

You can compare the size of the XML in text and the binary XML file created. Normally, the bigger the XML document, the more compression you will have.

Reading from Binary XML

You can use Oracle XDK APIs to read XML documents stored in Oracle binary XML format. The following example reads from binary XML files and creates a *Scalable DOM* object (*BinaryXMLRead.java*).

```
package xmlbook.chp04;

import java.io.File;
import oracle.xml.binxml.BinXMLDecoder;
import oracle.xml.binxml.BinXMLProcessor;
import oracle.xml.binxml.BinXMLProcessorFactory;
import oracle.xml.parser.v2.XMLDOMImplementation;
import oracle.xml.parser.v2.XMLDocument;
import oracle.xml.scalable.InfosetReader;
import oracle.xml.binxml.BinXMLStream;

public class BinaryXMLRead {

    public static void main(String[] args) throws Exception {
        try {
            XMLDocument doc =
                readBinaryXML(new File("src/xml/contact_list.bxml"));
            doc.print(System.out);
        } catch (Exception ex) {
            ex.printStackTrace();
        }
    }

    public static XMLDocument readBinaryXML(File binXMLFile) throws Exception
{
        BinXMLProcessor proc = BinXMLProcessorFactory.createProcessor();
        BinXMLStream bstr = proc.createBinXMLStream(binXMLFile);
        BinXMLDecoder dec = bstr.getDecoder();
        InfosetReader reader = dec.getReader();

        XMLDOMImplementation domi = new XMLDOMImplementation();
        domi.setAttribute(XMLDocument.SCALABLE_DOM, true);
        domi.setAttribute(XMLDocument.ACCESS_MODE, XMLDocument.UPDATEABLE);
        XMLDocument doc = (XMLDocument)domi.createDocument(reader);
        return doc;
    }
}
```

In this example, the readBinaryXML() function reads the binary XML from files. In this function, the first step is to create an *InfosetReader* to read binary XML data:

```
BinXMLProcessor proc = BinXMLProcessorFactory.createProcessor();
BinXMLStream bstr = proc.createBinXMLStream(binXMLFile);
```

To create an *InfosetReader* for binary XML, you first need to create a *BinXMLProcessor* from *BinXMLProcessorFactory* and then create the *BinXMLStream* using the BinXMLProcessor .createBinXMLStream(java.io.File file) function. In Oracle XDK, you can create a *BinaryXMLStream* from other sources, including *BLOBs, InputStream, OutputStream, byte array,* and an *URL*:

```
BinXMLStream createBinXMLStream(java.sql.Blob blob)
BinXMLStream createBinXMLStream(byte[] array)
BinXMLStream createBinXMLStream(java.io.InputStream in)
BinXMLStream createBinXMLStream(java.io.OutputStream out)
BinXMLStream createBinXMLStream(java.net.URL url)
```

The BinXMLProcessor.createBinXMLStream() function returns *BinXMLStream.*

```
BinXMLDecoder dec = bstr.getDecoder();
InfosetReader reader = dec.getReader();
```

From *BinXMLStream,* you can get *BinXMLDecoder,* which provides *InfosetReader* to read the binary XML stream. In Oracle XDK, you can create DOM access to the XML data from *InfosetReader*:

```
XMLDOMImplementation domi = new XMLDOMImplementation();
domi.setAttribute(XMLDocument.SCALABLE_DOM, true);
domi.setAttribute(XMLDocument.ACCESS_MODE, XMLDocument.UPDATEABLE);
XMLDocument doc = (XMLDocument)domi.createDocument(reader);
```

Note that, in this example, the *XMLDocument* object is created as a Scalable DOM with "lazy" DOM manifestation.

Summary

This chapter explains the XML parsing process. It's an important step to prepare for further XML processing. In Oracle XDK, you can parse XML in SAX or DOM, using JAXP or the native Oracle XDK APIs. In Oracle XML DB, XML parsing is performed when constructing XMLTypes or processing with DBMS_XMLPARSER. In Oracle Database 11*g*, the new binary XML and Scalable DOM provide a high performance and scalable DOM parsing, which is useful for building enterprise XML applications.

CHAPTER 5

Validating XML

ML parsing checks the XML syntax to ensure XML *well-formedness*. XML validation validates XML documents against XML Schema or DTD (Document Type Definition) to ensure that XML is conformed to the data model defined by XML Schema or DTD. The defined XML data model includes the XML elements and attributes, their data types, content restrictions, and the document structure.

In this chapter, we begin by reviewing some basic concepts of DTD and XML Schema (http://www.w3.org/2001/XMLSchema). We then learn how to perform XML validations in Oracle XML DB and Oracle XDK Java. We conclude by exploring how to use XML Schema and JAXB (Java Architecture for XML Binding) in XML applications.

DTD Validation

DTD defines the XML structure with a list of elements, attributes, and entities. DTD is widely used in document-centric applications. DTD can be stored as a file or embedded in XML documents. The DTDs included within an XML document are called "internal DTDs." An example is shown as follows (*contact_list_in.xml*):

```
<?xml version = '1.0' encoding = 'UTF-8'?>
<!DOCTYPE contact_list[
<!ELEMENT contact_list (contact+)>
<!ELEMENT contact (first_name,last_name)>
<!ELEMENT first_name (#PCDATA)>
<!ELEMENT last_name (#PCDATA)>
<!ATTLIST contact id CDATA #REQUIRED>
<!ENTITY author "John Smith">
<!ENTITY book "Oracle Database 11g: Building Oracle XML DB Applications">
]>
<contact_list>
<contact id="1">
 <first_name>John</first_name>
 <last_name>Smith</last_name>
</contact>
<contact id="2">
 <first_name>Richard</first_name>
 <last_name>Liu</last_name>
</contact>
</contact_list>
```

The DTDs defined as an external file of an XML document are called "external DTDs." An example is shown as follows (*contact_list_ex.xml*):

```
<?xml version = '1.0' encoding = 'UTF-8'?>
<!DOCTYPE contact_list SYSTEM "contact_list.dtd">
<contact_list>
<contact id="1">
 <first_name>John</first_name>
 <last_name>Smith</last_name>
```

```
</contact>
<contact id="2">
 <first_name>Richard</first_name>
 <last_name>Liu</last_name>
</contact>
</contact_list>
```

The following is the external DTD defined in a file (*contact_list.dtd*):

```
<!ELEMENT contact_list (contact+)>
<!ELEMENT contact (first_name,last_name)>
<!ELEMENT first_name (#PCDATA)>
<!ELEMENT last_name (#PCDATA)>
<!ATTLIST contact id CDATA #REQUIRED>
<!ENTITY author "John Smith">
<!ENTITY book "Oracle Database 11g: Building Oracle XML DB Applications">
```

In each of the preceding examples, DTD is an integral part of the XML document. This means DTD will be parsed during the XML parsing process.

Oracle XDK Tip: Why do I still get DTD parsing errors after turning off DTD validation?

After turning off DTD validation, the XML document will not be validated against DTD. However, DTD itself will be parsed by the XML parser. Therefore, if there is any syntax error in DTD, the XML parser will report the parsing error (*contact_list_dtderr.xml*):

```
XML-20100: (Fatal Error) Expected 'DOCTYPE'.
Error while parsing input file: ...(Expected 'DOCTYPE'.)
```

Let's learn how you can perform DTD validations using Oracle XDK and in XML DB.

Using Oracle XDK Command-Line Utility

Using the Oracle XDK Java command-line utility *oracle.xml.parser.v2.oraxml*, you can perform DTD validations as follows:

Listing 5-1 *Using Oracle XDK Command-Line Utility to Perform DTD Validation*

```
>java oracle.xml.parser.v2.oraxml -dtd contact_list_in.xml
The input XML file is parsed without errors using DTD validation mode.
>java oracle.xml.parser.v2.oraxml -dtd contact_list_ex.xml
The input XML file is parsed without errors using DTD validation mode.
```

To turn off DTD validation in *oracle.xml.parser.v2.oraxml*, you can use the *novalidate* option.

Using Oracle XDK Java APIs

Using XDK Java APIs, you can perform DTD validations with either the DOM parser or the SAX parser. The following example performs DTD validation using the Oracle XDK DOM parser (*DTDDOMValidation.java*):

Listing 5-2 *DTD Validation Using Oracle XDK DOM Parser*

```
package xmlbook.chp05;

import java.io.OutputStreamWriter;
import oracle.xml.parser.v2.DOMParser;
import oracle.xml.parser.v2.DTD;
import oracle.xml.parser.v2.XMLDocument;
import oracle.xml.parser.v2.XMLParser;
import oracle.xml.util.XMLUtil;

public class DOMDTDValidation {
    public static void main(String[] argv) {
        XMLDocument doc;
        DOMParser dp = new DOMParser();
        dp.setValidationMode(XMLParser.DTD_VALIDATION);
        try {
            dp.parse(XMLUtil.createURL("src/xml/contact_list_in.xml"));
            doc = dp.getDocument();
            OutputStreamWriter out = new OutputStreamWriter(System.out);
            doc.print(out);
            DTD dtd = (DTD)doc.getDoctype();
            System.out.println("The XML document has the following DTD:");
            dtd.print(out);
        } catch (Exception ex) {
            ex.printStackTrace();
        }
    }
}
```

In this DOM parsing, DTD validation is set up with the following command:

```
dp.setValidationMode(XMLParser.DTD_VALIDATION);
```

Whether the validation is set to *true* or *false*, the XML DOM object will be created containing a parsed DTD stored as the *org.w3c.dom.DocumentType* object. In Oracle XDK, this object is extended to an *oracle.xml.parser.v2.DTD* object. In the example, we can get the DTD object and print it out using the following command:

```
DTD dtd = (DTD) doc.getDoctype();
dtd.print(out);
```

To turn off DTD parsing for "external" DTDs, you can use the following settings:

```
dp.setAttribute(XMLParser.STANDALONE, Boolean.TRUE);
```

If you turn off external DTD parsing, but still have DTD validation on, you will get the "element not defined" error (i.e., *oracle.xml.parser.v2.XMLParseException: Element 'contact_list' used but not declared*).

Oracle XDK Tip: What is returned by the Oracle XDK DOM parser?
JAXP DOM parsing APIs by default returns the *org.w3c.dom.Document* object. When the Oracle XDK parser is used, the DOM *Document* object can be cast to the *oracle.xml.parser.v2.XMLDocument* object. Because Oracle XDK *XMLDocument* extends the W3C *Document* object by adding an XMLDocument.print() function, it is convenient to create an output from the parsed XML document.

The following example performs the DTD validation using the Oracle XDK SAX parser (*SAXDTDValication.java*):

Listing 5-3 *DTD Validation Using Oracle XDK SAX Parser*

```
package xmlbook.chp05;

import java.io.File;
import java.io.PrintStream;
import javax.xml.parsers.SAXParser;
import javax.xml.parsers.SAXParserFactory;
import oracle.xml.parser.v2.XMLSAXSerializer;
import org.xml.sax.SAXException;
import org.xml.sax.SAXParseException;
import org.xml.sax.XMLReader;

public class SAXDTDValidation {
    public static void main(String[] argv) {
        SAXParserFactory spf = SAXParserFactory.newInstance();
        spf.setValidating(true);
        try {
          MyXMLSAXSerializer ss = new MyXMLSAXSerializer(System.out);
          SAXParser sp = spf.newSAXParser();
          sp.setProperty("http://xml.org/sax/properties/lexical-handler",ss);
          sp.setProperty("http://xml.org/sax/properties/declaration-handler",ss);
          sp.parse(new File("src/xml/contact_list_err.xml"), ss);
        } catch (SAXParseException ex) {
            System.out.println(ex.getMessage());
        } catch (Exception ex) {
            ex.printStackTrace();
            System.out.print("error");
        }
    }

    private static class MyXMLSAXSerializer extends XMLSAXSerializer {
        MyXMLSAXSerializer(PrintStream p) {
            super(p);
```

```
        }
        public void warning(SAXParseException e) throws SAXException {
            System.out.println("Warning: ");
            printInfo(e);
        }
        public void error(SAXParseException e) throws SAXException {
            System.out.println("Error: ");
            printInfo(e);
        }
        public void fatalError(SAXParseException e) throws SAXException {
            System.out.println("Fatal error: ");
            printInfo(e);
        }
        private void printInfo(SAXParseException e) {
            System.out.println("Public ID: " + e.getPublicId());
            System.out.println("System ID: " + e.getSystemId());
            System.out.println("Line number: " + e.getLineNumber());
            System.out.println("Column number: " + e.getColumnNumber());
            System.out.println("Message: " + e.getMessage());
        }
    }
}
```

In the SAX validation, this command turns on the validation option:

```
(SAXParserFactory) spf.setValidating(true);
```

Oracle XDK Tip: Why do I get the *Element used but not declared* error?

If you turn on the validation by setting *(SAXParserFactory) spf.setValidating(true)* but don't have XML Schema or DTD assigned to the parser, you will get errors such as the following:

> **XML-20149:** *(Error) Element 'contact_list' used but not declared.*
> **XML-20137:** *(Warning) Attribute 'id' used but not declared.*

In the SAX parser, you need to set the error handling functions to report validation errors. In this example, we use Oracle XDK *oracle.xml.parser.v2.XMLSAXSerializer* as the SAX content handler. This class implements *org.xml.sax.ErrorHandler* but doesn't implement the error reporting functions. Therefore, we create an extended class *MyXMLSAXSerializer* from *XMLSAXSerializer*, which implements the error reporting functions, including the warning(), error(), and fatalError() functions.

For DTD validation, you need another two SAX handlers, org.xml.sax.ext.DeclHandler and org.xml.sax.ext.Lexicalhander. The DeclHandler handles DTD declarations. To set DeclHandler to a SAX parser, you need to use setProperty() with propertyId to be `"http://xml.org/sax/properties/declaration-handler"`. The LexicalHandler provides lexical information about an XML document, such as comments and CDATA section boundaries. It also handles startDTD() and endDTD() events. To set LexicalHandler to a SAX parser, you need to use setProperty() with propertyId to be `"http://xml.org/sax/properties/lexical-handler"`.

From the preceding example, *XMLSAXSerializer* implements both classes. Therefore, we can set the *MyXMLSAXSerilaizer* class to handle both events:

```
MyXMLSAXSerializer ss = new MyXMLSAXSerializer(System.out);
SAXParser sp = spf.newSAXParser();
sp.setProperty("http://xml.org/sax/properties/lexical-handler",ss);
sp.setProperty("http://xml.org/sax/properties/declaration-handler",ss);
sp.parse(new File(argv[0]), ss);
```

Otherwise, not all of the DTD information will be parsed.

Using Oracle XDK Java, we can parse DTD in a separate process. Then, we can assign the parsed DTD object to XML parsers for validations. The following is an example (*DOMDTDSetValidation.java*):

Listing 5-4 *DTD Caching*

```
package xmlbook.chp05;
import oracle.xml.parser.v2.DOMParser;
import oracle.xml.parser.v2.XMLDocument;
import oracle.xml.parser.v2.DTD;
import oracle.xml.parser.v2.XMLElement;
import oracle.xml.parser.v2.XMLParser;
import oracle.xml.util.XMLUtil;

public class DOMDTDSetValidation {
    static public void main(String[] argv) {
        try {

            DOMParser parser = new DOMParser();
            parser.parseDTD(XMLUtil.createURL("src/xml/contact_list.dtd"),
                            "contact_list");
            DTD exdtd = parser.getDoctype();
            parser.setErrorStream(System.err);
            parser.setValidationMode(DOMParser.DTD_VALIDATION);
            parser.showWarnings(true);
            parser.parse(XMLUtil.createURL("src/xml/contact_list_ex.xml"));
            XMLDocument doc = parser.getDocument();
           ((XMLElement)doc.getDocumentElement()).validateContent(exdtd);
           doc.print(System.out);
      } catch (Exception e) {
            System.out.println(e.toString());
        }
    }
}
```

In JAXP 1.3, there is no DTD parsing APIs. Therefore, we have to use Oracle XDK native APIs. The XDK DOM parser can parse DTD with the following:

```
parser.parseDTD(XMLUtil.createURL("src/xml/contact_list.dtd"), "contact_list");
DTD exdtd = parser.getDoctype();
```

In the parseDTD() function, the first parameter is the DTD document URL, and the second parameter is the XML document's root element name. Then the DTD object can set to DOM Document and Element to validate the content:

```
((XMLElement)doc.getDocumentElement()).validateContent(exdtd);
```

With this setup, we can keep the parsed DTD object in memory, and then use it to validate multiple XML documents/element to improve the efficiency of the XML processing.

Using Oracle XML DB

In Oracle XML DB, you can perform DTD validations. For inline DTD, the validation is done by default when creating XMLTypes:

```
SELECT XMLType('<?xml version = ''1.0'' encoding = ''UTF-8''?>
<!DOCTYPE contact_list[
<!ELEMENT contact_list (contact+)>
<!ELEMENT contact (first_name,last_name)>
<!ELEMENT first_name (#PCDATA)>
<!ELEMENT last_name (#PCDATA)>
<!ATTLIST contact id CDATA #REQUIRED>
<!ENTITY author "John Smith">
<!ENTITY book "Oracle Database 11g: Building Oracle XML DB Applications">
]>
<contact_list>
<contact id="1">
<first_name>John</first_name>
<last_name>Smith</last_name>
</contact>
<contact id="2">
<last_name>Liu</last_name>
<first_name>Richard</first_name>
</contact>
</contact_list>') FROM DUAL;
```

The example will raise DTD validation errors due to the incorrect order of <last_name> and <first_name> in the second contact. The error is shown as follows:

```
ERROR:
ORA-31011: XML parsing failed
ORA-19202: Error occurred in XML processing
LPX-00103: Warning: document structure does not match DTD
Error at line 17
ORA-06512: at "SYS.XMLTYPE", line 310
ORA-06512: at line 1
```

Oracle XML DB Tip: Why do I get the *"External DTD not found"* error when creating XMLTypes?

Just as with Oracle XDK parsers, the XML DB XMLType() function will parse DTD whether you turn on validation or not. If you have an external DTD reference, the XMLType() function must be able to access the DTD file. In Oracle XML DB, the file URL needs to be an XML DB Repository URL. Otherwise, you will get the "External DTD not found" error. Please refer to Chapter 4 to understand why DTD is parsed during the XML parsing. To turn off DTD parsing in Oracle XML DB sessions, run the following command:

```
alter session set events ='31156 trace name context forever, level 2';
```

XML Schema Validation

XML Schema is an XML-based language that extends the capability of DTD by adding *namespace* and *datatype* definitions and to define more complex data models. In Oracle XML DB applications, you can use Oracle XDK Java and XMLType() functions to perform XML Schema validations.

XML Schema and Namespaces

For the most part, the XML Schema concept is easy to understand, but the namespaces need some clarifications.

XML Schema has three namespaces. The first is the XML Schema namespace, which refers to XML Schema definitions such as *datatypes* and XML Schema *elements/attributes*, shown as follows:

```
<xsd:schema xmlns:xsd="http://www.w3.org/2001/XMLSchema"...>
```

The second namespace is the *target namespace* defined for XML documents:

```
<xsd:schema xmlns:xsd="http://www.w3.org/2001/XMLSchema"
            targetNamespace="http://www.xmlbook.com" ..
```

In XML Schema, you can specify if the defined document elements or attributes are qualified by the defined *target namespace* using the following XML Schema attributes:

```
elementFormDefault   = (qualified| unqualified) : unqualified
attributeFormDefault = (qualified| unqualified) : unqualified
```

The choice is between `qualified` and `unqualified`. When `elementFormDefault` is set to `qualified`, all the elements defined in the XML Schema must have a namespace by using a namespace *prefix* or setting a *default namespace*. This is called *explicitly qualified*. An `unqualified` setting means that only the globally declared elements must be *explicitly qualified* with a namespace, while the locally declared elements must not be qualified. Qualifying a local element declaration will raise an error. When `attributeFormDefault` is set to `qualified`, all attributes in the instance document must be explicitly qualified using a namespace prefix.

Remember, the default namespace doesn't apply to attributes. Hence, we can't use a default namespace declaration to qualify attributes. *Unqualified attributes* implies the attributes inherit the namespace of the containing element.

XML schemas can be imported and included in another XML schema. The XML Schema *<import>* is used to add multiple schemas with different target namespaces to an XML schema. The *namespace* attribute in <import> specifies the *target namespaces* of the imported XML schema. The *schemaLocation* attribute provides the URI as a clue to the location of the imported XML schema document. The following is an example:

```
<xs:import schemaLocation="http://www.xmlbook.com/contact.xsd" namespace="http://
www.xmlbook.com/contact/schema"/..>
```

The XML Schema *<include>* is used to add multiple schemas with the same *target namespace*. The *SchemaLocation* attribute provides the URI as a clue to the location of the included XML schema document:

```
<xs:include  schemaLocation="http://www.xmlbook.com/contact.xsd">
```

The third namespace is the XML Schema instance namespace. The namespace is specified in XML documents to qualify XML *noNamespaceSchemaLocation* and *schemaLocation* attributes, shown as follows:

```
<Contact xmlns:xsi="http://www.w3.org/2001/XMLSchema-instance"
xsi:noNamespaceSchemaLocation="contact.xsd"> ....</Contact>

<Contact xmlns:xsi="http://www.w3.org/2001/XMLSchema-instance"
xsi:schemaLocation="contact.xsd"> ....</Contact>
```

The *noNamespaceSchemaLocation* attribute is used to specify the XML Schema document for XML instances with no namespace. The *schemaLocation* attribute is used to specify the XML Schema document for XML instance with namespaces.

Using Oracle XDK Command-Line Utility

Using Oracle XDK Java command-line utility *oracle.xml.parser.v2.oraxml*, we can perform the XML Schema validation if the document has a *noNamespaceSchemaLocation* attribute or a *schemaLocation* attribute to specify the associated XML schema. The command is shown as follows:

Listing 5-5 *Using Oracle XDK Command-Line Utility to Perform XML Schema Validation*

```
>java oracle.xml.parser.v2.oraxml -schema john_smith.xml
The input XML file is parsed without errors using Schema validation mode.
```

Using Oracle XDK Java APIs

Using Oracle XDK Java, you can perform XML Schema validation with either the SAX or DOM parser. When performing XML Schema validations, you need two processors: the XML Schema processor which builds the XML Schema objects, and an XML parser which parses the XML document and validates against the pre-set XML Schema object.

Oracle XDK Tip: Can I validate an XML DOM element?

In Oracle XDK Java, in addition to document-level XML Schema/DTD validation, you can perform validation on the XML elements. Here is a list of XML Schema validation functions from an *XMLElement*:

- **Boolean validateContent(DTD dtd)** Validates the content of the element against the given DTD.
- **Boolean validateContent(XMLSchema schema)** Validates the content of the element against given XML Schema.
- **Boolean validateContent(XMLSchema schema, java.lang.String mode)** Validates the content of the element against given XML Schema in the given validation mode.
- **XMLNode validateContent(XSDValidator validator, boolean flag)** Validates the content of the element using the given XML Schema validator.

Let's look at this SAX parser validation example (*SAXXSDValidation.java*):

Listing 5-6 *XML Schema Validation in Oracle XDK Java SAX Parser*

```
// Build the XML Schema object
XSDBuilder builder = new XSDBuilder();
XMLSchema schemadoc = (XMLSchema)builder.build(createURL("src/xml/contact.xsd"));

//Parse the input XML document with the XML Schema validation
SAXParser parser = new SAXParser();
XMLSAXSerializer ss = new XMLSAXSerializer(System.out);
parser.setXMLSchema(schemadoc);
parser.setValidationMode(XMLParser.SCHEMA_VALIDATION);
parser.setContentHandler(ss);
parser.parse(createURL("src/xml/john_smith.xml"));
```

In the preceding example, the *oracle.xml.parser.schema.XSDBuilder* class creates the *oracle.xml.parser.schema.XMLSchema* object from the XML schema document. The *XMLSchema* object is then passed to *SAXParser*. With the validation mode set to *XMLParser.SCHEMA_VALIDATION*, the SAX parser will perform the STRICT XML Schema validation during the parsing process.

There are also two XML Schema validation modes: LAX and STRICT. STRICT XML Schema validation (*oracle.xml.parser.v2.XMLParser.SCHEMA_VALIDATION* or *oracle.xml.parser.v2.XMLParser.SCHEMA_STRICT_VALIDATION*) validates all elements/attributes in the XML document against the XML schema; LAX validation (*oracle.xml.parser.v2.XMLParser.SCHEMA_LAX_VALIDATION*) skips the element/attributes that are not defined within the XML schema.

The DOM validation process is very similar to the SAX XML Schema validation. The example code is shown as follows (*DOMXSDValiation.java*):

Listing 5-7 *XML Schema Validation in Oracle XDK Java DOM Parser*

```
package xmlbook.chp05;

import oracle.xml.parser.schema.XMLSchema;
```

```
import oracle.xml.parser.schema.XSDBuilder;
import oracle.xml.parser.v2.DOMParser;
import oracle.xml.parser.v2.XMLDocument;
import oracle.xml.parser.v2.XMLParser;
import oracle.xml.util.XMLUtil;

public class DOMXSDValidation {
    public static void main(String argv[]) {

        try {
            // Build the XML schema object
            DOMParser parser = new DOMParser();
            XSDBuilder builder = new XSDBuilder();
            XMLSchema schemadoc = (XMLSchema)builder.build(XMLUtil.createURL
("src/xml/contact.xsd"));

            parser.setValidationMode(XMLParser.SCHEMA_VALIDATION);
            parser.showWarnings(true);
            parser.parse(XMLUtil.createURL("src/xml/john_smith.xml"));
            System.out.println("XML Schema Validation is OK");

            XMLDocument doc = parser.getDocument();
            doc.print(System.out);

        } catch (Exception ex) {
            ex.printStackTrace();
        }
    }
}
```

The only difference is that we change from *SAXParser* to *DOMParser*.

Oracle XDK supports element-level and document-level XML Schema validations. The following is an element-level XML Schema validation example (*DOMNodeXSDValidation.java*):

```
package xmlbook.chp05;

import oracle.xml.parser.schema.XMLSchema;
import oracle.xml.parser.schema.XSDBuilder;
import oracle.xml.parser.v2.DOMParser;
import oracle.xml.parser.v2.XMLDocument;
import oracle.xml.parser.v2.XMLElement;
import oracle.xml.parser.v2.XMLParser;
import oracle.xml.util.XMLUtil;

import org.w3c.dom.NodeList;

public class DOMNodeXSDValidation {
    public static void main(String argv[]) {
        XMLDocument doc;

        try {
            // Build the XML schema object
```

```
            DOMParser parser = new DOMParser();
            XSDBuilder builder = new XSDBuilder();
            XMLSchema schemadoc =
(XMLSchema)builder.build(XMLUtil.createURL("src/xml/contact.xsd"));
            parser.parse(XMLUtil.createURL("src/xml/contact_list.xml"));
            doc = parser.getDocument();
            NodeList nl = doc.selectNodes("/contact_list/contact");
            for(int i=0; i< nl.getLength(); i++){
              XMLElement node = (XMLElement)nl.item(i);
              node.validateContent(schemadoc);
              System.out.println("XML Schema Validation for contact "+i+" is
OK.");
            }
        } catch (Exception ex) {
            ex.printStackTrace();
        }
    }
}
```

Using Oracle XDK, you can perform XML Schema validation at either the document or XML element level using the validateContent() function.

Using Oracle XML DB

XML Schema is extensively used in Oracle XML DB to validate XML documents and define XML Schema–based XMLTypes. Let's learn how to use either XMLType.validate() or DBMS_XMLSCHEMA.validate() to perform XML Schema validations in Oracle XML DB.

Oracle XML DB Tip: What are the LAX and STRICT XML Schema validations in Oracle XML DB?

In Oracle Database 11*g*, there are also two modes of XML Schema validations: LAX and STRICT. The LAX validation performs checking on elements/attributes defined in the XML schema. The STRICT validation performs on all the elements/attributes in the input XML documents. The LAX validation is performed for all XML Schema–based XMLTypes during creation. This LAX validation only checks on the XML data to ensure the XML document can be stored in XMLType objects.

Registering XML Schemas

In Oracle XML DB, you need to register an XML schema before using it for validation.

Oracle XML DB Tip: Why do I get the ORA-01031: *Insufficient privileges* error when registering my XML schema?

This is because you don't have the necessary privilege to complete the XML Schema registration, such as create object types, alter sessions, and so on.

```
grant alter session to XMLDEMO;
```

The following function is used to register XML schemas to Oracle XML DB:

```
DBMS_XMLSCHEMA.REGISTERSCHEMA(
    schemaurl          IN  VARCHAR2,
    schemadoc          IN  VARCHAR2,
    local              IN  BOOLEAN := TRUE,
    gentypes           IN  BOOLEAN := TRUE,
    genbean            IN  BOOLEAN := FALSE,
    gentables          IN  BOOLEAN := TRUE,
    force              IN  BOOLEAN := FALSE,
    owner              IN  VARCHAR2 := NULL,
    enablehierarchy    IN  PLS_INTEGER := DBMS_XMLSCHEMA.ENABLE_CONTENTS,
    options            IN  PLS_INTEGER := 0);
```

schemaurl is the unique URL to identify the XML schema in XML DB. *schemadoc* is where you provide the XML schema content. The parameter can be VARCHAR2, BLOB, BFILE, XMLType, DBUriType, or CLOB. The *local* parameter indicates whether the registered XML schema is local to the current user or global to all database users. We use *gentypes* to create object types with XML schema (default is TRUE), *genbean* to create Java beans (default is FALSE), *gentables* to create default tables (default is TRUE), and *force* to suppress errors during registration (default is FALSE). You can also specify the owner for the XML schema and whether you want to enable hierarchy table creation. It is important to set the *options* parameter to *DBMS_XMLSCHEMA.REGISTER_BINARYXML* if you will use the registered XML schema for binary XMLTypes.

Oracle XML DB Tip: Why do I get the ORA-44424: *BINARY XML storage requires XML Schema registered for BINARY usage* error when creating XML Schema–based binary XMLType?

This is because you haven't set up the *options* parameter to DBMS_XMLSCHEMA.REGISTER_BINARYXML during the XML schema registration.

Refer to Listing 2-8 in Chapter 2 for the details on registering an XML schema.

Oracle XML DB Tip: Why do I get the ORA-31094: *Incompatible SQL type error "CLOB" for attribute or element "last_name"*?

For binary XML schema registration, you don't need to annotate the XML schema. After you remove all of the *xsd:datatype* annotations, this error will not appear.

To make sure you provide a unique URL when registering a new XML schema, you can check the USER_XML_SCHEMAS view to find out the registered XML schemas:

```
SQL> desc USER_XML_SCHEMAS
Name                                       Null?    Type
----------------------------------------- -------- ---------------------------
```

```
SCHEMA_URL                                  VARCHAR2(700)
LOCAL                                       VARCHAR2(3)
SCHEMA                                      SYS.XMLTYPE
INT_OBJNAME                                 VARCHAR2(4000)
QUAL_SCHEMA_URL                             VARCHAR2(767)
HIER_TYPE                                   VARCHAR2(11)
BINARY                                      VARCHAR2(3)
SCHEMA_ID                                   RAW(16)
HIDDEN                                      VARCHAR2(3)
```

Normally, you just need to select the *schema_url* and *local* columns from the USER_XML_SCHEMAS view:

```
SELECT schema_url, local
FROM USER_XML_SCHEMAS
ORDER BY schema_url;
```

The *schema_url* column is the URL to identify the registered XML schema. The *local* column indicates whether the XML schema is only available to the current user (*local=yes*) or is global to all DB users (*local=no*).

You can turn on `events = '31098 trace name context forever'` to debug the XML schema registration:

```
ALTER SESSION SET events = '31098 trace name context forever'
```

The trace file is created in the USER_DUMP_DEST (i.e., $ORACL_HOME/diag/rdbms/oracl11g/oracl11g/trace) directory. The detailed locations can be found if you log in as a SYS user (SYSDBA) and run the following command:

```
SQL> show parameter user_dump_dest
NAME                                TYPE VALUE
-------------------- ------- ----------- -----------------------------
user_dump_dest string C:\Oracle\Database \diag\rdbms\orcl11g\orcl11g\trace
```

Go to this folder and find the latest *.trc file. An example trace file is shown as follows:

```
*** SESSION ID:(170.7) 2010-03-29 23:19:59.434
*** CLIENT ID:() 2010-03-29 23:19:59.434
*** SERVICE NAME:(SYS$USERS) 2010-03-29 23:19:59.434
*** MODULE NAME:(SQL*Plus) 2010-03-29 23:19:59.434
*** ACTION NAME:() 2010-03-29 23:19:59.434

 ------------ QMTS Executing SQL ------------
CREATE OR REPLACE TYPE "XMLDEMO"."contact821_T" AS OBJECT ("SYS_XDBPD$"
"XDB"."XDB$RAW_LIST_T",
"id" NUMBER(38),"first_name" VARCHAR2(4000 CHAR),"last_name" VARCHAR2(4000
CHAR))FINAL INSTANTIABLE
/
-----------------------------------------
*** 2010-03-29 23:20:00.374
```

```
select * from user_errors where name = 'contact821_T';
 ------------ QMTS Executing SQL ------------
CREATE TABLE "XMLDEMO"."contact822_TAB" OF SYS.XMLTYPE  XMLSCHEMA "http://
xmlbook.com/contact.xsd"
ID 'F9D1FFBACBB44713870F09C2960D821C' ELEMENT "contact" ID 5023  TYPE
"XMLDEMO"."contact821_T"
VARRAY XMLDATA."SYS_XDBPD$" STORE AS LOB SYS_XDBPD$823_L VARRAY XMLEXTRA
.EXTRADATA STORE AS
LOB EXTRADATA824_L VARRAY XMLEXTRA.NAMESPACES STORE AS LOB NAMESPACES825_L
/
--------------------------------------------
*** 2010-03-29 23:20:01.752
 ------------ QMTS Executing SQL ------------
begin
xdb.dbms_xdbz.enable_hierarchy('"XMLDEMO"','"contact822_TAB"',DBMS_XDBZ
.ENABLE_CONTENTS,TRUE); end;
/
```

We will explore the details of the storage in later chapters.

Performing XML Schema Validations

With the XML schemas registered, we can then perform XML Schema validations. XMLType provides two functions: XMLType.schemaValidate() and XMLType.isSchemaValid(). We can also use the SQL function CHECK(XMLISValid(XMLType)) to perform the XML Schema validation. Let's look at some examples.

First, let's create a new XML document using the XMLType() function. Then, we validate it against a registered XML schema *http://xmlbook.com/sample/contact.xsd* using XMLType .isSchemaValid() (*xsd_validation.sql*).

```
SELECT XMLType ('<?xml version = ''1.0'' encoding = ''UTF-8''?><contact id="1">
<first_name>John</first_name>
</contact>').isSchemaValid('http://xmlbook.com/sample/contact.xsd') FROM DUAL;
```

If the call returns 1 (one), then the XML document is valid against the specified XML schema; otherwise, it's invalid. Using XMLType.isSchemaValid(), you can specify the root XML element. This is useful if your XML schema defined many top-level elements.

Second, we can use the XMLType.schemaValidate() function. When using XMLType .schemaValidate(), you need to make sure that the XML *schemaLocation* attribute is specified in the XML document. XMLType.schemaValidate() can be used within INSERT and UPDATE triggers to ensure that all instances stored in the table are validated. The following is an example when we create an XML Schema–based XMLType table (*xsd_validation_in_trigger.sql*):

```
CREATE TABLE contact_tbl OF XMLType
  XMLSCHEMA "http://xmlbook.com/sample/contact.xsd" ELEMENT "contact";

CREATE TRIGGER contact_trig BEFORE INSERT OR UPDATE ON contact_tbl FOR EACH ROW
BEGIN
  XMLTYPE.schemavalidate(:new.OBJECT_VALUE);
```

```
END;
/
INSERT INTO contact_tbl values(XMLType ('<?xml version = ''1.0'' encoding =
''UTF-8''?><contact xmlns="http://xmlbook.com/sample/contact.xsd"  id="1">
<first_name>John</first_name>
<last_name>Smith</last_name>
</contact>'));

insert into contact_tbl values(XMLType ('<?xml version = ''1.0'' encoding =
''UTF-8''?><contact xmlns="http://xmlbook.com/sample/contact.xsd" id="1">
<first_name>John</first_name>
</contact>'));
```

The second data insertion will raise an XML Schema validation error.

Third, we can also create an XMLType table to enforce STRICT XML Schema validation for each inserted XML record (*xsd_validation_tbl.sql*):

```
CREATE TABLE contact_strict_tbl OF XMLType
   (CHECK (XMLIsValid(OBJECT_VALUE) = 1))
   XMLSCHEMA "http://www.xmlbook.com/contact.xsd" ELEMENT "contact";
```

Oracle XML DB Tip: Why do I get the following error when validating my XML document?

```
ERROR at line 4:
ORA-06553: PLS-306: wrong number or types of arguments in call to
'SCHEMAVALIDATE'
```

The XMLType.schemaValidate() function doesn't allow you to specify the XML schema URLs. You need to have the XML schema location specified in the XML document using the *schemaLocation* attributes.

Using JAXB with XML Schemas

XML schema can be used beyond validation. When building XML applications, you can create XML documents from XML schemas using JAXB (Java XML Binding). The following XML schema is designed to specify the configuration document of an application (*configure.xsd*):

```
<?xml version="1.0" encoding="UTF-8"?>
<xsd:schema targetNamespace="http://xmlns.xmlbook.com/sample/XSU"
          elementFormDefault="qualified"
         xmlns:xsd="http://www.w3.org/2001/XMLSchema">
 <xsd:element name="config">
  <xsd:complexType>
   <xsd:sequence>
    <xsd:element name="jdbc">
```

```
      <xsd:complexType>
       <xsd:sequence>
        <xsd:element name="username" type="xsd:string"/>
        <xsd:element name="password" type="xsd:string"/>
        <xsd:element name="connection" type="xsd:string"/>
       <xsd:sequence>
      </xsd:complexType>
     </xsd:element>
     <xsd:element name="query" type="xsd:string"/>
     <xsd:element name="output">
      <xsd:complexType>
       <xsd:attribute name="filename" type="xsd:string" use="optional"/>
      </xsd:complexType>
     </xsd:element>
     <xsd:element name="validation" minOccurs="0">
      <xsd:complexType>
        <xsd:attribute name="enable" type="xsd:boolean" use="required"/>
        <xsd:attribute name="xsd_file" type="xsd:string" use="required"/>
      </xsd:complexType>
     </xsd:element>
      <xsd:element name="transformation" minOccurs="0">
      <xsd:complexType>
       <xsd:attribute name="enable" type="xsd:boolean" use="required"/>
       <xsd:attribute name="xsl_file" type="xsd:string" use="required"/>
      </xsd:complexType>
     </xsd:element>
    </xsd:sequence>
    <xsd:attribute name="name" type="xsd:string" use="required"/>
   </xsd:complexType>
  </xsd:element>
</xsd:schema>
```

In this XML schema, we define the target namespace to be

```
<xsd:schema targetNamespace="http://xmlns.xmlbook.com/sample/XSU"....>
```

In JAXB, this target namespace will be translated to be the Java classes' package name. The <config> element is defined as the document element with a *name* attribute to specify the configuration file name. The <config> element includes the following elements for setting up the application:

- **<jdbc>** Specifies the JDB connections. The <jdbc> element has sub-elements <username> for the database user name, <password> for the database user password, and <connection> for the JDBC connection string.
- **<query>** Specifies the SQL query.
- **<output>** Specifies the output file name with its *filename* attribute.
- **<validation>** Specifies whether we will validate the output with the *enable* attribute. The *xsd_file* attribute provides the XML schema file if XML Schema validation is enabled.
- **<transformation>** Specifies whether we will apply XSL transformation to the query output with the *enable* attribute. The *xsl_file* attribute specifies the XSL stylesheet.

The elements' content is mostly *xsd:string* except that the "enable" attributes are defined as *xsd:boolean*. JAXB generates the Java classes to create and read XML documents. Let's create a Oracle JDeveloper project and add the XML schema document to the project. Then, right-clicking the XML schema file, you will see the Generate JAXB 2.0 Content Model option shown in Figure 5-1.

You can modify the JAXB class generation with customized files and specify the package name. This example uses the defaults by leaving the options blank, as shown in Figure 5-2.

The result of the generation is the set of classes shown in Figure 5-3.

If you look at the *Config* class, the Java classes give you the correct access to the configuration data with the *get** and *set** functions. You can create a Java program using the generated Java class (*CreateConfigFile.java*):

```
package xmlbook.chp05;

import com.xmlbook.xmlns.sample.xsu.*;

import javax.xml.bind.JAXBContext;
import javax.xml.bind.Marshaller;
```

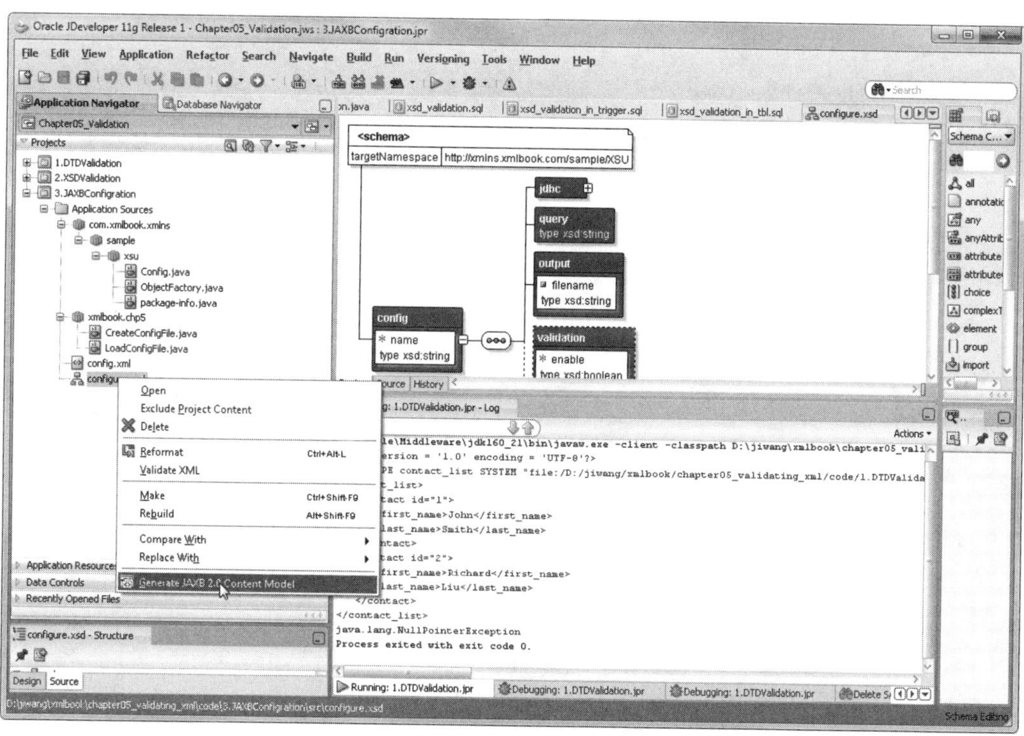

FIGURE 5-1. *Generating JAVA classes using JAXB in Oracle JDeveloper*

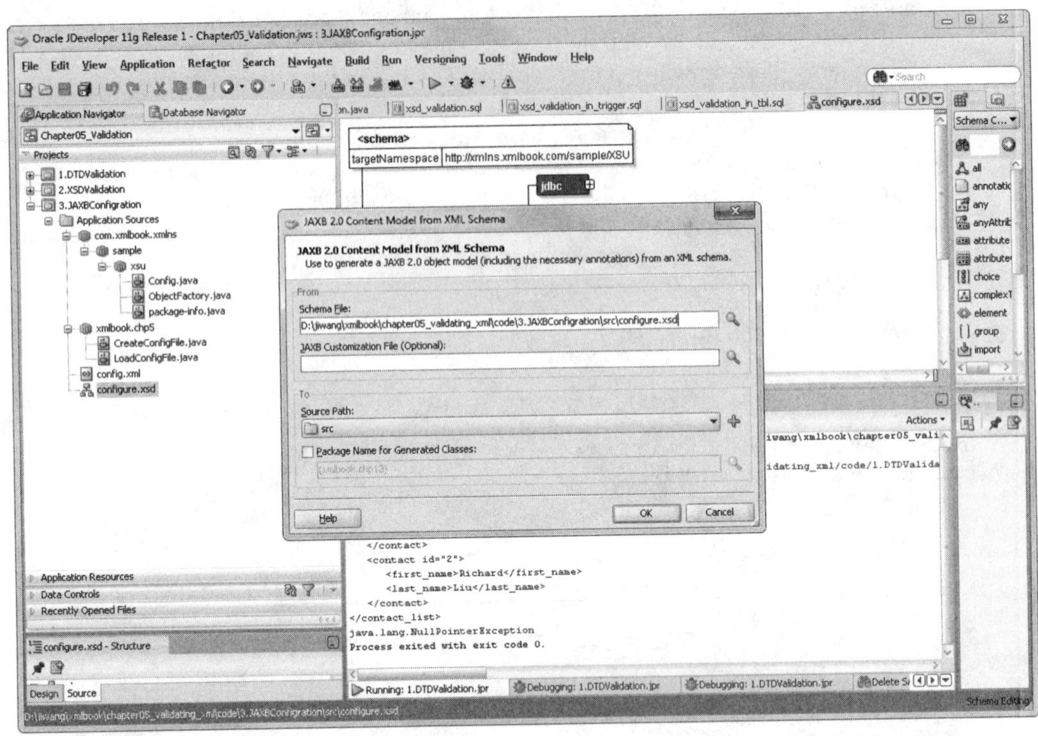

FIGURE 5-2. *JAXB 2.0 content model from XML Schema*

```
public class CreateConfigFile {
    public static void main(String[] args) {

        try {
            JAXBContext jaxbContext =
JAXBContext.newInstance("com.xmlbook.xmlns.sample.xsu");

            ObjectFactory of = new ObjectFactory();
            Config cf = of.createConfig();
            cf.setName("reational_table_small.xml");
            Config.Jdbc jdbc_o = of.createConfigJdbc();
            jdbc_o.setConnection("jdbc:jdbc:thin:@localhost:1521:ORCL");
            jdbc_o.setUsername("xmldemo");
            jdbc_o.setPassword("xmldemo");
            cf.setJdbc(jdbc_o);
            cf.setQuery("select * from contacta_tbl");
            Config.Output out = of.createConfigOutput();
            out.setFilename("output/rt_s_out.xml");
            cf.setOutput(out);
```

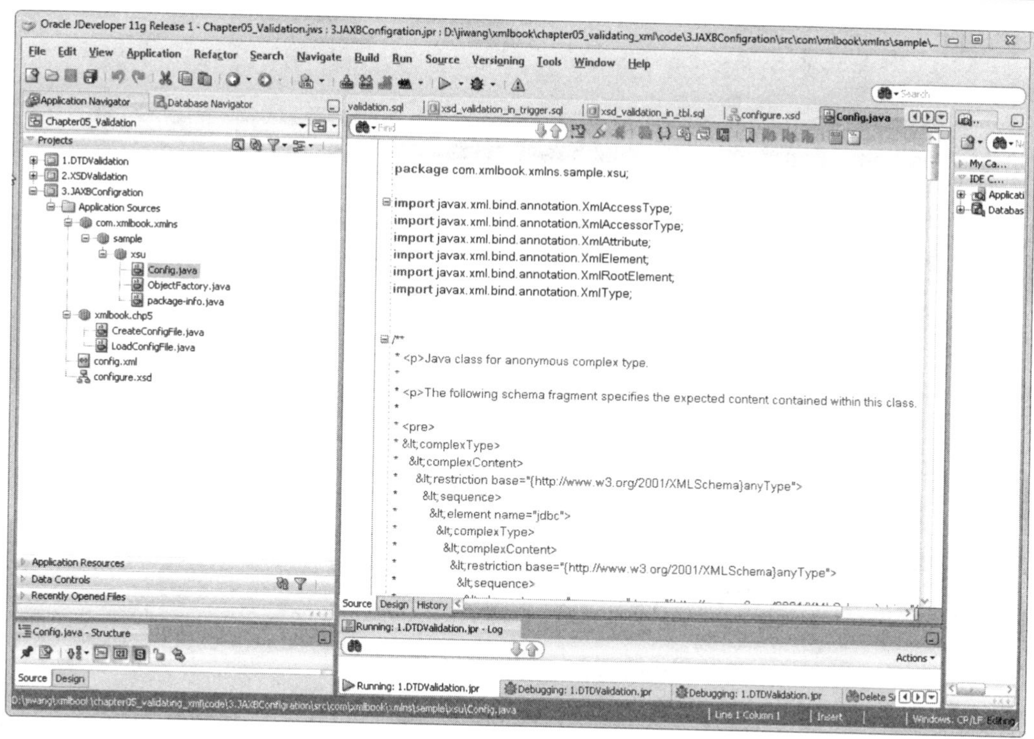

FIGURE 5-3. *JAXB generation result in Oracle JDeveloper*

```
            // Marshal to System.out
            Marshaller marshaller = jaxbContext.createMarshaller();
            marshaller.setProperty(Marshaller.JAXB_FORMATTED_OUTPUT,
                                   Boolean.TRUE);
            marshaller.marshal(cf, System.out);


        } catch (Exception ex) {
            ex.printStackTrace();
        } finally {
        }
    }
}
```

Running the Java program, we can create the following XML configuration file:

```
<?xml version="1.0" encoding="UTF-8" standalone="yes"?>
<config xmlns="http://xmlns.xmlbook.com/sample/XSU" name="reational_table_
small.xml">
    <jdbc>
```

```
        <username>xmldemo</username>
        <password>xmldemo</password>
        <connection>jdbc:jdbc:thin:@localhost:1521:ORCL</connection>
    </jdbc>
    <query>select * from contacta_tbl</query>
    <output filename="output/rt_s_out.xml"/>
</config>
```

You can also load XML to JAXB classes (unmarshaller) (*LoadConfigFile.java*):

```
package xmlbook.chp05;

import com.xmlbook.xmlns.sample.xsu.*;
import java.io.File;
import javax.xml.bind.JAXBContext;
import javax.xml.bind.Unmarshaller;

public class LoadConfigFile {
    public static void main(String[] args) {

        try {
            JAXBContext jaxbContext =
JAXBContext.newInstance("com.xmlbook.xmlns.sample.xsu");

            Unmarshaller unmarshaller =
                    jaxbContext.createUnmarshaller();

            Config conf  = (Config)
                unmarshaller.unmarshal(new File("src/config.xml"));

            System.out.println("Configuration File Name:"+conf.getName());
            System.out.println("Configuration Query:"+conf.getQuery());

        } catch (Exception ex) {
            ex.printStackTrace();
        } finally {
        }
    }
}
```

Summary

Whether we use DTD or XML Schema, defining the XML data model helps validate the XML documents. It's an important process to ensure the integrity of XML data. In addition, the XML data model further helps to define XML DB storage, and even to simplify and optimize XML processing.

CHAPTER 6

Navigating XML with XPath

ML Path Language (XPath) is used within SQL/XML, XSLT, and XQuery as the basis for accessing XML content and performing operations. W3C XPath standard (http://www.w3.org/TR/xpath) has two versions: XPath 1.0 and XPath 2.0. Both are supported in Oracle XML DB 11*g*. In this chapter, we will review some essential topics on what XPath is and how to use it in Oracle XML applications.

XPath Basics

XPath expressions navigate and retrieve XML content similar to traversing a file system's directory structure, except that XPath works on an XML document tree (also called XML *DOM* tree).

In XPath, the *root* node of an XML document is defined as a slash (/). Then, a location path, which is another slash (/) along with the element's name, steps down the XML DOM tree and selects the specified XML element. For example, the XPath expression */contact* returns the *<contact>* element. The */contact/first_name* returns the *<first_name>* element, which is a child element of *<contact>*.

The most important type of XPath expressions is the *location path*, which consists of a sequence of location steps. Each step has three components: an axis, a node test, and zero or more predicates. An XPath expression is evaluated with respect to a context node. An axis specifies the navigation direction from the context node. The node test contains node type test and node name test. The predicates are used to filter the XML nodes. The commonly used XPath axes are as follows:

- **Hierarchical Axes** *self, child, parent, decedent, ancestor*
- **Horizontal Axes** *following-sibling, preceding-sibling*
- **Attribute** *attribute*

XPath uses different symbols to specify different types of XML nodes:

- **node()** Matches any nodes except attributes.
- **@** Matches an attribute of an XML element.
- **comment()** Matches an XML comment.
- **processing-instruction()** Matches an XML processing instruction.
- **text()** Matches the text content in an XML element.

The default XPath node is an XML element. For element or attribute nodes, the node test can include the name test. Wildcards (*) can be used to match any name. The following are some common XPath wildcards:

- * Matches any child element.
- @* Matches any attribute of the context element.
- //* Matches any element node in the input document.

XML Tip: What are the differences between */contact* and */contact/*?*

/contact returns the *<contact>* element. */contact/** returns all child elements of the *<contact>* element: i.e., *<first_name>*, *<last_name>*, etc. This is used quite often in XQuery to query XMLTypes and XML DB Repository resources.

Within XPath, you can specify conditions with XPath predicates, written as expressions in square brackets, to filter out selected nodes.

Predicate ([...]) is a boolean expression returning either *true* or *false*. Multiple predicates can be specified. The predicates are applied to the result node set one by one.

Let's learn XPath through an example (*xpath_evaluation.sql*):

Listing 6-1 *XPath Evaluation Using XMLTable()*

```
SELECT c.*
FROM XMLTable('$r' PASSING XMLTYPE('<contact id="715">
<first_name>John</first_name>
<last_name>Smith</last_name>
<email>John.Smith@xmlbook.com</email>
<!-- Working History-->
<work_history>
<work company="Oracle" name="Oracle SES" start_date="1998-08-13"
title="Principal Product Manager"/>
<work company="McGraw-Hill" name="Book Writer" start_date="1993-08-13"
end_date="1994-08-13" title="Author">- Authored XML Book</work>
<work company="Oracle" name="Oracle XDK" start_date="1994-08-13"
end_date="13-Jun-2008" title="Sr.Product Manager">
- Define market requirement and function requirements.</work>
</work_history>
</contact>') AS "r" COLUMNS
   first_name XMLType PATH '/contact/first_name',
   first_name_text VARCHAR2(100) PATH '/contact/first_name/text()',
   contact_id NUMBER PATH '/contact/@id',
   latest_job XMLType PATH '/contact/work_history/work[1]',
   all_jobs XMLType PATH '/contact/work_history/work[@company="Oracle"]',
   my_comment XMLType PATH
 '/contact/comment()[local-name(following-sibling::*)="work_history"]',
   total_job_num NUMBER PATH 'count(/contact/work_history/work)',
   distinct_companies xmltype
    PATH 'distinct-values(/contact/work_history//work/@company)') c;
```

Table 6-1 summaries the XPath expressions and the results returned from the XPath evaluations.

XPath expressions #1, #2, and #3 in Table 6-1 are straightforward. They select an XML element, a text node, and an attribute node. In XPath #4, the DOM node position is used to pick up the first *<work>* element under *<work_history>*. In DOM tree, each sibling element node is

Request	XPath Expression

1. Find John Smith's first name element	`/contact/first_name`
	Result:
	`<first_name>John</first_name>`

2. Find the text content of John Smith's first name element	`/contact/first_name/text()`
	Result:
	`John`

3. Find John's contact id attribute	`/contact/@id`
	Result:
	`715`

4. Find John Smith's latest job	`/contact/work_history/work[1]`
	Result:
	`<work company="Oracle" name="Oracle SES" start_date="1998-08-13" title="Principal Product Manager"/>`

5. Find all jobs John has worked at Oracle	`/contact/work_history/work[@company='Oracle']`
	Result:
	`<work company="Oracle" name="Oracle SES" start_date="1998-08-13" title="Principal Product Manager"/>`
	`<work company="Oracle" name="Oracle XDK" start_date="1994-08-13" end_date="13-Jun-2008" title="Sr.Product Manager">- Define market requirement and function requirements.</work>`

6. Find the comments before the <work_history> element	`/contact/comment()[following-sibling::node()/local-name()='work_history']`
	Result:
	`<!-- Working History-->`

TABLE 6-1. *XPath Expression for Content Retrieval*

assigned to a position number. We can use either the position() function to get the position number or use the [position_number] predicate. In this example, we choose the first *<work>* element under *<work_history>* using */contact/work_history/work[1]*. The XPath #5 shows how to use the XPath predicates. We choose the *<work>* element, which has the attribute *company* equal to *Oracle*. In XPath #6, the *following-sibling* axis is used to find the sibling node right after the comment() node. We will only choose the comment node if its immediately following sibling node is an XML element named *work_history*. The local-name() XPath function returns the XML element's name without a namespace.

Using XPath expressions, you can also perform operations with the XPath functions. These functions include operations such as string updates, number and date calculations, and others. Table 6-2 lists some examples.

Request	XPath Expression
7. Find out how many jobs John Smith has had so far	`count(/contact/work_history/work)` Result: 3

8. Find all of the companies John Smith has worked for (distinct values)	`distinct-values(/contact/work_history//work/@company)`
	Result:
	`Oracle, McGraw-Hill`

TABLE 6-2. *XPath Expressions with XPath Functions*

XML Tip: Can I get the XML prolog using XPath?

No, the XML declaration (prolog) is not part of XPath Data Model. Therefore, you can't get its data using XPath. It's not treated as a processing instruction in the XML document. XPath also doesn't include CDATA sections, entity references, and DTD declarations. However, CDATA section data and entity reference data are returned as part of the text() content.

The count() and distinct-values() are XPath functions. For a complete list of XPath functions, please refer to the W3C XPath specification.

Let's look at another example, in which we use XPath operations in XSLT. In this example, we first need to open a received email in a new window by double-clicking the email title in Microsoft Outlook. Then, we select the View | Message Source menu, as shown in Figure 6-1.

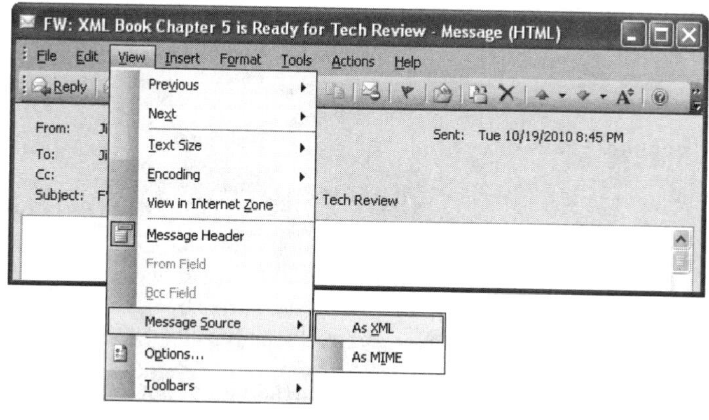

FIGURE 6-1. *Email in XML from Microsoft Outlook*

We see an XML document of the email in SOAP message format. Copy the *<TOReceivers/>* element from this message and create a new XML document (*to_receivers.xml*):

Listing 6-2 *XPath String Operations in XSLT*

```
<?xml version="1.0" encoding="windows-1252" ?>
<TOReceivers>
 <Item>
  <Address>"John Smith" &lt;John.Smith@oracle.com&gt;</Address>
  <Participant EID="334B:3BF0:user:CB3F97695BD24114B65149D2E4CC842E000000011763"/>
  <Directives/>
  <Status>DELIVERED</Status>
 </Item>
 <Item>
  <Address>"Raji Metha" &lt;RAJI.Metha@ORACLE.COM&gt;</Address>
  <Participant EID="334B:3BF0:user:0BF3BED41EC441538A80F6769E73DB83000000000D9F"/>
  <Directives/>
  <Status>DELIVERED</Status>
 </Item>....
</TOReceivers>
```

Run the following XSLT against the XML document (*create_distribution_list.xsl*):

```
<?xml version="1.0" encoding="windows-1252" ?>
<xsl:stylesheet version="2.0" xmlns:xsl="http://www.w3.org/1999/XSL/Transform">
 <xsl:output method="text" media-type="text/plain" />
  <xsl:template match="/TOReceivers">
   <xsl:for-each select="Item">
   <xsl:value-of select="lower-case(concat(substring-before(substring-
after(Address, '&lt;'), '&gt;'), ';'))"/>
   </xsl:for-each>
  </xsl:template>
</xsl:stylesheet>
```

Please refer to Chapter 16 for the steps to run XSLT in Oracle JDeveloper 11*g*. You will get the following result:

```
john.smith@oracle.com;raji.metha@oracle.com;
```

Let's look at the XPath expression in this XSL stylesheet:

```
lower-case(concat(substring-before(substring-after(Address, '&lt;'), '&gt;'), ';'))
```

There are four string functions used in this expression: substring-after(), substring-before(), concat(), and lower-case(). The substring-after() function extracts the string character from the *<Address>* element and removes *<*. The substring-before() function extracts the string by removing ">" from the result. We add ";" to the end of the extracted emails using the concatenation function, concat():

```
concat(substring-before(substring-after(Address, '&lt;'), '&gt;'), ';').
```

Finally, the lower-case() function changes all the characters to lowercase.

XML Tip: Why do I get the LPX-00601: *Invalid token* error from my XPath expression?

The expressions in XPath are case sensitive. Therefore, you need to use lowercase for XPath function and logic operators. Otherwise, you will get the LPX-00601: *Invalid token* error:

```
//*[contains(., "book") AND contains(.,"XML"]')
LPX-00601: Invalid token in: '//*[contains(., "book") AND contains(.,"XML")]'
```

Processing XPath in Java

Let's look at how to perform streaming XPath-based XML content evaluation.

The following example calls Oracle XDK to evaluate the XPath expression without building a DOM object in memory. The example only works on a subset of XPath functions and axes (including child, descendant, attribute, text, parent, and ancestor).

Listing 6-3 *XPath Evaluation with Oracle XDK Scalable DOM*

```
package xmlbook.chp06;

import java.io.File;
import java.io.FileInputStream;
import java.net.URL;
import javax.xml.xpath.XPath;
import javax.xml.xpath.XPathConstants;
import javax.xml.xpath.XPathFactory;
import oracle.xml.parser.v2.DOMParser;
import oracle.xml.parser.v2.FilePageManager;
import oracle.xml.parser.v2.XMLDocument;
import oracle.xml.scalable.BinaryStream;
import oracle.xml.util.XMLUtil;

public class StreamingXPath {
    DOMParser dp;
    XMLDocument doc;
    String xpath_expr;
    FilePageManager fpm;

    public StreamingXPath(String xmlName) {
        dp = new DOMParser();
        System.out.println("XDK version: " + dp.getReleaseVersion());
        try {
            FileInputStream xmlInFile = new FileInputStream(xmlName);
            fpm = new FilePageManager("tmp.bin", "new");
```

```
            dp.setAttribute(DOMParser.PARTIAL_DOM, Boolean.TRUE);
            dp.setAttribute(BinaryStream.BINARY_FORMAT,
                                 BinaryStream.XDB_BINXML);
            dp.setAttribute(XMLDocument.ACCESS_MODE,
                                 XMLDocument.FORWARD_READ);
            dp.setAttribute(DOMParser.PAGE_MANAGER, fpm);
            dp.setAttribute(DOMParser.BASE_URL, XMLUtil.createURL("."));
            dp.setPreserveWhitespace(true);
            dp.parse(xmlInFile);
            doc = dp.getDocument();
        } catch (Exception ex) {
            ex.printStackTrace();
        }
    }

    public void process() throws Exception {
        System.setProperty(XPathFactory.DEFAULT_PROPERTY_NAME + ":" +
                           XPathFactory.DEFAULT_OBJECT_MODEL_URI,
                           "oracle.xml.xpath.JXPathFactory");
        XPathFactory xpfac = XPathFactory.newInstance();
        XPath xpath = xpfac.newXPath();
        String expr = "count(//work)";
        double numValue =
             (Double)xpath.evaluate(expr, doc, XPathConstants.NUMBER);
        System.out.println("Number of nodes selected " + numValue);
    }

    public static void main(String[] args) throws Exception {
        StreamingXPath sxpath = new StreamingXPath(args[0]);
        sxpath.process();
    }
}
```

In this example, we create an *XPathFactory* instance *xpfac* and then create a new XPath object called *xpath*. The xpath.evaluate() function is called to evaluate the XPath. Because we are using Scalable DOM with the *XMLDocument.FORWARD_READ* setup, the in-memory objects are "lazily" created (i.e., created only when needed) and the nonused objects are automatically freed up. This improves the operation's scalability.

Extracting XPath from XML Documents

In previous sections, we discussed using XPath to navigate and access XML content. In this section, we will discuss how to extract XPaths from an XML document. We will extract XPaths using SAX parsing to improve the processing's scalability. There are several key components in this process:

- Creating a stack to keep track of the XPath
- Using SAX to push the XPath elements to the stack and record the XPaths

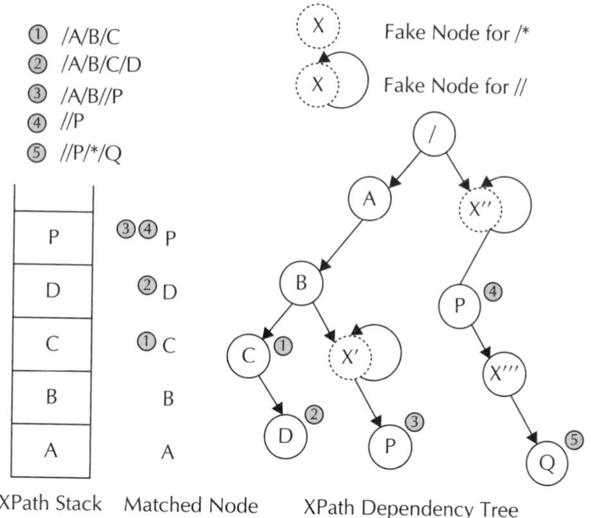

FIGURE 6-2. *Using Stack Record XPath Traversal*

The XPath stack is implemented in the *XPathStack* class in the following listing (*XPathStack.java*). The *XPathStack* class has two member variables: *s_XPathValue* is a hash table keeping track of a unique XPath-Value pair; *m_XPathStack* is a vector that maintains a stack to keep track of XPath traversal status, as shown in Figure 6-2.

```
public class XPathStack {
    public XPathStack(boolean useName, boolean has_content){
        m_useName = useName;
        s_XPathValue = new Hashtable();
        m_XPathStack = new Vector();
        m_hasContent= has_content;
    }

    public void printStack(PrintStream out) {
        Enumeration eKeys = s_XPathValue.keys();
        while (eKeys.hasMoreElements()) {
            String key = (String)eKeys.nextElement();
            out.println(key + "\t" + s_XPathValue.get(key));
        }
    }

    public void init() {
        m_curElement = null;
    }
```

```
public int push(String qName, Attributes attrs, String content) {

    // Update the XPATH stack
    int length = m_XPathStack.size();
    if (length > 0) {
        m_curElement = (XPathStackElement)m_XPathStack.get(length - 1);
        if (m_useName) {
            m_XPathStack.add(new XPathStackElement(m_curElement.m_childNum
+
                                                    1, 0, qName));
        } else {
            m_XPathStack.add(new XPathStackElement(m_curElement.m_childNum
+
                                                    1, 0));
        }
    } else {
        if (m_useName) {
            m_XPathStack.add(new XPathStackElement(0, 0, qName));
        } else {
            m_XPathStack.add(new XPathStackElement(0, 0));
        }
    }
    // Update XMLElement content
    m_curElement = (XPathStackElement)m_XPathStack.get(length);
    m_curElement.m_name = qName;
    m_curElement.m_XPath = getCurrentXPath();
    m_curElement.m_attrs = attrs;
    m_curElement.m_content = content;

    //Add XML element's XPath to XPath Collection
    //Processing duplicate XPaths
    if (s_XPathValue.containsKey(m_curElement.m_XPath)) {
        s_XPathValue.put(m_curElement.m_XPath + "[0]",
                         s_XPathValue.get(m_curElement.m_XPath));
        s_XPathValue.remove(m_curElement.m_XPath);
        m_curElement.m_XPath = m_curElement.m_XPath + "[1]";
    } else
        s_XPathValue.put(m_curElement.m_XPath, "");
    // Add attributes' XPaths Collection
    for (int i = 0; i < m_curElement.m_attrs.getLength(); i++) {
        s_XPathValue.put(m_curElement.m_XPath + "@" +
                         m_curElement.m_attrs.getQName(i),
                         m_curElement.m_attrs.getValue(i));
    }
    return length;
}

public void pop(String content) {
    int length = m_XPathStack.size();
    //Adding XML content with no mixed XML content
```

```
        if (content != null) {
            s_XPathValue.remove(m_curElement.m_XPath);
            s_XPathValue.put(m_curElement.m_XPath, content);
            updateXPathContent(length, content);
        } else {
            if(m_hasContent)
                s_XPathValue.remove(m_curElement.m_XPath);
        }
        if (length > 1) {
            m_curElement = (XPathStackElement)m_XPathStack.get(length - 2);
            m_curElement.m_childNum = m_curElement.m_childNum + 1;
            m_XPathStack.setSize(length - 1);
        }
    }

    public void updateXPathContent(int pos, String content) {
        XPathStackElement xse =
            (XPathStackElement)m_XPathStack.elementAt(pos - 1);
        xse.m_content = content;
        m_curElement.m_content = content;
    }

    protected String getCurrentXPath() {
        String temp_xpath = "/";
        if (m_useName) {
            for (int i = 0; i < m_XPathStack.size(); i++) {
                temp_xpath =
                        temp_xpath + ((XPathStackElement)m_XPathStack
.elementAt(i)).m_name + "/";
            }
        } else {
            for (int i = 1; i < m_XPathStack.size() - 1; i++) {
                temp_xpath = temp_xpath + "*[" + ((XPathStackElement)
m_XPathStack.elementAt(i)).m_nodePos + "]/";
            }
        }
        return temp_xpath;
    }

    public Hashtable getXPathValues() {
        return s_XPathValue;
    }
    boolean m_useName = true;
    boolean m_hasContent = false;
    XPathStackElement m_curElement;
    Vector m_XPathStack;
    Hashtable s_XPathValue;
}
```

XPathStackElement is used by *XPathStack* to tokenize each element in XPath:

```
class XPathStackElement {
    public int m_nodePos = 0;
    public int m_childNum = 0;
    public String m_name;
    public String m_XPath;
    public Attributes m_attrs;
    public String m_content;
    public XPathStackElement(int pos, int num) {
        m_nodePos = pos;
        m_childNum = num;
    }
    public XPathStackElement(int pos, int num, String qName) {
        m_nodePos = pos;
        m_childNum = num;
        m_name = qName;
    }
    public void printContent(PrintStream out) {
        if (m_content != null) {
            out.println(m_XPath);
            out.println(m_content);
        }
    }

    public void printXPath(PrintStream out) {
        printElementXPath(out);
        printAttrsXPath(out);
    }
    public void printElementXPath(PrintStream out) {
        if (m_content != null)
            out.print(m_XPath + "\t" + m_content);
        else
            out.print(m_XPath + "\t" + m_content);
    }
    public void printAttrsXPath(PrintStream out) {
        for (int i = 0; i < m_attrs.getLength(); i++) {
            out.print(m_XPath + "@" + m_attrs.getQName(i));
            out.print("\t");
            out.println(m_attrs.getValue(i));
        }
    }
}
```

The XPath extraction operation is performed within a SAX parsing process. This is implemented in an *XPathExtraction* class which extends the Oracle XDK *XMLMultiHandler* class as follows:

```
class XPathExtraction extends XMLMultiHandler {
    public XPathExtraction(boolean useName, boolean has_content) {
        m_XPathStack = new XPathStack(useName, has_content);
    }
```

```
    public void startDocument() throws SAXException {
        m_XPathStack.init();
    }
    public void startElement(String namespaceURI, String localName,
                             String qName,
                             Attributes atts) throws SAXException {
        m_XPathPos = m_XPathStack.push(qName, atts, null);
        m_content = null;
    }

    public void characters(char[] text, int start, int length) {
        StringBuffer sb = new StringBuffer();
        for (int i = start; i < start + length; i++) {
            sb.append(text[i]);
        }
        String str = sb.toString();
        if (str.trim().length()>0) m_content = str;
        else m_content = null;
    }
    public void endElement(String namespaceURI, String localName,
                           String qName) throws SAXException {
        m_XPathStack.pop(m_content);
        m_content = null;
    }
    void extract(URL fileURL) throws IOException, SAXException {
        InputSource is = new InputSource(fileURL.openStream());
        SAXParser parser = new SAXParser();
        parser.setContentHandler(this);
        parser.parse(is);
    }

    public XPathStack getXPathStack() {
        return m_XPathStack;
    }

    XPathStack m_XPathStack;
    String m_content;
    int m_XPathPos;
}
```

In this class, the extract() function starts SAX processing on the given XML document. Then, for each new XML document the *XPathStack* class is initialized in the startDocument() callback function. Then the XML element and its attributes are pushed to *XPathStack* in StartElement(). In endElement(), the same XML element is popped up from *XPathStack*. In characters(), the current element content is collected and is stored in the *m_content* variable. After the SAX parsing, the *m_XPathStack* instance should contain the XPath records of the XML document.

To call the XPath process, we use the following function (*RunXPathExtraction.java*):

Listing 6-4 *Extracting XPath Using SAX Processing in Java*

```
public static void checkFiles(String pathRoot, PrintStream out) {
        Vector cfiles = XMLUtility.getFileList(pathRoot, "xml");
        if (cfiles != null) {
            try {
                for (int i = 0; i < cfiles.size(); i++) {
                    XPathExtraction xe = new XPathExtraction(true,false);
                    String fp = pathRoot + cfiles.elementAt(i).toString();
                    xe.extract(XMLUtility.createURL(fp));
                    out.println(fp);
                    xe.getXPathStack().printStack(out);
                }
            } catch (Exception ex) {
                ex.printStackTrace();
            }
        }
    }
```

After XMLUtility.getFileList() gets all of the files from the folder specified by the *pathRoot* parameter, the XPathExtraction.extract() function is invoked for each file. Then the XPathExtraction .getXPathStack().printStack() function prints out the extracted XPath and its values. An example XPath output is as follows:

```
/contact/
/contact/@xmlns    http://xmlbook.com/sample/contact.xsd
/contact/@id       1
/contact/category/        customer
/contact/first_name/      Jennifer
/contact/last_name/       Wang
/contact/phone/    (86)1068739218
/contact/cellphone/       (86)1784462953
/contact/email/    jennifer.wang@acme.com
/contact/business/
/contact/business/title/       Director
/contact/business/company/     Acme Corporation
/contact/business/department/ Research and Development Center
```

We will use this processor in Chapter 17 to review XML content in XML DB Repository. This processing is also useful for loading XML into the database and performing XPath-based updates.

Summary

XPath is a compact expression that provides an easy way to navigate and access XML content. You will use it extensively in XSLT, XQuery, and XMLType functions. In later chapters, you will find more examples showing how to use XPath to perform XML operations and to review XML content in Oracle XML DB applications.

CHAPTER 7

XSL Transformations

XSL transformations (http://www.w3.org/1999/XSL/Transform) are used to transform XML documents, especially when there is a need to publish XML on the Web, translate XML from one vocabulary to another, or merge or split XML documents.

Figure 7-1 explains the XSL transformations (XSLT) process, in which the XSLT processor takes one or multiple XML documents as the inputs, applies the transformation instructions described in XSL stylesheets, and creates *new* XML or non-XML documents as the transformation outputs.

In this chapter, we will discuss basic XSLT techniques, explain some useful XSLT 1.0 and 2.0 features, and provide examples on how to run XSLT using Oracle XDK and Oracle XML DB.

Understanding XSLT Processing

XSLT is template-based processing, which operates on the tree-structured XML infoset (*source tree*). For example, let's run XSLT on this simple XML document (*john_smith.xml*):

```
<?xml version="1.0" encoding="UTF-8"?>
<contact xmlns="http://xmlbook.com/sample/contact.xsd" id="1">
  <category>customer</category>
  <first_name>John</first_name>
  <last_name>Smith</last_name>
  <email>john.smith@hfarm.com</email>
</contact>
```

The transformation traverses the document *source tree*, starting from the *<contact>* element and followed by its child nodes including the XML elements, attributes, text nodes, and others.

An XSL stylesheet is an XML document. In an XSL stylesheet, there are one or multiple *templates* defined by the *<xsl:template match="xpath pattern">* element. The *match="XPath Pattern"* attribute specifies the matched nodes in the source document to which the template

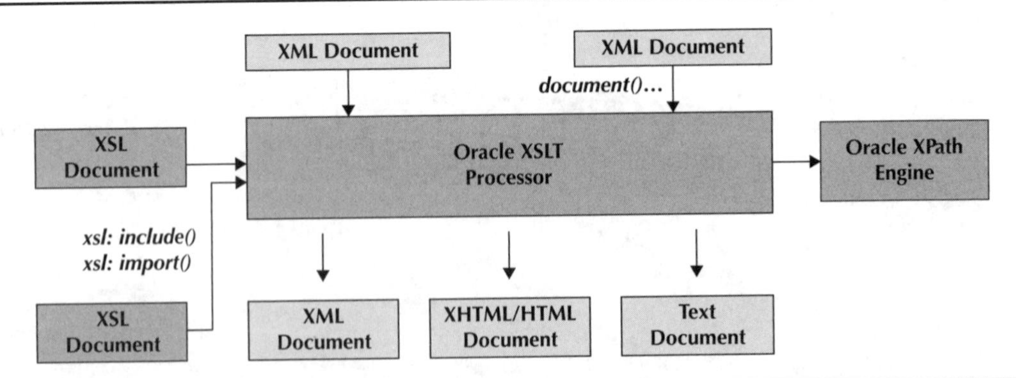

FIGURE 7-1. *The XSLT process*

should apply. Within each template element, there are a set of XSL transformation rules defined to construct the transformation *result tree*. The following is a simple XSL stylesheet (*copy.xsl*):

Listing 7-1 *Copying Documents with XSLT*

```
<xsl:stylesheet version="1.0" xmlns:xsl="http://www.w3.org/1999/XSL/Transform">
  <xsl:template match="@*|node()">
    <xsl:copy>
      <xsl:apply-templates select="@*|node()"/>
    </xsl:copy>
  </xsl:template>
</xsl:stylesheet>
```

There is only one XSL template in the stylesheet, which applies to all XML elements and attributes. During the XSLT process, the template is called from the first element in the *source tree*. The XSLT process creates a copy of the element using *<xsl:copy>*, and then calls *<xsl:apply-templates select="@*|node()"/>* to apply XSL templates to the current element's child nodes. The XSLT process continues on the XML sub-elements/attributes recursively until there are no attributes or elements left to be processed. The *result tree* is a copy of the input document's elements and attributes.

XML Tip: Can I update input XML documents with XSLT?

No. Whereas DOM operations update the input XML documents, XSLT only creates new documents.

Let's look at another example to further explain the XSLT process. The input document is shown as follows (*image_list.xml*):

```
<?xml version="1.0" encoding="windows-1252" ?>
<photourl>http://www.oracleimg.com/ocom/groups/public/@ocom/documents/
digitalasset/151997.gif;http://www.oracleimg.com/ocom/groups/public/@ocom/
documents/digitalasset/162216.gif;http://www.oracleimg.com/ocom/groups/public/
@ocom/documents/digitalasset/162217.gif;http://www.oracleimg.com/ocom/groups/
public/@ocom/documents/digitalasset/152000.gif</photourl>
```

The following XSL stylesheet creates an HTML page to display all images in an HTML table (*show_images.xsl*):

Listing 7-2 *Making Recursive Calls in XSLT*

```
<xsl:stylesheet version="1.0" xmlns:xsl="http://www.w3.org/1999/XSL/Transform">
  <xsl:output indent="yes"/>
  <xsl:template match="/">
  <table>
   <tr>
    <xsl:if test="normalize-space(photourl)!=''">
```

```
        <xsl:call-template name="create_image_td">
          <xsl:with-param name="photourl" select="photourl"/>
        </xsl:call-template>
      </xsl:if>
      </tr>
      </table>
    </xsl:template>

    <xsl:template name="create_image_td">
     <xsl:param name="photourl"/>
     <xsl:choose>
       <xsl:when test="contains($photourl,';')">
         <td valign="top">
          <img src="{substring-before($photourl,';')}" height="101"/>
         </td>
        <xsl:call-template name="create_image_td">
         <xsl:with-param name="photourl" select="substring-
after($photourl,';')"/>
        </xsl:call-template>
          </xsl:when>
          <xsl:otherwise>
          <xsl:if test="$photourl !=''">
            <td valign="top">
              <img src="{$photourl}" height="101"/>
            </td>
          </xsl:if>
          </xsl:otherwise>
        </xsl:choose>
    </xsl:template>
  </xsl:stylesheet>
```

The process starts by calling the *<xsl:template match="/">* template, in which the *create_image_td* template is called with the *<photourl>* element content. Within the *create_image_td* template, an *<img>* element is created within a *<td>* element with the *src* URL to be the string before the first ';'. This string is extracted by calling the XPath string function substring-before($photourl,';'). Then, the *create_image_td* template is called recursively with the new *photourl* string containing the remaining URL content returned by substring-after($photourl,';'). The recursive call ends when there is no ';' left in *$photourl* detected by *<xsl:when test="contains ($photourl,';')">*. The example transformation result is shown as follows:

```
<?xml version = '1.0' encoding = 'UTF-8'?>
<table>
<tr>
  <td valign="top"><img src="http://www.oracleimg.com/ocom/groups/public/@ocom/
documents/digitalasset/151997.gif" height="101"/></td>
  <td valign="top"><img src="http://www.oracleimg.com/ocom/groups/public/@ocom/
documents/digitalasset/162216.gif" height="101"/></td>
  <td valign="top"><img src="http://www.oracleimg.com/ocom/groups/public/@ocom/
documents/digitalasset/162217.gif" height="101"/></td>
```

```
  <td valign="top"><img src="http://www.oracleimg.com/ocom/groups/public/@ocom/
documents/digitalasset/152000.gif" height="101"/></td>
</tr>
</table>
```

Because of the template-based processing, it's very common to perform such recursive calls in XSLT.

Next, constructing the *result tree* is the main process in XSLT. Let's look at two examples. The first removes namespaces from an XML document (*ns_remove.xsl*):

Listing 7-3 *Removing Namespace from XML Documents with XSLT*

```
<?xml version="1.0" encoding="UTF-8"?>
<xsl:stylesheet version="1.0"
     xmlns:xsl="http://www.w3.org/1999/XSL/Transform">
  <xsl:output method="xml" version="1.0" encoding="UTF-8" indent="yes"/>
  <xsl:template match="*">
    <xsl:element name="{local-name()}">
    <xsl:for-each select="@*">
      <xsl:attribute name="{local-name()}">
         <xsl:value-of select="."/>
       </xsl:attribute>
    </xsl:for-each>
  <xsl:apply-templates/>
  </xsl:element>
  </xsl:template>
</xsl:stylesheet>
```

This example shows how you can control the *result tree* construction in XSLT using local_name() to specify the element/attribute names without a namespace.

The second example adds a namespace back into the XML document (*ns_add.xsl*):

Listing 7-4 *Adding Default Namespace to XML Documents with XSLT*

```
<?xml version="1.0" encoding="windows-1252" ?>
<xsl:stylesheet version="2.0" xmlns:xsl="http://www.w3.org/1999/XSL/Transform"
xmlns="http://xmlbook.com/sample/contact.xsd">
  <xsl:template match="*" priority="2">
    <xsl:element name="{local-name()}" namespace="http://xmlbook.com/sample/
contact.xsd" >
      <xsl:apply-templates select="@*|node()" />
    </xsl:element>
  </xsl:template>
  <xsl:template match="@*|node()">
  <xsl:copy>
   <xsl:apply-templates select="@*|node()"/>
  </xsl:copy>
 </xsl:template>
</xsl:stylesheet>
```

This example also shows how you can control XSLT result tree construction by changing the template execution priority using the *priority* attribute in the XSL template. The XSLT processor only applies one template on a node. When choosing which template to use, the XSL template with a higher priority is executed first.

Usually, the template has a lower priority when it has a more general template matching rule. In other words, the more specific the matching rule is, the higher priority the template has. By default, the *<xsl:template match="*">* template is set to a very low priority, which will not be executed before the *<xsl:template match="@*|node">* template. In order to add namespaces before copying the elements/attributes to the XSLT *result tree,* we change the execution order by increasing the priority of the *<xsl:template match="*">* template to "2".

In summary, the XSLT process traverses the input *source tree* starting from the primary document's root element. When a node in the source matches the rules specified by XSL templates, the XSLT processor will pick up a template to execute based on the template's execution priority. Then, rules in templates are applied to construct the XSLT *result tree.* If the template contains a process to select other nodes to process, the sequences of node matching and template execution will continue until there is no node left to be processed. Table 7-1 lists the commonly used XSLT elements and functions. The XSLT 2.0–related elements are highlighted in **bold**.

Use	XSLT Elements/Functions
Defining inputs	document()
Creating nodes	<xsl:element>, <xsl:attribute>, <xsl:text>
Copying nodes	<xsl:copy-of>, <xsl:copy>
Looping	<xsl:for-each>, **<xsl:for-each-group>**
Sorting	<xsl:sort> (always within looping elements or <xsl:apply-templates>)
Conditional processing	<xsl:choose> (<xsl:when><xsl:otherwise>), <xsl:if>
Computing values	<xsl:value-of>
Defining variables/ parameters	<xsl:variable>, <xsl:param>
Defining templates	<xsl:template>
Applying template rules	<xsl:template>, <xsl:apply-templates>, <xsl:call-template>
Combining stylesheets	<xsl:import>, <xsl:include>
Building lookup indexes	<xsl:key>
Defining outputs	<xsl:output>, **<xsl:result-documents>**
Whitespace stripping	<xsl:strip-space>, <xsl:preserve-space>

TABLE 7-1. *Commonly Used XSLT Elements and Functions*

Basic XSLT Features

Now, let's learn how to use the XSLT 1.0 features to create useful XSL transformations.

Multiple XML Inputs

XSLT inputs must be XML documents, but there is no limit on how many XML documents can be used. The XSL document() function allows XSLT to have multiple XML documents as the inputs.

A typical example is to use XSLT to merge XML documents (*contact_resume_merge.xsl*):

Listing 7-5 *Merging XML Documents with XSLT*

```
<xsl:stylesheet version="1.0" xmlns:xsl="http://www.w3.org/1999/XSL/Transform"
                xmlns:book="http://xmlbook.com/sample/contact.xsd">
 <xsl:output method="xml" omit-xml-declaration="no" indent="yes"/>
 <xsl:template match="@*|node()">
  <xsl:choose>
   <xsl:when test="local-name()= 'contact'">
    <xsl:element name="contact"
                 namespace="http://xmlbook.com/sample/contact.xsd">
     <xsl:attribute name="id">
       <xsl:value-of select="book:contact/@id"/>
     </xsl:attribute>
     <xsl:variable name="resume_file"
                   select="concat('resume/', ./book:first_name/text(),'_', ./
book:last_name/text(), '.xml')"/>
     <xsl:variable name="email" select="./book:email/text()"/>
     <xsl:apply-templates
         select="document($resume_file)[ book:resume/book:header/book:email/
text() = $email]"/>
      <xsl:apply-templates/>
    </xsl:element>
   </xsl:when>
   <xsl:otherwise>
    <xsl:copy>
     <xsl:apply-templates select="@*|node()"/>
    </xsl:copy>
   </xsl:otherwise>
  </xsl:choose>
 </xsl:template>
</xsl:stylesheet>
```

In this example, the document() function retrieves the resume document to merge into a contact XML document using the contact's first name and last name. For example, when transforming the *john_smith.xml* file, the resume document will be *john_smith.xml* in the resume folder:

```
<xsl:variable name="resume_file"
 select="concat('resume/', ./book:first_name/text(),'_', ./book:last_name/
text(), '.xml')"/>
```

We can add other XPath expressions to document(). In the example, we check if *<email>* in the resume has the same value as the *<email>* content in the contact document:

```
document($resume_file)[book:resume/book:header/book:email/text() = $email]
```

In the XSL stylesheet, the *$email* XSL variable is used to simplify the XPath construction.

XML Tip: How do I determine the URI for the document() function?
When using the document() function, you need be aware of the XSL *base URL*. Normally, it is the same location as the XSL document. For example, when using Oracle JDeveloper 11*g*'s default XSLT processor, the base URL is the *XSL Source Paths* setting. For example, if the XSL file is in the *D:\xslt_samples\src\xsl directory and* your *document is in the D:\xslt_samples\src\resume\john_smith.xml directory, the document path should be document('../resume/john_smith.xml').*

Building an XSL Index

You can simplify your XSL stylesheet processing by building indexes. Let's look at performing an in-place document update. The source document is shown as follows (*xmlbook_ann_tpl.xml*):

```
<email_template>
  <attachment>
     <imageContent baseurl="http://localhost:8081/public/chp17/event/
xmlbook_ann/images/">
        <image id="001">book_cover.jpg</image>
        <image id="002">learnmore.gif</image>
     </imageContent>
     <attachedContent baseurl="http://localhost:8081/public/chp17/event/
xmlbook_ann/files/">
        <file>sample_chapter.pdf</file>
     </attachedContent>
   </attachment>
  <xsl_content>
  <xsl:stylesheet version="1.0" xmlns:xsl="http://www.w3.org/1999/XSL/
Transform">
  <xsl:template match="/">
  <table bgcolor="#ffffff" border="0" bordercolor="#ffffff"
  width="492" height="236">
  <tbody>
  <tr bgcolor="#ffffff">
   <td valign="top"><img src="cid:002"/></td>
   </tr>
   <tr bgcolor="#ffffff">
    <td valign="top">
     <p>Hi <xsl:value-of select="/book:contact/book:first_name"/>,</p>
     <p> Oracle Database 11g: Building Oracle XML DB Applications is
published.<br/>
     <img src="cid:001" href="http://community.oraclepressbooks.com/
```

```
profile.php?aid=1284"/></p>
      <table>
       <tr>
        <td>Feel free to send me your comments, suggestions and questions. <br/>
  Sincerely,<br/>
        Jinyu</td>
       </tr>
     </table>
    </td></tr>
  </tbody>
</table>
</xsl:template>
</xsl:stylesheet>
</xsl_content>
</email_template>
```

The document contains an index table in the *<imageContent>* element listing the image IDs and the file names. The *baseurl* attribute in the *<imageContent>* element indicates the actual URL location of the image files. Within the *<xsl_content>* element, the *<img>* elements use image IDs with the *cid* prefix to refer to the images files.

We need to create an XSL stylesheet, which creates a new document by replacing the image *cid:IDs* with the image URL specified by the *<imageContent>* element. The XSL stylesheet is defined as follows (*gen_preview_stylesheet.xsl*):

Listing 7-6 *XML Content Update Using XSLT*

```
<xsl:stylesheet version="1.0" xmlns:xsl="http://www.w3.org/1999/XSL/Transform">
  <xsl:variable name="image_baseurl"
                select="/email_template/attachment/imageContent/@baseurl"/>
  <xsl:key name="image_index"
           match="/email_template/attachment/imageContent/image" use="@id"/>
  <xsl:template match="img">
    <xsl:variable name="current_id" select="substring-after(./@src, ':')"/>
    <xsl:element name="img">
      <xsl:attribute name="src">
        <xsl:value-of select="$image_baseurl"/>
        <xsl:value-of select="key('image_index', $current_id)/text()"/>
      </xsl:attribute>
    </xsl:element>
  </xsl:template>
  <xsl:template match="@*|node()">
    <xsl:copy>
      <xsl:apply-templates select="@*|node()"/>
    </xsl:copy>
  </xsl:template>
</xsl:stylesheet>
```

In this example, we define one global XSL variable (*image_baseurl*) and one lookup index (*image_index*). The *image_index* is an index of the *<image>* elements using their image ID attribute as the *index keys*. The *image_baseurl* keeps the image files' *base URL*. When the

<xsl:template match="img"> template finds an *<img>* element, the *current_id* of the image is retrieved using a substring function:

```
<xsl:variable name="current_id" select="substring-after(./@src, ':')"/>
```

Using *$current_id* as the key, we find the *<image>* element. Using the *<image>* element content and *image_baseurl*, we can construct the new *<img> src* attributes. The XSL transformation result is as follows:

```
<?xml version = '1.0' encoding = 'UTF-8'?>
<email_template>
  <attachment>
     <imageContent baseurl="http://localhost:8081/public/chp17/event/
xmlbook_ann/images /">
       <image id="001">book_cover.jpg</image>
       <image id="002">learnmore.gif</image>
     </imageContent>
<attachedContent baseurl="http://localhost:8081/public/chp17/event/xmlbook_ann/
files/">
       <file>sample_chapter.pdf</file>
     </attachedContent>
   </attachment>
  <xsl_content>
  <xsl:stylesheet xmlns:xsl="http://www.w3.org/1999/XSL/Transform"
version="1.0">
  <xsl:template match="/">
  <table bgcolor="#ffffff" border="0" bordercolor="#ffffff" width="492"
height="236">
  <tbody>
  <tr bgcolor="#ffffff">
   <td valign="top"><img src="http://localhost:8081/public/chp17/event/
xmlbook_ann/images/learnmore.gif"/></td>
   </tr>
   <tr bgcolor="#ffffff">
    <td valign="top">
     <p>Hi <xsl:value-of select="/book:contact/book:first_name"/>,</p>
     <p> Oracle Database 11g: Building Oracle XML DB Applications is
published.<br/>
     <img src="http://localhost:8081/public/chp17/event/xmlbook_ann/images/
book_cover.jpg"/></p>
     <table>
      <tr>
       <td>Feel free to send me your comments, suggestions and questions. <br/>
  Sincerely,<br/>
       Jinyu</td>
      </tr>
    </table>
   </td></tr>
  </tbody>
</table>
</xsl:template>
```

```
</xsl:stylesheet>
</xsl_content>
</email_template>
```

Creating XSLT Extensions

XSLT allows extensions. Using Oracle XDK Java, you can write XSLT extensions in Java. Let's look at how to do this. In this example, we create an extension title-case() function to convert a string to title-case format.

First, we create an *xmlbook.chp07.StringOperations* class in Java (*StringOperations.java*):

```
package xmlbook.chp07;

import java.util.StringTokenizer;

import oracle.xml.parser.v2.XMLDOMStringList;

public class StringOperations {
    public StringOperations() {
    }

    public static String toTitleCase(String input){
        String result="", temp;
        StringTokenizer st = new StringTokenizer(input, " ");

        while (st.hasMoreTokens()) {
         temp = st.nextToken();
         result=result+temp.substring(0,1).toUpperCase()+
                temp.subSequence(1,temp.length())+" ";
        }
        return result;
    }

}
```

The Java toTitleCase() function tokenizes the string into a set of words using whitespaces, and then changes the first character of each token to uppercase. At the end, the string tokens are concatenated.

Second, we compile the Java code in Oracle JDeveloper 11*g* and make sure the class is part of the Java CLASSPATH. In Oracle JDeveloper 11*g*, the compiled Java classes are automatically added to the Java CLASSPATH.

Third, in an XSL stylesheet, we declare the namespace for the Java class and call the method using the defined namespace (*extension_function.xsl*):

Listing 7-7 *Using Java Extensions in XSLT*

```
<?xml version="1.0" encoding="UTF-8"?>
<xsl:stylesheet version="2.0" xmlns:xsl="http://www.w3.org/1999/XSL/Transform"
xmlns:str="http://www.oracle.com/XSL/Transform/java/xmlbook.chp07
.StringOperations">
```

```
 <xsl:template match="@*|node()" priority="0">
  <xsl:choose>
   <xsl:when test="local-name() = 'street1'">
    <xsl:element name="street1">
     <xsl:value-of select="str:toTitleCase(text())"/>
    </xsl:element>
   </xsl:when>
   <xsl:otherwise>
    <xsl:copy>
     <xsl:apply-templates select="@*|node()"/>
    </xsl:copy>
   </xsl:otherwise>
  </xsl:choose>
 </xsl:template>
</xsl:stylesheet>
```

When using Oracle XDK, the namespace must begin with *http://www.oracle.com/XSL/Transform/java/*, followed by *java_class.method_name*.

Advanced XSLT Features

Here we will learn about advanced XSLT features offered in XSLT 2.0, including grouping, multiple outputs, and temporary tree features. We will use XSLT to create a dictionary for search applications.

Oracle Secure Enterprise Search (SES) is Oracle's enterprise search product. Oracle SES provides the "Did you mean?" search feature. With this feature, suggestions are given when users type in queries. Therefore, users can check typos, or expand acronyms to their full names for more effective search and a better user experience. For example, when people search for "oracle db," the search query can be extended to "oracle database." This feature is based on the *alternative words* dictionary.

To build a comprehensive dictionary, we have a tool to extract acronyms from multiple data sources and create an XML document in the format shown as follows (*altwords_1.xml*):

```
<AltWords>
  <Item>
    <A>gpug</A>
    <E>global product user group</E>
  </Item>
  <Item>
    <A>dug</A>
    <E>defense users group</E>
  </Item>...
</AltWords>
```

We also have an Excel spreadsheet that lists the alternative words (*altwords_3.xml*):

```
<?xml version="1.0"?>
<?mso-application progid="Excel.Sheet"?>
<Workbook xmlns="urn:schemas-microsoft-com:office:spreadsheet"
          xmlns:o="urn:schemas-microsoft-com:office:office"
          xmlns:x="urn:schemas-microsoft-com:office:excel"
```

```
         xmlns:ss="urn:schemas-microsoft-com:office:spreadsheet"
         xmlns:html="http://www.w3.org/TR/REC-html40">
<DocumentProperties xmlns="urn:schemas-microsoft-com:office:office">
 <LastAuthor>jinyu wang</LastAuthor>
 <Created>2010-07-01T07:12:35Z</Created>
 <Version>11.9999</Version>
</DocumentProperties>
<OfficeDocumentSettings xmlns="urn:schemas-microsoft-com:office:office">
 <DownloadComponents/>
 <LocationOfComponents HRef="file:///C:\Temp\rksinst\"/>
</OfficeDocumentSettings>
<ExcelWorkbook xmlns="urn:schemas-microsoft-com:office:excel">
 <WindowHeight>9975</WindowHeight>
 <WindowWidth>20955</WindowWidth>
 <WindowTopX>240</WindowTopX>
 <WindowTopY>75</WindowTopY>
 <ProtectStructure>False</ProtectStructure>
 <ProtectWindows>False</ProtectWindows>
</ExcelWorkbook>
<Styles>
 <Style ss:ID="Default" ss:Name="Normal">
  <Alignment ss:Vertical="Bottom"/>
  <Borders/>
  <Font/>
  <Interior/>
  <NumberFormat/>
  <Protection/>
 </Style>
 <Style ss:ID="s23">
  <Font x:Family="Swiss"/>
 </Style>
</Styles>
<Worksheet ss:Name="2009_additional">
 <Table ss:ExpandedColumnCount="2" ss:ExpandedRowCount="90" x:FullColumns="1"
        x:FullRows="1">
  <Column ss:AutoFitWidth="0" ss:Width="230.25"/>
  <Column ss:AutoFitWidth="0" ss:Width="113.25"/>
  <Row>
   <Cell ss:StyleID="s23">
    <Data ss:Type="String">Database</Data>
   </Cell>
   <Cell ss:StyleID="s23">
    <Data ss:Type="String">DB</Data>
   </Cell>
  </Row>
  <Row>
   <Cell ss:StyleID="s23">
    <Data ss:Type="String">Database Upgrade Assistant</Data>
   </Cell>
   <Cell ss:StyleID="s23">
```

```
      <Data ss:Type="String">DBUA</Data>
     </Cell>
    </Row>
...
```

The goal is to combine all of the provided alternative words into one file with a consistent format, to merge duplicate words, and to calculate the unique alternative word number. For each alternative word, we also calculate the number of occurrences from the input to determine its popularity. Do you think we can do all of this in a single XSLT? The answer is yes! Let's learn how in detail.

Modularizing XSLT Processing with Temporary Trees

The first operation is to combine multiple XML inputs. Because there is one document in the Excel spreadsheet, we first need to convert its format using the following XSL stylesheet (*file_extract.xsl*):

```
<?xml version="1.0" encoding="windows-1252" ?>
<xsl:stylesheet version="1.0" xmlns:xsl="http://www.w3.org/1999/XSL/Transform"
                xmlns:ss="urn:schemas-microsoft-com:office:spreadsheet">
   <xsl:template name="file_extract">
      <xsl:param name="content"/>
      <AltWords>
         <xsl:for-each select="$content/ss:Workbook/ss:Worksheet/ss:Table/
ss:Row">
            <Item>
               <A>
                  <xsl:value-of select="ss:Cell[2]/ss:Data/text()"/>
               </A>
               <E>
                  <xsl:value-of select="ss:Cell[1]/ss:Data/text()"/>
               </E>
            </Item>
         </xsl:for-each>
      </AltWords>
   </xsl:template>
</xsl:stylesheet>
```

This XSL stylesheet is quite simple: we just loop all of the *Row* elements in the spreadsheet and create a new XML document based on alternative word input format.

The following XSL stylesheet completes the file merge (*file_merge.xsl*):

Listing 7-8 *Using Temporary Tree to Merge Documents in XSLT*

```
<?xml version="1.0" encoding="windows-1252" ?>
<xsl:stylesheet version="2.0" xmlns:xsl="http://www.w3.org/1999/XSL/Transform">
    <xsl:import href="file_extract.xsl"/>
    <xsl:variable name="extracted_from_excel">
        <xsl:call-template name="file_extract">
            <xsl:with-param name="content" select="document('altwords_3.xml')"/>
```

```
        </xsl:call-template>
    </xsl:variable>
    <xsl:variable name="input">
        <xsl:apply-templates select="document('altwords_1.xml')/AltWords/Item"/>
        <xsl:apply-templates select="document('altwords_2.xml')/AltWords/Item"/>
        <xsl:copy-of select="$extracted_from_excel"/>
        <xsl:apply-templates select="document('altwords_4.xml')/AltWords/Item"/>
        <xsl:apply-templates select="document('altwords_5.xml')/AltWords/Item"/>
    </xsl:variable>
    <xsl:template name="file_merge">
        <AltWords num="{count($input/Item)}">
            <xsl:sequence select="$input"/>
        </AltWords>
    </xsl:template>
    <xsl:template match="@*|node()">
        <xsl:copy>
            <xsl:apply-templates select="@*|node()"/>
        </xsl:copy>
    </xsl:template>
    <xsl:template match="E">
        <xsl:element name="E">
            <xsl:value-of select="normalize-space(lower-case(.))"/>
        </xsl:element>
    </xsl:template>
    <xsl:template match="A">
        <xsl:element name="A">
            <xsl:value-of select="lower-case(.)"/>
        </xsl:element>
    </xsl:template>
</xsl:stylesheet>
```

The key part of the file merge is included in the definitions of the two global variables: *$extracted_from_excel* and *$input*. Both are created using a new XSLT 2.0 feature, the *temporary tree*.

In XSLT 1.0, intermediate XSL transformation results or XSL variables (created by *<xsl:variable>*, *<xsl:param>*, or *<xsl:with-param>*) are stored as strings. In XSLT 2.0, these contents are stored as XML document nodes, called *temporary trees*. Temporary trees can be constructed via calling templates or other XSL content construction operations. With temporary trees, you can evaluate the content of a variable or a parameter using the XPath expressions, e.g., *count($input/Item)*.

With this new feature, we can easily modularize complex XSL transformations and apply iterative processing to the XML documents using XSL variables and parameters.

Merging Duplicates with Grouping

To merge duplicate alternative words and calculate the number of occurrences for each word, we need to use the XSLT 2.0 grouping feature (*item_merge.xsl*):

```
<?xml version="1.0" encoding="windows-1252" ?>
<xsl:stylesheet version="2.0" xmlns:xsl="http://www.w3.org/1999/XSL/Transform">
  <xsl:template name="item_merge">
    <xsl:param name="content"/>
```

```
        <xsl:for-each-group select="$content/AltWords/Item" group-by="E">
          <xsl:sort select="A"/>
          <altWord name="{distinct-values(current-group()/A/text())}"
weight="{count(current-group()/E)}">
            <alternate>"<xsl:value-of select="distinct-values
(current-group()/E/text())"/>"</alternate>
            <autoExpansion>false</autoExpansion>
          </altWord>
        </xsl:for-each-group>
  </xsl:template>
</xsl:stylesheet>
```

In the example, *<xsl:for-each-group>* is used to select all *<Item>* elements and create groups based on the criterion specified by *group-by*. In this example, *group-by="E"* means to group the *<Item>* elements based on the content in its *<E>* sub-element, which is the acronym extension. Within the *<xsl:for-each-group>* element, the *<xsl:sort>* element sorts the current groups based on the alphabetical order of the *<A>* element content. Then, it creates one *<altWord>* per group, which refers to the current group node-set using the current-group() function, and calculates the number of occurrences using the count (current-group()/E) function call.

In the previous example, we grouped the elements based on the element content. The following are the available grouping rules in XSLT 2.0:

- **group-by** Groups selected items by evaluating the expression specified in the *group-by* expression and ignoring the order in which the items appear in the selected sequence.
- **group-adjacent** Only groups adjacent items with the same value.
- **group-starting-with** Contains a pattern that matches the first node in each group.
- **group-ending-with** Contains a pattern that matches the last node in each group.

Creating Outputs with Multiple Outputs

The final XSL stylesheet integrates all of the processes (*gen_altword_list.xsl*):

```
<?xml version="1.0" encoding="windows-1252" ?>
<xsl:stylesheet version="2.0" xmlns:xsl="http://www.w3.org/1999/XSL/Transform">
    <xsl:import href="file_extract.xsl"/>
    <xsl:import href="file_merge.xsl"/>
    <xsl:import href="item_merge.xsl"/>
    <xsl:import href="item_merge_ses.xsl"/>
    <xsl:output media-type="text/xml" indent="yes" name="altword-format"/>
    <xsl:variable name="merged_file">
        <xsl:call-template name="file_merge"/>
    </xsl:variable>
    <xsl:template match="/">
        <xsl:result-document href="../output/altwords_merged_ses.xml"
                             format="altword-format">
            <xsl:call-template name="item_merge_ses">
                <xsl:with-param name="content" select="$merged_file"/>
            </xsl:call-template>
        </xsl:result-document>
      <xsl:result-document href="../output/altwords_merged.xml"
```

```
                                    format="altword-format">
        <xsl:call-template name="count_total">
            <xsl:with-param name="content">
                <xsl:call-template name="item_merge">
                    <xsl:with-param name="content" select="$merged_file"/>
                </xsl:call-template>
            </xsl:with-param>
        </xsl:call-template>
        </xsl:result-document>
    </xsl:template>
    <xsl:template name="count_total">
        <xsl:param name="content"/>
        <AltWords num="{count($content/altWord)}">
            <xsl:copy-of select="$content"/>
        </AltWords>
    </xsl:template>
</xsl:stylesheet>
```

Now let's explain this XSL stylesheet.

First, multiple XSL stylesheets, including *file_extract.xsl*, *file_merge.xsl*, *item_merge.xsl*, and *item_merge_ses.xsl*, are imported to the *gen_altword_list.xsl* XSL stylesheet using the *<xsl:import>* elements shown as follows:

```
<xsl:import href="file_extract.xsl"/>
<xsl:import href="file_merge.xsl"/>
<xsl:import href="item_merge.xsl"/>
<xsl:import href="item_merge_ses.xsl"/>
```

Second, the *file_merge* template (defined in *file_merge.xsl*) is called to merge all of the alternative word files. The merged result is assigned to the *$merged_file* XSL variable:

```
<xsl:variable name="merged_file">
    <xsl:call-template name="file_merge"/>
</xsl:variable>
```

Third, the XSL stylesheet creates two outputs defined by *<xsl:result-document>*. Each output calls different templates to create the output files. This uses the XSLT 2.0 feature, *Multiple Outputs*. The two output files, *altwords_merged_ses.xml* and *altwords_merged.xml*, are created in addition to the default transformation output (*out.xml*). The output format is defined using *<xsl:output>*. In this example, the output format is an indented XML file format:

```
<xsl:output media-type="text/xml" indent="yes" name="altword-format"/>
```

The first XSLT result document is created in the Oracle SES defined alternative words document format (*altwords_merged_ses.xml*):

```
<xsl:result-document href="../output/altwords_merged_ses.xml"
                     format="altword-format">
    <xsl:call-template name="item_merge_ses">
        <xsl:with-param name="content" select="$merged_file"/>
    </xsl:call-template>
</xsl:result-document>
```

It calls the *item_merge_ses* template, given the content from the *$merged_file* variable. The *item_merge_ses* template is shown here (*item_merge_ses.xsl*):

```
<?xml version="1.0" encoding="windows-1252" ?>
<xsl:stylesheet version="2.0" xmlns:xsl="http://www.w3.org/1999/XSL/Transform"
                xmlns:search="http://xmlns.oracle.com/search">
  <xsl:template name="item_merge_ses">
    <xsl:param name="content"/>
    <search:config productVersion="11.1.2.0.0"
                   xmlns:search="http://xmlns.oracle.com/search">
      <search:altWords>
        <xsl:for-each-group select="$content/AltWords/Item" group-by="E">
          <xsl:sort select="A"/>
          <search:altWord>
            <search:keyword>
              <xsl:value-of select="distinct-values(current-group()/A/
text())"/>
            </search:keyword>
            <search:altKeyword>
              <xsl:value-of select="distinct-values(current-group()/E/
text())"/>
            </search:altKeyword>
            <search:autoExpand>false</search:autoExpand>
          </search:altWord>
        </xsl:for-each-group>
      </search:altWords>
    </search:config>
  </xsl:template>
</xsl:stylesheet>
```

The *item_merge_ses* template is similar to the *item_merge* template (defined in *item_merge.xsl*), discussed in the previous section. The *item_merge_ses* template merges duplicate alternative words using the XSLT 2.0 grouping feature. In addition, it creates the merged alternative word output in the Oracle SES defined format and in the Oracle SES namespace (*xmlns:search="http://xmlns.oracle.com/search"*).

The second XSLT output also performs the item merging, but with the *item_merge* template defined in *item_merge.xsl*. In addition to the item merging, the total number of alternative words is calculated using the *count_total* template:

```
<xsl:template match="/">
  ...
  <xsl:result-document href="../output/altwords_merged.xml"
                       format="altword-format">
  <xsl:call-template name="count_total">
     <xsl:with-param name="content">
        <xsl:call-template name="item_merge">
           <xsl:with-param name="content" select="$merged_file"/>
        </xsl:call-template>
     </xsl:with-param>
   </xsl:call-template>
</xsl:result-document>
```

```
</xsl:template>
<xsl:template name="count_total">
        <xsl:param name="content"/>
        <AltWords num="{count($content/altWord)}">
            <xsl:copy-of select="$content"/>
        </AltWords>
    </xsl:template>
```

The calculation result is assigned to the *num* attribute of the *<AltWords>* element. An example result is shown as follows (*altwords_merged.xml*):

```
<?xml version = '1.0' encoding = 'UTF-8'?>
<AltWords num="259">
   <altWord name="acs" num="4">
      <alternate>"applied computer solutions"</alternate>
      <autoExpansion>false</autoExpansion>
   </altWord>
   <altWord name="addm" num="4">
      <alternate>"automatic database diagnostic monitor"</alternate>
      <autoExpansion>false</autoExpansion>
   </altWord>
....
</AltWords>
```

Because multiple results are created in a single XSLT process, the XSLT 2.0 *Multiple Output* feature improves the efficiency of the XSL transformations.

Running XSLT

To run XSLT, you can use the Oracle XDK *oraxsl* command-line utility, call Oracle XDK or XML DB XSLT APIs, or run XSLT in Oracle JDeveloper 11*g* (based on the Oracle XDK *oraxsl* command-line utility). In this chapter, we only discuss XSLT using Oracle XDK and using Oracle XML DB in SQL. Chapter 11 discusses how to run *oraxsl* and Chapter 16 discusses running XSLT using Oracle JDeveloper 11*g*.

Using Oracle XDK Java

Oracle XDK Java supports both XSLT 1.0 and XSLT 2.0. The Oracle XDK XSLT processor exposes two Java classes for XSLT: *oracle.xml.parser.v2.XSLStylesheet* and *oracle.xml.parser.v2.XSLProcessor*. The *XSLStylesheet* object keeps the compiled XSL stylesheet. *XSLProcessor* applies the XSL transformations. The following is an example (*XSLTransform.java*):

```
package xmlbook.chp07;

import java.net.URL;
import oracle.xml.parser.v2.DOMParser;
import oracle.xml.parser.v2.XMLDocument;
import oracle.xml.parser.v2.XSLStylesheet;
import oracle.xml.parser.v2.XSLProcessor;
import oracle.xml.util.XMLUtil;
import java.net.MalformedURLException;
```

```
import java.io.File;

public class XSLTransform {
    public static void main(String[] args) throws Exception {
        try {
            if (args.length != 2) {
                // Must pass in the names of the XSL and XML files
                System.err.println("Usage: java XSLTransform xmlfile xslfile");
                System.exit(1);
            }
            XSLTransform xsltrans = new XSLTransform();
            xsltrans.transform(XMLUtil.createURL(args[0]),
                               XMLUtil.createURL(args[1]));
        } catch (Exception e) {
            e.printStackTrace();
        }
    }

    private void transform(URL xmlURL, URL xslURL) throws Exception {
        // Parse xsl and xml documents
        DOMParser parser = new DOMParser();
        parser.parse(xmlURL);
        XMLDocument xml = parser.getDocument();
        parser.parse(xslURL);
        XMLDocument xsldoc = parser.getDocument();

        // instantiate a stylesheet
        XSLProcessor processor = new XSLProcessor();
        processor.showWarnings(true);
        processor.setErrorStream(System.err);
        XSLStylesheet xsl = processor.newXSLStylesheet(xsldoc);
        processor.processXSL(xsl, xml, System.out);
    }
}
```

Oracle XDK Tip: Is there a requirement to print out the XSLT result in Java?
If an XSL stylesheet contains *<xsl:output>*, you need to use the *OutputWriter* Java class to ensure the *<xsl:output>* instructions are interpreted correctly.

In the Java process, you need to parse the XML document:

```
(XMLDocument) xml = parser.getDocument();
```

And you need to parse the XSL document to create *XSLStylesheet*:

```
parser.parse(xslURL);
(XMLDocument) xsldoc = parser.getDocument();
XSLProcessor processor = new XSLProcessor();
XSLStylesheet xsl = processor.newXSLStylesheet(xsldoc);
```

Then you can apply *XSLStylesheet* to the XML document by calling the XSLProcessor.processXSL() function:

```
processor.processXSL(xsl, xml, System.out);
```

In Oracle Database 11*g*, you can parse XML documents using Scalable DOM and then provide the *XMLDocument* object to the Oracle XDK XSLT processor. Scalable DOM parsing is explained in Chapter 4.

Using Oracle XML DB

In Oracle Database 11*g*, you can use the XMLTransform() SQL function, the XMLType.transform() function, or the DBMS_XSLPROCESSOR PL/SQL package to perform XSLT. All of the functions and packages only support XSLT 1.0. The following is an XSLT example, which passes in XSLT parameters to XMLTransform() (*contact_extract.sql*):

```
Set long 1000000
select xmltransform(xmltype('<contact><first_name>john</first_name>
<address country="US"><street> xyz street</street><state>ca</state><zip>94065</
zip></address></contact>'),
xmltype('<xsl:stylesheet xmlns:xsl="http://www.w3.org/1999/XSL/Transform"
version="1.0">
<xsl:param name="pattern" select="/contact"/>
<xsl:template match="/">
   <xsl:copy-of  select="$pattern"/>
</xsl:template>
</xsl:stylesheet>'), 'pattern="/contact/address "') result
from dual;
```

The result is

```
RESULT
------------------------------
<address country="US">
  <street> xyz street</street>
  <state>ca</state>
  <zip>94065</zip>
</address>
```

Summary

XSLT is a very powerful XML processing tool. XSLT is very useful in creating web pages (HTML), generating reports (PDF), and transforming XML data from one format to another. In Chapter 16, we will discuss further how to run XSLT in Oracle JDeveloper 11*g* and create a Java Stored Procedure to run the XSLT 2.0 stylesheets in Oracle Database 11*g*.

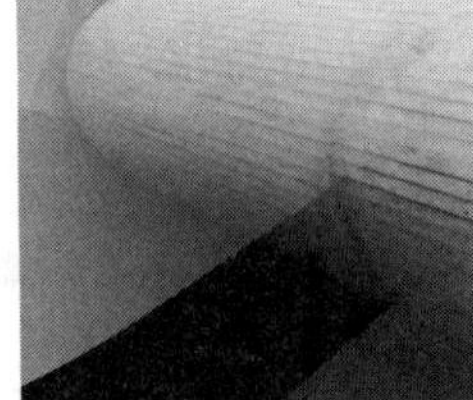

CHAPTER 8

XML Query

racle XML DB 11*g* XQuery supports the W3C XML Query (XQuery) 1.0 standard (http://www.w3.org/TR/xquery/). In Oracle Database 11*g*R2, XQuery is supported mainly by two SQL/XML functions, XMLQuery() and XMLTable(). The XMLQuery() function takes an XQuery expression as the input to query XML. The XMLTable() function maps the result of an XQuery evaluation into relational rows and columns.

In Oracle Database 11gR2, XQuery functions are replacing Oracle SQL functions and becoming the standard to query XML in the Oracle database. The XMLQuery() and XMLTable() functions replace the SQL functions extract() and XMLSequence() respectively. In addition, XMLCast() is used with the XMLQuery() function to replace extractValues() to get the result as an XMLType or a scalar value. XMLExists() replaces existsNode() to evaluate XQuery as a predicate in the SQL *where* clause.

Oracle XML DB Tip: Deprecating SQL functions with XQuery functions

You can still use XMLType.extract() and XMLType.extractValues() as the XMLType methods to query XML content.

In this chapter, let's learn XQuery and how to use the XMLQuery() function. We will discuss the XMLTable() function in Chapter 9.

XQuery Expressions

An XQuery can be as simple as a single XPath expression or as complicated as a query with functional calls, conditional processes, and XML result constructions. In general, XQuery syntax is a FLWOR (pronounced "*flower*") expression. *FLWOR* stands for *for, let, where, order by,* and *return*:

- For Iterates over a sequence of items, each of which could be XML nodes or atomic values.
- Let Declares variables that can be sequences of XML nodes or atomic values.
- Where Defines the conditions for filtering the result.
- Order By Specifies the sorting order of the result.
- Return Returns the result content.

The following is a typical XQuery example with a *FLWOR* expression (*xq_flwor.sql*):

Listing 8-1 *XQuery FLWOR Expression in XMLQuery()*

```
SELECT XMLQuery('declare namespace book="http://xmlbook.com/sample/contact
.xsd"; (: :)
for $cd in collection("/public/contact/xml")/book:contact
  let $last_name:=$cd/book:last_name/text(),
      $first_name:=$cd/book:first_name/text(),
      $email:=$cd/book:email/text()
  where not(empty($email))
  order by $last_name
  return <contact>{$first_name},{$last_name}</contact>'
  returning content) result
FROM dual;
```

In this query, the *for* statement iterates the *<contact>* elements (assigned as the *$cd* variable) from the files stored in the */public/contact/xml* folder in XML DB Repository. The *where* clause restricts to select *<contact>* elements with a non-empty *<email>* element. The *<contact>* elements are processed in the order of their *<last_name>* element content as specified by the *order by* statement. The *let* statement retrieves the text content of *<first_name>* and *<last_name>* and assigns them to query variables. These variables are used in the *return* statement to construct the XML result.

In practice, you don't have to use all of the FLWOR clauses in XQuery.

Using XMLQuery()

In Oracle XML DB, XQuery expressions need to be evaluated by SQL/XML functions such as XMLQuery():

```
XMLQUERY (XQuery-expression
   [PASSING value-expression [AS identifier]]
    RETURNING CONTENT
   [NULL ON EMPTY]
    )
```

The XMLQuery() function has two required arguments, an XQuery expression and a RETURNING CONTENT statement. The *value-expression* is used in the PASSING expression to pass in a sequence of XML nodes or atomic values to XQuery. You can assign a name alias to the passed-in XML data using the *AS* operator. RETURNING CONTENT returns the XQuery output. XMLQuery() can operate on different data sources. Normally, XMLQuery() operates on the following types of XML data sources:

- **XMLType objects** Constructed from the XMLType() constructor, a value from an XMLType column or XMLType table, or an XMLType PL/SQL variable.
- **XML files in Oracle XML DB Repository** Use the fn:doc() or fn:collection() function (also can be shortened to doc() or collection()) to load the document(s).
- **XMLType from relational tables/columns** Use the fn:collection() function to access relational tables/views in XML.

Let's learn about these types through examples.

Querying XMLType Objects

The XMLType objects can be passed to the XMLQuery() function.

XMLType Constructed from XMLType()

The simplest way to pass in XML to XMLQuery() is to construct XML directly via the XMLType() function. The following is an example (*xq_xmltype.sql*):

Listing 8-2 *Passing Multiple XML Objects Created by XMLType() to XMLQuery()*

```
SELECT XMLQuery('for $cd in $c/contact, $cp in $b/companyList/company
   let $last_name:=$cd/last_name/text(),
```

```
        $first_name:=$cd/first_name/text(),
        $email:=$cd/email/text(),
        $contact_company_id:=$cd/@company_id,
        $company_id:=$cp/@id,
        $company_name:=$cp/text()
    where not(empty($email)) and $company_id=$contact_company_id
    order by $last_name
    return <contact company="{$company_name}">{$first_name},{$last_name}
</contact>'
    passing XMLType('<contact company_id="1">
<first_name>John</first_name>
<last_name>Smith</last_name>
<email>jsmith@xmlbook.com</email>
</contact>') AS "c",
        XMLType('<companyList>
        <company id="1">Oracle</company>
        <company id="2">McGraw-Hill</company>
        </companyList>') AS "b"
    returning content) result
FROM dual;
```

This example passes in two XML objects to XMLQuery(). The contact document is passed in as "c" and the company index document is passed in as "b". Both are created using the XMLType() construction function. After passing in the documents, we can refer to them via the alias in the XQuery expression.

To handle the two XML inputs, the XQuery performs a typical content look-up and update:

```
    for $cd in $c/contact, $cp in $b/companyList/company
    let $last_name:=$cd/last_name/text(),
        ... ...
        $contact_company_id:=$cd/@company_id,
        $company_id:=$cp/@id,
        $company_name:=$cp/text()
    where not(empty($email)) and $company_id=$contact_company_id
    order by $last_name
    return <contact company="{$company_name}">{$first_name},{$last_name}
</contact>'
```

The *for* statement loops on all *<contact>* and *<company>* elements. Then, the company id is selected from the contact document and is assigned to the *$contact_company_id* variable. Another company id and its company name are selected from the *<company>* element. They are assigned to *$company_id* and *$company_name*, respectively. When the *<company>* element's company id (*$company_id*) equals the contact document's company id (*$contact_company_id*), the corresponding company name value (*$company_name*) is assigned to the output. The output is as follows:

```
<contact company="Oracle">John,Smith</contact>
```

Querying from PL/SQL Variables

XMLQuery() can process XML documents in PL/SQL variables. Let's look at the following example (*xq_plsql_variable.sql*):

Listing 8-3 *Querying from PL/SQL Variables in XMLQuery()*

```
DECLARE
  v_tpl xmltype;
  v_out CLOB;
  v_xsl_path varchar2(4000)
        :='/public/email_template/xsl/gen_preview_stylesheet.xsl';
  v_tpl_path varchar2(4000)
       :='/public/email_template/xmlbook_ann_tpl.xml';
BEGIN
  SELECT xmltransform( xdburitype(v_xsl_path).getxml(),
                       xdburitype(v_tpl_path).getxml())
  INTO v_tpl  FROM dual;

  SELECT XMLSerialize(content XMLQuery('$r/email_template/xsl_content/*'
  passing v_tpl AS "r" returning content) AS CLOB)
  INTO v_out  FROM dual;
  dbms_output.put_line(v_out);
END;
```

In the XML query, the XSL transformation result is passed into XMLQuery() using the PL/SQL variable *var_tpl*. The parameters of the xdburitype() functions are set using the PL/SQL variables *v_xsl_path* and *v_tpl_path*.

Querying SQL XMLType Columns

XMLQuery() can be used in a SQL query where we pass in an XMLType column. To run the following examples, first log into the Oracle database as XMLDEMO user and create a table as follows (*xq_xmltype_column.sql*):

```
CREATE TABLE contact_file_tbl(filename varchar2(255), xml XMLType);
```

Then insert the file into the table:

```
INSERT into contact_file_tbl(filename, xml)
VALUES ('john_smith.xml', XMLType(bfilename('XML_DIR', 'chp08/john_smith
.xml'),0));
```

Then query the XMLType column in the table using XMLQuery():

Listing 8-4 *Querying an XMLType Column with XMLQuery()*

```
select XMLQuery('declare namespace book="http://xmlbook.com/sample/contact
.xsd"; (: :)
for $c in /book:contact
return $c/book:first_name' PASSING a.xml RETURNING CONTENT)
from contact_file_tbl a;
```

The PASSING statement passes the XMLType column in the *contact_file_xtbl* table using *a.xml* to XMLQuery().

Querying XML DB Repository

When querying XML DB Repository in XMLQuery(), the easiest way is to use the fn:doc() and fn:collection() functions to retrieve document(s). With the XML DB Repository URL, the fn:doc() function returns one document, and the fn:collection() function returns a set of documents.

For example, the following query reads the */public/chp08/events.xml* file, extracts the data, and creates a new *<eventReport>* (*xq_doc.sql*):

Listing 8-5 *Calling fn:doc() in XMLQuery()*

```
SELECT XMLQuery('for $ev in doc("/public/chp08/events.xml")/eventList/event
   let $event_name := $ev/@name
   where $event_name="xmlbook_ann_2010"
   return <event name="{$event_name}" desc="{$ev/description}" date="{$ev/@
date}"/>'
   returning content) result
FROM dual;
```

This example shows that you can add XPath after the fn:doc() function to retrieve XML content within the document. The fn:collection() function has a similar syntax; you can find an example of it in Listing 8-9.

You can perform string operations in XMLQuery(). The following example selects a set of *<image>* elements and concatenates the values with ":" to a string (*xq_generate_string_list.sql*):

Listing 8-6 *Using XMLQuery() to Create a Concatenated String*

```
SELECT XMLQuery('for $i in fn:doc("/public/chp17/event/xmlbook_ann/xmlbook_
ann_tpl.xml")/email_template/attachment/imageContent/image
return concat($i/text(),":")'
returning content) as result
from dual;
```

The example output is

```
oracle_view.jpg: learnmore.gif:
```

This kind of string output can be used to create an index look-up table in Oracle APEX applications using the apex_util.string_to_table() function. We will use this function in Chapter 17.

You can pass PL/SQL variables to the fn:doc() or fn:collection() functions. The following is an example (*xq_passing_plsql_variable_to_doc_func.sql*):

Listing 8-7 *Setting fn:doc() Path with a PL/SQL Parameter*

```
DECLARE
  v_email_template VARCHAR2(4000) :=
          '/public/chp17/event/xmlbook_ann/xmlbook_ann_tpl.xml';
```

```
  v_imagelist      VARCHAR2(4000);
BEGIN
  SELECT rtrim(xmlserialize(content
  xmlquery('for $i in fn:doc($p)/email_template/attachment/imageContent/image
return concat($i/text(),":")'
  passing v_email_template AS "p" returning content) AS VARCHAR2(4000)),':')
  INTO v_imagelist
  FROM dual;
  dbms_output.put_line(v_imagelist);
END;
```

In this example, the path of the fn:doc() function is specified by the *v_email_template* PL/SQL variable. Note that we don't need to add double quotes around the *$p* alias in fn:doc(). The example output is

```
oracle_view.jpg: learnmore.gif
```

Querying Relational Tables

When using XMLQuery() to query relational tables/views, you can use the fn:collection() function.

> **Oracle XML DB Tip: Replacing ora:view() with fn:collection()**
> In Oracle Database 11*g*R2 (11.2.0.2), the ora:view() function is replaced by the XQuery standard fn:collection() function. The fn:collection() function takes a URL for a table or a view that could be a relational table/view or an XMLType table/view.

For example, we can query the *contact_file_tbl* as follows (*xq_collection_relational.sql*):

Listing 8-8 *Using ora:view() in XMLQuery()*

```
SELECT XMLQuery('fn:collection("oradb:/XMLDEMO/CONTACT_FILE_TBL")' returning
content) result
FROM dual;
```

This example uses the simplest format of XMLQuery(). It just provides an XPath expression to the fn:collection() function. An example output is as follows (*xq_collection_relational.sql*):

```
<ROW>
  <FILENAME>john_smith.xml</FILENAME>
  <_xFFFF_XML><contact xmlns="http://xmlbook.com/sample/contact.xsd" id="1">
  <category>customer</category>
   ….
   </contact></_xFFFF_XML>
</ROW>
```

You can see that each row in the relational table is represented by a *<ROW>* element, and the columns values are enclosed by an XML element with its capitalized column name as the element name *<COLUMN-NAME>*. The value of the *<COLUMN-NAME>* element is the content from the table. If the column is XMLType, the element name is in the format of <_FFFF_COLUMN-NAME>. You can query the content within the XMLType column as follows:

Listing 8-9 *Querying an XMLType Column Using ora:view()*

```
SELECT XMLQuery('declare namespace book="http://xmlbook.com/sample/contact
.xsd"; (: :)
for $c in fn:collection("oradb:/XMLDEMO/CONTACT_FILE_TBL")/ROW/_xFFFF_XML/
book:contact
return $c' returning content) result
FROM dual;
```

An example output is

```
<contact xmlns="http://xmlbook.com/sample/contact.xsd" id="1">
  <category>customer</category>...</contact>
```

The */ROW/x_FFFF_XML/contact* is used to retrieve the *<contact>* element within the XMLType column in the *contact_file_tbl* table. To retrieve a sub-element in *<contact>*, you can use the following XQuery (*xq_collection_relational.sql*):

```
SELECT XMLQuery('declare namespace book="http://xmlbook.com/sample/contact
.xsd"; (: :)
for $c in fn:collection("oradb:/XMLDEMO/CONTACT_FILE_TBL")/ROW/_xFFFF_XML/
book:contact/*
return $c' returning content) result
FROM dual;
```

An example output is

```
<category xmlns="http://xmlbook.com/sample/contact.xsd">customer</category>
<first_name xmlns="http://xmlbook.com/sample/contact.xsd">John
</first_name>
<last_name xmlns="http://xmlbook.com/sample/contact.xsd">Smith</last_name>
<email xmlns="http://xmlbook.com/sample/contact.xsd">john.smith@hfarm.com
</email>
...
```

XQuery Beyond the Basics

XQuery can perform complex operations. Let's look at some examples.

Using Functions

We have used some functions in the previous examples. In Listing 8-1, we used empty() and not() functions in the *where* clause to select contacts with non-empty emails using *not(empty($email))*. In Listings 8-7 and 8-8, we used fn:doc() and fn:collection() to retrieve documents from XML DB Repository and relational tables. There are many other functions defined by W3C XQuery 1.0 and XPath 2.0 standards, which we can use to perform different operations. Please refer to the *Oracle XML DB Developer's Guide* and *W3C Standards* to learn more about the available functions.

Nested XQuery Expressions

XQuery expressions can be more complex than FLWOR expressions. For example, multiple XQuery expressions that can be nested. This means you can include an XQuery expression within another XQuery expression. Let's look at an example (*xq_nested.sql*):

Listing 8-10 *Nested XQuery Expressions in XMLQuery()*

```
SELECT XMLQuery('declare namespace book="http://xmlbook.com/sample/contact
.xsd"; (: :)
for $ev in doc("/public/chp08/events.xml")/eventList/event
   let $path:=$ev/@path,
       $event_name := $ev/@name
   where $event_name="xmlbook_ann_2010"
   return <event desc="{$ev/description}" date="{$ev/@date}" path="{$path}">
    {
     for $cd in fn:collection($path)/book:contact
     let $last_name:=$cd/book:last_name/text(),
         $first_name:=$cd/book:first_name/text(),
     $email:=$cd/book:email/text()
     where not(empty($email))
     order by $last_name
     return
       <contact first_name="{$first_name}" last_name="{$last_name}">{$email}
</contact>
    }
      </event>' returning content) result
FROM dual;
```

There are two XQuery statements in this example. The first XQuery gets the event information and sets up the *<event>* element with its *description, date,* and *path* attributes:

```
SELECT XMLQuery(''declare namespace book="http://xmlbook.com/sample/contact
.xsd"; (: :)
for $ev in fn:doc("/public/chp08/events.xml")/eventList/event
   let $path:=$ev/@path,
       $event_name := $ev/@name
   where $event_name="xmlbook_ann_2010"
   return <event desc="{$ev/description}" date="{$ev/@date}" path="{$path}">
   ...
    </event>' returning content) result
FROM dual;
```

The second XQuery retrieves all of the contacts involved in the event by reading all of the documents in the path specified in the *<event>* element's *path* attribute:

```
{
     for $cd in fn:collection($path)/book:contact
     let $last_name:=$cd/book:last_name/text(),
         $first_name:=$cd/book:first_name/text(),
     $email:=$cd/book:email/text()
     where not(empty($email))
```

```
     order by $last_name
     return
       <contact first_name="{$first_name}" last_name="{$last_name}">{$email}
</contact>
}
```

The query works on two sets of data: events and contacts. The *contact* query is nested within the *event* query. An example output is as follows:

```
<event desc="Send Announcement of the XML Book" date="31-Mar-2010"
path="/public/chp08/xmlbook_ann_2010/contacts">
  <contact first_name="Lawrence"
           last_name="Liu">lawrence.liu@abcshopping.com</contact>
  <contact first_name="Mark"
           last_name="Richardson">mark.richardson@xmlbook.com</contact>
  <contact first_name="John"
           last_name="Smith">john.smith@hfarm.com</contact>
  <contact first_name="Jennifer"
            last_name="Wang">jennifer.wang@acme.com</contact>
</event>
```

Numeric Calculations

XQuery can perform numeric calculations. For example, we can update the previous XQuery to include a new *contact_num* attribute in the *<event>* element to indicate how many contacts are included in an event. The query is shown as follows (*xq_nested_count.sql*):

Listing 8-11 *XQuery Numeric Calculation in XMLQuery()*

```
SELECT XMLQuery('declare namespace book="http://xmlbook.com/sample/contact
.xsd"; (: :)
for $ev in doc("/public/chp08/events.xml")/eventList/event
   let $path:=$ev/@path,
       $event_name := $ev/@name,
       $contact_num := count(collection($path))
 where $event_name="xmlbook_ann_2010"
   return <event desc="{$ev/description}" date="{$ev/@date}" path="{$path}"
   contact_num="{$contact_num}">
    {
     for $cd in fn:collection($path)/book:contact
     let $last_name:=$cd/book:last_name/text(),
         $first_name:=$cd/book:first_name/text(),
     $email:=$cd/book:email/text()
     where not(empty($email))
     order by $last_name
     return
       <contact first_name="{$first_name}" last_name="{$last_name}">{$email}
</contact>
    }
      </event>' returning content) result
FROM dual;
```

This *count(collection($path))* returns the number of *contacts* in the specified folder. An example output is:

```
<event desc="Send Announcement of the XML Book" date="31-Mar-2010"
path="/public/chp08/xmlbook_ann_2010/contacts" contact_num="4">
  <contact first_name="Lawrence"
           last_name="Liu">lawrence.liu@abcshopping.com</contact>
  <contact first_name="Mark"
           last_name="Richardson">mark.richardson@xmlbook.com</contact>
  <contact first_name="John"
           last_name="Smith">john.smith@hfarm.com</contact>
  <contact first_name="Jennifer"
            last_name="Wang">jennifer.wang@acme.com</contact>
</event>
```

You can add a more functional process by counting contacts with distinct emails (*xq_nested_count_distinct_emails.sql*):

```
count(distinct-values(collection($path)/book:contact/book:email/text()))
```

Oracle XQuery Extensions

Oracle XML DB provides some useful XQuery extension functions, which are summarized in Table 8-1.

All of these functions have the XML DB namespace *http://xmlns.oracle.com/xdb* defined with the ora prefix. Let's review their functionality in this section.

Function Name	Description
ora:contains(input_text, text_query, [policy_name] [,policy_owner])	Returns positive number if **input_text** has full-text matches of **text_query**.
ora:matches(target_string, match_pattern [, match_parameter])	Uses regular expressions to match text similar to the SQL REGEXP_LIKE condition. The function returns **true** if **target_string** matches the regular expression **match_pattern**. Otherwise, it returns **false**.
ora:replace(target_string, match_pattern, replace_string [, match_parameter])	Replaces **target_string** with **replace_string** if **match_pattern** is met (**true**).
ora:tokenize(target_string, match_pattern [, match_parameter])	Allows you to use a regular expression to split the input string specified in **target_string** into a sequence of strings.

TABLE 8-1. *Oracle XML DB XQuery Extension Functions*

ora:contains()

The ora:contains() function is used by XMLQuery() to perform full-text searches. ora:contains() returns a number that indicates whether the text query matches the text content. A positive number indicates a match. Otherwise, it returns zero. Let's perform the following XQuery (*xq_oracontains.sql*):

Listing 8-12 *Using ora:contains() in XMLQuery()*

```
SELECT XMLQuery('for $c in fn:doc("/public/chp08/contact_category.xml")/
contact_category/category
where ora:contains($c/@name, "friends")>0
return $c' returning content)
FROM dual;
```

This query returns all the contact categories that contain the word *friends* in their name.

ora:matches()

The ora:matches() function uses a regular expression to match text. It is similar to the SQL REGEXP_LIKE condition. The function returns *true* if there is a match. Otherwise, it returns *false.*

> **Oracle XML DB Tip**
> REGEXP_LIKE uses regular expression syntax based on the POSIX standard. The XQuery ora:matches() function uses PERL-based regular expression syntax.

Here are two examples (*xq_oramatches.sql*).

Listing 8-13 *Using ora:matches() in XMLQuery()*

```
SELECT XMLQuery('declare namespace book="http://xmlbook.com/sample/contact
.xsd"; (: :)
for $c in fn:collection("/public/contact/xml")/book:contact/book:email
 where ora:matches($c/text(), "[A-Za-z0-9._%+-]+@([A-Za-z0-9-]+\.)+[A-Za-z]
{2,4}")
 return $c' returning content) AS contact_with_valid_emails
FROM dual;

SELECT XMLQuery('for $c in fn:doc("/public/contact/contact_category.xml")/
contact_category/category
where ora:matches($c/@name, "/friends/neighbor/*")
 return $c' returning content)
FROM dual;
```

In the first example, ora:matches() finds the *<email>* elements with a valid email address. In the second example, ora:matches() lists all the categories that have names starting with */friends/neighbor*. With the *contact_category.xml* as follows:

```
<contact_category>
  <category name="/friends/work/oracle"/>
  <category name="/friends/neighbor/austin"/>
  <category name="/friends/neighbor/bayarea"/>
  <category name="/friends/university/usc"/>
  <category name="/friends/university/njtu"/>
  <category name="/business/partner"/>
  <category name="/business/customer"/>
</contact_category>
```

The second query returns the following result:

```
<category name="/friends/neighbor/austin"/>
<category name="/friends/neighbor/bayarea"/>
```

ora:replace()

ora:replace(target_string, match_pattern, replace_string) extends the ora:matches() function by replacing target_string with replace_string if match_pattern is met. The new string is returned. Like ora:matches(), ora:replace() uses regular expressions to match the text. The following is an example (*xq_orareplace.sql*):

Listing 8-14 *Using ora:replace() in XMLQuery()*

```
SELECT XMLSerialize(content XMLQuery('for $c in fn:doc("/public/chp08/contact_
category.xml")/contact_category/category
 let $new_name := ora:replace($c/@name, "/friends/neighbor/*","/friends/
region/")
 where ora:matches($c/@name, "/friends/neighbor/*")
 return <category name="{$new_name}"/>' returning content) as clob indent
size=2)
 result
FROM dual;
```

The following result is returned:

```
<category name="/friends/region/austin"/>
<category name="/friends/region/bayarea"/>
```

Summary

Just as SQL is used to query relational tables, XQuery is designed to query XML. In Oracle XML DB, XQuery can process relational tables, XMLType columns/tables, XML DB Repository, and even PL/SQL parameters. Using the XMLQuery() function, along with the XPath/XQuery functions, XML DB extension functions, and SQL functions, you easily process the XML data in Oracle Database 11*g*.

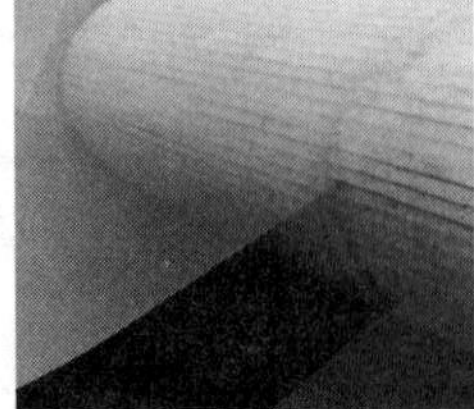

CHAPTER 9

XML and Relational Tables

n Oracle Database 11*g*, most of the data are stored in relational tables. This chapter discusses how to create XML from relational tables, create a relational view from XML data, and load XML data into relational tables.

Creating XML from Relational Tables

Figure 9-1 shows an Entity-Relationship (ER) map of a set of relational tables storing purchase orders.

The seven tables include ORDER_TBL, ORDER_ITEM_TBL, CUSTOMER_TBL, PRODUCT_TBL, SUPPLIER_TBL, ACCOUNT_MGR_TBL, and COUNTRY_TBL tables (*po_create_tables.sql*) to store customers, sales, and order information (data inserted with *po_insert_data.sql*). Let's use these tables to learn how to create XML from relational tables.

Using SQL/XML Functions

SQL/XML functions can be used to create XML document. Table 9-1 lists the SQL/XML functions in Oracle Database 11*g*.

ORDER
ORDER_ID VARCHAR2(40)
CUSTOMER_ID CHAR(20)
ORDER_DATE CHAR(10)
ACCOUNT_MGR_ID CHAR(10)

CUSTOMER
CUSTOMER_ID CHAR(20)
NAME VARCHAR2(40)
EMAIL VARCHAR2(100)
PHONE VARCHAR2(30)
COUNTRY_ID CHAR2(20)

ORDER_ITEM
ORDER_ITEM_ID VARCHAR2(40)
ORDER_ID CHAR(20)
PRODUCT_ID CHAR(20)
QUANTITY DEC (18,6)

ACCOUNT MANAGER
ACCOUNT_MGR_ID CHAR(20)
NAME VARCHAR2(40)
EMAIL VARCHAR2(100)
PHONE VARCHAR2(30)
COUNTRY_ID CHAR2(20)

COUNTRY
COUNTRY_ID CHAR2(40)
NAME VARCHAR2(50)

PRODUCT
PRODUCT_ID CHAR(20)
PRODUCT_CODE VARCHAR(40)
PRODUCT_NAME VARCHAR(40)
SUPPLIER_ID CHAR(20)

SUPPLIER
SUPPLIER_ID CHAR(20)
COUNTRY_ID CHAR(20)
SUPPLIER_CODE VARCHAR(40)
SUPPLIER_NAME CHAR(20)

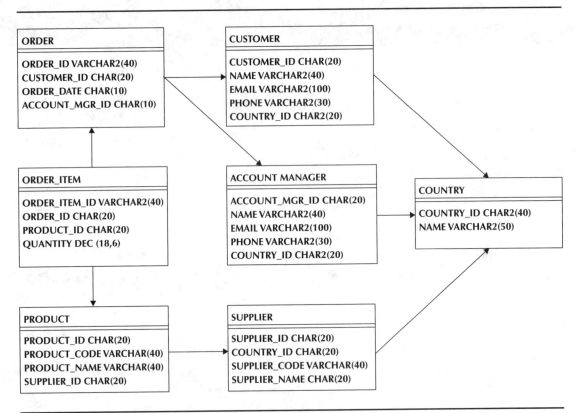

FIGURE 9-1. *Purchase Order database Entity-Relationship map*

Function	Description
XMLRoot()	Creates an XML document element.
XMLElement()	Creates an XML element.
XMLAttributes()	Creates XML attributes.
XMLForest()	Creates an XML fragment.
XMLCDATA()	Creates a CDATA section.
XMLPI()	Creates an XML processing instruction.
XMLComment()	Creates an XML comment.
XMLNamespaces()	Creates XML namespaces.
XMLConcat()	Combines multiple XML values into an XML fragment.
XMLAgg()	Combines a set of XML elements into an XML fragment.
XMLParse()	Parses and generates an XML instance.

TABLE 9-1. *SQL/XML Functions*

There are two types of SQL/XML functions:

- **SQL/XML functions that create XML entities** These functions include XMLElement(), XMLAttributes(), XMLRoot(), XMLCDATA(), XMLForest(), XMLPI(), XMLComment(), and XMLNamespaces(). Each of these functions creates an XML entity such as an element, an attribute, an XML fragment, and so on.
- **SQL/XML functions that specify construction operations** These functions include XMLConcat(), XMLAgg(), and XMLParse(), which specify XML concatenation, aggregation, and parsing operations, respectively.

The following example uses SQL/XML functions to create a purchase order XML document view (*po_create_sqlxml_vw.sql*):

Listing 9-1 *Creating XML Using SQL/XML Functions*

```
CREATE OR REPLACE VIEW po_sqlxml_vw AS SELECT XMLRoot(
        XMLElement("PurchaseOrder",
          XMLAttributes(o.order_id as "id", o.order_code as "order_code",
                        o.order_date as "order_date"),
          XMLElement("Customer",
            XMLForest(cu.name as "Name" ,.email as "Email",
                      cu.phone as "Phone", co.name as "Country")),
          XMLElement("Account_Manager",
            XMLForest(am.name as "Name" , am.email as "Email",
                      am.phone as "Phone", am.name as "Country")),
          XMLElement("Order_Items",
            (select XMLAGG(
```

```
                XMLElement ("Item",
                  XMLAttributes(order_item_id as "order_item_id",
                              oi.product_id as "product_id",
                              quantity as "quantity"),
                  XMLForest(pr.product_name as "ProductName",
                          pr.product_code as "ProductCode",
                          s.supplier_code as "SupplierCode",
                          s.supplier_name as "SupplierName")))
              from order_item_tbl oi, product_tbl pr, supplier_tbl s
              where oi.order_id=o.order_id and pr.product_id=oi.product_id
                    and pr.supplier_id=s.supplier_id ))),
          VERSION '1.0', STANDALONE YES) as purchase_order
from order_tbl o, country_tbl co, customer_tbl cu, account_mgr_tbl am
where o.customer_id=cu.customer_id and co.country_id= cu.country_id
      and o.account_mgr_id=am.account_mgr_id;
```

An example output is shown as follows:

Listing 9-2 *Creating Purchase Order Document via SQL/XML View*

```
<?xml version="1.0" standalone="yes"?>
<PurchaseOrder id="ORDER000000000000006" order_code="O006"
order_date="2007-12-15">
  <Customer>
    <Name>Vincent Zhang</Name>
    <Email>vzhang@xmbook.com</Email>
    <Phone>(86)1352257624</Phone>
    <Country>China</Country>
  </Customer>
  <Account_Manager>
    <Name>Richard Liu</Name>
    <Email>rliu@xmlbook.com</Email>
    <Phone>(86)1397459948</Phone>
    <Country>Richard Liu</Country>
  </Account_Manager>
  <Order_Items>
    <Item order_item_id="ORDERITEM00000000008" product_id="PRODUCT0000000000002"
 quantity="10">
      <ProductName>iPad</ProductName>
      <ProductCode>P001</ProductCode>
      <SupplierCode>S001</SupplierCode>
      <SupplierName>APPLE Inc</SupplierName>
    </Item>
</PurchaseOrder>
```

Let's explain this SQL query in detail. First, to create a *<PurchaseOrder>* element, we need the following SQL to query the ORDER_TBL table:

```
select XMLElement("PurchaseOrder",
        XMLAttributes(o.order_id as "id", o.order_code as "order_code",
                      o.order_date as "order_date"))
from order_tbl o;
```

The example output is

```
<PurchaseOrder id="ORDER000000000000001" order_code="0001" order_date="2006-
04-05"/> </PurchaseOrder>
```

Next, we create the *<Order_Items>* element with a nested SQL query. This SQL query uses XMLAgg() to include multiple order *<Item>* elements from the ORDER_ITEM_TBL table, given that they belong to the purchase order identified by the same *order_id*:

```
Select XMLElement("PurchaseOrder",
        XMLAttributes(o.order_id as "id", o.order_code as "order_code",
                      o.order_date as "order_date"),
        XMLElement("Order_Items",
         (select XMLAgg(XMLElement ("Item",
               XMLAttributes(order_item_id as "id",
                             quantity as "quantity")))
          from order_item_tbl oi
          where oi.order_id=o.order_id))) as "result"
from order_tbl o;
```

Then, to add a set of child elements for the *Item* items, such as *<ProductName>*, *<ProductCode>*, *<SupplierCode>*, and *<SupplierName>* elements, we use the XMLForest() function to create an XML fragment by querying more tables:

```
Select XMLElement("PurchaseOrder",
        XMLAttributes(o.order_id as "id", o.order_code as "order_code",
                      o.order_date as "order_date"),
        XMLElement("Order_Items",
         (select XMLAGG(XMLElement ("Item",
               XMLAttributes(order_item_id as "order_item_id",
                             quantity as "quantity"),
               XMLForest(pr.product_name as "ProductName",
                         pr.product_code as "ProductCode",
                         s.supplier_code as "SupplierCode",
                         s.supplier_name as "SupplierName")))
          FROM order_item_tbl oi, product_tbl pr, supplier_tbl s
          WHERE oi.order_id=o.order_id and pr.product_id=oi.product_id and pr
.supplier_id=s.supplier_id))) as "result"
FROM order_tbl o;
```

To add the customer information to the *<PurchaseOrder>* element, we create an XML element *<Customer>* and attach a set of child elements as we did for the order *<Item>* element using XMLForest(), as highlighted here:

```
Select XMLElement("PurchaseOrder",
        XMLAttributes(o.order_id as "id", o.order_code as "order_code",
                      o.order_date as "order_date"),
        XMLElement("Customer",
           XMLForest(cu.name as "Name" , cu.email as "Email",
                     cu.phone as "Phone", co.name as "Country")),
        XMLElement("Order_Items",
```

```
          (select XMLAGG(XMLElement ("Item",
             XMLAttributes(order_item_id as "order_item_id",
                           quantity as "quantity"),
            XMLForest(pr.product_name as "ProductName",
                      pr.product_code as "ProductCode",
                      s.supplier_code as "SupplierCode",
                      s.supplier_name as "SupplierName")))
           from order_item_tbl oi, product_tbl pr, supplier_tbl s
           where oi.order_id=o.order_id and pr.product_id=oi.product_id and
pr.supplier_id=s.supplier_id))) as "result"
from order_tbl o, country_tbl co, customer_tbl cu
where o.customer_id=cu.customer_id and co.country_id= cu.country_id;
```

The same applies to the *<Account_Manager>* element.

The SQL/XML function works well with other SQL functions. The following example uses the SQL *CASE* function to avoid missing the *<Email/>* XML element when the *email* column in the customer table (*customer_tbl*) is *null* (*po_create_sqlxml_with_case.sql*):

Listing 9-3 *Creating Purchase Order XML with SQL/XML and SQL CASE Functions*

```
CREATE OR REPLACE VIEW po_sqlxml_vw as select XMLRoot(
        XMLElement("PurchaseOrder",
          XMLAttributes(o.order_id as "id", o.order_code as "order_code",
                        o.order_date as "order_date"),
          XMLElement("Customer",
         XMLForest(cu.name as "Name",cu.phone as "Phone", co.name as "Country"),
                 CASE WHEN cu.email is not null
                 THEN XMLElement ("Email",cu.EMAIL)
                 ELSE XMLElement ("Email", ' ') END),
          XMLElement("Account_Manager",
            XMLForest(am.name as "Name" ,am.email as "Email",
                      am.phone as "Phone",am.name as "Country")),
          XMLElement("Order_Items",
            (select XMLAGG(
                XMLElement ("Item",
                  XMLAttributes(order_item_id as "order_item_id",
                    oi.product_id as "product_id", quantity as "quantity"),
                  XMLForest(pr.product_name as "ProductName",
                          pr.product_code as "ProductCode",
                          s.supplier_code as "SupplierCode",
                          s.supplier_name as "SupplierName")))
              from order_item_tbl oi, product_tbl pr, supplier_tbl s
              where oi.order_id=o.order_id and pr.product_id=oi.product_id
                    and pr.supplier_id=s.supplier_id))),
          VERSION '1.0', STANDALONE YES) as purchase_order
from order_tbl o, country_tbl co, customer_tbl cu, account_mgr_tbl am
where o.customer_id=cu.customer_id and co.country_id= cu.country_id
      and o.account_mgr_id=am.account_mgr_id;
```

In the bolded section, the SQL CASE statement creates *<Email>* elements with " " values when the email content is *null*. Without this SQL CASE statement, the *<Email>* element will not be created when the *email* column content in the *customer_tbl* is *null*.

Using XQuery

The same purchase order XML document can be created using the following XQuery (*po_create_xquery_vw.sql*):

Listing 9-4 *Creating One Purchase Order XML with XMLQuery()*

```
CREATE OR REPLACE VIEW po_xquery_vw AS
SELECT XMLQuery(
'for $po in collection("oradb:/XMLDEMO/ORDER_TBL")
  let $customer_id :=$po/ROW/CUSTOMER_ID/text(),
      $po_orderid := $po/ROW/ORDER_ID/text(),
      $account_mgr_id := $po/ROW/ACCOUNT_MGR_ID/text()
  return
  <PurchaseOrder id="{$po/ROW/ORDER_ID}" order_code="{$po/ROW/ORDER_CODE}"
order_date="{$po/ROW/ORDER_DATE}">
   { for $cu in collection("oradb:/XMLDEMO/CUSTOMER_TBL")
   let $cu_name :=$cu/ROW/NAME/text(),
       $cu_phone:=$cu/ROW/PHONE/text(),
       $cu_email:=$cu/ROW/EMAIL/text(),
       $cu_countryid:=$cu/ROW/COUNTRY_ID/text()
   where $cu/ROW/CUSTOMER_ID/text() = $customer_id
   return
   <Customer>
     <Name>{$cu_name}</Name>
     <Phone>{$cu_phone}</Phone>
     <Email>{$cu_email}</Email>
     {for $co in collection("oradb:/XMLDEMO/COUNTRY_TBL")
      where $co/ROW/COUNTRY_ID/text()=$cu_countryid
      return
      <Country>{$co/ROW/NAME/text()}</Country>
     }
   </Customer>
   }
   { for $am in collection("oradb:/XMLDEMO/ACCOUNT_MGR_TBL")
   let $am_name :=$am/ROW/NAME/text(),
       $am_phone:=$am/ROW/PHONE/text(),
       $am_email:=$am/ROW/EMAIL/text(),
       $am_countryid:=$am/ROW/COUNTRY_ID/text()
   where $am/ROW/ACCOUNT_MGR_ID/text() = $account_mgr_id
   return
   <Account_Manager>
     <Name>{$am_name}</Name>
     <Phone>{$am_phone}</Phone>
     <Email>{$am_email}</Email>
     {for $co in collection("oradb:/XMLDEMO/COUNTRY_TBL")
      where $co/ROW/COUNTRY_ID/text()=$am_countryid
```

```
    return
    <Country>{$co/ROW/NAME/text()}</Country>
   }
  </Account_Manager>
  }
  <Order_Items>
   {for $oi in collection("oradb:/XMLDEMO/ORDER_ITEM_TBL"),
        $pr in collection("oradb:/XMLDEMO/PRODUCT_TBL"),
        $s in collection("oradb:/XMLDEMO/SUPPLIER_TBL")
    let $oi_orderid := $oi/ROW/ORDER_ID/text(),
        $oi_quantity:= $oi/ROW/QUANTITY/text(),
        $oi_productid:= $oi/ROW/PRODUCT_ID/text(),
        $pr_supplierid :=$pr/ROW/SUPPLIER_ID/text()
    where $oi_orderid=$po_orderid
          and $pr/ROW/PRODUCT_ID/text()=$oi_productid
          and $s/ROW/SUPPLIER_ID/text()=$pr_supplierid
    return
        <Item id="{$oi_orderid}" quantity="{$oi_quantity}">
        <ProductName>{$pr/ROW/PRODUCT_NAME/text()}</ProductName>
        <ProductCode>{$pr/ROW/PRODUCT_CODE/text()}</ProductCode>
        <SupplierName>{$s/ROW/SUPPLIER_NAME/text()}</SupplierName>
        <SupplierCode>{$s/ROW/SUPPLIER_CODE/text()}</SupplierCode>
        </Item>
    }
  </Order_Items>
 </PurchaseOrder>' returning content) as purchase_order
from dual;
```

Let's explain this XQuery step by step. First we start with a simple XQuery to create a *<PurchaseOrder>* element:

```
Select XMLQuery(
'for $po in collection("oradb:/XMLDEMO/ORDER_TBL")
 return
  <PurchaseOrder id="{$po/ROW/ORDER_ID}" order_code="{$po/ROW/ORDER_CODE}"
order_date="{$po/ROW/ORDER_DATE}">
  </PurchaseOrder>' returning content)
 from dual;
```

The *collection("oradb:/XMLDEMO/ORDER_TBL")* expression is used to retrieve data from the ORDER_TBL table. The purchase order XML document is constructed directly in the XQuery *return* statement.

Next, we add the customer information to the query:

```
Select XMLQuery(
'for $po in collection("oradb:/XMLDEMO/ORDER_TBL")
  let $customer_id :=$po/ROW/CUSTOMER_ID/text()
  return
  <PurchaseOrder id="{$po/ROW/ORDER_ID}" order_code="{$po/ROW/ORDER_CODE}"
order_date="{$po/ROW/ORDER_DATE}">
  { for $cu in collection("oradb:/XMLDEMO/CUSTOMER_TBL")
```

```
  let $cu_name :=$cu/ROW/NAME/text(),
      $cu_phone:=$cu/ROW/PHONE/text(),
      $cu_email:=$cu/ROW/EMAIL/text(),
      $cu_countryid:=$cu/ROW/COUNTRY_ID/text()
  where $cu/ROW/CUSTOMER_ID/text() = $customer_id
  return
  <Customer>
    <Name>{$cu_name}</Name>
    <Phone>{$cu_phone}</Phone>
    <Email>{$cu_email}</Email>
    {for $co in collection("oradb:/XMLDEMO/COUNTRY_TBL")
     where $co/ROW/COUNTRY_ID/text()=$cu_countryid
     return
     <Country>{$co/ROW/NAME/text()}</Country>
    }
  </Customer>
  }
  </PurchaseOrder>' returning content)
from dual;
```

In XQuery, the ORDER_TBL.CUSTOMER_ID column value is assigned to the *$customer_id* variable so that it can be used in the XQuery *where* clause to join the CUSTOMER table. Within the *<Customer>* element construction, we query the country information for each customer. A similar approach is used to create the *<ACCOUNT_MANAGER>* and *<ORDER_ITEM>* elements.

To create an XML view with each row representing a purchase order, we need to do some modifications and create the view as follows (*po_create_xquery_item_vw.sql*):

Listing 9-5 *Creating XML View with Multiple Rows Using XMLQuery()*

```
CREATE OR REPLACE VIEW po_xquery_vw AS
SELECT XMLQuery(
'for $po in collection("oradb:/XMLDEMO/ORDER_TBL")
  let $customer_id :=$po/ROW/CUSTOMER_ID/text(),
      $po_orderid := $po/ROW/ORDER_ID/text(),
      $account_mgr_id := $po/ROW/ACCOUNT_MGR_ID/text()
   where $po_orderid=$id
   return
  <PurchaseOrder id="{$po/ROW/ORDER_ID}" order_code="{$po/ROW/ORDER_CODE}"
order_date="{$po/ROW/ORDER_DATE}">
   { for $cu in collection("oradb:/XMLDEMO/CUSTOMER_TBL")
   let $cu_name :=$cu/ROW/NAME/text(),
       $cu_phone:=$cu/ROW/PHONE/text(),
       $cu_email:=$cu/ROW/EMAIL/text(),
       $cu_countryid:=$cu/ROW/COUNTRY_ID/text()
   where $cu/ROW/CUSTOMER_ID/text() = $customer_id
   return
   <Customer>
     <Name>{$cu_name}</Name>
     <Phone>{$cu_phone}</Phone>
     <Email>{$cu_email}</Email>
```

```
      {for $co in collection("oradb:/XMLDEMO/COUNTRY_TBL")
       where $co/ROW/COUNTRY_ID/text()=$cu_countryid
       return
       <Country>{$co/ROW/NAME/text()}</Country>
      }
    </Customer>
    }
    { for $am in collection("oradb:/XMLDEMO/ACCOUNT_MGR_TBL")
    let $am_name :=$am/ROW/NAME/text(),
        $am_phone:=$am/ROW/PHONE/text(),
        $am_email:=$am/ROW/EMAIL/text(),
        $am_countryid:=$am/ROW/COUNTRY_ID/text()
    where $am/ROW/ACCOUNT_MGR_ID/text() = $account_mgr_id
    return
    <Account_Manager>
      <Name>{$am_name}</Name>
      <Phone>{$am_phone}</Phone>
      <Email>{$am_email}</Email>
      {for $co in collection("oradb:/XMLDEMO/COUNTRY_TBL")
       where $co/ROW/COUNTRY_ID/text()=$am_countryid
       return
       <Country>{$co/ROW/NAME/text()}</Country>
      }
    </Account_Manager>
    }
    <Order_Items>
     {for $oi in collection("oradb:/XMLDEMO/ORDER_ITEM_TBL"),
          $pr in collection("oradb:/XMLDEMO/PRODUCT_TBL"),
          $s in collection("oradb:/XMLDEMO/SUPPLIER_TBL")
      let $oi_orderid := $oi/ROW/ORDER_ID/text(),
          $oi_quantity:= $oi/ROW/QUANTITY/text(),
          $oi_productid:= $oi/ROW/PRODUCT_ID/text(),
          $pr_supplierid :=$pr/ROW/SUPPLIER_ID/text()
      where $oi_orderid=$po_orderid
            and $pr/ROW/PRODUCT_ID/text()=$oi_productid
            and $s/ROW/SUPPLIER_ID/text()=$pr_supplierid
      return
          <Item id="{$oi_orderid}" quantity="{$oi_quantity}">
          <ProductName>{$pr/ROW/PRODUCT_NAME/text()}</ProductName>
          <ProductCode>{$pr/ROW/PRODUCT_CODE/text()}</ProductCode>
          <SupplierName>{$s/ROW/SUPPLIER_NAME/text()}</SupplierName>
          <SupplierCode>{$s/ROW/SUPPLIER_CODE/text()}</SupplierCode>
          </Item>
     }
    </Order_Items>
  </PurchaseOrder>' passing by value order_id as "id" returning content) as
purchase_order
FROM order_tbl;
```

In this example, we pass in the *ORDER_ID* column from ORDER_TBL as the "id" to establish a limit of one purchase order per each query.

Using DBMS_XMLGEN or XMLType()

To create XML directly from a SQL query, you can use DBMS_XMLGEN or XMLType() (*create_xml_from_sql.sql*):

Listing 9-6 *Creating XML Using DBMS_XMLGEN and XMLType()*

```
SELECT DBMS_XMLGEN.getxml('select * from po_xquery_vw') from dual;

SELECT XMLType(cursor(select * from po_xquery_vw)) from dual;
```

DBMS_XMLGEN is a PL/SQL package in XML DB to generate XML in the Oracle predefined XML format. When using XMLType() to construct XML from SQL cursors, the format is the same as the XML format used by DBMS_XMLGEN. The format includes the SQL query result set in an *<ROWSET>* element. Each row of the result is represented as a *<ROW>* element. The column data are included in an XML element with the capitalized column name as its element name. The *ROWSET* and *ROW* tags can be overridden by the users to specify their own tags. DBMS_XMLGEN supports a fetch interface so that you can retrieve the XML iteratively.

Using Oracle XDK Java

In Oracle Database 11*g* Java applications, you can use Oracle XDK XML SQL Utility (XSU) to create the XML from the SQL queries or retrieve XMLType objects. The following is an example, in which XML is retrieved from the XMLType objects (*XMLGen.java*):

Listing 9-7 *Getting XML in Java from Queries Returning XMLType Objects*

```
package xmlbook.chp09;
import java.io.FileOutputStream;
import java.io.OutputStream;
import java.sql.Connection;
import java.sql.DriverManager;
import oracle.jdbc.OracleConnection;
import oracle.jdbc.driver.OracleDriver;
import oracle.xml.parser.v2.XMLDocument;
import oracle.xml.sql.query.OracleXMLQuery;

public class XMLGen {
    static OutputStream m_out;
    static String m_jdbc_conn = "jdbc:oracle:thin:@localhost:1522:ORCL11GB";
    static String m_jdbc_user = "xmldemo";
    static String m_jdbc_pwd = "xmldemo";
    static String m_filename = "domout.xml";
    static String m_query = "select * from po_sqlxml_vw";

    public static void main(String[] args) {
        // Check the command-line input
        XMLGen SXMLGen = new XMLGen();
        SXMLGen.generate();
    }
```

```
    public static void generate() {
        try {
            //Open an output file or print out to System.out
            if (m_filename != null)
                m_out = new FileOutputStream(m_filename);
            else
                m_out = System.out;
            // Open JDBC connection
            DriverManager.registerDriver(new OracleDriver());
            Connection conn =
                DriverManager.getConnection(m_jdbc_conn, m_jdbc_user,
                                            m_jdbc_pwd);
            ((OracleConnection)conn).setDefaultRowPrefetch(50);
            // Initialize the OracleXMLQuery
            OracleXMLQuery qry = new OracleXMLQuery(conn, m_query);
            XMLDocument my_result= (XMLDocument)qry.getXMLDOM();
            my_result.print(m_out);
            System.out.println("Output file " + m_filename + " created.");
        } catch (Exception ex) {
            ex.printStackTrace();
        }
    }
}
```

As shown in Listing 9-7, after initializing *OracleXMLQuery*, we can use query.getXMLDOM() to get an *XMLDocument* from the returned XMLType object.

EXAMPLE SETUP
To run the Java program, please include $ORACLE_HOME/LIB/xsu12.jar *($ORACLE_HOME refers to the home folder of the Oracle database) in the JAVA CLASSPATH.* The xsu12.jar *has the definition of the* OracleXMLQuery *class.*

If the SQL query doesn't return XMLTypes, Oracle XDK XSU can create the XML in the Oracle predefined ROWSET-ROW format. Differing from the previous approach, this approach allows us to create an XML document in a SAX stream (*StreamingXMLGen.java*):

```
package xmlbook.chp09;

import java.sql.Connection;
import java.sql.DriverManager;
import oracle.jdbc.OracleConnection;
import oracle.xml.sql.query.OracleXMLQuery;
import oracle.xml.parser.v2.XMLSAXSerializer;
import java.io.OutputStream;
import java.io.FileOutputStream;

public class StreamingXMLGen {
```

```
    static OutputStream m_out;
    static String m_jdbc_conn = "jdbc:oracle:thin:@localhost:1522:ORCL11G";
    static String m_jdbc_user = "xmldemo";
    static String m_jdbc_pwd = "xmldemo";
    static String m_filename = "saxout.xml";
    static String m_query = "select * from order_tbl";

    static public void main(String[] args) {
        StreamingXMLGen SXMLGen = new StreamingXMLGen();
        SXMLGen.generate();
    }

    static public void generate() {
        try {
            //Open an output file or print out to System.out
            if (m_filename != null)
                m_out = new FileOutputStream(m_filename);
            else
                m_out = System.out;
            // Open JDBC connection
            DriverManager.registerDriver(new oracle.jdbc.driver.OracleDriver());
            Connection conn =
                DriverManager.getConnection(m_jdbc_conn, m_jdbc_user,
                                            m_jdbc_pwd);
            ((OracleConnection)conn).setDefaultRowPrefetch(50);
            // Initialize the OracleXMLQuery
            OracleXMLQuery qry = new OracleXMLQuery(conn, m_query);
            // Setup the output serializer
            XMLSAXSerializer sample = new XMLSAXSerializer(m_out);
            qry.getXMLSAX(sample);
            sample.flush();
            System.out.println("Output file " + m_filename + " created.");
        }
        catch (Exception ex) {
            ex.printStackTrace();
        }
    }
}
```

In this example, Oracle XDK implements a *XMLSAXSerializer* class to serialize SAX input to an XML output.

Oracle XML DB Tip: How do I choose between Oracle XDK Java and SQL/XML?
In general, it is recommended to use the SQL/XML generation functions when possible since these are standards-based.

Creating a Relational View on XML Data

Next, let's look at matters from the other way around. If you have a set of XML documents, how do you access the data via relational SQL queries? Some Oracle database applications, such as APEX applications, are created mainly to work on relational database schemas. How can you enable these applications to access XML content? In Oracle XML DB 11*g*, the best approach is to create relational views using XMLTable().

The XMLTable() function can set up the mapping between the XML data and relational data using the XQuery and XPath expressions. The following is an example (*create_email_template_img_vw.sql*):

Listing 9-8 *Creating XML View in XML DB Repository Using XMLTable()*

```
CREATE OR REPLACE VIEW email_template_img_vw AS
  SELECT xdburitype(a.any_path).getblob() AS photo,
                  c.filename AS filename,
                  c.mimetype AS mimetype,
                   a.any_path
  FROM resource_view a,
    XMLTable( XMLNamespaces(DEFAULT 'http://xmlns.oracle.com/xdb/XDBResource
.xsd'),
    'for $i in . return $i/Resource'
     passing a.res COLUMNS
     filename VARCHAR2(100) path 'DisplayName',
     mimetype VARCHAR2(4000) path 'ContentType') c
  WHERE a.any_path like '/public/chp17/event/%images%' and mimetype
!='application/octet-stream';
```

In this example, we create a relational view called *email_template_vw* by passing in all of the resources **a.res** in the XML DB Repository */public/chp17/event/*/images/** directory. Then, the XQuery *content-selection* expression *'for $i in . return $i/Resource'* iterates through all of the resources' *<Resource>* element using the */Resource* XPath expression to create rows in the relational view. The XMLTable() COLUMNS clause defines the columns in the relational view with their names, data types, and XPath expressions to extract content from the XML data selected from the XQuery *content-selection* expression. In Chapter 17, we will use this to set up an image file indexing view.

In the example, the XMLTable() view is used along with RESOURCE_VIEW so that we can select the XML DB resources' BLOB content using XDBUriType(a.any_path).getblob(), and the metadata is extracted from the source using XMLTable().

Loading XML into Relational Tables

Loading XML data into relational tables is needed when we receive XML data from other applications. The available approaches include using the XMLTable() function, creating SQL/XML or XQuery views instead of triggers, using DBMS_XMLSTORE, and using the Oracle XDK Java XSU *oracle.xml.sql.dml.OracleXMLSave* package. Among these approaches, using XMLTable() is the easiest approach and thus is the method we will discuss now.

To load XML data into relational tables with XMLTable(), you need to insert XML from the relational view created by XMLTable(). For example, the following table stores email templates (*loading_xml.sql*):

Listing 9-9 *Inserting Data to Relational Table Using XMLTable() View*

```
CREATE TABLE email_template_tbl (photo BLOB, file_name varchar2(100), mime_
type varchar2(4000), any_path varchar2(4000));

INSERT INTO email_template_tbl
  SELECT XDBUriType(a.any_path).getblob() AS photo,
           c.filename AS filename, c.mimetype AS mimetype, a.any_path
  FROM RESOURCE_VIEW a,
    XMLTable(XMLNamespaces(DEFAULT 'http://xmlns.oracle.com/xdb/XDBResource
.xsd'),
    'for $i in . return $i/Resource'
     passing a.res COLUMNS
     filename VARCHAR2(100) path 'DisplayName',
     mimetype VARCHAR2(4000) path 'ContentType') c
    WHERE a.any_path like '/public/chp17/event/%images%' and mimetype
!='application/octet-stream';
```

Oracle XML DB Tip: How do I avoid XMLTable() execution failure?

1. The XPath defining each column has to return one item; otherwise, the XMLTable() execution will fail.
2. The XPath returned value has to match the data type specified. In this example, `'work_history/work[@num="1"]/@start_date'` has to return the valid database date string `"1994-08-13"`. If you put data in the wrong format (for example, "18-Aug-1994"), you will get the following error:

```
ERROR at line 1:
ORA-01858: a non-numeric character was found where a numeric was
expected
```

Loading Excel Spreadsheet Content into Relational Tables

Now that we've looked at the basic processing techniques, let's look at a more complex example that loads Microsoft Excel spreadsheet content stored in XML format (*sessions.xml*) into the Oracle database relational tables.

Oracle Database Tip: How do I load Excel spreadsheets into the Oracle database?

In addition to the approach discussed in this chapter, you can use Oracle SQL*Loader or Oracle Application Express (APEX) to load Excel data into the Oracle database.

The key elements to be processed are in the *<Table>* element:

```
<Table ss:ExpandedColumnCount="18" ss:ExpandedRowCount="1959" x:FullColumns="1"
x:FullRows="1">
...
<Row>
<Cell><Data ss:Type="String">ABSTRACT</Data></Cell>
<Cell><Data ss:Type="String">DATE</Data></Cell>
<Cell><Data ss:Type="String">DATETIME</Data></Cell>
<Cell><Data ss:Type="String">DAY</Data></Cell>
<Cell><Data ss:Type="String">DOCUMENTURL</Data></Cell>
<Cell><Data ss:Type="String">DURATION</Data></Cell>
<Cell><Data ss:Type="String">LANGUAGE</Data></Cell>
<Cell><Data ss:Type="String">SESSIONID</Data></Cell>
<Cell><Data ss:Type="String">SESSIONTYPE</Data></Cell>
<Cell><Data ss:Type="String">SES_DESCRIPTION</Data></Cell>
<Cell><Data ss:Type="String">SES_TITLE</Data></Cell>
<Cell><Data ss:Type="String">SES_URL</Data></Cell>
<Cell><Data ss:Type="String">SPEAKER</Data></Cell>
<Cell><Data ss:Type="String">TIME</Data></Cell>
<Cell><Data ss:Type="String">TITLE</Data></Cell>
<Cell><Data ss:Type="String">TRACK</Data></Cell>
<Cell><Data ss:Type="String">TYPE</Data></Cell>
<Cell><Data ss:Type="String">VENUE</Data></Cell>
</Row>
<Row>
<Cell ss:StyleID="s21">
<Data ss:Type="String">Since Release 3.2, the Oracle Forms migration toolkit
has been part of Oracle Application Express. This toolkit is not a silver
bullet, so for complex forms, labor-intensive adjustments in Oracle Application
Express will be necessary. To preserve investments in Oracle Forms and to
prevent large investments in Oracle Application Express, it is an advantage if
you can integrate your existing Oracle Forms with Oracle Application Express.
In this session, you will learn how to integrate your existing Oracle Forms in
Oracle Application Express pages and how you can make these two technologies
work closely together.</Data></Cell>
<Cell><Data ss:Type="DateTime">2009-10-11T00:00:00.000</Data></Cell>
<Cell><Data ss:Type="String">10/11/2009; 08:00-09:00</Data></Cell>
<Cell><Data ss:Type="String">Sunday</Data></Cell>
<Cell><Data ss:Type="String">[http://www20.cplan.com/cc221_new/session_details
.jsp?isid=307387&amp;ilocation_id=221-1&amp;ilanguage=english]</Data></Cell>
<Cell><Data ss:Type="String">60 minutes</Data></Cell>
<Cell><Data ss:Type="String">english</Data></Cell>
<Cell><Data ss:Type="String">S307387</Data></Cell>
<Cell><Data ss:Type="String">User Group Forum (Sunday only)</Data></Cell>
<Cell ss:StyleID="s21">
<Data ss:Type="String">Since Release 3.2, the Oracle Forms migration toolkit
has been part of Oracle Application Express. This toolkit is not a silver
bullet, so for complex forms, labor-intensive adjustments in Oracle Application
```

```
Express will be necessary. To preserve investments in Oracle Forms and to
prevent large investments in Oracle Application Express, it is an advantage if
you can integrate your existing Oracle Forms with Oracle Application Express.
In this session, you will learn how to integrate your existing Oracle Forms in
Oracle Application Express pages and how you can make these two technologies
work closely together.</Data></Cell>
<Cell><Data ss:Type="String">It's Great to Integrate: Combining Oracle Forms
and Oracle Application Express</Data></Cell>
<Cell><Data ss:Type="String">[http://www20.cplan.com/cc221_new/session_details
.jsp?isid=307387&amp;ilocation_id=221-1&amp;ilanguage=english&amp;venue=Moscone+West
+L2%2C+Room+2012&amp;datetime=10%2F11%2F2009%3B+08%3A00-09%3A00]</Data></Cell>
<Cell><Data ss:Type="String">Roel Hartman, Logica</Data></Cell>
<Cell><Data ss:Type="String"> 08:00 - 09:00</Data></Cell>
<Cell><Data ss:Type="String">It's Great to Integrate: Combining Oracle Forms
and Oracle Application Express</Data></Cell>
<Cell><Data ss:Type="String">DATABASE: Database</Data></Cell>
<Cell><Data ss:Type="String">SESSION</Data></Cell>
<Cell><Data ss:Type="String">Moscone West L2, Room 2012</Data></Cell>
</Row>
......
</Table>
```

Each *<Row>* element represents a row of data in the Excel spreadsheet. The *<Data>* element in the *<Cell>* elements includes the data for each Excel cell. The *ss:Type* attribute specifies the data type of each cell in the Excel spreadsheet.

Creating a Table

After loading an Excel XML document into Oracle XML DB Repository, we first can use the *<Row>* element in the spreadsheet to create a table to store the Excel data. The following XSL stylesheet creates a SQL statement to create the table (*create_table_from_excel.xsl*):

Listing 9-10 *XSL Stylesheet Generating Table Creation SQL Statements*

```
<?xml version="1.0" encoding="UTF-8"?>
<xsl:stylesheet version="1.0" xmlns:xsl="http://www.w3.org/1999/XSL/Transform"
xmlns:ss="urn:schemas-microsoft-com:office:spreadsheet">
  <xsl:output method="text" version="1.0" encoding="UTF-8" indent="yes"/>
  <xsl:template match="/">
   <xsl:text>create table </xsl:text><xsl:value-of select="/ss:Workbook/
ss:Worksheet/@ss:Name"/>_tbl (<xsl:for-each select="/ss:Workbook/ss:Worksheet/
ss:Table/ss:Row[1]/ss:Cell">
       <xsl:value-of select="ss:Data/text()"/><xsl:text>_col
</xsl:text><xsl:call-template name="get_datatype">
      <xsl:with-param name="content" select="/ss:Workbook/ss:Worksheet/
ss:Table/ss:Row[2]"/>
      <xsl:with-param name="seq" select="position()"/>
    </xsl:call-template><xsl:if test="position() != last()"><xsl:text>,
</xsl:text></xsl:if> </xsl:for-each><xsl:text>)</xsl:text>
```

```
  </xsl:template>
  <xsl:template name="get_datatype">
     <xsl:param name="content"/>
     <xsl:param name="seq"/>
       <xsl:if test="$content/ss:Cell[$seq]/ss:Data[@ss:Type='DateTime']"><xsl
:text>DATE</xsl:text></xsl:if>
        <xsl:if test="$content/ss:Cell[$seq]/ss:Data[@ss:Type='Number']"><xsl:
text>NUMBER</xsl:text></xsl:if>
       <xsl:if test="$content/ss:Cell[$seq]/ss:Data[@ss:Type='String']"><xsl:
text>VARCHAR2(4000)</xsl:text></xsl:if>
   </xsl:template>
</xsl:stylesheet>
```

Running the XSLT, the following SQL statement is created:

```
CREATE TABLE sessions_tbl (ABSTRACT_col  VARCHAR2(4000),  DATE_col  DATE,
DATETIME_col  VARCHAR2(4000),  DAY_col  VARCHAR2(4000),  DOCUMENTURL_col
VARCHAR2(4000),  DURATION_col  VARCHAR2(4000),  LANGUAGE_col  VARCHAR2(4000),
VARCHAR2(4000), SPEAKER_col  VARCHAR2(4000),  TIME_col  VARCHAR2(4000),
TITLE_col  VARCHAR2(4000), TRACK_col  VARCHAR2(4000),  TYPE_col
VARCHAR2(4000),  VENUE_col  VARCHAR2(4000))
```

Note that this XSLT operation requires the Excel spreadsheet to have its first row of data list the title of each column.

The following PL/SQL code runs the generated SQL statement using the Oracle database's *Dynamic SQL* feature (*create_table_from_excel.sql*):

```
DECLARE
  v_sql_stmt VARCHAR2(800);
BEGIN
  SELECT XMLCAST(XMLTransform(
    XDBUriType('/public/chp09/openworld2009_sessions.xml').getXML(),
    XDBUriType('/public/chp09/create_table_from_excel.xsl').getXML()) as
VARCHAR2(4000)) INTO v_sql_stmt FROM DUAL;
  EXECUTE IMMEDIATE v_sql_stmt;
END;
```

If the SQL runs successfully, a table called *sessions_tbl* is created.

Oracle Database Tip: Why I get the ORA-00911: *Invalid character* error when running dynamic SQL?

When generating an SQL statement for dynamic SQL, you don't need to add the semicolon (;) at the end of the statement. Otherwise, you will get the following error:

```
ERROR at line 1:
ORA-00911: invalid character
ORA-06512: at line 8
```

Loading XML Data

The following XSL stylesheet transforms an Excel XML document (*session.xml*) into a set of SQL data insertion commands (*create_data_inserts_from_excel.xsl*):

```
<xsl:stylesheet version="2.0" xmlns:xsl="http://www.w3.org/1999/XSL/Transform"
xmlns:ss="urn:schemas-microsoft-com:office:spreadsheet">
    <xsl:output method="html" version="1.0" encoding="UTF-8" indent="yes"/>
    <xsl:template match="/">
        <xsl:text>Begin
        </xsl:text>
        <xsl:for-each select="/ss:Workbook/ss:Worksheet/ss:Table/ss:Row">
              <xsl:if test="position() != 1">
               <xsl:text>insert into </xsl:text><xsl:value-of select=
"/ss:Workbook/ss:Worksheet/@ss:Name"/><xsl:text>_tbl(</xsl:text><xsl:for-each
select="/ss:Workbook/ss:Worksheet/ss:Table/ss:Row[1]/ss:Cell">
         <xsl:value-of select="ss:Data/text()"/>_col<xsl:if test="position() !=
last()"><xsl:text>, </xsl:text></xsl:if></xsl:for-each><xsl:text>)
         values(</xsl:text>
             <xsl:for-each select="ss:Cell">
                  <xsl:choose>
            <xsl:when test="ss:Data[@ss:Type='DateTime']">to_date
('<xsl:value-of select="substring(ss:Data/text(),0,11)"/>','YYYY-MM-DD')</
xsl:when>
                    <xsl:otherwise>'<xsl:value-of
select="ss:Data/text()"/>'</xsl:otherwise>
              </xsl:choose><xsl:if test="position() != last()"><xsl:text>,
        </xsl:text></xsl:if></xsl:for-each><xsl:text>);
               </xsl:text>
              </xsl:if>
         </xsl:for-each>
        <xsl:text>End;
        </xsl:text>
    </xsl:template>
</xsl:stylesheet>
```

Note that we use *<xsl:output method="html"..>* to make sure the XML characters are escaped.

Oracle XML DB Tip: How do I escape XML characters in XMLTransform()?

XMLTransform() will raise the following error if XML characters in XSL stylesheets are not properly escaped (for example, *&* has to be escaped to *&*):

```
ERROR:
ORA-31011: XML parsing failed
ORA-19202: Error occurred in XML processing
LPX-00209: PI names starting with XML are reserved
Error at line 1
```

The following PL/SQL code calls the generated SQL from XSLT (*insert_data_from_excel.sql*):

```
DECLARE
  v_sql_stmt CLOB;
BEGIN
  SELECT XMLSerialize(content XMLTransform(
  XDBUriType('/public/chp09/sessions.xml').getXML(),
  XDBUriType('/public/chp09/create_data_inserts_from_excel.xsl').getXML()) as
CLOB)
  into v_sql_stmt FROM DUAL;
  EXECUTE IMMEDIATE v_sql_stmt;
END;
```

Because the approach generates a SQL command for data insertions, the single quote in the Excel spreadsheet has to be replaced by two single quotes. This is needed to avoid generating invalid SQL commands.

Oracle Database Tip: Why do I get the PL/SQL: ORA-00972: *Identifier is too long* error when using dynamic SQL?

Make sure you use ' (single quotes) instead of " (double quotes) for the string input. Otherwise, you will get the following error:

```
ERROR at line 1:
ORA-06550: line 3, column 296:
PL/SQL: ORA-00972: identifier is too long
ORA-06550: line 3, column 6:
PL/SQL: SQL Statement ignored
ORA-06512: at line 9
```

Oracle Database Tip: Why do I get the ORA-00911: *Invalid character* error when using dynamic SQL?

Make sure you include the insert statement within "Begin... End". Otherwise, you will get the following error:

```
ERROR at line 1:
ORA-00911: invalid character
ORA-06512: at line 9
```

Creating a PL/SQL Procedure

To simplify the loading process, we can create a PL/SQL procedure (*loadexceltodb.sql*):

```
CREATE OR REPLACE PROCEDURE loadExceltoDB (p_inputFilePath VARCHAR2:='/public/
chp09/openworld2009_sessions.xml') as
   sql_stmt_var1 VARCHAR2(4000);
   sql_stmt_var2 CLOB;
BEGIN
     dbms_output.put_line('Start the program');
     select XMLCAST(XMLTRANSFORM(
```

```
        xdbUriType(p_inputFilePath).getXML(),
        xdbUriType('/public/chp09/create_table_from_excel.xsl').getXML()) as
VARCHAR2(
4000)) into sql_stmt_var1 FROM dual;
    dbms_output.put_line(sql_stmt_var1);
    EXECUTE IMMEDIATE sql_stmt_var1;
    dbms_output.put_line('table created');

    select XMLTRANSFORM(
    XDBUriType(p_inputFilePath).getXML(),
XDBUriType('/public/chp09/create_data_inserts_from_excel.xsl').getXML())
.getCLOBVal() into sql_stmt_var2 FROM dual;
    dbms_output.put_line(dbms_lob.getlength('SQL text size:'||sql_stmt_var2));

    EXECUTE IMMEDIATE sql_stmt_var2;
    end;
/
show errors;
```

Oracle XML DB Tip: What's the difference between XMLCast() and XMLSerialize()?

XMLCast() is used to cast an XMLType value to a SQL scalar data type such as VARCHAR or NUMBER. XMLSerialize(), on the other hand, is used to serialize an XMLType value into a string. Typically, you use XMLSerialize() to generate a well-formed XML to be printed out. XMLSerialize() lets you control the indentation, pretty printing, etc.

Run the PL/SQL procedure as shown in the following command:

```
SQL> exec loadexceltodb;
```

After running the command, we have created a new table, and fed the data into the table.

Oracle Database Tip: Why do I get the ORA-01031: *Insufficient privileges* error when running dynamic SQL?

Because when dynamic SQL creates a table, you have to make sure that the database user running this dynamic SQL has the table creation privilege. If not, you will get the following error:

```
ORA-01031: insufficient privileges
```

You can grant this privilege by logging in to SYS and running the following command (the database user is XMLDEMO):

```
SQL>grant create any table to XMLDEMO;
```

In this example, we just copy the XML files to XML DB, and run the PL/SQL procedure to load the Excel spreadsheet data into the database table. This is a nice way to use XML to solve problems.

Oracle XML DB Tip: How can I escape SQL characters?

In this example, it's important to make sure that all of the single quotes are escaped in the XSLT output, because the XSLT output is a SQL statement that includes a lot of SQL inserts. Here we use Microsoft Excel's Replace feature to pre-process the XML document. You can also write a PL/SQL procedure to process the SQL statement for character-escaping. However, without proper escaping, you will get errors like these:

```
PLS-00103: Encountered the symbol "MARON" when expecting one of the
following::= . ( @ % ;
 PLS-00103: Encountered the symbol "=" when expecting one of the
following::= . ( @ % ;
PL/SQL: ORA-00917: missing comma
```

If this is the first time you encounter such errors, it will be difficult to discover the reason. Therefore, as we discussed, please DO pay attention to the special characters!

Summary

In this chapter, we learned how to create XML from relational tables, create relational views on XML data, and use the relational view to load XML data into relational tables.

CHAPTER 10

Searching XML

With the significant growth of unstructured content over the past few years, full-text search becomes more important to ensure that database users can find information efficiently. In this chapter, we will learn how to enable full-text search on XML data stored in the Oracle database.

EXAMPLE SETUP

To run the examples in this chapter, you need to finish running the examples in Chapter 9 and then create a materialized view in the XMLDEMO *user* (create_mv.sql):

```
create materialized view po_mv AS
SELECT * FROM po_xquery_vw;
```

To refresh po_mv, *you can use the DBMS_SNAPSHOT package to perform a COMPLETE refresh* (refresh_mv.sql):

```
execute dbms_snapshot.refresh('po_mv','c');
```

To run the CTX_DDL package, which manages the Oracle Text CONTEXT index, you also need to grant the XMLDEMO *user the CTXAPP role by logging in to SYS user (as SYSDBA) and running the following command:*

```
grant ctxapp to xmldemo;
```

Please make sure you set up the book example mentioned in the "About the Examples" section in the Introduction of this book and load the sample data files to Oracle XML DB Repository.

Using ora:contains()

The simplest XML full-text search is to use ora:contains() in the XMLExists() SQL function. Let's search the purchase orders from the *po_mv* view (*query_oracontains.sql*):

Listing 10-1 *Full-Text XML Query Using ora:contains()*

```
select XMLQuery('/PurchaseOrder/@id'
passing purchase_order returning content)
from po_mv
where XMLExists('/PurchaseOrder/Customer/Name[ora:contains(text(), "liu")>0]'
passing by value purchase_order);
```

When executing the query, Oracle XML DB will retrieve all of the data first, perform full-text analysis at run-time, and then deliver matched search results.

Using Oracle Text

The ora:contains() function is easy to use but not a good choice for large datasets or frequent full-text queries because run-time full-text analysis is a very resource-intensive process. Instead, for a large XML dataset, you need to create a full-text index using Oracle Text. Oracle Text is known as Oracle *InterMedia Text* in Oracle8*i*. One of the Oracle Text indexes, the CONTEXT index, can be used to enable full-text search.

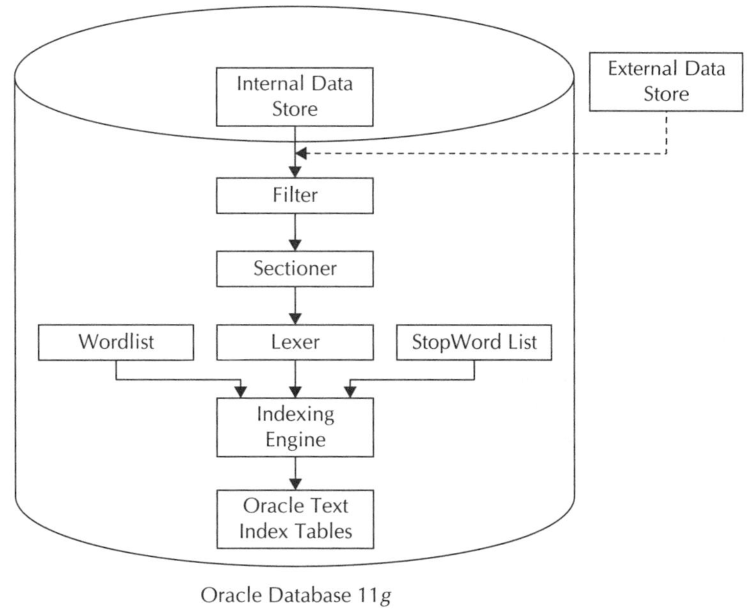

FIGURE 10-1. *Oracle Text indexing process*

Figure 10-1 illustrates the Oracle Text indexing process. Each step in the process is configurable.

First, the data is fetched from database tables or external data sources, such as files and web pages, which can be accessed from the Oracle database. Because the Oracle Text CONTEXT index is a *domain* index, you can only create the index on a table or a materialized view. Second, the fetched data is filtered by the Oracle Text built-in content filter to detect the data items, including document language and file format, and translate the content into an indexable text format. Third, the Oracle Text sectioner identifies the text units in the content and adds metadata based on the content structure. Fourth, the Oracle Text lexer performs linguistic analysis to create index tokens. This process is based on the wordlist, stopword list, and lexer's default linguistic analysis setups. Finally, the index tokens are stored in the Oracle Text index tables.

Basic Oracle Text Search on XML

You can create one CONTEXT index per table column as shown in the following code (*create_index.sql*):

Listing 10-2 *Creating Oracle Text CONTEXT Index on XML*

```
exec ctx_ddl.create_preference('po_lexer', 'auto_lexer');

create index po_context_idx
```

```
on po_mv(purchase_order)
indextype is ctxsys.context
parameters ('lexer po_lexer
            filter ctxsys.auto_filter
            sync (on commit)');
```

In this example, we choose AUTO_LEXER, a new lexer in Oracle Database 11*g*, to enable advanced multi-language support. In the index parameter setting, specify the content filter to be *ctxsys .auto_filter* and set up the Oracle Text index synchronization process to run after transaction *commits*. Another option is to synchronize the index as needed. You can use the following SQL query to check if there is a need for index synchronization (*check_pending_sync.sql*):

Listing 10-3 *Checking Oracle Text Index Status*

```
select pnd_index_name, pnd_rowid, to_char(pnd_timestamp,'dd-mon-yyyy') timestamp
from ctx_user_pending;
```

If there is a pending request, you can synchronize the index (*sync_text_idx.sql*):

Listing 10-4 *Synchronizing Oracle Text Index*

```
exec ctx_ddl.sync_index('po_context_idx','2M');
```

This is better than the transactional-based CONTEXT index setup, because when there is frequent index synchronization, the CONTEXT index can be fragmented. This will affect the query response time. To remove the fragments in the CONTEXT index, run the index optimization (*optimize_text_idx.sql*):

Listing 10-5 *Optimizing Oracle Text Index*

```
exec ctx_ddl.optimize_index('po_context_idx','FULL');
```

With the index created, you can then use the contains() SQL operator to perform full-text queries (*query_simple.sql*):

Listing 10-6 *Full-Text Search SQL Query*

```
select score(1) as score,
       XMLQuery('/PurchaseOrder/@id'
                passing purchase_order returning content)
from po_mv
where contains(purchase_order, 'liu and iphone',1)>0;
```

The SQL query returns a relevance score using the SCORE operator. The score is between 1 and 10. The higher the score, the more relevant the document for the given query. Note the third parameter **1** in the contains() function. This is the "Primary Invocation." The value of the number is arbitrary, but the same value must be used in the score() operator. Otherwise, you will get the following error:

```
ORA-29908: missing primary invocation for ancillary operator
```

Using XML Section Groups

Oracle Text provides three types of document sections for XML documents. AUTO_SECTION_GROUP indexes an XML document based on the element and attribute names. XML_SECTION_GROUP indexes an XML document based on the element and attribute names listed during the section group creation. PATH_SECTION_GROUP indexes all of the XML elements and attributes, maintaining the XPath information for each element and attribute.

Using PATH_SECTION_GROUP

PATH_SECTION_GROUP is the default section group for XMLTypes. To create a CONTEXT index with PATH_SECTION_GROUP, run the following command (*create_path_index.sql*):

Listing 10-7 *Creating CONTEXT Index with PATH_SECTION_GROUP*

```
drop index po_context_idx;
exec ctx_ddl.create_section_group('po_path_group','PATH_SECTION_GROUP');
create index po_context_idx
  on po_mv(purchase_order)
  indextype is ctxsys.context
  parameters ('lexer po_lexer
               filter ctxsys.auto_filter
               section group po_path_group
               sync (on commit)');
```

With PATH_SECTION_GROUP, you can use two operators, HASPATH() and INPATH(), in the SQL queries. HASPATH() returns *true* if the specified XPath exists in the XML document. INPATH() returns *true* if the specified text exists in XML content selected by the XPath expression. The following are examples (*query_path.sql*):

Listing 10-8 *SQL Query with HASPATH() and INPATH()*

```
select score(1) as score, XMLQuery('/PurchaseOrder/@order_code'
passing purchase_order returning content) as order_code
from po_mv
where contains(purchase_order, 'liu INPATH(/PurchaseOrder/Customer/
Name)',1)>0;

select score(1) as score, XMLQuery('/PurchaseOrder/@id'
passing purchase_order returning content) as order_id
from po_mv
where contains(purchase_order, 'HASPATH(/PurchaseOrder[@order_
code="o003"])',1)>0;
```

The first query uses INPATH() to check if we have *liu* showing in the */PurchaseOrder/Customer/Name* element. The second query checks if the XPath */PurchaseOrder[@order_code="o003"]* exists in the XML documents.

> **Oracle XML DB Tip: Are the XPaths in INPATH() and HASPATH() case sensitive?**
> Yes, the XPaths are case sensitive. Therefore INPATH(/PurchaseOrder) is different from INPATH(/purchaseorder).

Using XML_SECTION_GROUP

When you don't need to record the element/attribute names instead of the XPaths, you can use AUTO_SECTION_GROUP. If you'd like to further restrict the index to a subset of XML elements/attributes, you can use XML_SECTION_GROUP. The following example creates an XML_SECTION_GROUP index (*create_xmlsection_index.sql*):

Listing 10-9 *Creating Oracle Text Index with XML_SECTION_GROUP*

```
exec ctx_ddl.create_section_group('po_xml_group','XML_SECTION_GROUP');
exec ctx_ddl.add_zone_section('po_xml_group','customer_name_sec','Name');
exec ctx_ddl.add_zone_section('po_xml_group','order_item_sec','Order_Items');

drop index po_context_idx;
create index po_context_idx
on po_mv(purchase_order)
indextype is ctxsys.context
parameters ('lexer po_lexer
filter ctxsys.auto_filter
section group po_xml_group
sync (on commit)');
```

The SQL query needs to use the WITHIN operator:

Listing 10-10 *Oracle Text Query with XML_SECTION_GROUP Index*

```
exec ctx_doc.set_key_type('ROWID');
select score(1) as score,
       XMLQuery('/PurchaseOrder/@id'
                passing purchase_order returning content) as order_id,
       CTX_DOC.SNIPPET('po_context_idx', ROWID, 'liu') as snippet
from po_mv
where contains (purchase_order,'liu within customer_name_sec',1)>0;
```

In this example, we create a snippet, which is a summary of content based on the user's query created by Oracle Text. This is very useful for search users to find out how the record is returned as part of the search result.

Indexing Oracle XML DB Repository

To add an Oracle Text index for an XML file store in XML DB Repository, you can create the CONTEXT index using XDBUriType (*create_xdbrepository_tbl.sql*):

Listing 10-11 *Creating Oracle Text Index on XML DB Repository*

```
create table contact_uri_tbl (link varchar2(4000) primary key, url xdburitype);

insert into contact_uri_tbl (link, url) values('/public/resume/john_smith.xml',
xdburitype('/public/resume/john_smith.xml'));
insert into contact_uri_tbl (link, url) values('/public/resume/richard_liu.xml',
xdburitype('/public/resume/richard_liu.xml'));
```

Then, you can create a CONTEXT index on this column (*create_index_on_xdbrepository.sql*):

```
drop index contact_uri_idx;
create index contact_uri_idx on contact_uri_tbl(url)
indextype is ctxsys.context
parameters('section group ctxsys.path_section_group');
```

Then, query the content:

Listing 10-12 *Oracle Text Query on XML DB Repository*

```
select xdburitype(link).getxml().extract('/resume/header/firstname/text()') as
first_name, xdburitype(link).getxml().extract('/resume/header/surname/text()')
as last_name
from contact_uri_tbl where contains(url, 'stanford and $marketing')>0;
```

richard_liu.xml will be found. Note that in `$marketing`, we use the stem ($) operator to search for terms that have the same linguistic root as the query term. Therefore, although *richer_liu.xml* doesn't contain "marketing", we can find it because it has the word "market". There are many other advanced search features in Oracle Text that you can use in XML after the Oracle Text index is created.

Applying the same approach, you can create an Oracle Text index on files using other UriTypes; for example, the files accessible via HTTP using HTTPUriType.

Using Oracle Secure Enterprise Search

Distinct from Oracle Text, Oracle Secure Enterprise Search (SES) is a comprehensive secure enterprise search product. Oracle SES uses Oracle Text as its full-text index engine but offers many additional features.

First, Oracle SES provides out-of-box query and administration applications. Within these applications, there are many prebuild search features such as index data source management, content categorization, and query UI customizations. These features greatly simplify the process of building search applications on the data stored in Oracle Database 11*g*.

Second, Oracle SES provides built-in security to manage the search index so that unauthorized content access is not allowed.

Third, Oracle SES provides search crawlers. The database crawler can index multiple database tables/columns with a simple SQL statement. The other crawlers, such as web crawlers and enterprise application crawlers, can search web pages, files systems, and enterprise applications such as Oracle Universal Content Management System (UCM), Oracle WebCenter Suite, Oracle OBIEE, Oracle Siebel, Oracle E-Business Suite, and others. With Oracle SES, you can maintain all of the indexes in one place.

Fourth, Oracle SES provides an extensible development framework that allows building Java extensions and accessing query services via Web Service APIs.

There are many other advantages; we can't list them all here. Instead, let's build an Oracle SES search application to search XML documents. We will not go through the Oracle SES installation details. You can download Oracle SES from Oracle Technology Network (OTN) and install it on your machine. The installation steps are quite straightforward and are described in the Oracle SES Installation Guides. We will skip the security part of Oracle SES and focus on how to search XML content.

Preparing the Index Data

In Oracle SES, there are two types of indexes. Document content is indexed as *search content*. Document metadata, which describes the content, are indexed as *search attributes*.

To define *search content* and *attributes*, let's first review the search requirements. When searching the purchase order documents created from Listing 10-2, we need to allow the following actions:

- Search by Order ID
- Search the orders for customer *Mr. Liu*
- Search the orders for customer *Mr. Liu* in CY2010
- Search the orders for customer *Mr. Liu* purchasing *iPhone*
- Search the orders for all customers from China
- Search the customer orders for Microsoft
- Search the countries of the Microsoft customers
- Search the customers who purchased the same products as Mr. Liu
- Search the orders that contain more than two products (includes 2)

Based on these requirements, we need the metadata from the purchase order XML documents listed in Table 10-1.

Metadata Name	XPath
Customer Name	/PurchaseOrder/Customer/Name
Order Date	/PurchaseOrder@order_date
Customer Country	/PurchaseOrder/Customer/Country
Supplier Name	/PurchaseOrder/Order_Items/Item/SupplierName
Product Name	/PurchaseOrder/Order_Items/Item/ProductName
Order ID	/PurchaseOrder@id

TABLE 10-1. *Search Attributes and XPath for the Purchase Order Search*

We can create a SQL view to pull the search attributes and purchase order content (*create_search_vw.sql*):

```
create or replace view po_search_vw as
select c.*
from po_mv, XMLTable('for $e in $d
return <e>
  {$e/PurchaseOrder}
   <Suppliers>{fn:string-join($e/PurchaseOrder/Order_Items/Item/SupplierName/
text(), ";")}</Suppliers>
    <Products>{fn:string-join($e/PurchaseOrder/Order_Items/Item/ProductName/
text(), ";")}</Products>
<Order_Item_Num>{fn:count($e/PurchaseOrder/Order_Items/Item)}</Order_Item_Num >
    </e>'
PASSING purchase_order as "d"
COLUMNS
customer_name varchar2(100) PATH '/e/PurchaseOrder/Customer/Name/text()',
customer_country varchar2(100) PATH '/e/PurchaseOrder/Customer/Country/text()',
order_date varchar2(4000) PATH '/e/PurchaseOrder/@order_date',
order_id varchar2(4000) PATH '/e/PurchaseOrder/@id',
supplier_name varchar2(4000) PATH '/e/Suppliers',
product_name varchar2(4000) PATH '/e/Products',
order_item_num number PATH '/e/Order_Item_Num/text()',
po_content XMLType PATH '/e/PurchaseOrder') c;
```

Because we will perform number operations on the *order_item_num* column, we convert the *order_item_num* value to a *number* datatype. In this statement, we call the fn:string-join() function to concatenate multiple suppliers into one *<Suppliers>* element. The same is used for *<Products>* element.

To further simplify the SQL access of the data, we create another view to eliminate the XMLType operations:

```
create or replace view po_xml_search_vw as
select customer_name, customer_country,
       order_date, order_id, supplier_name, product_name, order_item_num,
       XMLSerialize(DOCUMENT po_content AS CLOB) as po_content
from po_search_vw;
```

With the SQL view created, the index data is ready for the Oracle SES database source.

Creating a Database Data Source

Before setting up the Oracle SES database source, we need to find a way for the Oracle SES query application to display the purchase order on the Web. In Oracle Database 11*g*, the Oracle XML DB servlet can create a web view of all Oracle database tables and views via a URL. For the *po_xml_search_vw* view, the following URL is shown:

```
http://localhost:8080/oradb/XMLDEMO/PO_XML_SEARCH_VW/ROW[ORDER_
ID="ORDER000000000000004"]
```

Note that in this example, the XML DB HTTP port is 8080. Using the *xmldemo* database user login, the web output is shown here:

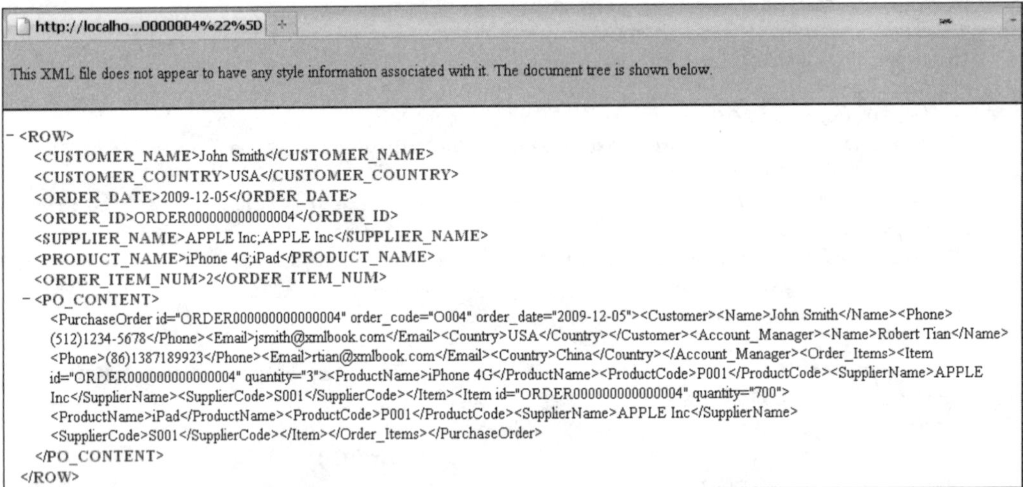

Now, we can use Oracle SES to create an XML search application:

1. Log in to Oracle SES Administration UI. Choose the Home | Sources tab, and then select the Database source from the Source Type drop-down menu, as shown here:

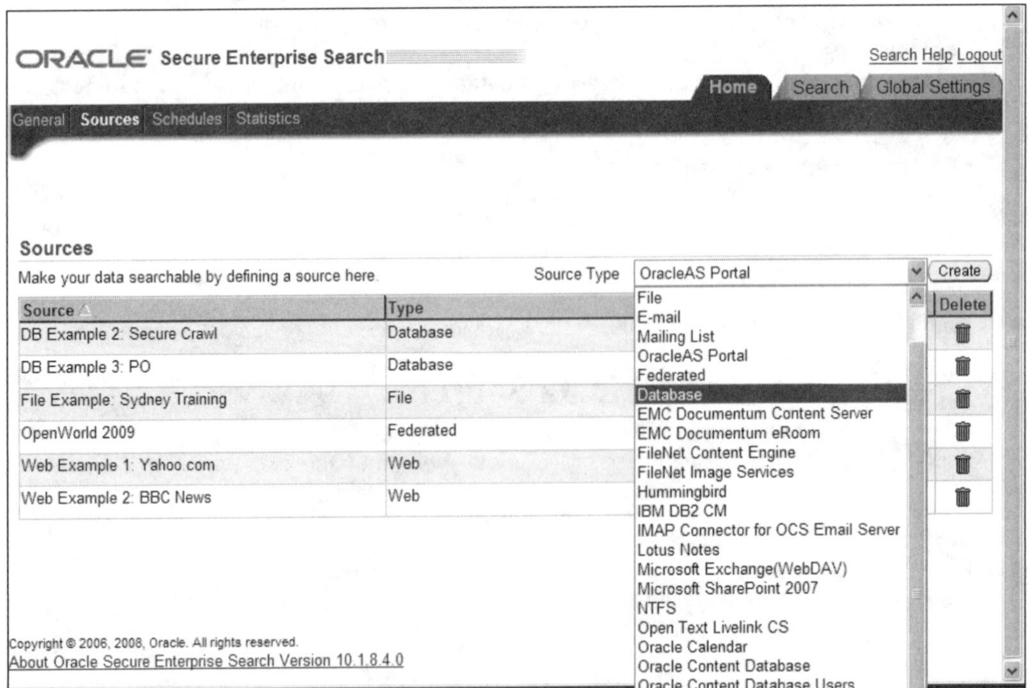

2. After clicking the Create button with the Database source selected, you see the database source setup page:

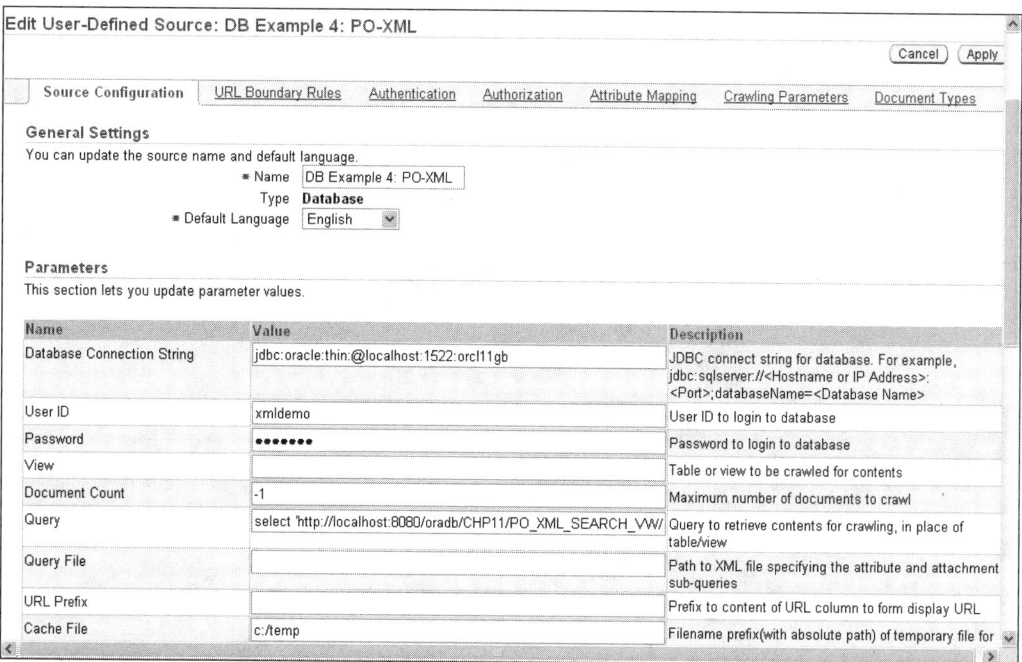

3. In the database source setup, we need to set up the JDBC connection, the database user login info (in the example, we use *xmldemo*), and the SQL query to retrieve the search content/attributes. An example input is as follows:

```
Name: DB Example 4: PO-XML
Database Connection String: jdbc:oracle:thin:@localhost:1522:orcl11gb
User ID: xmldemo
Password: xmldemo
Document Count: -1
Query: select 'http://localhost:8080/oradb/XMLDEMO/PO_XML_SEARCH_VW/
ROW[ORDER_ID='''||c.order_id||''']' as url, c.order_id as key, c.po_
content as content, c.order_id||': '||c.customer_name||' order on '||
c.product_name as title, c.order_date as order_date, c.customer_name
as customer_name, c.customer_country as country_name, c.supplier_name
as supplier_name, c.product_name as product_name, c.order_item_num as
order_item_num, to_date(sysdate) as lastmodifieddate,'EN' as lang from
po_xml_search_vw c
Cache File: c:/temp
Path Separator: #
Parse Attributes: false
Remove deleted documents: false
Attachment Link Authentication Type: PUBLIC
```

Note that we don't include ";" at the end of the SQL query for the query setup. There are required attributes by Oracle SES. URL is the display URL of the search record. KEY is the unique identifier of the search record. CONTENT is the search content. LASTMODIFIEDDATE is the time when the search record is last updated. LANG is the content language. With all these setups, you can click Next to continue.

4. We create a public source, and then we select the No Access Control List option in the Authorization section, as shown next:

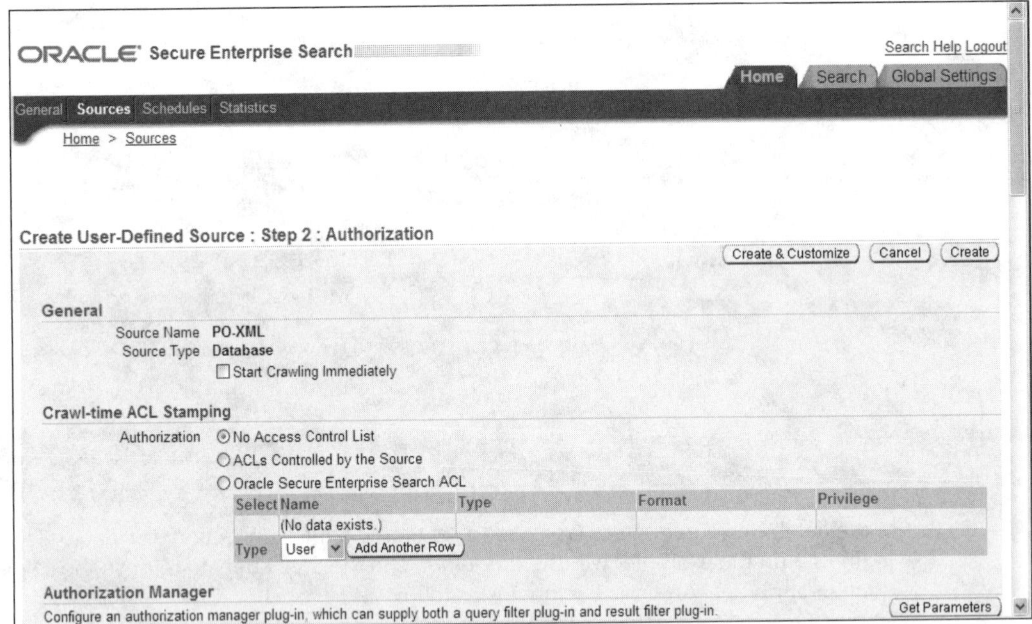

5. Clean up the Plug-in Class Name and Jar File Name fields in the Authorization Manager section and click Create.

After the creation, you will find a new source, "DB Example 4: PO-XML," in the Oracle SES data source list. Using an approach that differs from Oracle Text, we create one index across multiple table columns with a simple SQL statement. The search index is also automatically maintained by Oracle SES.

Crawling the XML Data

Now we can start the crawling process to fetch the data and build the full-text index in Oracle SES:

1. After clicking Schedules in the Home tab, you see a schedule with the same name as the data source created by Oracle SES, as shown next.

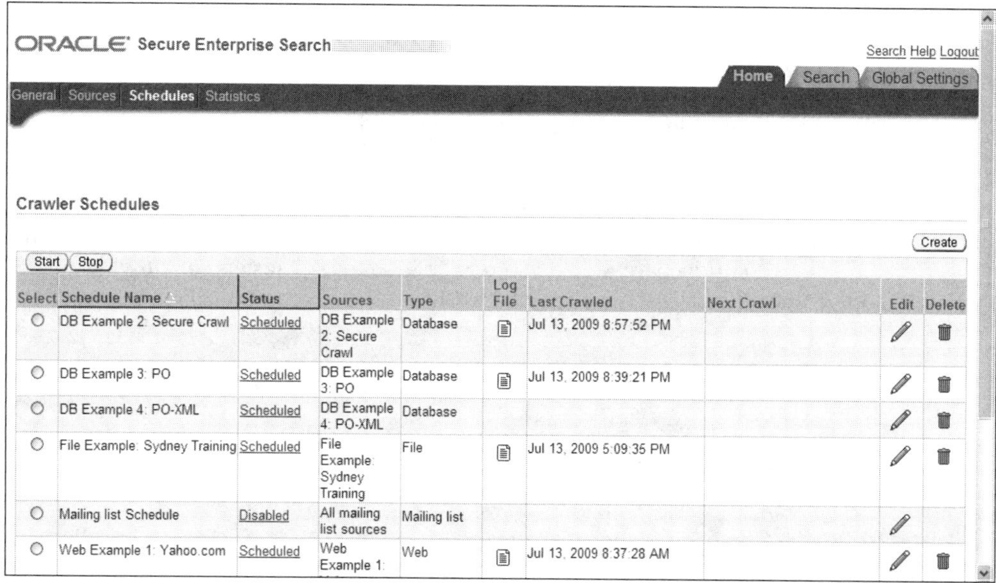

2. To start the crawl, click the radio button in the Select column and then the Start button. The status of the schedule will change from *Scheduled* to *Launching*.
3. Click the Launching link to see the schedule running status. You can get the detailed Crawler Progress Summary, shown here, by clicking Statistics.

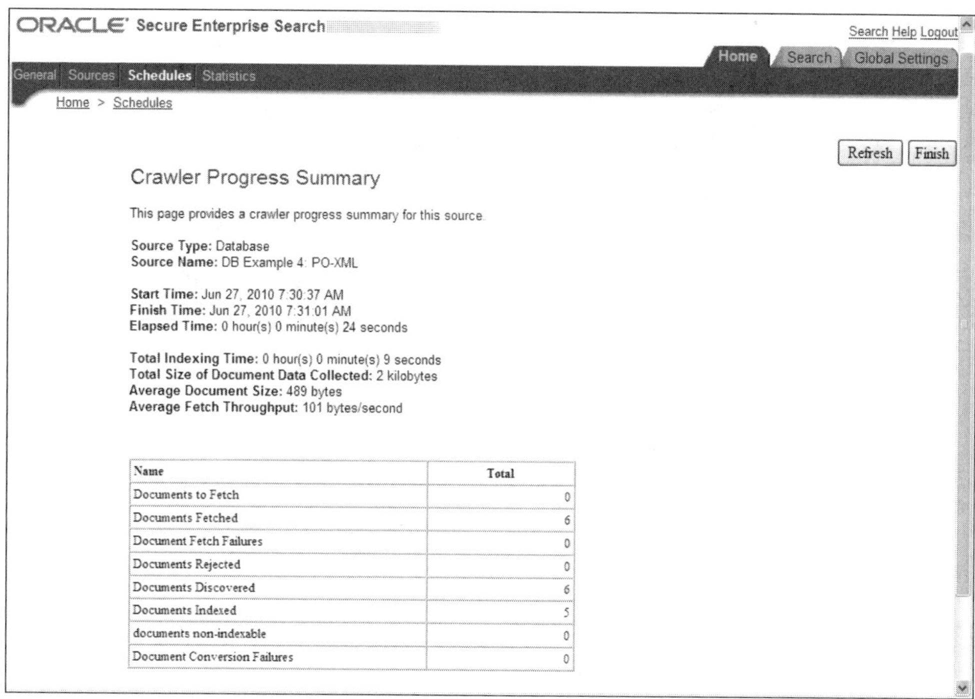

After the crawling is done, the data is ready to be searched.

Enabling XML Content Navigation

Oracle SES allows you to categorize data using the defined search attributes. To set this up:

1. Click the Global Settings tab. In the Out-of-Box Query Application section, click the Clustering Configuration link. In the Query-time Clustering Configuration, update the Minimum Number Of Document Per Node to be 1 instead of the default 3, and the Minimum Occurrence for Single Word Extraction to be 1 instead of 2 (by default). Click Apply. Then choose the Metadata in the Cluster Type menu and click Create.

Topic Clustering Metadata Extraction

Enter configuration information for query-time topic clustering metadata extraction.

Single Word Extraction

Minimum occurrence: 1

Maximum number of words to extract: 20

Phrase Extraction

Minimum occurrence: 2

Maximum number of phrases to extract: 10

Maximum phrase length: 6

The phrase length is the number of words in a phrase

Cluster Trees

Select and configure clustering trees. Cluster Type: Metadata Create

Select a tree and... Move up Move down

Select	Tree name	Cluster Type	Attributes	Status	Edit	Delete
O	Topic	Topic	Keywords, Title, eqsnippet, eqtopphrases	Enabled		
O	Customer	Metadata	customer_name	Enabled		
O	Path	Metadata	Infosource Path	Enabled		

2. First, we create the cluster based on customer name.

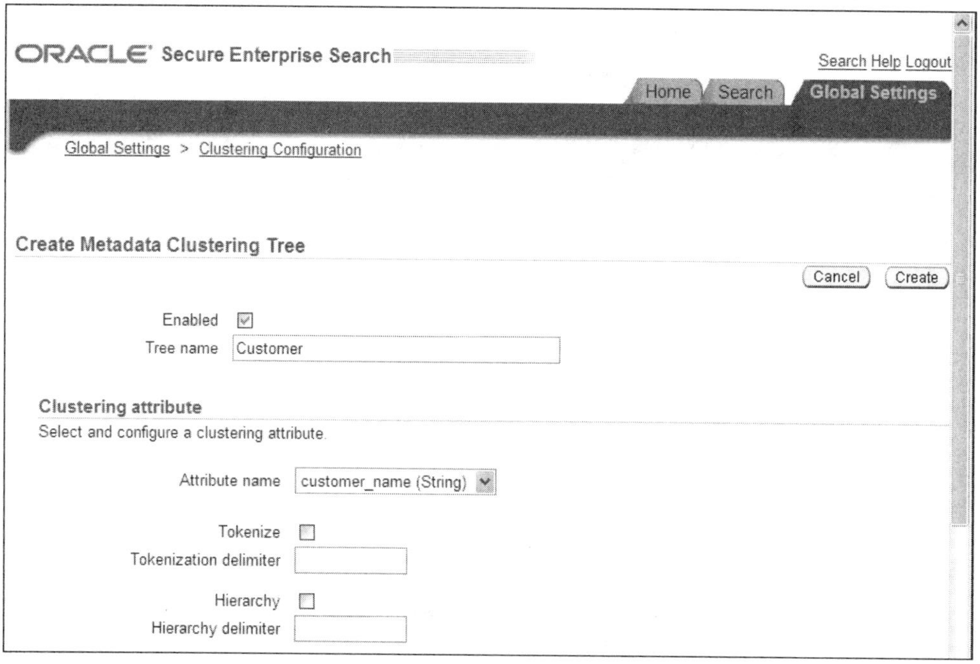

3. Then we add another cluster based on product names.

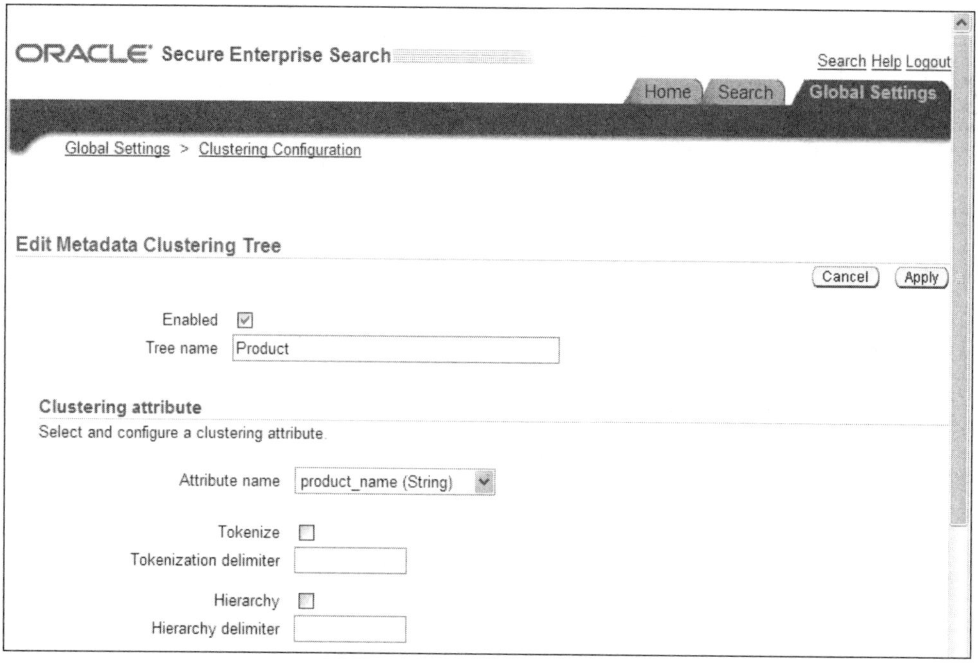

4. And add a third cluster based on order date.

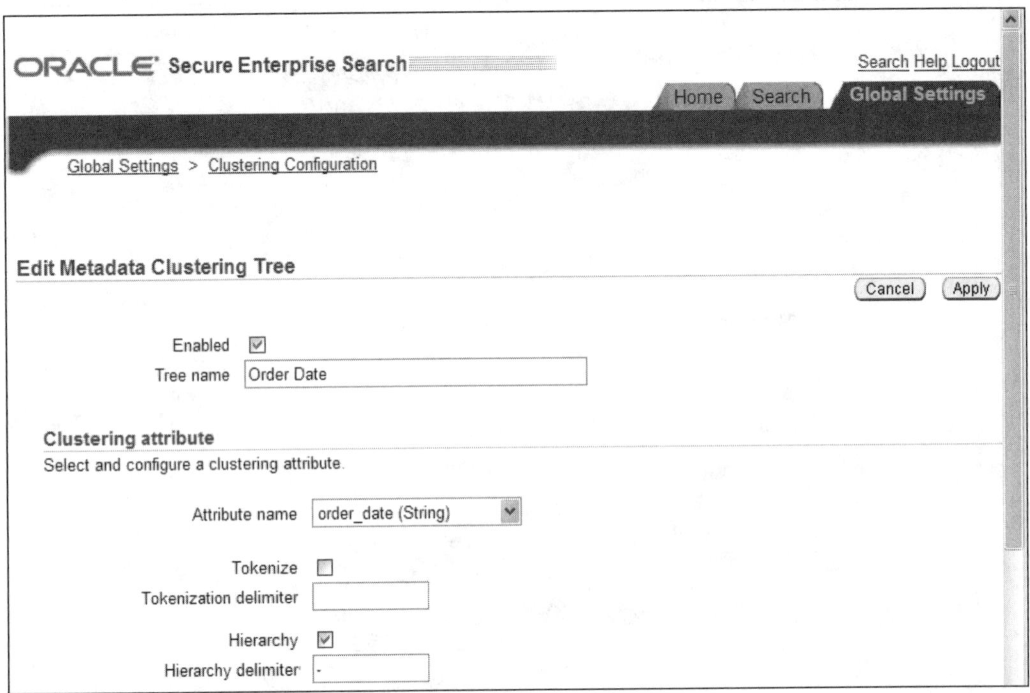

In this cluster, we enable the hierarchy based on the "-" because the date format is YYYY-MM-DD. With "-" serving as the delimiter, we can drill down into the data based on year, month, and date.

Creating a Source Group

Oracle SES allows you to create an index from multiple sources, and you can group a set of sources so you can search within them. To set this up:

1. Click the Search tab and choose Source Groups. Click the Create button.
2. Specify the name of the source group as *PO in XML* and then click Proceed To Step 2.
3. Select the Database Source Type and click the Go button.
4. You can find *DB Example 4: PO-XML source*. Move this source to the Assigned Sources. Then click Finish to complete the source group creation.

5. Next, click the Search link at the top right of the Oracle SES administration page to open the Oracle SES query UI. You will find the created source group (*PO in XML*) listed at the top of the search text box, as shown here:

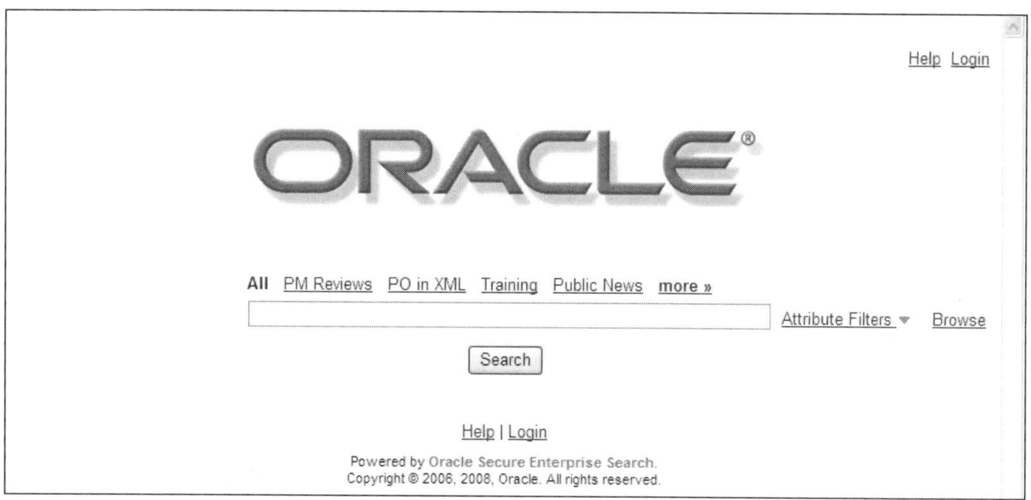

You can try some simple searches (e.g., "iphone") to see the search results.

UI Customization

The default result doesn't show the key data in the purchase order, such as customer name and country, ordered product name, and so on. In Oracle SES, we can easily change to display these along with the search result. This makes the search result more meaningful to the application users. Additionally, we can display different results based on the source groups.

To set this up:

1. We first need to create an XSL stylesheet. In this XSL stylesheet, we need to transform the result set by adding search attributes we want to show.

```
<xsl:template match="result[contains(eqdatasourcename,'DB Example 4:
PO-XML')]">
<table border="0">
  <!-- Title -->
  <tr>
    <td>
      <a href="http://{url}">
        <span class="title">
          <!-- Replace '[[' with '<b>' and ']]' with '</b>' -->
          <xsl:call-template name="process-hilite-attr">
            <xsl:with-param name="str" select="title" />
          </xsl:call-template>
        </span>
      </a>
    </td>
```

```
    </tr>
    <table cellpadding="0" cellspacing="0" border="0">
      <tr>
        <td>
          <!-- Display description if available, otherwise display snippet
-->
          <xsl:choose>
            <xsl:when test="description[.!='']">
              <span class="description">
                <!-- Replace '[[' with '<b>' and ']]' with '</b>' -->
                <xsl:call-template name="process-hilite-attr">
                  <xsl:with-param name="str" select="description" />
                </xsl:call-template>
              </span>
              <br />
            </xsl:when>
            <xsl:otherwise>
              <!-- Display snippet if non-empty -->
              <xsl:if test="eqsnippet[.!='']">
                <span class="snippet">
                  <!-- Replace '[[' with '<b>' and ']]' with '</b>' -->
                  <xsl:call-template name="bold-template">
                    <xsl:with-param name="str" select="eqsnippet" />
                    <xsl:with-param name="startdelim" select="'[['" />
                    <xsl:with-param name="enddelim" select="']]'" />
                    <xsl:with-param name="doe" select="'yes'" />
                  </xsl:call-template>
                </span>
                <br />
              </xsl:if>
            </xsl:otherwise>
          </xsl:choose>

           <!-- Display Author if non-empty -->
          <xsl:if test="customer_name[.!='']">
              <b><xsl:text>Customer: </xsl:text></b>
              <!-- Replace '[[' with '<b>' and ']]' with '</b>' -->
              <xsl:call-template name="process-hilite-attr">
                <xsl:with-param name="str" select="customer_name" />
              </xsl:call-template>
             <xsl:text>       
</xsl:text>
          </xsl:if>

      <!-- Display Author if non-empty -->
          <xsl:if test="product_name[.!='']">
              <b><xsl:text>Ordered Products: </xsl:text></b>
              <!-- Replace '[[' with '<b>' and ']]' with '</b>' -->
              <xsl:call-template name="process-hilite-attr">
                <xsl:with-param name="str" select="product_name" />
```

```
            </xsl:call-template>
          <br />
        </xsl:if>

      <!-- Display Author if non-empty -->
        <xsl:if test="country_name[.!='']">
            <b><xsl:text>Country: </xsl:text></b>
            <!-- Replace '[[' with '<b>' and ']]' with '</b>' -->
            <xsl:call-template name="process-hilite-attr">
              <xsl:with-param name="str" select="country_name" />
            </xsl:call-template>
           <xsl:text>       
</xsl:text>
        </xsl:if>

        <!-- Display Author if non-empty -->
        <xsl:if test="order_item_num[.!='']">
            <b><xsl:text>Number of Products Ordered: </xsl:text></b>
            <!-- Replace '[[' with '<b>' and ']]' with '</b>' -->
            <xsl:call-template name="process-hilite-attr">
              <xsl:with-param name="str" select="order_item_num" />
            </xsl:call-template>
            <br/>
        </xsl:if>

    <!-- Display "URL - Content Length - Last Modified Date - Cached
Links" -->
    <span class="lastModified">
      <!-- Display URL -->
      <span class="displayUrl">
        <xsl:value-of select="url" /><xsl:text> - </xsl:text>
      </span>
      <!-- Normalized content length -->
      <span class="contentLength">
        <xsl:call-template name="normalize-cl">
          <xsl:with-param name="contentLength" select=
"eqcontentlength" />
        </xsl:call-template>
        <xsl:text> - </xsl:text>
      </span>
      <!-- Display last modified date if non-empty -->
      <xsl:if test="lastmodifieddate[.!='']">
        <span class="lastModified"><xsl:value-of
select="lastmodifieddate" /></span><xsl:text> - </xsl:text>
      </xsl:if>
      <!-- Cached link -->
      <a class="cacheUrl" href="{eqcacheurl}">
        <xsl:call-template name="translate">
         <xsl:with-param name="strKey" select="'CACHED'" />
         </xsl:call-template>
```

```
          </a>
          <xsl:text> </xsl:text>
             <!-- Links link -->
             <a class="cacheUrl" href="{eqlinksurl}">
               <xsl:call-template name="translate">
                 <xsl:with-param name="strKey" select="'LINKS'" />
               </xsl:call-template>
             </a>
           </span>
         </td>
       </tr>
     </table>
   </table>
   </xsl:template>
```

The updates of the default XSL stylesheet are highlighted.

2. After you have the XSL stylesheet, choose the Global Settings tab and then select Out-of-Box Query Application | Configure Search Result List.
3. Select Use Advanced Configuration and include the search attributes that need to be shown with the search result. In this example, we choose *country_name, customer_name, order_item_num, product_name,* and *supplier_name,* as shown here:

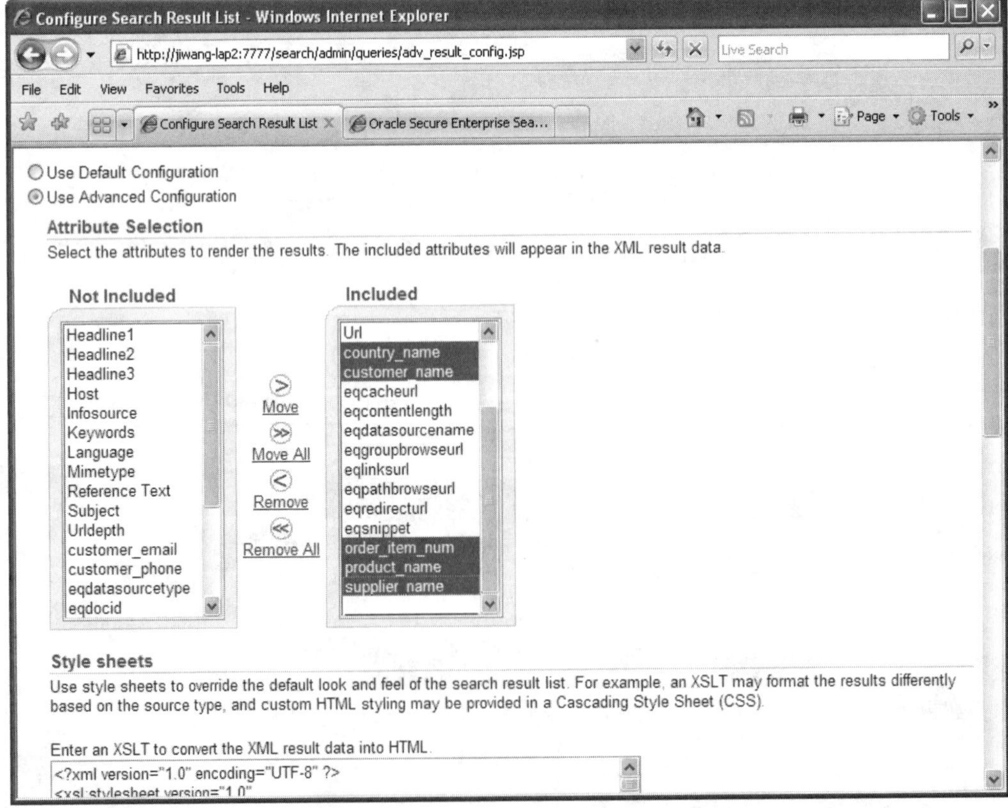

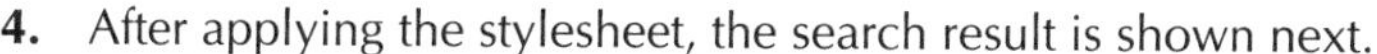

4. After applying the stylesheet, the search result is shown next.

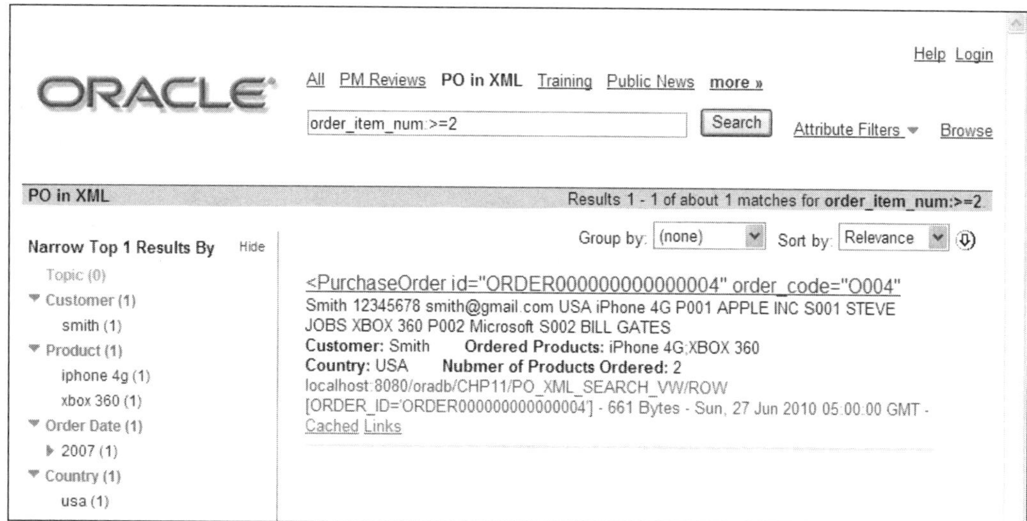

Because Oracle SES customization is based on XSL transformation, you can easily add new templates for new sources and display results in different formats. With the search result customization, you can also link the result to user applications so that users can access the application system directly from the search results and then perform the necessary actions.

Searching XML

Now, we have a full-text search index created for the purchase orders. Let's answer the questions from the list discussed earlier in the chapter.

Search by Order ID With a full-text search, we can use the *wildcard* search feature in Oracle SES to search *order*1* for order with ID *ORDER000000000000001*, as shown in Figure 10-2.

Search the orders for customer Mr. Liu This is another simple filtered search. We use the *customer_name* search attribute to restrict *liu* to be from the customer name as *customer_name:liu*, as shown in Figure 10-3.

Search the orders for customer Mr. Liu in CY2010 We need to extend the previous search by constraining the order date to the year 2010. We don't have to update the search query. Because we have categorized our search results with the order date, we can click the 2010 category to list the purchase orders from Liu to CY2010, as shown in Figure 10-4.

Search the orders for customer Mr. Liu purchasing iPhone For this query we just add an iPhone, so now it appears as *customer_name:liu iphone*, as shown in Figure 10-5.

Search the orders for all customers from China This is similar to the second query. We need an attribute filter search, *country:china*, as shown in Figure 10-6.

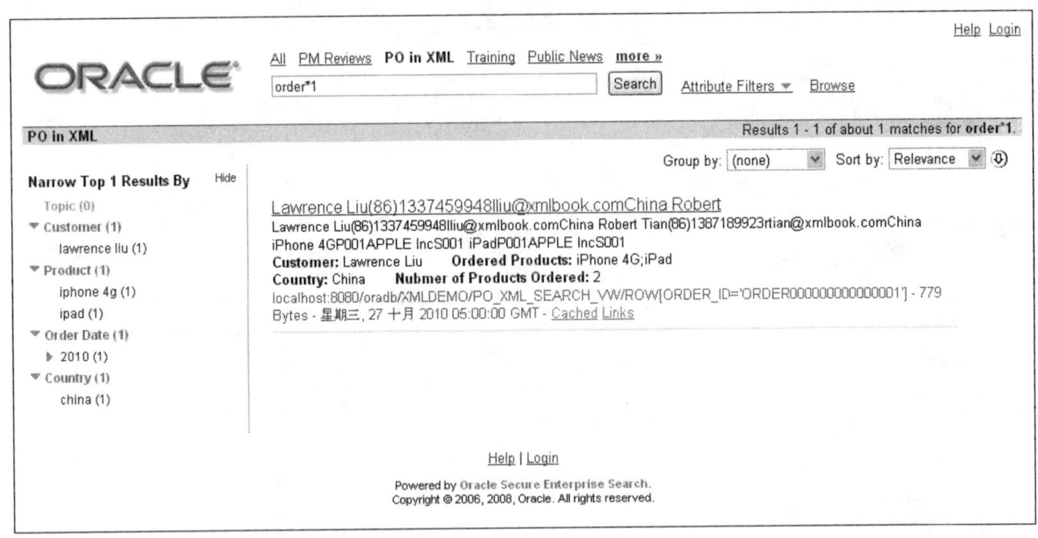

FIGURE 10-2. *Oracle SES query with wildcard*

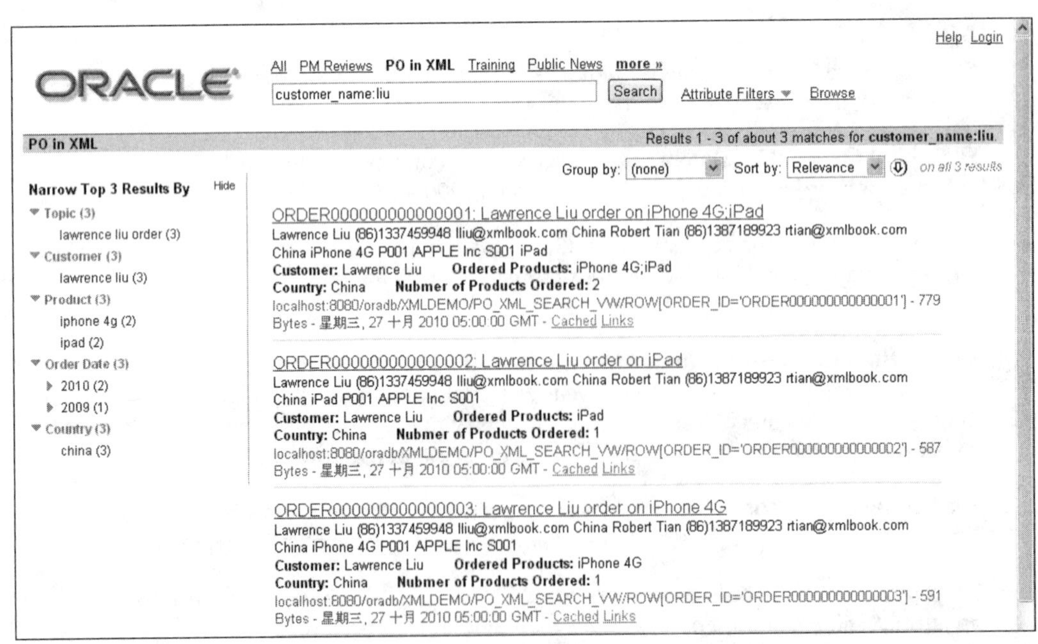

FIGURE 10-3. *Oracle SES query with attribute/metadata filtering*

FIGURE 10-4. *Oracle SES query with clustering navigation*

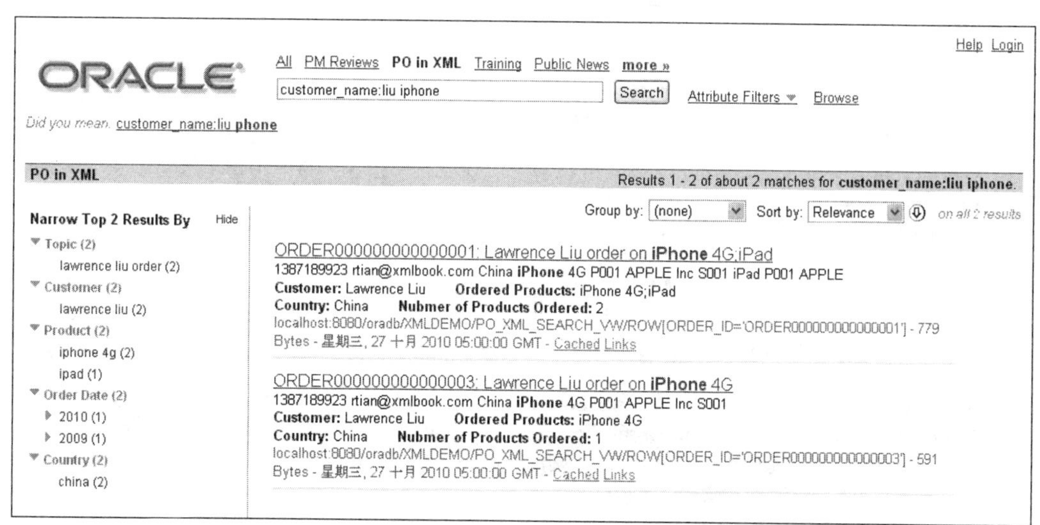

FIGURE 10-5. *Oracle SES query with text and attribute filtering*

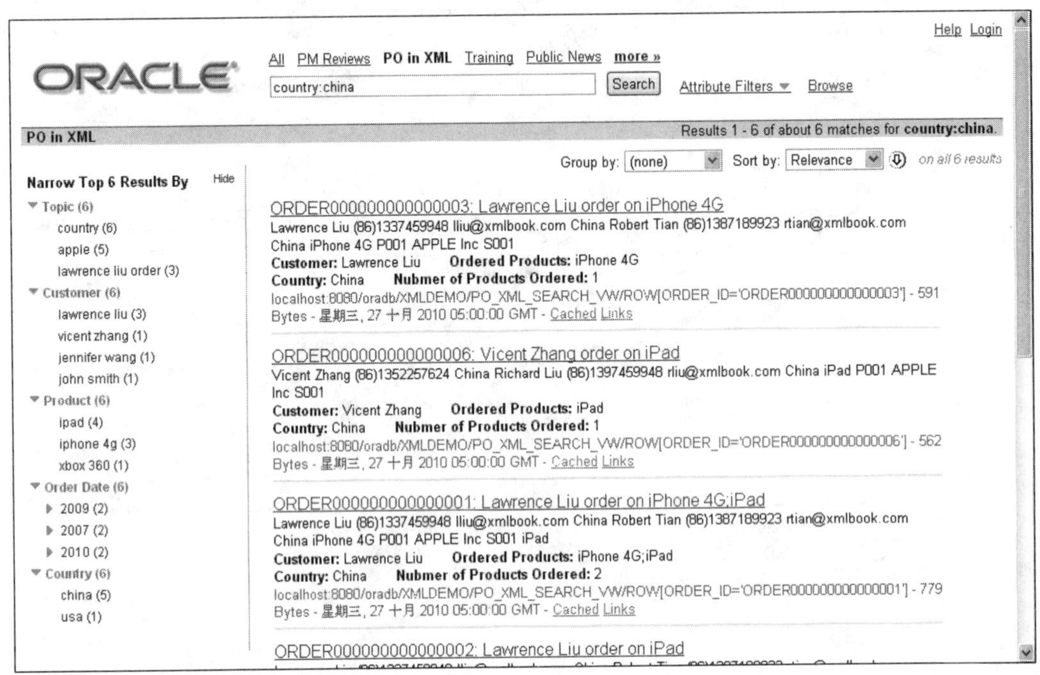

FIGURE 10-6. *Oracle SES query with attribute filtering*

Search the customer orders for Microsoft This requires a search using the supplier name. If you don't remember the search attribute name, you can use the Oracle SES *Inline Attribute Filtering* feature shown in Figure 10-7.

This feature will list the available search attributes to simplify the query restrictions.

Search the countries of the Microsoft customers We don't need to have a new search. Looking at the search result shown in Figure 10-7, in the categorization window, we see that for the two Microsoft customer orders, one came from China and the other from the United States.

Search the customers who purchased the same products as Mr. Liu First, search for All Orders from *Mr. Liu* to find all of the products ordered. Then search which customers ordered those products. We find out that *Mr. Liu* (*customer_name:liu*) has two orders, as shown in Figure 10-3, in which he ordered *iphone 4g* and *ipad*. Then search both *("iphone 4g" | ipad)*. John Smith is listed as another customer in the search result; clicking *john smith*, we can see John's order in Figure 10-8.

Search the orders that contain more than two products (includes 2). This query can be done because we have prepared the data and calculated the number of order items in each purchase order using the count() XPath function in XMLTable(). We used the *order_item_num* attribute to keep the data. Therefore we can search orders with more than two products, as shown in Figure 10-9.

This is the same result as if you had typed the query *order_item_num:>=2*.

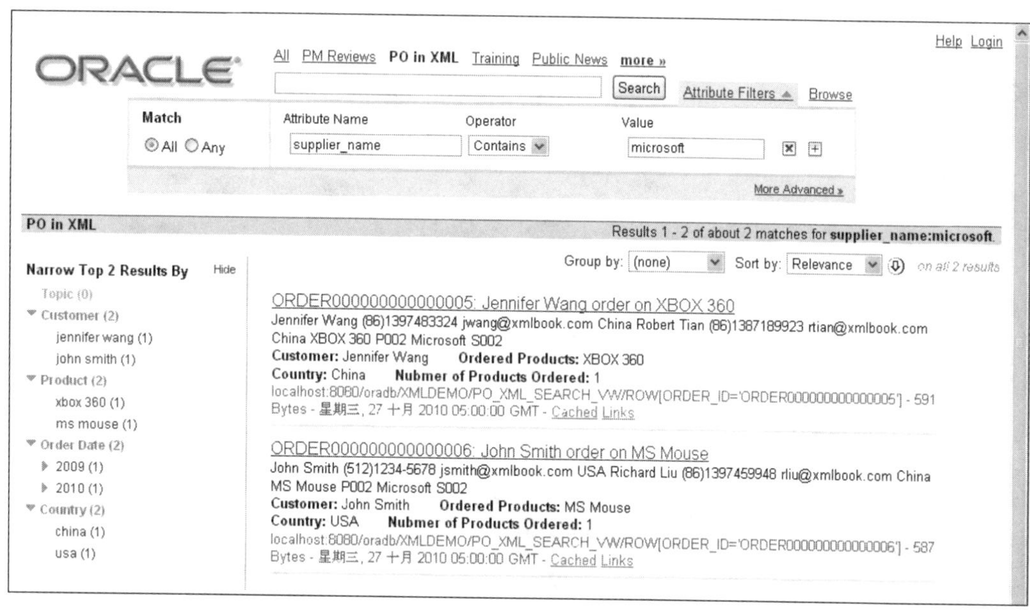

FIGURE 10-7. *Oracle SES query with inline attribute filter*

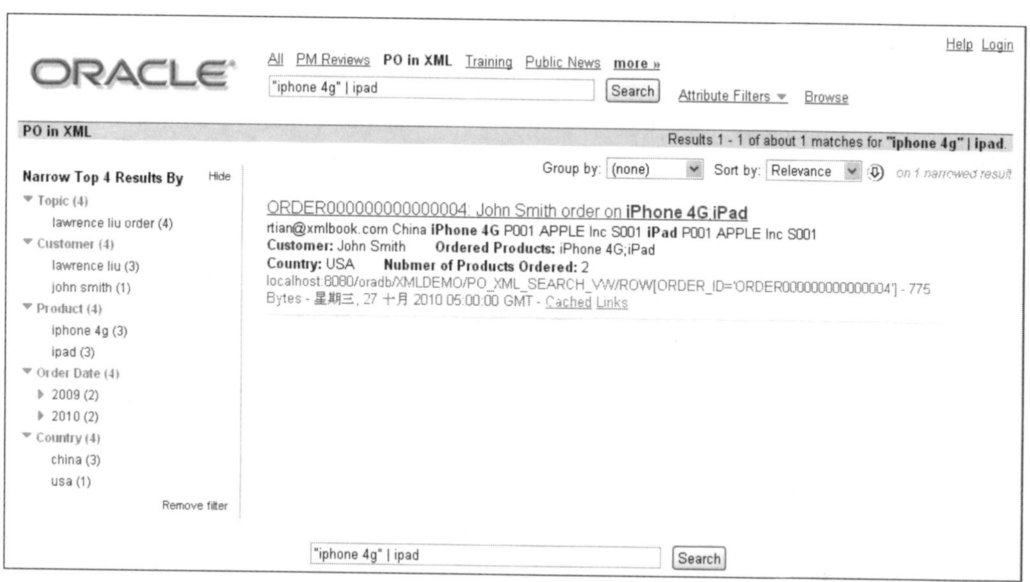

FIGURE 10-8. *Oracle SES second query with logical operator*

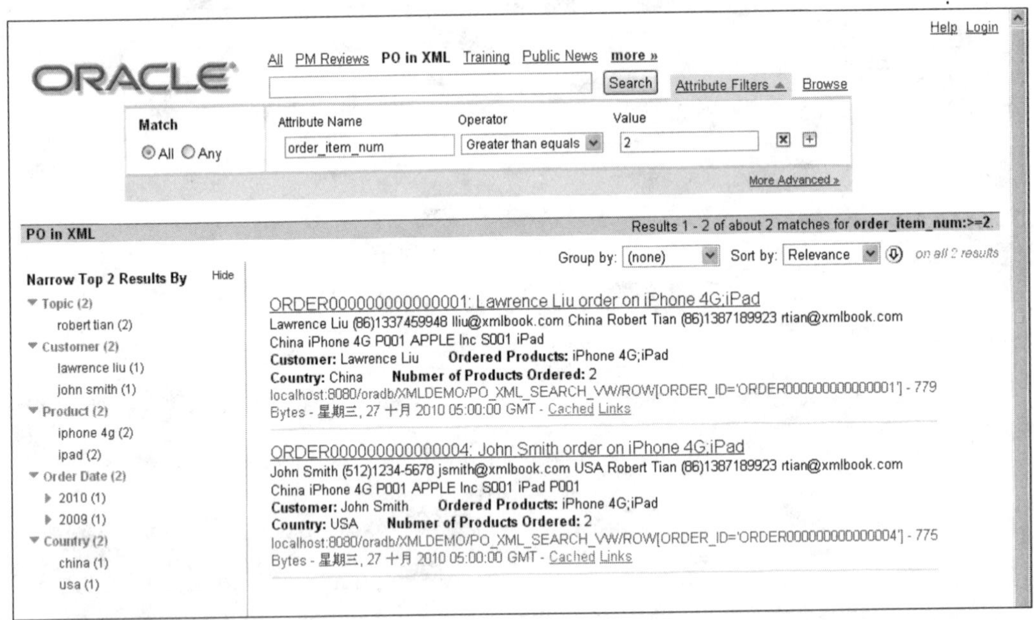

FIGURE 10-9. *Number filtering*

Refining the Search Result Cache

Oracle SES provides the search result cache. Within the cache, the matched keywords are highlighted. By default, the XML documents are not well formatted in the cache window. Let's see how to make this result look better.

The cache result in Oracle SES is based on its *content*. In the SQL query, we simply provide the XML document as *content*. This is good for a content search, but the output is not well formatted. The best way to do this is to apply an XSLT before passing the content to Oracle SES, shown as follows (*po_show.xsl*):

```
<?xml version="1.0" encoding="UTF-8"?>
<xsl:stylesheet version="1.0" xmlns:xsl="http://www.w3.org/1999/XSL/Transform"
xmlns:fo="http://www.w3.org/1999/XSL/Format">
<xsl:template match="/">
<html>
    <body>
    <table border="1">
             <tr>
            <td colspan="2"><b>Purchase Order <xsl:value-of select=
"PurchaseOrder/@order_id"/></b></td>
        </tr>
```

```
        <tr>
            <td><b>Order Code:</b><xsl:value-of select="PurchaseOrder/
@order_code"/></td>
            <td><b>Order Date:</b><xsl:value-of select="PurchaseOrder/
@order_date"/></td>
        </tr>
        <tr>
            <td colspan="2"><b>Customer</b></td>
        </tr>
......
        <tr>
            <td><b>Supplier:</b></td><td><xsl:value-of
select="SupplierName"/></td>
        </tr>
        <tr>
            <td><b>Supplier Code:</b></td><td><xsl:value-of
select="SupplierCode"/></td>
        </tr>
        </xsl:for-each>
    </table>
</body>
</html>
</xsl:template>
</xsl:stylesheet>
```

The SQL view for Oracle SES search is now updated as follows (*create_search_vw_with_cache.sql*):

```
create or replace view po_xml_search_vw as
select customer_name, customer_country,
       order_date, order_id, supplier_name, product_name, order_item_num,
       XMLSerialize(DOCUMENT xmltransform(po_content, xdburitype('/public/
chp10/po_show.xsl').getxml()) AS CLOB) as po_content from po_search_vw;
```

The XMLTransform() function is called to apply the XSL transformation. We then use XMLSerialize() to serialize the XSL transformation result to CLOB. The content is now in HTML format, with MIME type as *text/html*. We need to update the database crawler query by adding the content type info. Otherwise, the crawler will set the default of the content type to be text/plain.

```
select 'http://localhost:8080/oradb/XMLDEMO/PO_XML_SEARCH_VW/ROW[ORDER_
ID='''||c.order_id||''']' as url, c.order_id as key, c.po_content as content,
c.order_id||': '||c.customer_name||' order on '|| c.product_name as title,
c.order_date as order_date, c.customer_name as customer_name, c.customer_
country as country_name, c.supplier_name as supplier_name, c.product_name as
product_name, c.order_item_num as order_item_num, to_date(sysdate) as
lastmodifieddate,'EN' as lang, 'text/html' as contenttype from po_xml_search_
vw c
```

After we set up the new query, we can recrawl the data. Then submit the "*liu iphone*"query and look at our cache result. The result is shown in Figure 10-10 as well-formatted HTML.

ORACLE

Puchase Order	
Order Code:O001	**Order Date:**2010-04-05
Customer	
Name:	Lawrence **Liu**
Phone:	(86)1337459948
Email:	lliu@xmlbook.com
Country:	China
Order Details	
Product:	**iPhone** 4G
Product Code:	P001
Quantity:	500
Supplier:	APPLE Inc
Supplier Code:	S001
Product:	iPad
Product Code:	P001
Quantity:	200
Supplier:	APPLE Inc
Supplier Code:	S001

FIGURE 10-10. *Oracle SES cache output in HTML*

Summary

From the simplest ora:contains() function in SQL query, to building indexes with Oracle Text inside the Oracle database, and then to using Oracle SES to create a secure enterprise search application, you can enable full-text search on XML stored in Oracle Database 11*g* via different approaches. The ora:contains() function is ideal for a quick query on a small set of XML data. Oracle Text indexes XML stored within the database and allows you to provide real-time transactional index updates. However, if you are looking for "Google-like" searches across database tables/schemas and even applications, Oracle Secure Enterprise Search is the best choice, because it allows you to easily build an integrated XML search solution to securely search data across multiple repositories.

In general, you can also combine the three approaches. Using Oracle SES *suggested content* (compliant with Google *OneBox*), you can easily federate Oracle Text and ora:contains() query results into Oracle SES applications.

PART II

Managing Oracle XML Database

CHAPTER 11

XML DB Installation

To enable Oracle XML DB application development, you need to set up Oracle XML DB and Oracle XDK. Oracle XML DB provides the native XML storage and retrieval inside the Oracle database. Oracle XDK includes the tools and utilities in Java, C, and C++ for developing XML applications. This chapter discusses how to set up these products in your development environment.

Installing Oracle XML DB

Oracle XML DB is a component of the Oracle database. Oracle Database installations include Oracle XML DB by default. Therefore, the first step is to verify whether Oracle XML DB is already installed.

Simple Installation Review

If you are a developer, you can perform a simple three-step check of the XML DB installation.

Step 1: Check XML DB and the Related Components

You can query DBA_REGISTRY to verify whether XML DB and its related components are loaded to the Oracle database (*check_xmldb_registry.sql*):

```
column comp_name format a20
column status format a10
column version format a10
select comp_name,status,version
from dba_registry
where comp_name in ('Oracle XML Database', 'Oracle XDK', 'Oracle Text');
```

The following result shows that XML DB and its related components are loaded into the database successfully:

```
Oracle XML Database  VALID      11.2.0.2.0
Oracle Text          VALID      11.2.0.2.0
Oracle XDK           VALID      11.2.0.2.0
```

Step 2: Check the XMLType Object

You can check whether the XMLType object is defined and ready-to-use with the following SQL command:

```
SQL> desc XMLType
METHOD
------
 STATIC FUNCTION CREATEXML RETURNS XMLTYPE
 Argument Name                  Type                    In/Out Default?
 ------------------------------ ----------------------- ------ --------
 XMLDATA                        CLOB                    IN
...
```

If you get a detailed description of the XMLType object and its methods, then the XMLType object is ready for use.

Step 3: Check XML DB Repository

To check whether XML DB Repository is installed, run the following command:

```
SQL>desc resource_view
Name        Null?     Type
 --------- -------- ---------------------------
 RES            SYS.XMLTYPE(XMLSchema
               "http://xmlns.oracle.com/xdb/XDBResource.xsd" Element "Resource")
 ANY_PATH       VARCHAR2(4000)
 RESID          RAW(16)
```

Then, calculate the number of resources in XML DB Repository as follows:

```
SQL> select count(any_path) from resource_view;
7500
```

If there are not many resources, you can list them in XML DB Repository using the following command:

```
SQL> select any_path from resource_view;
/OLAP_XDS
/OLAP_XDS/dsclass.xml
/home
/home/john_smith.xml
/images
/images/16admin.gif
...
```

If both the RESOURCE_VIEW and the resource files in XML DB Repository are shown without errors, then XML DB Repository is normally ready for use.

Detailed Installation Review

If you are a DBA, you need a more detailed review of the XML DB installation, so let's take a closer look.

Step 1: Check the XML DB Users

You need to verify the database users created or needed by Oracle XML DB. They are listed as follows:

- **SYS** This is the database user that owns the XMLType object.
- **XDB** This is the database user that maintains the XML DB dictionary, SQL functions, and PL/SQL packages.
- **ANONYMOUS** The ANONYMOUS user is created to allow for unauthenticated HTTP access to Oracle XML DB Repository. The ANONYMOUS user is initially LOCKED.

> **Oracle XML DB Tip: A cautionary note about removing XML DB**
> Unless you need unauthenticated access to Oracle XML DB Repository, please ***do not*** unlock the ANONYMOUS user.

Let's check the XML DB related users (*check_xmldb_users.sql*):

```
column username format a10
column account_status format a18
column default_tablespace a20
select username, account_status,default_tablespace
from dba_users
where username in ('XDB', 'ANONYMOUS');
```

An example result is shown as follows:

```
USERNAME   ACCOUNT_STATUS     DEFAULT_TABLESPACE
---------- ------------------ ------------------------------
ANONYMOUS  EXPIRED & LOCKED   SYSAUX
XDB        EXPIRED & LOCKED   SYSAUX
```

By default, the XDB user is locked. You can run the following commands in the SYS user to unlock the XDB user:

```
alter user xdb account unlock;
alter user xdb identified by xdbpwd;
```

In this example, the XDB user password is set to *xdbpwd*. You can choose your own password as needed.

Step 2: Check the XML DB Database Roles

Oracle XML DB creates a set of database roles in Oracle Database 11*g*, which are listed as follows:

- **XDBADMIN** Allows the grantee to register an XML schema globally, as opposed to registering it for use or access only by its owner. It also lets the grantee bypass Access Control List (ACL) checks when accessing Oracle XML DB Repository.
- **XDB_SET_INVOKER** Allows the grantee to define invoker's rights handlers and to create or update the resource configuration for XML repository triggers. By default, Oracle Database grants this role to the DBA role but not to the XDBADMIN role.
- **XDB_WEBSERVICES** Allows the grantee to access Oracle Database Web services over HTTPS. However, it does not provide the user access to objects in the database that are public. To allow public access, you need to grant the user the XDB_WEBSERVICES_WITH_PUBLIC role. For a user to use these Web services, SYS must enable the Web service servlets.
- **XDB_WEBSERVICES_OVER_HTTP** Allows the grantee to access Oracle Database Web services over HTTP. However, it does not provide the user access to objects in the database that are public. To allow public access, you need to grant the user the XDB_WEBSERVICES_WITH_PUBLIC role.
- **XDB_WEBSERVICES_WITH_PUBLIC** Allows the grantee access to public objects through Oracle Database Web services.

You can check the database roles by running the following SQL query (*check_xmldb_roles.sql*):

```
select role
from dba_roles
where role in ('XDBADMIN','XDB_SET_INVOKER','XDB_WEBSERVICES','XDB_WEBSERVICES_
WITH_PUBLIC',
'XDB_WEBSERVICES_OVER_HTTP');
```

By default the following roles should be defined:

```
ROLE
------------------------------
XDBADMIN
XDB_SET_INVOKER
XDB_WEBSERVICES
XDB_WEBSERVICES_WITH_PUBLIC
XDB_WEBSERVICES_OVER_HTTP
```

Step 3: Check the XML DB Objects

You need to check the XMLType object owned by the SYS user as follows (*check_xmltype.sql*):

```
col object_name format a35
col owner format a12
col status format a8
select object_name, owner, object_type, status
from dba_objects
where object_name='XMLTYPE';
```

An example result is shown here:

```
OBJECT_NAME                         OWNER        OBJECT_TYPE         STATUS
----------------------------------- ------------ ------------------- --------
XMLTYPE                             SYS          TYPE BODY           VALID
XMLTYPE                             SYS          TYPE                VALID
XMLTYPE                             PUBLIC       SYNONYM             VALID
```

Then, you check the database objects owned by the XDB user as follows (*check_xmldb_objects.sql*):

```
select version from v$instance;

select *
from dba_objects
where status='invalid' and OWNER in ('XDB');
```

There should not be an invalid object under XDB.

If all of the checking steps run smoothly, the Oracle XML DB is ready for use.

Installing Oracle XML DB

If you don't have Oracle XML DB installed, you can install it by logging into the Oracle database as SYS user with SYSDBA privileges, and then performing the following installation steps (*install_xmldb.sql*):

1. Create a new *XDB* tablespace.

```
CREATE TABLESPACE "XDB"
  LOGGING DATAFILE D:\app\jiwang\oradata\orcl11g\xdb01.dbf' SIZE 50M
REUSE
  AUTOEXTEND ON   NEXT 50M   MAXSIZE 1500M
  EXTENT MANAGEMENT LOCAL SEGMENT SPACE MANAGEMENT AUTO;
```

   Note that you need to update the DATAFILE path based on your system setup. It's important to create a separate tablespace for the XDB user when storing large numbers of documents in XML DB.

2. Create the XDB user, and grant the necessary privileges to the XDB user by running the *catqm.sql* script. The script also creates the XML DB database tables and views, SQL functions, and PL/SQL packages:

```
catqm.sql <XDBUSER_password> <XDB_TS_NAME> <TEMP_TS_NAME> <SECURE_
FILES_REPO>
```

   An example call is shown as follows:

```
SQL > @?/rdbms/admin/catqm XDBPW XDB TEMP YES
```

   In SQL*Plus, the "?" (question mark) locates the home directory of the Oracle database. The example command creates the XDB user using the **XDB** tablespace and sets the temporary tablespace to **TEMP**. The password for the XDB user is **XDBPW**. Because of setting SECURE_FILES_REPO to **YES**, the XML DB Repository resources will be stored as SecureFiles. Otherwise, LOBs (CLOBs or BLOBs) will be used. Note that to use SecureFiles, the database compatibility must be set to *11.2*.

3. Ensure that there are no invalid objects in the Oracle database:

```
SQL> @?/rdbms/admin/utlrp.sql
```

Oracle XML DB Tip: Do I still need to run *catxdbj.sql* during the Oracle XML DB installation?

In Oracle Database 11*g*, all of the functions provided by *catxdbj.sql* are not used. Therefore, you don't need to run *catxdbj.sql* during the XML DB installation.

Reinstall Oracle XML DB

If you don't need XML DB, you can remove it by connecting to the Oracle database as the SYS user with SYSDBA role and running the following commands.

Oracle XML DB Tip: A cautionary note about removing XML DB
You need to know that after you have removed XML DB by running the following commands, all registered XML schemas and their associated XMLTypes, and any XMLType columns that are stored as binary XMLTypes, will be *invalid.*

```
SQL >sqlplus "SYS/<sys_password> as sysdba"
SQL >spool "d:\temp\xdb_reinstall.log"
SQL >@?/rdbms/admin/catnoqm.sql
```

catnoqm.sql is located in the *$ORACLE_HOME/rdbms/admin* directory. ($ORACLE_HOME is the Oracle database home directory.) After running the script, you can assess XML DB's availability with two-step checking:

```
SQL> describe xmltype
SQL> select count(1) from resource_view;
```

You can still find the XMLType definitions, but you will get an error when checking the XML DB Repository resources:

```
SQL> select count(1) from resource_view
ERROR at line 1:
ORA-00942: table or view does not exist
```

The Oracle XML DB registry is also removed from *dba_registry* (*check_xmldb_registry.sql*):

```
column comp_name format a20
column status format a10
column version format a10
select comp_name,status,version from dba_registry
where comp_name in ('Oracle XML Database', 'Oracle XDK', 'Oracle Text');
```

Now, only Oracle Text and Oracle XDK are shown:

```
COMP_NAME            STATUS     VERSION
-------------------- ---------- ----------
Oracle Text          VALID      11.2.0.2.0
Oracle XDK           VALID      11.2.0.2.0
```

Then, shut down and restart the Oracle database. It's important to do this before reinstalling the Oracle XML DB.

```
SQL> shutdown immediate;
SQL> startup
```

Run the XML DB installation as described in the previous section (*install_xmldb.sql*):

```
SQL>sqlplus "SYS/<sys_password> as sysdba"
SQL>CREATE TABLESPACE "XDB"
  LOGGING DATAFILE 'D:\app\jiwang\oradata\orcl11g\xdb01.dbf' SIZE 50M REUSE
  AUTOEXTEND ON   NEXT 50M   MAXSIZE 1500M
  EXTENT MANAGEMENT LOCAL SEGMENT SPACE MANAGEMENT AUTO;
```

```
SQL>@?/rdbms/admin/catqm.sql xdb XDB TEMP YES
SQL>@?/rdbms/admin/utlrp.sql
SQL>spool off
```

You can check XML DB's availability as described earlier. An example XML DB reinstallation log file is included as part of the sample code of this chapter. You can use it as a reference for your reinstallation (*xmldb_reinstall.log*).

Set Up XML DB Repository

XML DB Repository provides file-based metaphors in the Oracle database. Oracle XML DB Repository is installed with Oracle XML DB. However, the protocol servers that enable the Internet protocol access to XML DB Repository are not enabled by default.

Let's learn how to set up the protocol servers for XML DB Repository access.

Step 1: Set Up the DISPATCHERS

DISPATCHERS is a database system parameter. The parameter is needed by the XML DB protocol servers to register to the Oracle database listener. To set up the dispatcher, you need to add the DISPATCHERS parameter to the database SPFILE as follows:

```
dispatchers="(PROTOCOL=TCP) (SERVICE=<SID>XDB)"
```

<SID> is the database System ID (SID). For example,

```
SQL> alter system set dispatchers='(PROTOCOL=TCP)(SERVICE=ORCL11gXDB)';
SQL> show parameters dispatchers
 NAME                         TYPE        VALUE
---------------------------- ----------- ------------------------------
dispatchers                  string      (PROTOCOL=TCP) (SERVICE=ORCL11gXDB)
```

If the listener hasn't been started, start it using the following command:

```
D:\>lsnrctl start
```

You can see that the dispatcher is set up to respond to the *orcl11gXDB* service:

```
d:\>lsnrctl status
LSNRCTL for 32-bit Windows: Version 11.2.0.2.0 - Production on …
Copyright (c) 1991, 2010, Oracle.  All rights reserved.
Connecting to (DESCRIPTION=(ADDRESS=(PROTOCOL=IPC)(KEY=EXTPROC1522)))
STATUS of the LISTENER
------------------------
Alias                     LISTENER
Version                   TNSLSNR for 32-bit Windows: Version 11.2.0.2.0 -
                          Production
Start Date                26-MAY-2011 23:08:38
Uptime                    0 days 0 hr. 7 min. 33 sec
Trace Level               off
Security                  ON: Local OS Authentication
SNMP                      OFF
Listener Parameter File   D:\app\jiwang\product\11.2.0\dbhome_1\network\admin\
                          listener.ora
```

```
Listener Log File         d:\app\jiwang\diag\tnslsnr\jsmith-lap2\listener\
alert\log.xml
Listening Endpoints Summary...
  (DESCRIPTION=(ADDRESS=(PROTOCOL=ipc)(PIPENAME=\\.\pipe\EXTPROC1522ipc)))
  (DESCRIPTION=(ADDRESS=(PROTOCOL=tcp)(HOST=jsmith-lap2.us.oracle.com)
(PORT=1522
)))
Services Summary...
Service "CLRExtProc" has 1 instance(s).
  Instance "CLRExtProc", status UNKNOWN, has 1 handler(s) for this service...
Service "orcl11g" has 1 instance(s).
  Instance "orcl11g", status READY, has 1 handler(s) for this service...
Service "orcl11gXDB" has 1 instance(s).
  Instance "orcl11g", status READY, has 1 handler(s) for this service...
The command completed successfully
```

You won't see the HTTP and FTP servers run, because the LOCAL_LISTENER parameter still needs to be set up.

Step 2: Set Up the LOCAL_LISTENER

If the database listener does not use the default 1521 port (e.g., 1522), then the XML DB FTP and HTTP services can't dynamically register to the listener. You need to set up the LOCAL_LISTENER parameter. By default, the *local_listener* entry in the database SPFILE file refers to the TNSNAME entry specified in the *$ORACLE_HOME/network/admin/tnsname.ora* file. Here is an example *tnsname.ora* file:

```
# tnsnames.ora Network Configuration File: D:\app\jiwang\product\11.2.0\
dbhome_1\network\admin\tnsnames.ora
# Generated by Oracle configuration tools.

ORACLR_CONNECTION_DATA =
  (DESCRIPTION =
    (ADDRESS_LIST =
      (ADDRESS = (PROTOCOL = IPC)(KEY = EXTPROC1522))
    )
    (CONNECT_DATA =
      (SID = CLRExtProc)
      (PRESENTATION = RO)
    )
  )

ORCL11G =
  (DESCRIPTION =
    (ADDRESS = (PROTOCOL = TCP)(HOST = jsmith-lap2.us.oracle.com)(PORT =
1522))
    (CONNECT_DATA =
      (SERVER = DEDICATED)
      (SERVICE_NAME = orcl11g)
```

```
    )
  )

LISTENER_ORCL11G =
  (ADDRESS = (PROTOCOL = TCP)(HOST = jsmith-lap2.us.oracle.com)(PORT = 1522))
```

You can list the current LOCAL_LISTENER as follows:

```
SQL> show parameters local_listener;
NAME                                 TYPE        VALUE
------------------------------------ ----------- ----------------
local_listener                       string      LISTENER_ORCL11G
```

If the parameter is not set, you then need to update LOCAL_LISTENER to the following format:

```
LOCAL_LISTENER = "(ADDRESS=(PROTOCOL=TCP)(HOST=<hostname>)(port=<port>))"
```

And then run the following SQL command:

```
alter system set local_listener="(ADDRESS=(PROTOCOL=TCP)(HOST=localhost)
(port=1522))" scope=SPFILE;
```

Step 3: Set Up the HTTP and FTP Ports

To enable HTTP and FTP access, run the following commands:

```
SQL> call DBMS_XDB.setHttpPort(8081);
SQL> call DBMS_XDB.setFTPPort(2121);
```

The SQL commands change the default ports for both HTTP and FTP from the default value (0) to the ports assigned. In this example, we choose port *8081* for HTTP and port *2121* for FTP. You need to make sure that there is no port conflict on your machine.

Now, when we check the listener status, we get the following output:

```
d:\>lsnrctl status
LSNRCTL for 32-bit Windows: Version 11.2.0.2.0 - Production on 01-JUN-2011
08:56:40
Copyright (c) 1991, 2010, Oracle.  All rights reserved.
Connecting to (DESCRIPTION=(ADDRESS=(PROTOCOL=IPC)(KEY=EXTPROC1522)))
STATUS of the LISTENER
------------------------
Alias                     LISTENER
Version                   TNSLSNR for 32-bit Windows: Version 11.2.0.2.0 -
                          Production
Start Date                01-JUN-2011 08:50:17
Uptime                    0 days 0 hr. 6 min. 23 sec
Trace Level               off
Security                  ON: Local OS Authentication
SNMP                      OFF
Listener Parameter File   D:\app\jiwang\product\11.2.0\dbhome_1\network\admin\
                          listener.ora
Listener Log File         d:\app\jiwang\diag\tnslsnr\jsmith-lap2\listener\alert\
```

```
log.xml
Listening Endpoints Summary...
  (DESCRIPTION=(ADDRESS=(PROTOCOL=ipc)(PIPENAME=\\.\pipe\EXTPROC1522ipc)))
  (DESCRIPTION=(ADDRESS=(PROTOCOL=tcp)(HOST=jiwang oracle.com)(PORT=1522)))
  (DESCRIPTION=(ADDRESS=(PROTOCOL=tcp)(HOST=jiwang.oracle.com)(PORT=8081
))(Presentation=HTTP)(Session=RAW))
  (DESCRIPTION=(ADDRESS=(PROTOCOL=tcp)(HOST=jiwang.oracle.com)(PORT=2121
))(Presentation=FTP)(Session=RAW))
Services Summary...
Service "CLRExtProc" has 1 instance(s).
  Instance "CLRExtProc", status UNKNOWN, has 1 handler(s) for this service...
Service "orcl11g" has 1 instance(s).
  Instance "orcl11g", status READY, has 1 handler(s) for this service...
Service "orcl11gXDB" has 1 instance(s).
  Instance "orcl11g", status READY, has 1 handler(s) for this service...
The command completed successfully
```

You can see the FTP and HTTP listeners in the database listeners' status report as highlighted.

You can also configure the XML DB Repository HTTP and FTP port using Oracle Database Control (also called Oracle Enterprise Manager). In the Oracle Database Control Schema tab, you will find the Oracle XML DB management options as shown here:

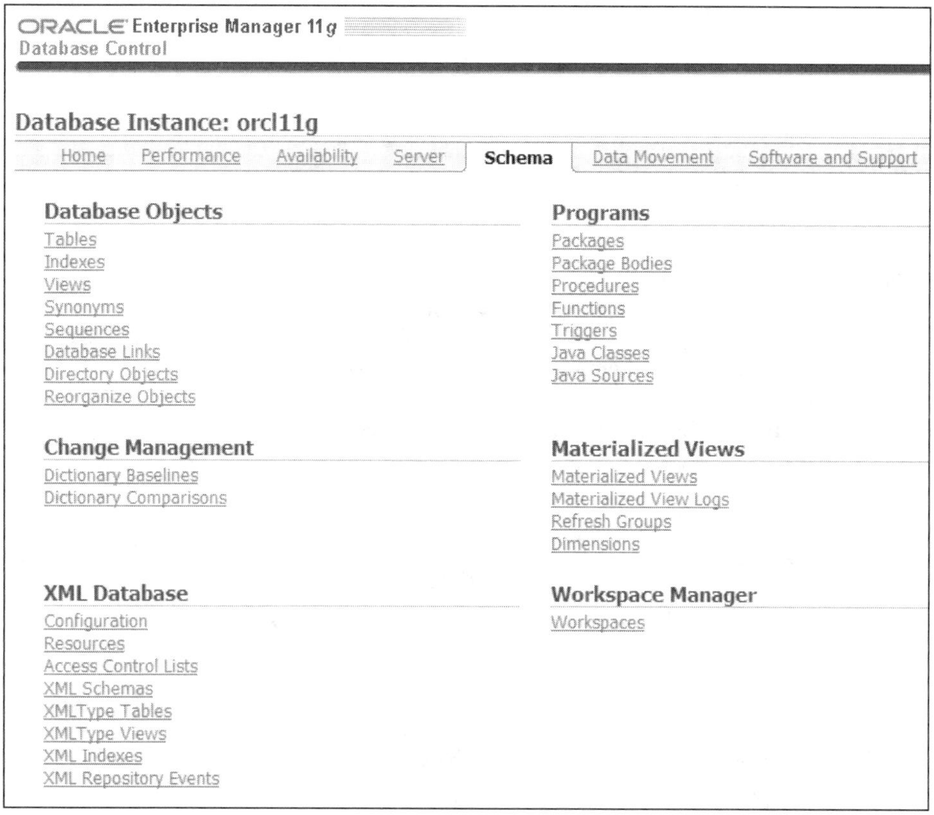

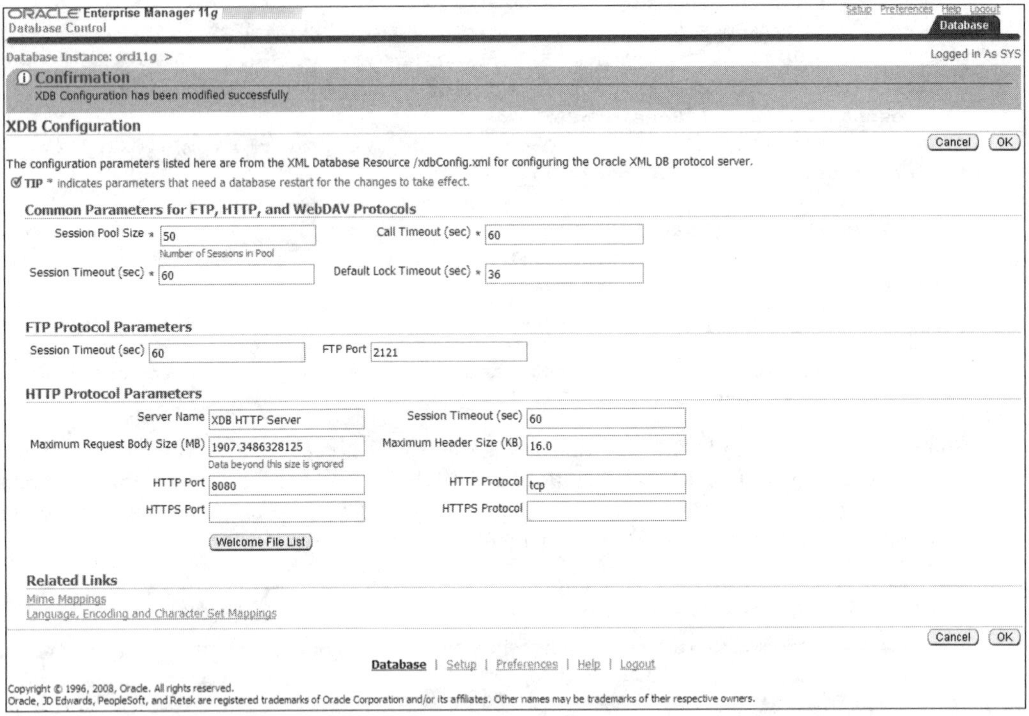

FIGURE 11-1. *Oracle XML DB Configuration in Enterprise Manager*

Click the Configuration link in the XML Database section to set up the XML DB Repository port shown in Figure 11-1.

In Oracle JDeveloper 11*g*, you can set up a database connection for SYS user. Then, right-click the connection and choose the XML DB Protocol Server Configuration option to configure the HTTP/FTP port. Figure 11-2 shows the XML DB FTP and HTTP set up page in Oracle JDeveloper 11*g*.

Step 4: Set Up the HTTP Access

After the Oracle database listener setup, you can then work on getting HTTP access. You can type `http://<host_name>:<xdb_http_port>/` (i.e., `http://localhost:8081`) in your browser to get the access.

A login dialog will pop up for user authentication. You can log in as any valid database user. However, you can only see public and the database user–owned content in the XML DB Repository. You can't see XML DB Repository *system* files if not logged in as the *XDB* user.

Step 5: Set Up the WebDav Access

Let's set up WebDav access, using the Windows (on Windows 7) WebDav setup as the example,

1. Right-click the Network icon and choose the Map Network Drive… menu.
2. In the Map Network Drive dialog, click the "Connect to a Web site that you can use to store your documents and pictures" link. The Add Network Location wizard dialog will pop up.

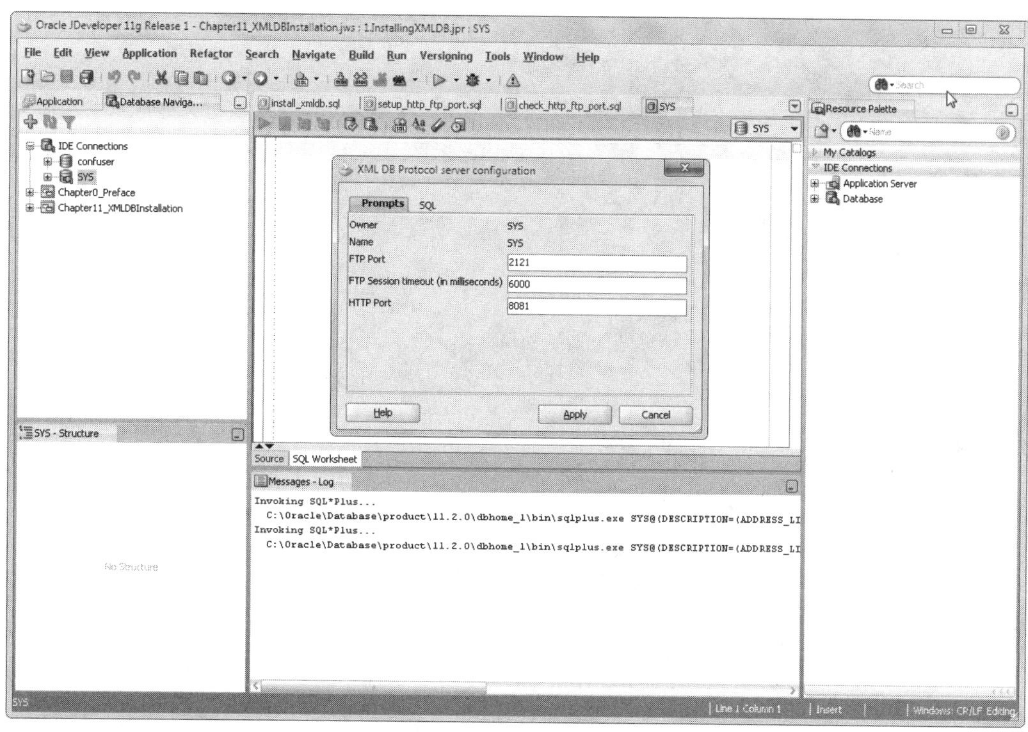

FIGURE 11-2. *Oracle XML DB protocol server set up in Oracle JDeveloper 11*g

3. Click the Next button in the Add Network Location wizard dialog to continue.
4. Choose the Choose A Custom Network Location option and then click the Next button.
5. Add the *http://<host_name>:<xmldb_http_port>/* (i.e., **http://localhost:8081**) to the Internet Or Network Address field and then click Next.
6. Specify a name for the WebDav Folder and then click Next.
7. Check the Open This Network Place When I Click Finish box and then click Finish.

You will be asked to log in to XML DB Repository. Again, you can log in as any valid Oracle database user. An example XML DB folder is shown in Figure 11-3.

Note that both Windows Vista and Windows 7 restrict the access to WebDav servers using the Basic HTTP authentication on non-SSL connections. Because Oracle XML DB 11*g* WebDav server only supports Basic HTTP authentication, you have to change a registry key on Windows 7 or Windows Vista to set up the WebDav access. The steps are described as follows:

1. Click Start, and then click Run.
2. In the Open box, type **regedit**, and then click OK.

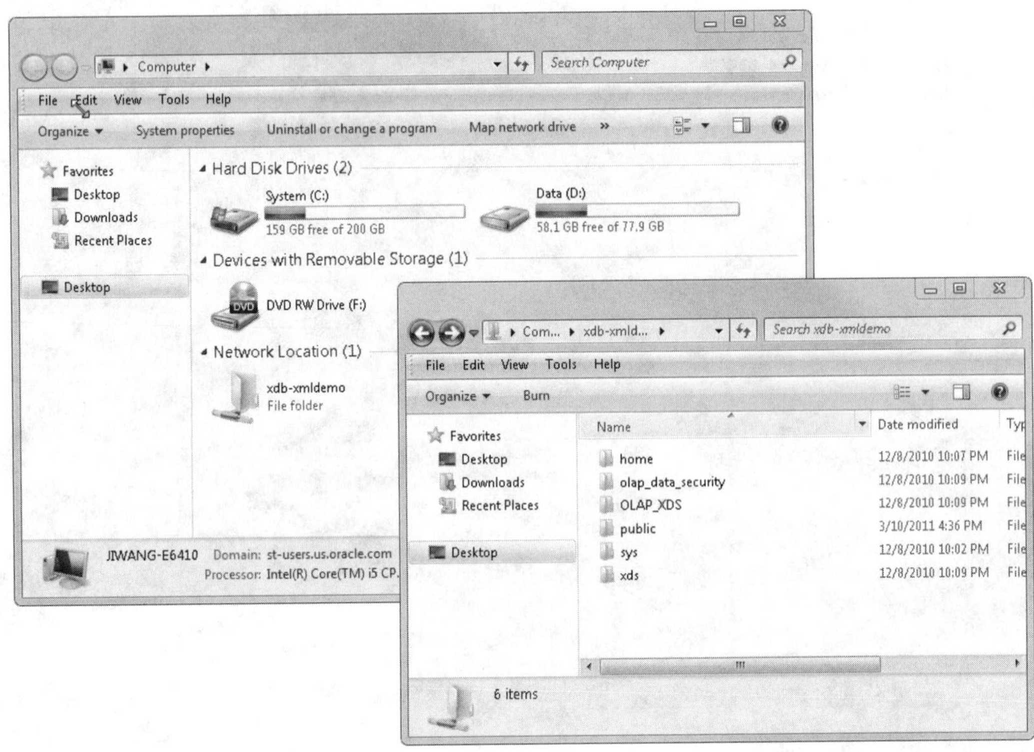

FIGURE 11-3. *WebDav access to XML DB Repository*

3. Locate and then click the following registry key:

   HKEY_LOCAL_MACHINE\SYSTEM\CurrentControlSet\Services\WebClient\Parameters
4. On the Edit menu, point to New, and then click DWORD (32bit) Value. Type **BasicAuthLevel**, and then press ENTER. If the BasicAuthLevel parameter already exists, skip this step.
5. On the Edit menu, click Modify with the BasicAuthLevel parameter selected. In the Value data box, type **2**, and then click OK. Note that BasicAuthLevel has to be set to 2 or greater to enable Basic HTTP authentication for SSL shares and for non-SSL shares.
6. Exit Registry Editor, and then restart the computer.

You can refer to Microsoft support note (*http://support.microsoft.com/kb/841215*) for more information.

Oracle XML DB Tip: What should I do if the Windows WebDav access is broken?

Sometimes, when you access the XML DB Repository WebDav folders, you may see the "Documents in the folder are not available. The folder may have been moved or deleted, or network problems may be preventing a connection to the server" error.

This doesn't mean the XML DB Repository is broken. Sometimes, it's a Windows error. Don't try to reinstall Oracle XML DB. Instead, verify whether XML DB and XML DB Repository are still in service. You can do a quick check with the following commands:

```
SQL>select count(any_path) from resource_view;
SQL>show parameter dispatchers
```

If everything is OK, just use another WebDav client for the Oracle XML DB WebDav access.

Step 6: Set Up the FTP Access

To set up the FTP access, you can open any FTP client or use the FTP command-line tool, shown as follows:

```
ftp> open localhost 2121
Connected to jsmith-lap2.us.oracle.com.
220\- jsmith-lap2
Unauthorized use of this FTP server is prohibited and may be subject to civil
and criminal prosecution.
220 jsmith-lap2 FTP Server (Oracle XML DB/Oracle Database) ready.
User (jsmith-lap2.us.oracle.com:(none)): xmldemo
331 pass required for XDB
Password:
230 XMLDEMO logged in
ftp> ls
200 PORT Command successful
150 ASCII Data Connection
OLAP_XDS
images
olap_data_security
public
sys
xdbconfig.xml
226 ASCII Transfer Complete
ftp: 66 bytes received in 0.00Seconds 66000.00Kbytes/sec.
```

With HTTP, FTP, and WebDav access, you can create folders and copy files to a folder just like you do in a normal file system. The difference is that the created folder/files are the private content of the current database user and can only be accessed by that user.

Installing Oracle XDK

Oracle XDK is a set of Java and C/C++ libraries installed with Oracle Database 11*g*. To build Java XML applications, you need the following Oracle XDK and the dependent Java libraries:

- $ORACLE_HOME/LIB/**xmlparserv2.jar** Provides Java XML parsers (DOM, JAXP, SAX), XML schema validator, and XSL processor.
- $ORACLE_HOME/LIB/**xml.jar** Includes JAXB, XMLDiff, XML Pipeline, Transviewer, XSDValidator Bean, TransX, Compression Bean, DB Access Bean, and XSQL Servlet.
- $ORACLE_HOME/LIB/**xsu12.jar** Includes XML SQL Utility (XSU).
- $ORACLE_HOME/jlib/**xquery.jar** Includes the XQuery Java APIs.
- $ORACLE_HOME/RDBMS/jlib/**xdb.jar** Provides oracle.xdb.XMLType support.
- $ORACLE_HOME/jdbc/lib/**ojdbc6.jar** Provides the Oracle JDBC driver.
- $ORACLE_HOME/jlib/**orai18n.jar (orai18n-collation.jar)** Provides the language support for Java applications.

NOTE
Refer to Chapter 16 to learn how to add these libraries to Oracle JDeveloper projects.

Validate Oracle XDK Installation

After the Oracle database is installed, you can set up the Java CLASSPATH to pick up the Oracle XDK Java libraries. In Windows, you can set up the Java CLASSPATH:

```
SET ORACLE_HOME=C:\Oracle\Database\product\11.2.0\dbhome_1
SET CLASSPATH=%ORACLE_HOME%\LIB\xmlparserv2.jar;%CLASSPATH%
```

Here's how to set it up in Linux:

```
EXPORT ORACLE_HOME=/home/Oracle/Database/product/11.2.0/dbhome_1
EXPORT CLASSPATH=$ORACLE_HOME/LIB/xmlparserv2.jar;$CLASSPATH
```

After you set *xmlparserv2.jar* to the Java CLASSPATH, you can run the following command:

```
> java oracle.xml.parser.v2.oraxml -version
Parser version: Oracle XML Developers Kit 11.2.0.2.0 - Production
```

Within the Java application, you can check the Oracle XDK version using XMLParser.getReleaseVersion() as shown in Listing 11-1 (*XDKVersion.java*):

Listing 11-1 *Checking Oracle XDK Version*

```
import oracle.xml.parser.v2.XMLParser;
public class XDKVersion
{
   static public void main(String[] argv)
```

```
    {
        System.out.println("XDK Version from XMLParser.getReleaseVersion ");
        System.out.println(XMLParser.getReleaseVersion());
    }
}
```

Set Up Oracle XDK Command-line Utilities

Oracle XDK provides a set of command-line utilities. The command-line utilities are good for running a simple test of the Oracle XDK process. The following are the commonly used Oracle XDK command-line utilities.

oraxml

oraxml is an Oracle XDK command-line utility parsing XML documents. It checks for XML well-formedness and validity. The following are the options given by the *oraxml* utility:

```
d:\>oraxml
Error: Atleast one argument (file name) is required.
usage: oraxml options* <filename>
where the options are:
    -help                   Prints the help message
    -version                Prints the release version
    -novalidate             Checks whether the input file is well-formed
    -dtd                    Validates the input file with DTD Validation
    -schema                 Validates the input file with Schema Validation
    -log <logfile>          Writes the errors/logs to the output file
    -comp                   Compresses the input xml file
    -decomp                 Decompresses the input compressed file
    -enc                    Prints the encoding of the input file
    -warning                Show warnings
Oraxsl allows us to do quick XSL transformations
```

oraxsl

oraxsl is an Oracle XDK command-line utility performing XSL transformations. The following are the options given by the *oraxsl* utility:

```
d:\>oraxsl
oraxsl: Number of arguments specified (0) is illegal
usage: oraxsl options* source? stylesheet? result?
            -w                          Show warnings
            -e <error log>              A file to write errors to
            -l <xml file list>          List of files to transform
            -d <directory>              Directory with files to transform
            -x <source extension>       Extensions to exclude
            -i <source extension>       Extensions to include
            -s <stylesheet>             Stylesheet to use
            -r <result extension>       Extension to use for results
            -o <result directory>       Directory to place results
            -p <param list>             List of Params
```

```
          -t <# of threads>               Number of threads to use
          -v                              Verbose mode
          -debug                          Debug mode
          -m <version #>                  XSLT Version, 1 or 2
Please refer to the readme file for more information on the above options.
```

The Oracle XDK *oraxsl* is used by Oracle JDeveloper 11*g* for the built-in XSL transformation.

Summary

We have discussed the installations of Oracle XML DB and XDK in this chapter. Make sure you restart the Oracle database after deinstalling Oracle XML DB and before installing new XML DB. To find the XML DB installation files *catqm.sql* and *catnoqm.sql*, please visit the *$ORACLE_HOME/rdbms/admin* directory.

CHAPTER 12

XML DB Storage

n Oracle Database 11*g*, there are several XML storage options. This is primarily because XML is used in many different ways. XML data can vary from structured data like purchase orders and employee records to unstructured documents like reports and whitepapers. Thus, there is no single solution for XML storage. However, with XMLType datatype abstraction, you can have a single interface to access all XML data stored in the Oracle database. This chapter explains and compares XML storage options and gives examples on how to use and manage the XMLType storage.

EXAMPLE SETUP

To run the SQL examples in this chapter, you can log in as the XMLDEMO user created in the "About the Examples" section in the Introduction of this book. Also, grant additional privileges to the XMLDEMO user by logging in to SYS (as SYSDBA) and running the following commands (xmldemo_chp12_setup.sql):

```
grant select on v_$session to xmldemo;
grant select on v_$process to xmldemo;
```

XML Storage Options

In Oracle Database 11*g*, there are three XMLType storage options: relational tables with XMLType views, *object-relational* (O-R) XMLTypes, and *binary* XMLTypes. The relational table storage shreds XML documents and stores the data in one or more relational tables. XMLType views are created to generate XML and enable XML queries and updates on relational data. The object-relational (O-R) XMLTypes parse XML documents and store them in a set of object-relational tables defined by registered XML schemas. The binary XMLTypes store XML in a pre-parsed compact binary format designed to optimize XML-based operations.

Figure 12-1 summarizes the XML storage options. When XML contains highly structured data, you can shred the XML documents and store the data in one or more relational tables. You can also store the XML documents in O-R XMLTypes when you would like to preserve the XML format in the Oracle database. For an unstructured or semi-structured XML document, you can use binary XMLTypes.

Relational table storage is useful when XML is used to exchange data between business processes. Because XML is created as needed for data sharing, storing XML in relational tables simplifies data storage management. With Oracle XML DB, XML documents can easily be created whenever needed. XMLType views are usually used to simplify the process. You can find examples in Chapter 9, where we discussed how to store XML documents in relational tables and create XML from relational tables.

O-R XMLType is used for XML-centric applications where XML, structured or semi-structured, is preferred to be stored in a native XML format. O-R XMLType provides high-performance XML updates and query access. O-R XMLType requires a relatively stable XML Schema defined for the XML documents, although the *in-place XML schema evolution* is supported in Oracle Database 11*g*R2.

Binary XMLType replaces the CLOB XMLType in Oracle Database 11*g* and provides a native XML storage mainly for unstructured or semi-structured XML documents. As discussed, because the binary XMLType stores pre-parsed XML in a compact format, it saves the XML storage space and delivers high-performance data access. With *XMLIndex*, the performance of binary XMLTypes is comparable to that of O-R XMLType. In addition, the BLOB storage used by binary XMLType is

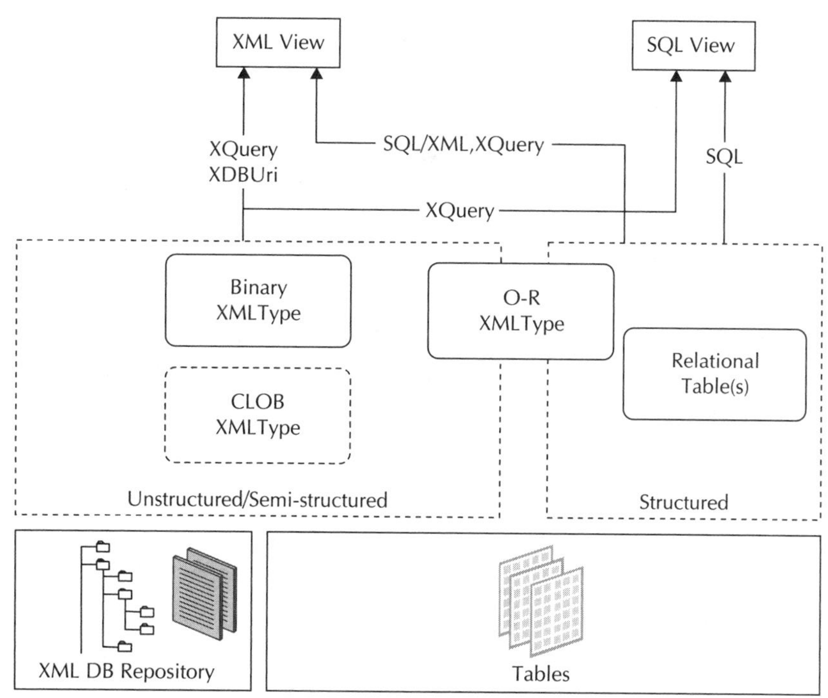

FIGURE 12-1. *XML storage options in Oracle Database 11*g

easier to manage than the set of object tables used by O-R XMLType. Binary XMLType can also handle XML formats with evolving XML schemas.

Oracle XML DB Tip: When do I use CLOB XMLTypes?
In Oracle Database 11gR2, you can use binary XMLTypes to replace CLOB (Character Large Object) XMLTypes. Binary XMLTypes are stored in a compressed and pre-parsed binary format. This data compression reduces the storage space. Binary XMLType optimizes the XML data access by voiding the DOM parsing required by the CLOB XMLType.

Next, we will look at examples of how to use O-R and binary XMLTypes.

Object-Relational XMLType

Creating object-relational (O-R) XMLTypes starts from the XML Schema registration. The XML registration process not only registers the XML Schema to Oracle XML DB, but also creates object-relational tables. The O-R table creation is based on the default setup in Oracle XML DB and the Oracle XML DB XML Schema annotations.

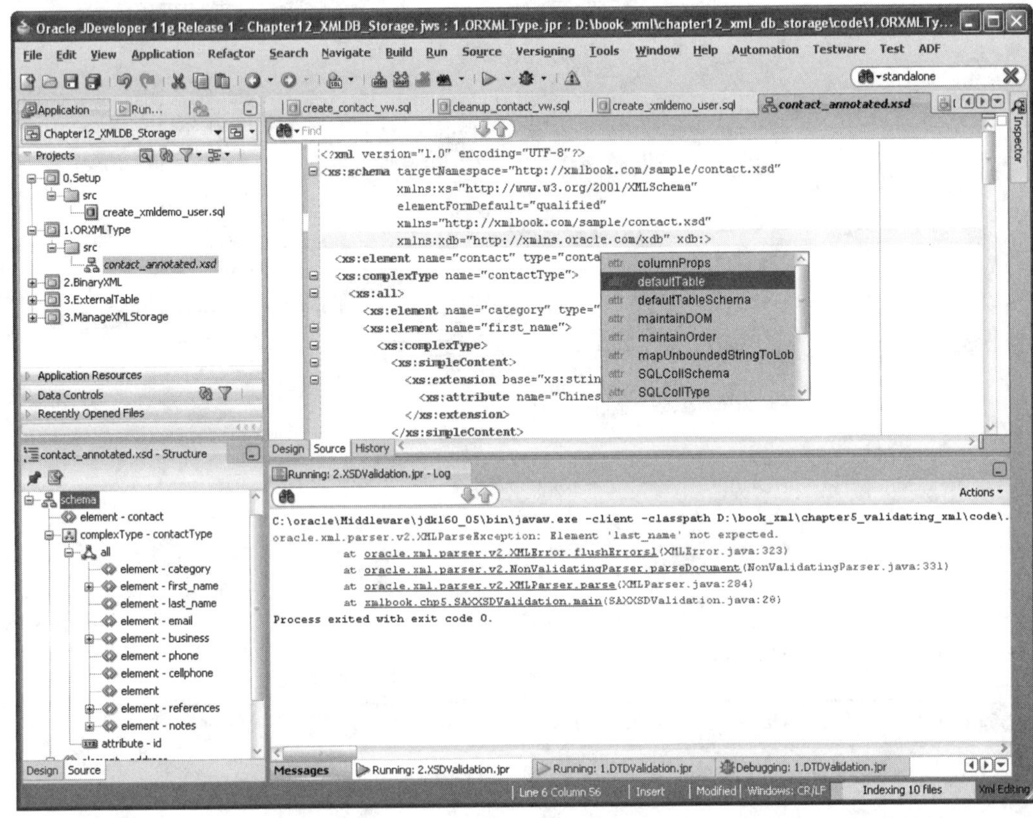

FIGURE 12-2. *Annotating XML schemas in Oracle JDeveloper 11g*

Figure 12-2 shows how you get in-line hints when adding XML DB annotations in Oracle JDeveloper 11*g*. The following is an example of an annotated XML schema (*contact_annotated.xsd*):

Listing 12-1 *Annotating XML Schemas for O-R XMLType Storage*

```
<?xml version="1.0" encoding="UTF-8"?>
<xs:schema targetNamespace="http://xmlbook.com/sample/contact.xsd"
           xmlns:xs="http://www.w3.org/2001/XMLSchema"
           elementFormDefault="qualified"
           xmlns="http://xmlbook.com/sample/contact.xsd"
           xmlns:xdb="http://xmlns.oracle.com/xdb" >
  <xs:element name="contact" type="contactType" xdb:defaultTable="contact_or_
tbl"/>
  <xs:complexType name="contactType">
    <xs:all>
```

```
      <xs:element name="category" type="xs:string" minOccurs="0"
xdb:SQLName="category"/>
      <xs:element name="first_name" xdb:SQLName="first_name">
        <xs:complexType>
          <xs:simpleContent>
            <xs:extension base="xs:string">
              <xs:attribute name="Chinese" type="xs:string"
xdb:SQLName="first_name_ch"/>
            </xs:extension>
          </xs:simpleContent>
        </xs:complexType>
      </xs:element>
      <xs:element name="last_name" type="xs:string" xdb:SQLName="last_name"/>
      <xs:element name="email" type="xs:string" minOccurs="0"
xdb:SQLName="email"/>
      <xs:element name="business" minOccurs="0" xdb:SQLName="business">
        <xs:complexType>
          <xs:all>
            <xs:element name="title" type="xs:string" minOccurs="0"/>
            <xs:element name="department" type="xs:string" minOccurs="0"/>
            <xs:element name="company" type="xs:string" minOccurs="0"/>
            <xs:element name="phone" type="phoneType" minOccurs="0"/>
            <xs:element name="email" type="xs:string" minOccurs="0"/>
            <xs:element ref="address" minOccurs="0"/>
            <xs:element name="notes" minOccurs="0">
              <xs:complexType mixed="true" xdb:SQLType="CLOB">
                <xs:sequence>
                  <xs:any namespace="http://www.w3.org/1999/xhtml"
                          processContents="lax" minOccurs="0"
                          maxOccurs="unbounded"/>
                </xs:sequence>
              </xs:complexType>
            </xs:element>
            <xs:element name="fax" minOccurs="0" xdb:SQLName="fax"/>
            <xs:element name="website" minOccurs="0" xdb:SQLName="website"/>
          </xs:all>
        </xs:complexType>
      </xs:element>
      <xs:element name="phone" type="phoneType" minOccurs="0"/>
      <xs:element name="cellphone" type="phoneType" minOccurs="0"/>
      <xs:element ref="address" minOccurs="0"/>
      <xs:element name="references" minOccurs="0">
        <xs:complexType xdb:SQLType="CLOB">
          <xs:sequence>
            <xs:element name="reference" maxOccurs="3">
              <xs:complexType>
                <xs:all>
                  <xs:element name="first_name"/>
                  <xs:element name="last_name"/>
                  <xs:element name="email"/>
```

```
                </xs:all>
                <xs:attribute name="relationship" type="xs:string"/>
              </xs:complexType>
            </xs:element>
          </xs:sequence>
        </xs:complexType>
      </xs:element>
      <xs:element name="notes" minOccurs="0">
        <xs:complexType mixed="true" xdb:SQLType="CLOB">
          <xs:sequence>
            <xs:any namespace="http://www.w3.org/1999/xhtml"
                    processContents="lax" minOccurs="0"
maxOccurs="unbounded"/>
          </xs:sequence>
        </xs:complexType>
      </xs:element>
    </xs:all>
    <xs:attribute name="id" type="xs:positiveInteger"/>
  </xs:complexType>
  <xs:element name="address">
    <xs:complexType>
      <xs:sequence>
        <xs:element name="street1"/>
        <xs:element name="street2" minOccurs="0"/>
        <xs:element name="city"/>
        <xs:element name="state"/>
        <xs:element name="zipcode"/>
        <xs:element name="country"/>
      </xs:sequence>
    </xs:complexType>
  </xs:element>
  <xs:simpleType name="phoneType">
    <xs:restriction base="xs:string">
      <xs:pattern value="(\(\d{3}\)\d{3}-\d{4})|(\(\d{2}\)\s\d{11})|(\
(\d{2}\)\s\d{10})"/>
    </xs:restriction>
  </xs:simpleType>
</xs:schema>
```

Oracle XML DB XML schema annotations are defined in the Oracle XML DB namespace (*xmlns:xdb="http://xmlns.oracle.com/xdb"*). There are many annotation options. You can refer to *Oracle XML DB Developer's Guide* for the complete list. Table 12-1 lists some commonly used ones.

In practice, specifying SQL names is useful because the system-generated names are not easy to remember. Additionally, using *xsd:SQLType="CLOB"* can avoid create unnecessary tables and objects.

Annotation	Description
xdb:storeVarrayAsTable	Tells Oracle XML DB to store all VARRAY elements in nested object tables. This annotation helps speed up the queries on the XML element that has *maxOccurs>1*.
xdb:mapUnboundedStringtoLob	Tells Oracle XML DB to map unbounded string to CLOB and unbounded binary data to BLOB with out-of-line storage.
xdb:defaultTable	Specifies the name of the table into which XML instances conforming to the XML schema should be stored. This should be specified on the definition of the XML document's root element.
xdb:tableProps	Specifies the default table properties in SQL syntax that is appended to the CREATE TABLE clause.
xdb:SQLName	Specifies the SQL object name for a given XML element.
xdb:SQLType	Specifies the SQL type for a given XML type or element.
xdb:SQLCollType	Specifies the SQL collection type corresponding to the XML element that has *maxOccurs>1*.
xdb:maintainDOM	Specifies whether *complexType* should maintain DOM fidelity.

TABLE 12-1. *Oracle XML DB Commonly Used XML Schema Annotations*

Oracle XML DB Tip: Should I capitalize all SQL names in Oracle XML DB XML schema annotations?

You should consider capitalizing the SQL names in the Oracle XML DB XML schema annotations. This avoids creating tables and objects with case-sensitive names in the database. All case-sensitive names in the Oracle database require the use of double quotes when referring to SQL objects.

To register an XML schema, run the following commands (*register_xsd.sql*):

Listing 12-2 *Registering XML Schema for O-R XMLTypes*

```
begin
  dbms_xmlschema.registeruri('http://xmlbook.com/sample/contact_annotated.xsd',
     '/public/chp12/contact_annotated.xsd',
     local=>true,
     gentypes=>true,
     genbean=>false,
     gentables=>true);
end;
/
```

After the successful XML schema registration, the XMLType table is created and ready for use.

Oracle XML DB Tip: Why do I get the ORA-30937: *No schema definition* error when registering XML schemas?

When adding XML DB annotations, there are restrictions on where to put them. For example, the *defaultTable* annotation needs to be specified on the top level XML element; Placing it in the *<xs:schema>* element will result in the *ORA-30937: No schema definition for 'defaultTable' (namespace 'http://xmlns.oracle.com/xdb') in parent '/schema'* error.

Another example is xdb:SQLName, which is not allowed on the XML schema complexType or simpleType definitions. Violation of this will raise the following error: *ORA-30937: No schema definition for 'SQLName'(namespace 'http://xmlns.oracle.com/xdb') in parent 'complexType'.*

To debug the XML schema registration process, you can issue the *alter session set events='31098 trace name context forever'* command before the XML schema registration. This command creates a trace file (**.trc*) in the USER_DUMP_DEST directory with a name in the format of *<database_SID_ora>_<sessionid>.trc* (e.g., *orcl11gb_ora_5816.trc*). This trace file includes the DDL used to create object tables and data types during the XML schema registration.

To locate a trace file, you can run the following command to report the current database session id (*register_xsd.sql*):

Listing 12-3 *Checking the Current DB Session ID*

```
SELECT a.spid
FROM v$process a, v$session b
WHERE a.addr=b.paddr and b.audsid=userenv('sessionid');
```

To locate the USER_DUMP_DEST directory, run the following SQL commands by logging in to SYS user:

Listing 12-4 *Checking USER_DUMP_DEST*

```
SELECT value FROM v$parameter WHERE name='user_dump_dest';
```

The following example inserts an XML document into the created O-R XMLType table (*insert_data_to_or_tbl.sql*):

Listing 12-5 *Inserting XML Document to an O-R XMLType Table*

```
INSERT INTO contact_or_tbl
    values(xdburitype('/public/contact/xml/john_smith.xml').getXML().
createschemabasedxml('http://xmlbook.com/sample/contact_annotated.xsd'));
```

For an XML document with the *xsi:schemaLocation* or *xsi:noNamespaceSchemaLocation* attribute, you don't need to use the createschemabasedxml() function. The XML insertion to the O-R table is done automatically when the document is loaded to XML DB Repository.

To optimize the performance of O-R tables, we can create B-Tree indexes or function-based indexes on the O-R tables. The following is an example:

Listing 12-6 *Creating B-Tree Index on O-R XMLTypes*

```
create index contact_email_idx on contact_or_tbl (object_value.xmldata.email);
```

Binary XMLType

Binary XML storage is a new XMLType storage format in Oracle Database 11*g*. It is created with the *STORE AS BINARY XML* syntax.

Creating Binary XMLType

The following example creates a binary XMLType column in a relational table (*create_bin_tbl.sql*):

Listing 12-7 *Creating a Binary XML Type Column*

```
CREATE TABLE contact_binary_tbl (id NUMBER, contact XMLType)
XMLType COLUMN contact
STORE AS SECUREFILE
BINARY XML (TABLESPACE USERS
            RETENTION AUTO KEEP_DUPLICATES
            COMPRESS HIGH
            STORAGE (INITIAL 4K NEXT 32K));
```

The binary XML storage is specified using the *XMLType COLUMN [column_name] STORE AS SECUREFILE BINARY XML* syntax. SECUREFILE, which is optional, allows the XMLType to be stored in Oracle *SecureFiles*.

Oracle XML DB Tip: Do I need to store binary XMLType in SecureFiles?

Yes, SecureFiles storage is more efficient to store binary XMLTypes. In addition, with SecureFiles storage, you have options to manage the storage. For example, you can specify the RETENTION AUTO KEEP_DUPLICATES option to keep duplicate documents, and you can compress the documents with the COMPRESS HIGH option.

In this example, the XMLType column *contact* is stored in the *USERS* tablespace, with initial storage set at 4KB. An additional 32KB of storage will be allocated when the initial 4KB proves insufficient. In the following listing, we create a binary XMLType object table (*create_bin_xtbl.sql*).

Listing 12-8 *Creating a Binary XMLType Table*

```
CREATE TABLE contact_binary_xtbl OF XMLType
XMLType STORE AS SECUREFILE
BINARY XML (TABLESPACE USERS
            RETENTION AUTO KEEP_DUPLICATES
            COMPRESS HIGH
            STORAGE (INITIAL 4K NEXT 32K));
```

Binary XML storage can be associated with one or multiple XML schemas. Here we register the following XML schema as we did in Listing 2-8 (*register_xsd.sql*):

Listing 12-9 *Registering XML Schema for Binary XMLTypes*

```
BEGIN
DBMS_XMLSCHEMA.registerSchema('http://localhost:8081/public/contact/contact.xsd',
XDBUriType('/public/contact/contact.xsd'),
LOCAL=>true,
GENTYPES=>false,
GENBEAN=>false,
GENTABLES=>false,
FORCE=>true,
OWNER=>'XMLDEMO',
OPTIONS=>DBMS_XMLSCHEMA.REGISTER_BINARYXML);
END;
/
```

Note that in this example GENTYPES is set to *false* to turn off creating object types. To check the registered XML schema, run the following command (*check_xsd.sql*):

Listing 12-10 *Checking Registered XML Schema*

```
SELECT schema_url FROM user_xml_schemas;

SELECT dbms_metadata.get_ddl('XMLSCHEMA', 'http://localhost:8081/public/contact/
contact.xsd') FROM dual;
```

The XML schema–based binary XMLType table can be created as follows (*create_bin_xstbl.sql*):

Listing 12-11 *Creating an XML Schema–based Binary XMLType Table*

```
CREATE TABLE contact_binary_xstbl OF XMLType
XMLType STORE AS SECUREFILE
BINARY XML (TABLESPACE USERS
            RETENTION AUTO KEEP_DUPLICATES
            COMPRESS HIGH
            STORAGE (INITIAL 4K NEXT 32K))
XMLSCHEMA "http://localhost:8081/public/contact/contact.xsd"
ELEMENT "contact";
```

With XML schema defined along with the XMLType, the XML documents to be stored in the *contact_binary_xstbl* table need to conform to the registered XML schema (*http://localhost:8081/public/contact/contact.xsd*). Oracle XML DB uses the XML schema to encode the stored documents into binary XML format and validate the documents.

Oracle XML DB Tip: Does Oracle XML DB perform XML Schema validation for all XML Schema–based XMLTypes?

Yes, the XML Schema validation will be performed, but it is a LAX and not STRICT XML Schema validation. LAX XML Schema validation doesn't validate the data types.

To enforce XML Schema restriction without limiting to a specific XML schema, you can use ANY SCHEMA storage option or simply ignore the XML schema setup (*create_bin_anyxsd_xstbl.sql*):

Listing12-12 *Creating an XML Schema-based Binary XMLType Table Allowing ANYSCHEMA*

```
CREATE TABLE contact_binary_anyxsd_xstbl OF XMLType
XMLType STORE AS SECUREFILE
BINARY XML (TABLESPACE USERS
            RETENTION AUTO KEEP_DUPLICATES
            COMPRESS HIGH
            STORAGE (INITIAL 4K NEXT 32K))
ALLOW ANYSCHEMA;
```

There are other options, including ALL NONSCHEMA, ALL ANYSCHEMA, and NONSCHEMA. You can find more information in *Oracle XML DB Developer's Guide.*

To check the binary XMLType table storage details, run the following command:

```
SELECT dbms_metadata.get_ddl('TABLE','CONTACT_BINARY_XSTBL') FROM dual;
```

To insert XML data into the binary XML table, we can use the XML DB Repository resources and do batch insert:

```
INSERT INTO contact_binary_xstbl
SELECT xdburitype(a.any_path).getxml()
FROM resource_view a
WHERE under_path(a.res,'/public/contact/xml')=1;
```

This command inserts the contact XML files in the */public/contact/xml* directory to the *contact_binary_xstbl* table.

You can calculate the size of each contact file stored in the binary XMLType table as follows (*check_bin_xmltype_size.sql*):

Listing 12-13 *Checking Binary XMLType Storage Size*

```
SELECT dbms_lob.getlength(xmldata) FROM contact_binary_xstbl;
```

You can estimate the total size of the binary XMLType table as follows (*check_bin_xmltype_total_size.sql*):

```
SELECT sum(dbms_lob.getlength(xmldata)) FROM contact_binary_xstbl;
```

Partitioning Binary XMLType

In Oracle Database 11*g*, Oracle XML DB offers three types of XMLType partitions: *range, hash,* and *list*. The *range* partition maps rows to partitions based on the ranges of column values. The *hash* partition maps rows to partitions based on a hash value of the partition key (normally a table column value). The *list* partition is defined by listing the values in a column that are to be assigned to a partition.

Let's look at an example of range partition on binary XMLTypes. In this example, we need to create a *virtual column* using XQuery to specify the partition ranges.

First, we need to create database tablespaces to store the partitioned XMLType data as follows (*create_ts.sql*):

```
CREATE TABLESPACE cpart1
DATAFILE 'd:\temp\cpart01.dbf' SIZE 10M
BLOCKSIZE 8192
EXTENT MANAGEMENT LOCAL UNIFORM SIZE 256K
SEGMENT SPACE MANAGEMENT AUTO
ONLINE;

CREATE TABLESPACE cpart2
DATAFILE 'd:\temp\cpart02.dbf' SIZE 10M
BLOCKSIZE 8192
EXTENT MANAGEMENT LOCAL UNIFORM SIZE 256K
SEGMENT SPACE MANAGEMENT AUTO
ONLINE;

CREATE TABLESPACE cpart3
DATAFILE 'd:\temp\cpart03.dbf' SIZE 10M
BLOCKSIZE 8192
EXTENT MANAGEMENT LOCAL UNIFORM SIZE 256K
SEGMENT SPACE MANAGEMENT AUTO
ONLINE;
```

Make sure that you update the paths of tablespace files in this SQL script based on your system setup.

Next, we can create the partitioned binary XMLType table as follows (*create_partitioned_bin_xtbl.sql*):

Listing 12-14 *Using Binary XMLType Range Partitioning*

```
CREATE TABLE contact_partitioned_xtbl OF XMLType
XMLType STORE AS SECUREFILE BINARY XML
VIRTUAL COLUMNS
 (contact_last_name AS (XMLCast(XMLQuery('/contact/last_name'
```

```
                                       PASSING OBJECT_VALUE RETURNING CONTENT)
                                 AS VARCHAR2(100))))
PARTITION BY RANGE (contact_last_name)
 (PARTITION contactA_G VALUES LESS THAN ('G%') TABLESPACE cpart1,
  PARTITION contactG_S VALUES LESS THAN ('S%') TABLESPACE cpart2,
  PARTITION contactS_Z VALUES LESS THAN (MAXVALUE) TABLESPACE cpart3);
```

In this example, we partition *contact_partitioned_xtbl* using the *<last_name>* element content and divide the content using the first character of the last name. XQuery is used to retrieve the last name values. The table is created as follows:

```
SQL> desc contact_partitioned_xtbl;
 Name                                      Null?    Type
 ----------------------------------------- -------- ----
TABLE of SYS.XMLTYPE STORAGE BINARY
```

Note that you wouldn't see the defined *virtual column* in the table description. We can insert the XML document into this partitioned table as follows (*insert_data_to_partitioned_bin_xtbl.sql*):

```
INSERT INTO contact_partitioned_xtbl
SELECT xdburitype(a.any_path).getxml()
FROM resource_view a
WHERE under_path(a.res,'/public/contact/xml')=1;
```

XMLIndex on Binary XMLType

It's important to create *XMLIndex* for binary XMLTypes. XMLIndex builds indexes based on XPaths. The following is an example (*create_xmlindex.sql*):

Listing 12-15 *Creating XMLIndex on Binary XMLType*

```
CREATE INDEX contact_xmlindex_idx ON contact_partitioned_xtbl (OBJECT_VALUE)
INDEXTYPE IS XDB.XMLIndex
PARAMETERS ('PATH TABLE contact_idx_path_table')
LOCAL;
```

Oracle XML DB Tip: Why do I get the *ORA-30978: The XML Index is not locally partitioned* error?

When creating XMLIndex on partitioned binary XMLTypes, you need to specify the LOCAL parameter; otherwise, you get the following error:

```
ERROR at line 1:
ORA-29958: fatal error occurred in the execution of ODCIINDEXCREATE routine
ORA-30978: The XML Index is not locally partitioned.
```

When defining XMLIndex, you need to specify a *path table*. XMLIndex uses the path table to store the indexes. In the example, the path table is the *contact_idx_path_table* table:

```
SQL> desc contact_idx_path_table;
 Name                                      Null?    Type
 ----------------------------------------- -------- ------------------
 RID                                                ROWID
 PATHID                                             RAW(8)
 ORDER_KEY                                          RAW(1000)
 LOCATOR                                            RAW(2000)
 VALUE                                              VARCHAR2(4000)
```

Each index record includes a row id (*RID*), an XPath (with *PATHID*), a locator (*LOCATOR*) to access document fragments, an order key (*ORDER_KEY*) to record the hierarchical position of the node in the XML document, and a text value of the XML node. Note that the text value is in VARCHR2(4000) with limited content size.

By default, XMLIndex creates an index on all of the possible XPath expressions. In practice, you normally need to limit the index to a set of XPaths. This reduces the index space, simplifies the index maintenance, and improves the query performance. There are two ways to specify the XPath expressions for XMLIndex:

- **Exclusion** Include all of the default XPath expressions but exclude the specified XPaths.
- **Inclusion** Exclude all of the default XPath expressions but include the specified XPaths.

The following example indexes only a set of XPaths (*create_xmlindex_inclusion.sql*):

```
CREATE INDEX contact_xmlindex_idx ON contact_partitioned_xtbl (OBJECT_VALUE)
INDEXTYPE IS XDB.XMLIndex
PARAMETERS ('PATH TABLE contact_idx_path_table
             PATHS (INCLUDE (/contact/first_name
                             /contact/email))')
LOCAL;
```

XMLIndex is a domain index. Therefore, you can create one XMLIndex per XMLType table. To review the index details, run the following command (*check_xmlindex_inclusion.sql*):

```
SELECT DBMS_METADATA.GET_DDL('INDEX', 'CONTACT_XMLINDEX_IDX') from dual;
```

To add an XPath to the XMLIndex, run the following command (*add_path_to_xmlindex.sql*):

```
ALTER INDEX contact_xmlindex_idx PARAMETERS ('PATHS (INCLUDE ADD(/contact/
last_name))');
```

Note that this is not an index rebuild. For a partitioned table, you have to rebuild the index one partition at a time. Therefore, for a global change (for all partitions), we use ALTER INDEX instead.

Managing XML DB Storage

In Oracle XML DB, you need to manage the registered XML schemas, XMLType tables, and XMLType views. All of them are listed in the database directories.

Directory	Description
DBA_XML_TABLES	Lists all XMLType tables in the database
USER_XML_TABLES	Lists all XMLType tables owned by the current user
ALL_XML_TABLES	Lists all XMLType tables usable by the current user.
DBA_XML_TAB_COLS	Lists all XMLType table columns in the database.
USER_XML_TAB_COLS	Lists all XMLType table columns in tables owned by the current user.
ALL_XML_TAB_COLS	Lists all XMLType table columns in tables usable by the current user.

TABLE 12-2. *XMLType Tables and Columns*

XMLType Tables and Columns

Table 12-2 lists the directories summarizing the XMLType tables and columns.

You can run the following SQL command after logging in to SYS user (as SYSDBA) to list all of the XMLType tables (*check_xmltype_tables.sql*):

```
SELECT owner,storage_type,count(*) "TOTAL"
FROM dba_xml_tables
GROUP by owner,storage_type;
```

An example output is

```
XDB                           CLOB                      1
XMLDEMO                       OBJECT-RELATIONAL         4
XDB                           OBJECT-RELATIONAL        24
XDB                           BINARY                   15
```

From the report shown, in this example database, we have 1 CLOB XMLType table, 28 object-relational XMLType tables, and 15 binary XMLType tables in XDB user. Outside the XDB user, the XMLDEMO user has created 4 object-relational XMLType tables. Let's look at these tables in detail:

```
SELECT owner, table_name ,storage_Type
FROM DBA_XML_TABLES
WHERE owner='XMLDEMO';
```

The example result is

```
XMLDEMO                          CONTACT_BINARY_ANYXSD_XSTBL    BINARY
XMLDEMO                          CONTACT_XTBL                   BINARY
XMLDEMO                          CONTACT_BINARY_XSTBL           BINARY
```

We can also check the XMLType columns in SYS (*check_xmltype_table_cols.sql*):

```
SELECT owner,storage_type,count(*) "TOTAL"
FROM DBA_XML_TAB_COLS
GROUP BY owner,storage_type;
```

An example output is

```
ORDDATA                         CLOB                         9
XDB                             CLOB                         6
XMLDEMO                         CLOB                         1
APEX_030200                     CLOB                         5
MDSYS                           CLOB                        24
SYS                             CLOB                         4
ORDSYS                          CLOB                         9
8 rows selected.
```

Let's look at the XMLDEMO user specifically:

```
SELECT owner, table_name ,storage_Type
FROM DBA_XML_TAB_COLS
WHERE owner='XMLDEMO';
```

The example result is

```
OWNER                          TABLE_NAME                     STORAGE_TYPE
------------------------------ ------------------------------ --------------
XMLDEMO                          CONTACT_BINARY_TBL             BINARY
XMLDEMO                          CONTACT_XTBL                   CLOB
```

You can change the script listed earlier to the directory tables starting with USER_* and ALL_* to find out the XMLType tables or columns owned by the current user and usable by the current user.

XMLType Views

There are a set of directories summarizing the XMLType views and XMLType view columns that are part of relational table views, as listed in Table 12-3.

Directory	Description
DBA_XML_VIEWS	Lists all XMLType views in the system.
USER_XML_VIEWS	Lists all XMLType views owned by the current user.
ALL_XML_VIEWS	Lists all XMLType views usable by the current user.
DBA_XML_VIEW_COLS	Lists all XMLType view columns in the system.
USER_XML_VIEW_COLS	Lists all XMLType view columns in views owned by the current user.
ALL_XML_VIEW_COLS	Lists all XMLType view columns in views usable by the current user.

TABLE 12-3. *XMLType Views and Columns*

Let's run the report in SYS with the following code (*check_xmltype_view.sql*):

```
SELECT owner,count(*) "TOTAL"
FROM dba_xml_views
GROUP by owner;
```

An example output is

```
XMLDEMO                                         1
```

To check the XML view columns (*check_xmltype_view_col.sql*):

```
SELECT owner,count(*) "TOTAL"
FROM DBA_XML_VIEW_COLS
GROUP BY owner;
```

An example output is

```
XMLDEMO                                         1
SYS                                             7
```

XML Schemas

After you have registered XML schemas, the XML schema registries are kept in the database directories listed in Table 12-4.

We can check the schemas using the following SQL command (*check_xmlschemas.sql*):

```
SELECT owner,count(*) "TOTAL"
FROM dba_xml_schemas
GROUP by owner;
```

The report looks like the following:

```
XMLDEMO                                2
MDSYS                                  4
EXFSYS                                 2
ORDSYS                                19
XDB                                   25
SYS                                   43
```

We have discussed how to check the XML schema details in Listing 12-10.

Directory	**Description**
DBA_XML_SCHEMAS	Lists all registered XML schemas in the system.
USER_XML_SCHEMAS	Lists all registered XML schemas owned by the current user.
ALL_XML_SCHEMAS	Lists all registered XML schemas usable by the current user.

TABLE 12-4. *XML Schema Management Directories*

XML DB Repository

You can check the XML DB Repository resources' details using the following SQL command (*check_xdbrepository.sql*):

```
SELECT distinct(a.username) "USER",count (r.xmldata) "TOTAL"
FROM dba_users a, xdb.xdb$resource r
WHERE sys_op_rawtonum (extractvalue (value(r),'/Resource/OwnerID/text()'))
=a.USER_ID
GROUP BY a.username;
```

The example output is

```
XMLDEMO                          1
MDSYS                            9
EXFSYS                           3
ORDSYS                          22
XDB                             28
SYS                          13342
```

XML Indexes

Oracle XML DB XML indexes are recorded in the database directories listed in Table 12-5.
The directory provides key XML index information:

```
SQL> desc DBA_XML_INDEXES
 Name                                      Null?    Type
 ----------------------------------------- -------- --------------------
 INDEX_OWNER                               NOT NULL VARCHAR2(30)
 INDEX_NAME                                NOT NULL VARCHAR2(30)
 TABLE_OWNER                               NOT NULL VARCHAR2(30)
 TABLE_NAME                                NOT NULL VARCHAR2(30)
 TYPE                                               VARCHAR2(10)
 INDEX_TYPE                                         VARCHAR2(27)
 PATH_TABLE_NAME                                    VARCHAR2(30)
 PARAMETERS                                         XMLTYPE
 ASYNC                                              VARCHAR2(9)
 STALE                                              VARCHAR2(5)
 PEND_TABLE_NAME                                    VARCHAR2(30)
 EX_OR_INCLUDE                                      VARCHAR2(8)
```

Directory	Description
DBA_XML_INDEXES	Lists all registered XML indexes in the system.
USER_XML_INDEXES	Lists all registered XML indexes owned by the current user.
ALL_XML_INDEXES	Lists all registered XML indexes usable by the current user.

TABLE 12-5. *Database Directories for XML Indexes*

An example summary review is

```
SELECT index_owner,type,count(*) "TOTAL"
FROM dba_xml_indexes
GROUP BY index_owner,type;
INDEX_OWNER                    TYPE            TOTAL
------------------------------ ---------- ----------
XMLDEMO                        BINARY              1
XDB                            BINARY              3
```

Summary

In this chapter, we have reviewed the XML storage options in Oracle XML DB and briefly discussed how to manage XML storage. In Oracle Database 11*g*, the new binary XMLType provides a compact storage format optimized for XML processing.

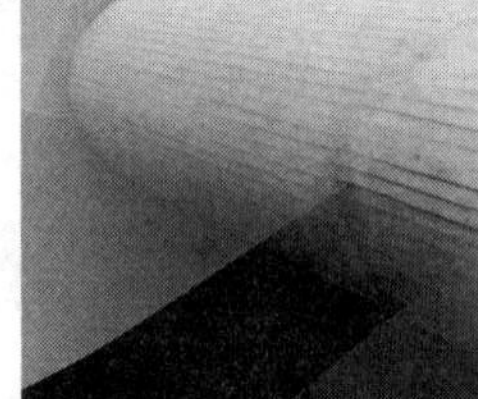

CHAPTER 13

XML DB Backup and Recovery

In Oracle Database 11*g*, you can back up XML documents stored in Oracle XML DB using Oracle Recovery Manager (RMAN) and the Oracle database *export/import* utilities. In this chapter, let's review these approaches, go over the setup steps, and explain the differences.

Back Up XML DB with RMAN

RMAN is the recommended solution to back up Oracle XML DB. RMAN provides comprehensive backup and recovery support for all Oracle data, including XMLTypes. Let's go through the basic steps to run RMAN.

To set up RMAN, we first need to start the RMAN client with the *rman* command:

```
D:\>rman
Recovery Manager: Release 11.2.0.2.0 - Production on Wed Jun 2 20:21:47 2010
Copyright (c) 1982, 2009, Oracle and/or its affiliates.  All rights reserved.
RMAN>
```

Then connect from the RMAN client to the target Oracle database using the *connect target* command. The following is an example:

```
RMAN> connect target sys@orcl11g
target database Password:
connected to target database: ORCL11G (DBID=815923617)
```

The Oracle Net service name is used to specify the target databases. The names can be found in the *$ORACLE_HOME/NETWORK/admin/tnsnames.ora* file ($ORACLE_HOME refers to the Oracle database home directory). In this example, we connect from RMAN to the target database, the *ORCL11G* database instance.

Back Up in NOARCHIVE Log Mode

After connecting to the target database, we can then use the RMAN *backup* command to back up the Oracle database. If the database is running in NOARCHIVE log mode, to have a consistent database backup, we need to shut down the database and start it in the *mounted* status.

Oracle Database Tip: How do I check if the Oracle database is running in archive log mode?

You can run the following command in SYS user:

```
SQL> archive log list;
Database log mode              No Archive Mode
Automatic archival             Disabled
Archive destination            USE_DB_RECOVERY_FILE_DEST
Oldest online log sequence     3
Current log sequence           5
```

Here are the steps:

```
RMAN> shutdown immediate;
using target database control file instead of recovery catalog
database closed
database dismounted
Oracle instance shut down

RMAN> startup mount
connected to target database (not started)
Oracle instance started
database mounted
Total System Global Area     535662592 bytes
Fixed Size                     1375792 bytes
Variable Size                398459344 bytes
Database Buffers             130023424 bytes
Redo Buffers                   5804032 bytes
```

We first shut down the target database and start it again in the *mounted* mode. Then, we can start the backup process by running the *backup* command:

```
RMAN> backup database;
Starting backup at 02-JUN-10
allocated channel: ORA_DISK_1
channel ORA_DISK_1: SID=133 device type=DISK
channel ORA_DISK_1: starting full datafile backup set
channel ORA_DISK_1: specifying datafile(s) in backup set
input datafile file number=00001 name=D:\APP\JIWANG\ORADATA\ORCL11G\SYSTEM01
.DBF
input datafile file number=00002 name=D:\APP\JIWANG\ORADATA\ORCL11G\SYSAUX01
.DBF
input datafile file number=00003 name=D:\APP\JIWANG\ORADATA\ORCL11G\UNDOTBS01
.DBF
input datafile file number=00005 name=D:\APP\JIWANG\ORADATA\ORCL11G\XDB01.DBF
input datafile file number=00004 name=D:\APP\JIWANG\ORADATA\ORCL11G\USERS01
.DBF
input datafile file number=00006 name=D:\APP\JIWANG\ORADATA\ORCL11G\
FLOW_1044606
354098968.DBF
channel ORA_DISK_1: starting piece 1 at 02-JUN-10
channel ORA_DISK_1: finished piece 1 at 02-JUN-10
piece handle=D:\APP\JIWANG\FLASH_RECOVERY_AREA\ORCL11G\BACKUPSET\2010_06_02\
O1_M
F_NNNDF_TAG20100602T221208_60G7DC5V_.BKP tag=TAG20100602T221208 comment=NONE
channel ORA_DISK_1: backup set complete, elapsed time: 00:03:26
channel ORA_DISK_1: starting full datafile backup set
channel ORA_DISK_1: specifying datafile(s) in backup set
including current control file in backup set
including current SPFILE in backup set
channel ORA_DISK_1: starting piece 1 at 02-JUN-10
channel ORA_DISK_1: finished piece 1 at 02-JUN-10
```

```
piece handle=D:\APP\JIWANG\FLASH_RECOVERY_AREA\ORCL11G\BACKUPSET\2010_06_02\
O1_M
F_NCSNF_TAG20100602T221208_60G7LSK2_.BKP tag=TAG20100602T221208 comment=NONE
channel ORA_DISK_1: backup set complete, elapsed time: 00:00:01
Finished backup at 02-JUN-10
```

After the backup, we can open the Oracle database using the following command:

```
RMAN> alter database open
database opened
```

We can look at the backup files in the backup directory or use the RMAN *list* command:

```
RMAN> LIST BACKUP OF DATABASE;
List of Backup Sets
===================
BS Key  Type LV Size       Device Type Elapsed Time Completion Time
------- ---- -- ---------- ----------- ------------ ---------------
1       Full    1.80G      DISK        00:03:24     02-JUN-10
        BP Key: 1   Status: AVAILABLE  Compressed: NO  Tag: TAG20100602T221208
        Piece Name: D:\APP\JIWANG\FLASH_RECOVERY_AREA\ORCL11G\BACKUPSET\2010_06_
02\O1_MF_NNNDF_TAG20100602T221208_60G7DC5V_.BKP
  List of Datafiles in backup set 1
  File LV Type Ckp SCN    Ckp Time  Name
  ---- -- ---- ---------- --------- ----
  1       Full 10455199   02-JUN-10 D:\APP\JIWANG\ORADATA\ORCL11G\SYSTEM01.DBF
  2       Full 10455199   02-JUN-10 D:\APP\JIWANG\ORADATA\ORCL11G\SYSAUX01.DBF
  3       Full 10455199   02-JUN-10 D:\APP\JIWANG\ORADATA\ORCL11G\UNDOTBS01.DBF
  4       Full 10455199   02-JUN-10 D:\APP\JIWANG\ORADATA\ORCL11G\USERS01.DBF
  5       Full 10455199   02-JUN-10 D:\APP\JIWANG\ORADATA\ORCL11G\XDB01.DBF
  6       Full 10455199   02-JUN-10 D:\APP\JIWANG\ORADATA\ORCL11G\FLOW_104460635
4098968.DBF
```

After the full database backup, you can perform incremental database backups to reduce overall backup times. For example, a typical backup strategy is having weekly full backups, followed by daily incremental backups. Refer to *Oracle Backup & Recovery User's Guide* for additional information.

Now let's test if we can perform a recovery process from the created backups. First we need to connect to the target database from RMAN:

```
RMAN> connect target sys@orcl11g
target database Password:
connected to target database: ORCL11G (DBID=815923617, not open)
```

We then need to start the database in mounted mode, and run the RMAN *restore* and *recover* commands:

```
RMAN> startup force mount;
RMAN> restore database;
Starting restore at 04-JUN-10
```

```
using target database control file instead of recovery catalog
allocated channel: ORA_DISK_1
channel ORA_DISK_1: SID=10 device type=DISK
channel ORA_DISK_1: starting datafile backup set restore
channel ORA_DISK_1: specifying datafile(s) to restore from backup set
channel ORA_DISK_1: restoring datafile 00001 to D:\APP\JIWANG\ORADATA\ORCL11G\
SYSTEM01.DBF
channel ORA_DISK_1: restoring datafile 00002 to D:\APP\JIWANG\ORADATA\ORCL11G\
SYSAUX01.DBF
channel ORA_DISK_1: restoring datafile 00003 to D:\APP\JIWANG\ORADATA\ORCL11G\
UNDOTBS01.DBF
channel ORA_DISK_1: restoring datafile 00004 to D:\APP\JIWANG\ORADATA\ORCL11G\
USERS01.DBF
channel ORA_DISK_1: restoring datafile 00005 to D:\APP\JIWANG\ORADATA\ORCL11G\
XDB01.DBF
channel ORA_DISK_1: restoring datafile 00006 to D:\APP\JIWANG\ORADATA\ORCL11G\
FLOW_1044606354098968.DBF
channel ORA_DISK_1: reading from backup piece D:\APP\JIWANG\FLASH_RECOVERY_AREA\
ORCL11G\BACKUPSET\2010_06_02\O1_MF_NNNDF_TAG20100602T221208_60G7DC5V_.BKP
channel ORA_DISK_1: piece handle=D:\APP\JIWANG\FLASH_RECOVERY_AREA\ORCL11G\
BACKUPSET\2010_06_02\O1_MF_NNNDF_TAG20100602T221208_60G7DC5V_.BKP
tag=TAG20100602T221208
channel ORA_DISK_1: restored backup piece 1
channel ORA_DISK_1: restore complete, elapsed time: 00:03:17
Finished restore at 04-JUN-10

RMAN> recover database;
Starting recover at 04-JUN-10
using channel ORA_DISK_1
starting media recovery
archived log for thread 1 with sequence 333 is already on disk as file D:\APP\
JIWANG\ORADATA\ORCL11G\REDO03.LOG
archived log for thread 1 with sequence 334 is already on disk as file D:\APP\
JIWANG\ORADATA\ORCL11G\REDO01.LOG
archived log for thread 1 with sequence 335 is already on disk as file D:\APP\
JIWANG\ORADATA\ORCL11G\REDO02.LOG
RMAN-08187: WARNING: media recovery until SCN 10455199 complete
Finished recover at 04-JUN-10
```

We then open the database:

```
RMAN> alter database open noresetlogs;
database opened
```

Now the backup and recovery are done.

Back Up in Archive Log Mode

For archive log mode backup, we don't need to shut down the database. To make sure the database is running in archive log mode, we can run the *archive log list* command first in SYS user.

Oracle Database Tip: How do I change the database to archive log mode?

We can run the following commands in SYS user:

```
alter system set log_archive_start=TRUE scope=spfile;
SQL> alter system set log_archive_dest_1='location=d:\temp' scope=spfile;
SQL> shutdown immediate;
SQL> startup mount;
SQL> alter database archivelog;
SQL> archive log list;
Database log mode              Archive Mode
Automatic archival             Enabled
Archive destination            d:\temp
Oldest online log sequence     1
Next log sequence to archive   3
Current log sequence           3
SQL> archive log start
SQL>alter database open
```

To back up with archive log mode using RMAN, we follow these steps:

```
RMAN> backup database plus archivelog;
```

This RMAN backup process backs up the database files and the archive log files.

Oracle XML DB data can be fully backed up and recovered with RMAN. We don't need to discuss the details any further. Refer to the *Oracle Backup & Recovery User's Guide* for full details on RMAN functionality, including the *incrementally updated backups*, which allow a backup copy on disk to be quickly refreshed in place using a current incremental backup.

Importing and Exporting XML with Data Pump

Oracle database *export* and *import* utilities are useful to back up XMLType tables and columns. However, *export* and *import* can't back up XML DB Repository data and its metadata, nor can they back up the XML DB management data, such as the registered XDB schemas, even in a full database export. Therefore, the utilities can only be used for XMLType table export/import.

Oracle XML DB Tip: Is XML Schema–based XMLType supported by Oracle Database 11*g* Data Pump export/import utilities?

Yes, it is supported in Oracle Database 11*g*.

However, the *export* and *import* utilities are still useful if you want to back up or transport content from XMLType tables. In Oracle Database 11*g*, we will use Oracle Data Pump import (*impdp*) and export (*expdp*) utilities for Oracle XML DB, which offer better performance. Let's learn how to use them.

Oracle XML DB Tip: Why can't I import/export data from older versions of XML DB?
Oracle Data Pump 11*g* utilities only support XMLTypes in Oracle Database 11*g*.

XMLType Stored as a Table Column

We have discussed that in Oracle Database 11*g* it is a good practice to store XML in binary XMLTypes. Therefore, we only discuss the import and export of binary XMLType tables and columns.

Log in as SYS user and create a new user *xmldemo_backup* schema to run the examples in this chapter (*create_user.sql*):

```
create user xmldemo_backup identified by xmldemo_backup;
grant connect,resource to xmldemo_backup;
```

We will use the database directory *xmlbook_dir* created earlier for data import and export and grant the new *xmldemo* and *xmldemo_backup* users read and write privileges:

```
grant write on directory xmlbook_dir to xmldemo;
grant read on directory xmlbook_dir to xmldemo_backup;
```

Let's create a binary XMLType column first and check its content (*create_binary_xml_column.sql*):

```
create table contact_backup_tbl (id number, profile xmltype)
xmltype profile store as binary xml;

insert into contact_backup_tbl values(1, '<contact>
 <first_name>John</first_name>
 <last_name>Smith</last_name>
</contact>');

set long 10000
column id format 99
column profile format a35
select * from contact_tbl;
```

We have the following content:

```
 ID PROFILE
--- -----------------------------------
  1 <contact>
      <first_name>John</first_name>
      <last_name>Smith</last_name>
    </contact>
```

Now we export this table using the *export* utility:

```
d:\>expdp xmldemo/xmldemo dumpfile=contact_tbl.dmp directory=xmlbook_dir
tables=contact_backup_tbl
Export: Release 11.2.0.2.0 - Production on Thu Jun 3 08:15:17 2010
Copyright (c) 1982, 2009, Oracle and/or its affiliates.  All rights reserved.
Connected to: Oracle Database 11g Enterprise Edition Release 11.2.0.2.0 -
Production
With the Partitioning, OLAP, Data Mining and Real Application Testing options
Starting "XMLDEMO"."SYS_EXPORT_TABLE_01":  xmldemo/******** dumpfile=contact_
backup_tbl.dm
p directory=xmlbook_dir tables=contact_backup_tbl
Estimate in progress using BLOCKS method...
Processing object type TABLE_EXPORT/TABLE/TABLE_DATA
Total estimation using BLOCKS method: 128 KB
Processing object type TABLE_EXPORT/TABLE/TABLE
. . exported "XMLDEMO"."CONTACT_BACKUP_TBL"          5.804 KB       1 rows
Master table "XMLDEMO"."SYS_EXPORT_TABLE_01" successfully loaded/unloaded
******************************************************************************
Dump file set for XMLDEMO.SYS_EXPORT_TABLE_01 is:
  D:\TEMP\CONTACT_XTBL.DMP
Job "XMLDEMO"."SYS_EXPORT_TABLE_01" successfully completed at 08:15:36
```

Oracle Database Tip: Multiple table import/export

If you have multiple tables, you can list them as `tables=Table1, Table2...`.

Now, we can import this data to the backup database schema *xmldemo_backup*:

```
d:\>Impdp xmldemo_backup/xmldemo_backup directory=xmlbook_dir dumpfile=contact_
backup_tbl.dmp remap_schema=xmldemo:xmldemo_backup
Import: Release 11.2.0.2.0 - Production on Thu Jun 3 10:15:46 2010
Copyright (c) 1982, 2009, Oracle and/or its affiliates.  All rights reserved.
Connected to: Oracle Database 11g Enterprise Edition Release 11.2.0.2.0 -
Production
With the Partitioning, OLAP, Data Mining and Real Application Testing options
Master table "XMLDEMO_BACKUP"."SYS_IMPORT_FULL_01" successfully loaded/unloaded
Starting "XMLDEMO_BACKUP"."SYS_IMPORT_FULL_01":  xmldemo_backup/********
directory=x
mlbook_dir dumpfile=contact_tbl.dmp remap_schema=xmldemo:xmldemo_backup
Processing object type TABLE_EXPORT/TABLE/TABLE
Processing object type TABLE_EXPORT/TABLE/TABLE_DATA
. . imported "XMLDEMO_BACKUP"."CONTACT_TBL"                  5.804 KB       1
rows
Job "XMLDEMO_BACKUP"."SYS_IMPORT_FULL_01" successfully completed at 10:15:56
```

Oracle Database Tip: Why do I get the *object not found* error when importing data?

When importing data, don't include the *tables* option if there is no table in the new schema. Otherwise, you will get the following error:

```
Impdp xmldemo_backup/xmldemo_backup tables=contact_backup_tbl
directory=xmlbook_dir dumpfile=contact_backup_xtbl.dmp remap_
schema=xmldemo:xmldemo_backup
......
ORA-39002: invalid operation
ORA-39166: Object XMLDEMO_BACKUP.CONTACT_BACKUP_TBL was not found.
```

We can check the table data by logging in to *xmldemo_backup*:

```
SQL> connect xmldemo_backup/xmldemo_backup
Connected.
SQL> select * from contact_backup_tbl;
 ID PROFILE
--- -----------------------------------
  1 <contact>
      <first_name>John</first_name>
      <last_name>Smith</last_name>
    </contact>
```

The table import and export is successful.

XMLType Tables

For non-XML-schema-based binary XMLType tables, we have to do something different. For the following table created in *xmldemo*:

```
create table contact_backup_xtbl of xmltype
xmltype store as binary xml

insert into contact_backup_xtbl values('<contact>
 <first_name>John</first_name>
 <last_name>Smith</last_name>
</contact>');
```

we export with the following command:

```
d:\>expdp xmldemo/xmldemo dumpfile=contact_backup_xtbl.dmp grants=y
directory=xmlbook_dir tables=contact_backup_xtbl
```

However, we can't directly load this to the *xmldemo_backup* schema. We will get an error with direct import:

```
d:\>Impdp xmldemo_backup/xmldemo_backup directory=xmlbook_dir
dumpfile=contact_backup_xtbl.dmp remap_schema=xmldemo:xmldemo_backup
...
```

```
ORA-39083: Object type TABLE:"XMLDEMO_BACKUP"."CONTACT_BACKUP_XTBL" failed to
create with error:
ORA-02304: invalid object identifier literal
```

This is because the object-relational table has a unique object id (OID) in the Oracle database and is exported. For export/import in different databases, this is acceptable. However, when importing to the same database, we need to create the table and perform table-content-only import. After we create the *contact_backup_xtbl* table in the *xmldemo_backup* schema, we can run the following command:

```
d:\>Impdp xmldemo_backup/xmldemo_backup directory=xmlbook_dir
dumpfile=contact_backup_xtbl.dmp remap_schema=xmldemo:xmldemo_backup
content=data_only
```

XML Schema–based XMLType Tables and Columns

Using the example table in Listing 2-9, we can create the following XML Schema–based binary XML table:

```
SQL> desc contact_xsxtbl;
 Name                                      Null?    Type
 ----------------------------------------- -------- ----------------------------
TABLE of SYS.XMLTYPE(XMLSchema "http://xmlbook.com/sample/contact.xsd" Element
"contact") STORAGE BINARY
```

To export the XML schema information, you need to grant the user the EXP_FULL_DATABASE privilege by logging in as SYS and running the following command:

```
SQ> grant EXP_FULL_DATABASE to xmldemo;
```

Let's do an export of the data:

```
d:\>expdp xmldemo/xmldemo dumpfile=contact_xsxtbl.dmp grants=y
directory=xmlbook_dir tables=contact_xstbl
Export: Release 11.2.0.2.0 - Production on Fri Jun 4 00:24:12 2010
Copyright (c) 1982, 2009, Oracle and/or its affiliates.  All rights reserved.
Connected to: Oracle Database 11g Enterprise Edition Release 11.2.0.2.0 -
Production
With the Partitioning, OLAP, Data Mining and Real Application Testing options
Legacy Mode Active due to the following parameters:
Legacy Mode Parameter: "grants=TRUE" Location: Command Line, ignored.
Legacy Mode has set reuse_dumpfiles=true parameter.
Starting "XMLDEMO"."SYS_EXPORT_TABLE_01":  xmldemo/******** dumpfile=contact_
xstbl.d
mp directory=xmlbook_dir tables=contact_xsxtbl reuse_dumpfiles=true
Estimate in progress using BLOCKS method...
Processing object type TABLE_EXPORT/TABLE/TABLE_DATA
Total estimation using BLOCKS method: 192 KB
Processing object type TABLE_EXPORT/TABLE/TABLE
Processing object type TABLE_EXPORT/TABLE/STATISTICS/TABLE_STATISTICS
```

```
. . exported "XMLDEMO"."CONTACT_XSTBL"                      6.093 KB       1 rows
Master table "XMLDEMO"."SYS_EXPORT_TABLE_01" successfully loaded/unloaded
******************************************************************************
Dump file set for XMLDEMO.SYS_EXPORT_TABLE_01 is:
  D:\TEMP\CONTACT_XSTBL.DMP
Job "XMLDEMO"."SYS_EXPORT_TABLE_01" successfully completed at 00:24:20
```

Since we're running the example on the same database, we have to create the table on the target user schema and then do table-content-only import. If we are importing to a separate database, we don't have to do this. We register the XML schema and create the table in *xmldemo_backup*. Then, we import the data shown as follows:

```
d:\>impdp xmldemo_backup/xmldemo_backup dumpfile=contact_xstbl.dmp
directory=xmlbook_dir content=data_only remap_schema=xmldemo:xmldemo_backup

Import: Release 11.2.0.2.0 - Production on Fri Jun 4 00:25:02 2010
Copyright (c) 1982, 2009, Oracle and/or its affiliates.  All rights reserved.
Connected to: Oracle Database 11g Enterprise Edition Release 11.2.0.2.0 -
Production
With the Partitioning, OLAP, Data Mining and Real Application Testing options
Master table "XMLDEMO_BACKUP"."SYS_IMPORT_FULL_01" successfully loaded/unloaded
Starting "XMLDEMO_BACKUP"."SYS_IMPORT_FULL_01":  xmldemo_backup/********
dumpfile=contact_xstbl.dmp directory=xmlbook_dir content=data_only remap_
schema=xmldemo:xmldemo_backup
Processing object type TABLE_EXPORT/TABLE/TABLE_DATA
. . imported "XMLDEMO_BACKUP"."CONTACT_XSTBL"               6.093 KB       1
rows
Job "XMLDEMO_BACKUP"."SYS_IMPORT_FULL_01" successfully completed at 00:25:06
```

Similar operations apply for XML Schema–based binary XMLType columns and O-R XMLType table and columns. We will not discuss these in detail in this book.

Summary

Because RMAN provides an easy-to-use approach for backing up all XML DB data and metadata, it is recommended for full XML DB backup. However, if you just need an XMLType table backup, the Data Pump *import* and *export* utilities can be useful.

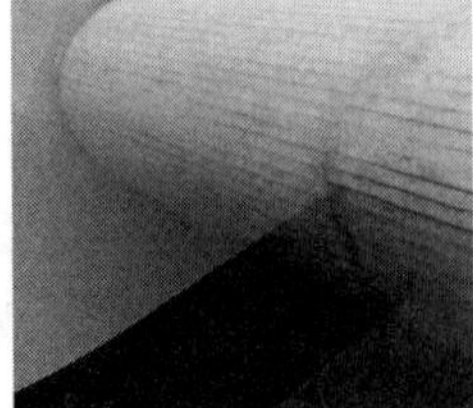

CHAPTER 14

XML DB Security and Performance Tuning

n this chapter, we will discuss two topics: XML DB security and performance tuning. Both of them are important for XML DB applications.

Oracle XML DB Security

In Oracle Database 11*g*, Access Control List (ACL)–based security is set up to prevent unauthorized data access and operations. The ACLs are specified in XML files called ACL files that are stored in the Oracle XML DB Repository. These ACL files include a list of object-level restrictions, called access control entities (ACEs), which are set up based on database users or roles, the database resources, and operations. In this section, we will discuss how to use ACLs to manage users' access to XML DB Repository resources and enable the access to external network services.

XML DB Repository ACLs

FULL ACCESS on all resources within XML DB Repository is granted to the XDBADMIN role. For other database users, before performing any operation on an XML DB Repository resource, privilege checking takes place against the assigned ACL files.

The *system ACL* files supplied by Oracle XML DB (under the */sys/acls* folder) include

- **bootstrap_acl.xml** Grants READ privilege to all users and FULL ACCESS to the XDBADMIN role and DBA.
- **all_all_acl.xml** Grants all privileges to all users.
- **all_owner_acl.xml** Grants all privileges to the resource owner (creator).
- **ro_all_acl.xml** Grants READ privilege to all users.

To check a document or a folder's ACL, run the following command (*check_acl.sql*):

```
select dbms_xdb.getacldocument('/public/contact').getStringVal() result from
dual;
```

An example result follows (*all_all_acl.xml*):

```
RESULT
--------------------------------------------------------------------------------
<acl description="Public:All privileges to PUBLIC"
     xmlns="http://xmlns.oracle.com/xdb/acl.xsd"
     xmlns:xsi="http://www.w3.org/2001/XMLSchema-instance"
xsi:schemaLocation="http://xmlns.oracle.com/xdb/acl.xsd  http://xmlns.oracle
.com/xdb/acl.xsd" shared="true">
  <ace>
    <grant>true</grant>
    <principal>PUBLIC</principal>
    <privilege>
      <all/>
    </privilege>
  </ace>
</acl>
```

The ACL file grants all users (*<principal>PUBLIC</principal>)* the access to the resource and allows all operations on the resource (*<privilege><all/></privilege>*).

To control the XML DB Repository resource access, you can create a new ACL file and assign it to the specific resource. For example, if you only give the read and write privilege of the */public/contact* folder to the XMLDEMO user, you can create the following ACL file by logging in as SYS (as SYSDBA) (*/sys/acls/all_xmldemo_acl.xml*) (*assign_acl.sql*):

```
declare
   v_res Boolean;
begin
   v_res := dbms_xdb.createFolder('/xmldemo');
   v_res := dbms_xdb.createResource('/xmldemo/all_xmldemo_acl.xml',
     '<acl description="READ/WRITE ONLY by XMLDEMO"
      xmlns="http://xmlns.oracle.com/xdb/acl.xsd"
      xmlns:xsi="http://www.w3.org/2001/XMLSchema-instance"
      xsi:schemaLocation="http://xmlns.oracle.com/xdb/acl.xsd
http://xmlns.oracle.com/xdb/acl.xsd" shared="true">
  <ace>
    <grant>true</grant>
    <principal>XMLDEMO</principal>
    <privilege>
      <all/>
    </privilege>
  </ace>
</acl>');
end;
/
```

The XMLDEMO user name needs to be capitalized in SQL commands. Otherwise, you will get the ORA-44416: *Invalid ACL: Unresolved principal 'XMLDEMO'* error.

You can check whether the ACL file is created (*check_xmldemo_acl.sql*):

```
select XDBUriType('/xmldemo/all_xmldemo_acl.xml').getXML() from dual;
```

Then, assign it to the */public/contact* folder (*assign_acl.sql*):

```
begin
  dbms_xdb.setacl('/public/contact', '/xmldemo/all_xmldemo_acl.xml');
end;
/
```

Then only the XMLDEMO user can access the */public/contact* folder. You can refer to *Oracle XML DB Developer's Guide* for other detailed setups on various privilege options.

To delete an ACL file, you first need to remove the references from resource files. Otherwise, you will get the ORA-31052: *Cannot delete ACL with other references* error. For example, to delete the *all_xmldemo_acl.xml* file, you need to perform the following operations (in SYS) (*delete_acl.sql*):

```
begin
  dbms_xdb.setacl('/public/contact', '/sys/acls/all_all_acl.xml');
  dbms_xdb.deleteresource('/xmldemo/all_xmldemo_acl.xml');
end;
/
```

Note that you need to *commit* after the set ACL and delete ACL operations.

Setting Up ACL for Network Services Access

In Oracle Database 11*g*, ACL files are used to manage database users' access to external network services. These ACLs restrict the connection from database servers to external network services via UTL_TCP, UTL_HTTP (including HTTPUriType), UTL_INADDR, UTL_MAIL, and UTL_SMTP.

Oracle Database Tip: Why do I get the ORA-24247: *Network access denied by access control list (ACL)* error?

If you don't have the correct ACL setup for HTTP, TCP, or SMTP access in the Oracle database, you will get the following error:

```
ERROR:
ORA-29273: HTTP request failed
ORA-06512: at "SYS.UTL_HTTP", line 1819
ORA-24247: network access denied by access control list (ACL)
ORA-06512: at "SYS.HTTPURITYPE", line 34
ORA-06512: at "SYS.HTTPURITYPE", line 97
```

Let's learn from an example where we set up the ACLs to access external network services via HTTP. The same setup can be applied to other network services.

First, log in to Oracle Database 11*g* using SYS user (as SYSDBA) to create an ACL file called *http_xmldemo_acl.xml* for the XMLDEMO user using the DBMS_NETWORK_ACL_ADMIN package (*create_http_connect_acl.sql*):

```
begin
  if (dbms_xdb.existsResource('/sys/acls/http_xmldemo_acl.xml')) then
    dbms_xdb.deleteresource('/sys/acls/http_xmldemo_acl.xml');
  end if;
  dbms_network_acl_admin.create_acl(
          acl             => 'http_xmldemo_acl.xml',
          description     => 'HTTP Access',
          principal       => 'XMLDEMO',
          is_grant        => TRUE,
          privilege       => 'connect',
          start_date      => null,
          end_date        => null
        );
end;
/
commit;
```

The *http_xmldemo_acl.xml* ACL file gives the XMLDEMO user the HTTP *connect* privilege with no time restrictions. The *http_xmldemo_acl.xml* file will be stored in the XML DB Repository */sys/acls* folder after we *commit* the SQL operation:

```
SELECT any_path
FROM resource_view
WHERE equals_path(res,'/sys/acls/http_xmldemo_acl.xml')=1;
```

An example result is

```
ANY_PATH
--------------------------------------------------------------------------------
/sys/acls/http_xmldemo_acl.xml
```

The ACL file's content is as follows:

```
select XMLSerialize(content
XMLQuery('declare namespace ns="http://xmlns.oracle.com/xdb/XDBResource
.xsd";(: :)
$r/ns:Resource/ns:Contents/*' passing res
as "r" returning content) as CLOB indent size=2) as content
from resource_view
where any_path='/sys/acls/http_xmldemo_acl.xml';
```

An example result is

```
Content
--------------------------------------------------------------------------------
<a:acl description="HTTP Access" xmlns:a="http://xmlns.oracle.com/xdb/acl.xsd"
xmlns:plsql="http://xmlns.oracle.com/plsql" xmlns:xsi="http://www.w3.org/2001/
XMLSchema-instance" xsi:schemaLocation="http://xmlns.oracle.com/xdb/acl.xsd
http://xmlns.oracle.com/xdb/acl.xsd" shared="true">
  <a:security-class>plsql:network</a:security-class>
  <a:ace>
    <a:grant>true</a:grant>
    <a:principal>XMLDEMO</a:principal>
    <a:privilege>
      <plsql:connect xmlns:plsql="http://xmlns.oracle.com/plsql"/>
    </a:privilege>
  </a:ace>
</a:acl>
```

The next step is to assign the ACL to the XMLDEMO user:

```
begin
  dbms_network_acl_admin.add_privilege(acl =>'http_xmldemo_acl.xml',
    principal =>'XMLDEMO',
    is_grant => true,
    privilege =>'resolve');
end;
/
```

We then need to assign accessible hosts and ports via the created *http_xmldemo_acl.xml* ACL file. We can enable each server access or give all hosts access using "*" as the *host* input:

```
begin
  dbms_network_acl_admin.assign_acl (
  acl => 'http_xmldemo_acl.xml',
  host => 'localhost',
  lower_port => 7777,
  upper_port => 7777);
end;
/
```

We then check the ACL file assigned to database users using the following command:

```
column acl format a25
column principal format a25
column is_grant format a25
select acl, principal, is_grant
from DBA_NETWORK_ACL_PRIVILEGES;
```

The sample result is

```
ACL                              PRINCIPAL              IS_GRANT
-------------------------------- ---------------------- ------------------------
/sys/acls/http_xmldemo_acl.xml    XMLDEMO               true
```

This result confirms that the */sys/acls/http_xmldemo_acl.xml* ACL file is granted to the XMLDEMO user.

We can then query the DBA_NETWORK_ACLS view to find out the access privileges included in the ACL file:

```
column host format a25
column lower_port format 9999
column lower_port format 9999
select host, lower_port, upper_port, aclid
from dba_network_acls
where ACL='/sys/acls/http_xmldemo_acl.xml';
```

An example result is

```
HOST                 LOWER_PORT  UPPER_PORT  ACLID
-------------------- ----------  ----------  --------------------------------
localhost            7777        7777        8CAA06342F754E0D87247C8A7D646BDB
```

In this example, the XMLDEMO user can access only the *localhost* using ports *7777*. This means that if you call a different website or call *localhost* with a port other than 7777, it will again fail with the ORA-24247 error. You can see that the ACL security restriction can be set at the granular level.

Next, connect to the XMLDEMO user and run the following SQL commands (*run_httpuritype_query.sql*):

Listing 14-1 *Retrieving Full-Text Search in RSS Feed*

```
set define off
select HTTPUriType('http://localhost:7777/search/query/feed.jsp?group=PO+in+
XML&q=lawrence+liu').getXML() from dual;
```

We will get the RSS feed (in XML) from the Oracle SES search application, which is set up in Chapter 10.

You can try another HTTPUriType query from the XMLDEMO user (*run_http_query_2.sql*):

```
set define off
select HTTPUriType('http://pressroom.oracle.com/search/feed?keyword=product:
%22database%22&group=PressReleases&start=1').getXML() from dual;
```

This is a website providing RSS feeds. To access the new service we need to add access to the website server in ACL (in SYS user as SYSDBA) (*grant_pressroom_access.sql*):

```
begin
  dbms_network_acl_admin.assign_acl (
  acl => 'http_xmldemo_acl.xml',
  host => 'pressroom.oracle.com',
  lower_port => 22,
  upper_port => 85);
end;
/
```

When running the SQL command behind a firewall, you will need to set up the proxy server access. Otherwise, you will get either the ORA-12535: *TNS: operation timed out* or ORA-29273: *HTTP request failed as the first time* error when making HTTP requests. This includes setting up the proxy in the database connection session and granting the proxy server access in ACL.

To set up the proxy in the database connection session, use the following command:

```
UTL_HTTP.set_proxy('[proxy_name]:[proxy_port]', NULL);
```

The following is an example (*set_proxy.sql*):

```
call UTL_HTTP.set_proxy('www-proxy.xmlbook.com:80', NULL);
```

To add the ACL privileges to access the proxy server, use the following command (*grant_proxy_access.sql*):

```
begin
  dbms_network_acl_admin.assign_acl (
  acl => 'http_xmldemo_acl.xml',
  host => 'www-proxy.xmlbook.com',
  lower_port => 22,
  upper_port => 85);
end;
/
```

In order for APEX applications to have external access via HTTP and other protocols, such as running a report from *HTTUriType* queries, we need to create an ACL for *APEX_030200 user* (*create_apex_acl.sql*):

```
delete from resource_view
where equals_path(res,'/sys/acls/apex_acl.xml')=1;

begin
```

```
  dbms_network_acl_admin.create_acl (
      acl=> 'apex_acl.xml',
      description=> 'http access',
      principal=> 'APEX_030200',
      is_grant=> true,
      privilege=> 'connect',
      start_date=> null,
      end_date=> null);

  dbms_network_acl_admin.add_privilege(acl => 'apex_acl.xml',
      principal => 'APEX_030200',
      is_grant => true,
      privilege => 'resolve');

  dbms_network_acl_admin.assign_acl (
      acl => 'apex_acl.xml',
      host => 'www-proxy.xmlbook.com');
  dbms_network_acl_admin.assign_acl (
      acl => 'apex_acl.xml',
      host => 'localhost');

  dbms_network_acl_admin.assign_acl (
       acl => 'apex_acl.xml',
       host => 'internal-mail-router.xmlbook.com'
       );
end;
/
commit;
```

Note that we give the APEX user the access to the *internal-mail-router.xmlbook.com* server. This is an email server which is used in Chapter 17 to send emails from the APEX applications. We will discuss this in detail in Chapter 17.

Oracle Database Tip: Can I assign an ACL to a database role and then grant the role to the APEX user?

No, you can't grant ACL access to a database role and then grant the database role to the APEX user. You will continue to get the ORA-24247: *Network access denied by access control list (ACL)* error.

Oracle XML DB Performance Tuning

To ensure the effective performance of Oracle XML DB applications, we need to well design the application and allocate proper resources to the application so that it can balance the use of the CPU/memory/disk I/Os resources. In this section, let's summarize performance tuning tips by looking at the key processes that need your attention, and discuss how to optimize their performance. These key processes include

- **Basic XML Processing** Includes XML parsing, transformations, and validations. To gain better performance in your applications, these basic processes are required to be completed quickly while using minimum memory spaces.
- **XML Data Insertion to Database** Is the process during which users bulk-load XML documents into the Oracle database. The goal of performance tuning is to shorten the data loading time.
- **XML Query** Queries XML stored in Oracle XML DB. How to quickly deliver query results is important for this process.

Let's start with the discussion of the basic XML processing.

Basic XML Processing Performance

XML parsing (including creating XMLTypes), transformation, and validations are very basic XML processing steps. The performance tuning is normally done via well-designed XML document format, selected XML storage type or in-memory object format, and the streamlined XML processing. Let's take a closer look.

Having a Simple XML Format

XML format affects the XML processing performance at the fundamental level. The following are some tips.

First, simplify the XML document structure. For example, using XML attributes instead of child XML elements can reduce the depths in an XML tree. Fewer levels of depths can save the XML storage space and the data accessing time.

Second, use consistent XML tag names across XML applications. When the XML documents are stored in Oracle XML DB as binary XMLTypes, you can save the XML storage space. In Oracle XML DB 11*g*, binary XMLTypes store distinct XML tag names in an index table. The indexed IDs are then used to replace the tag names within binary XMLTypes. The smaller set of the tag names means that a smaller storage space is required for the index table. The index lookup process is also faster.

Third, avoid including DTD (Document Type Definition) within each XML document especially when you have a large number of documents sharing the same DTD. When DTD is not used for entity references, it is optional for parsing XML documents. However, when DTD is included in XML documents, it is always parsed and stored with the XML objects. This could introduce big impacts. For example, if each XML document includes a small DTD—let's say 0.5KB—then storing DTDs for 10,000 XML documents would need 5000KB! Therefore, turning off DTD parsing can save the storage space. When you need DTD validation, you can use XDK Java to parse the DTD separately and use setDocType() to perform the DTD validation (refer to Chapter 5). This is more efficient because of avoiding the redundant DTD storage and parsing process.

Fourth, remove whitespaces if not used. Whitespaces can take up significant space if preserved in XMLTypes and DOM objects. Removing them can save space and content accessing time. In Oracle XML DB, all *insignificant whitespaces* are removed by default. You can easily create pretty-formatted XML using XMLSerialize() in SQL or XMLDocument.print() and *XMLSAXSerializer* in Java (refer to Chapter 4) to serialize XML in a pretty-print format.

Oracle XML DB Tip: How can I remove whitespaces?

To remove *insignificant whitespaces* from XML documents with DTDs, you can set up the Oracle XDK DOM parser as follows (*DOMParsingWS.java*):

```
DOMParser.setPreserveWhitespace(false);
```

For the Oracle XDK SAX parser, you need the following (*SAXParsingWS.java*):

```
SAXParser parser = new SAXParser();
parser.setPreserveWhitespace(false);
```

In XSLT, you can remove whitespace by adding *<xsl:strip-space elements="*"/>* in the XSL stylesheet (*contact_position_nws.xsl*):

Listing 14-2 *Removing XML Whitespaces in XSLT*

```
<?xml version="1.0"?>
<xsl:stylesheet version="1.0" xmlns:xsl="http://www.w3.org/1999/XSL/Transform">
   <xsl:output method="xml" indent="yes"/>
   <xsl:strip-space elements="*"/>
   <xsl:template match="*">
      <xsl:element name="{local-name()}">
         <xsl:if test="local-name()='contact'">
            <xsl:attribute name="rownum">
               <xsl:value-of select="position()"/>
            </xsl:attribute>
         </xsl:if>
         <xsl:apply-templates select="@*|node()"/>
      </xsl:element>
   </xsl:template>
</xsl:stylesheet>
```

If you don't want to strip spaces for all XML elements, you can use a comma-delimited string listing the elements in which you'd like to remove insignificant whitespaces:

```
<xsl:strip-space element="contact_groups,xmldb,contact">
```

Choosing XML Storage Types

In Oracle Database 11*g* you need to choose among XMLType storage types to optimize the content storage and query access. When using binary XMLType, you can choose Oracle *SecureFiles* to optimize the storage. In Oracle Database 11*g*, you can partition the XMLType storage tables to allow parallel queries. You can refer to Chapter 12 for more information.

Streamlined XML Processing

In Oracle XML DB, performance is affected by scalability challenges. This is addressed by the binary XMLTypes, Scalable DOM parsing, and SAX XML processing (discussed extensively in Chapters 2, 4, and 12). All of the approaches aim toward streamlining XML processing to minimize memory consumption and shorten the path to traverse XML documents.

Bulk XML Loading Performance

The typical XML document bulk-loading process that requires performance tuning is the loading of large XML documents. In Oracle Database 11*g*, you can use binary XMLTypes. Performance of binary XMLTypes data insertion is optimized for both XMLType tables and XML DB Repository. When bulk-loading XML documents, the indexes updates and the full XML schema validations need to be turned off. These operations can be performed after the data are inserted into the Oracle database.

Additionally, you can break down the large XML documents into a set of small documents. You can streamline the process by using SAX XML parsing. Please refer to Oracle Technology Network for an example of this. In Oracle Database 11*g*, you can also load the big XML document into XML DB Repository first and then use XMLTable() queries to extract the XML content.

XQuery Performance Tuning

In Oracle Database 11*g*, XQuery statements are rewritten by Oracle XML DB before the query executions. Therefore, XQuery performance tuning relies on analyzing the *XQuery rewrite* process and creating proper indexes to optimize the rewritten queries.

> **Oracle XML DB Tip: Which XQuery functions use XMLIndex?**
> There are four XQuery functions using XMLIndex: XMLQuery(), XMLTable(), XMLExists(), and XMLCast().

XQuery Rewrite and Indexing

Oracle XML DB rewrites XQuery in many ways, depending on how XML is stored in the database.

For XMLType views over relational tables and object-relational (O-R) XMLTypes, XQueries are rewritten to SQL queries. In this case, you can use relational table indexes, such as the B-Tree index, to optimize the rewritten SQL queries. You can find an example creating a B-Tree index on O-R XMLTypes in Listing 12-6. When CLOB is used in O-R XMLTypes or XMLType views to store XML document fragments, XQueries accessing those CLOBs are rewritten to XPath expressions. The XPath evaluation optimization requires creating an XMLIndex. The index-creation technique is the same as what we would use for binary XMLTypes.

For binary XMLTypes, XQueries are rewritten to a set of XPath expressions. The evaluation of these XPath expressions requires evaluation of the binary XML content and the XMLIndex lookups.

Learning More About XMLIndex

In the "Binary XMLType" section of Chapter 12, we briefly introduced XMLIndex with a few examples. In this chapter, let's learn more about XMLIndex.

First, XMLIndex is a *domain index* provided by Oracle XML DB to optimize the XML data access. A *domain index* extends the basic types of hash, bitmapped, and B-Tree indexes by allowing the developer to create his or her own index methods and apply them to a specific type of data set. Domain indexes typically use their own tables, sometimes including multiple tables, to store and manage the index. When using domain indexes, you need to know that you can't create multiple domain indexes on the same column list with the same index type. Otherwise, you will get the ORA-29879: *Cannot create multiple domain indexes on a column list using same indextype* error. For example, you can't create multiple XMLIndex on the same XMLType column.

Second, XMLIndex can be used in any part of the XQuery, including the XQuery expressions, and in SQL SELECT, FROM, and WHERE clauses.

Third, in Oracle Database 11g, XMLIndex has two types of components: *Structured* and *Unstructured* component. *Structured XMLIndex component,* also called *Structured XMLIndex,* is used for tuning queries on highly structured XML data. Structured XMLIndex creates one or more *content tables* to keep the indexes. *Unstructured XMLIndex component,* also called *Unstructured XMLIndex,* is used for tuning queries on unstructured XML data. Unstructured XMLIndex uses *path tables* to record XML nodes (using XPaths) and their values. Both Structured XMLIndex's *content tables* and Unstructured XMLIndex's *path tables* are relational tables. Therefore, you can create *secondary indexes* on the *path table* and *content table* to further improve the query performance.

In practice, you would need to create both Structured and Unstructured XMLIndex indexes on the same XML column to optimize different types of XQueries.

XQuery Tuning with XMLIndex

Let's learn how XMLIndex can be used for XQuery performance tuning. We use the binary XMLType table *contact_xsxtbl* created in Listing 2-9 shown as follows (*register_xsd_xdburi.sql, create_xmltype_xsd.sql, insert_xmltype_xsxtbl_batch.sql*):

```
CREATE TABLE contact_xsxtbl OF XMLTYPE
XMLTYPE STORE AS SECUREFILE BINARY XML
XMLSCHEMA "http://www.xmlbook.com/sample/contact.xsd" ELEMENT "contact";

SQL> desc contact_xsxtbl;
 Name                                      Null?    Type
 ----------------------------------------- -------- ----------------------------
TABLE of SYS.XMLTYPE(XMLSchema "http://www.xmlbook.com/sample/contact.xsd"
Element "contact") STORAGE BINARY
```

An unstructured XMLIndex is created (*create_xmlindex.sql*):

```
CREATE INDEX contact_xidx ON contact_xsxtbl (OBJECT_VALUE)
INDEXTYPE IS XDB.XMLIndex
PARAMETERS ('PATH TABLE contact_xidx_path_table');
```

To check on whether the XMLIndex is created, run the following command (*check_xmlindex .sql*):

```
SELECT INDEX_NAME FROM USER_INDEXES
  WHERE TABLE_NAME = 'CONTACT_XSXTBL' AND ITYP_NAME = 'XMLINDEX';

INDEX_NAME
------------------------------
CONTACT_XIDX
```

We can add a structured component to the created XMLIndex. Before doing this, it's good practice to test the query to be used in the index creation (*query_to_create_xmlindex.sql*):

```
select csx.*
from contact_xsxtbl cs,
     xmltable(XMLNamespaces(DEFAULT 'http://xmlbook.com/sample/contact.xsd'),
```

```
        '/contact'
        passing cs.object_value
        COLUMNS
          id NUMBER PATH '@id',
          first_name VARCHAR2(50) PATH 'first_name',
          last_name VARCHAR2(50) PATH 'last_name',
          email    VARCHAR2(50) PATH 'email') csx;
```

Then we create the following XMLIndex parameter and register it to the XMLIndex (*add_structured_idx.sql*):

```
exec DBMS_XMLINDEX.DROPPARAMETER ('CONTACT_METADATA_PARAMETER');

BEGIN
  DBMS_XMLINDEX.registerParameter('CONTACT_METADATA_PARAMETER',
      'ADD_GROUP GROUP CONTACT_G
       XMLTABLE contact_topmeta_tbl
       XMLNamespaces(DEFAULT ''http://xmlbook.com/sample/contact.xsd''),
       ''/contact''
       COLUMNS
         id NUMBER PATH ''@id'',
         first_name VARCHAR2(50) PATH ''first_name'',
         last_name VARCHAR2(50) PATH ''last_name'',
         email    VARCHAR2(50) PATH ''email''');
END;
/
ALTER INDEX CONTACT_XIDX PARAMETERS('PARAM CONTACT_METADATA_PARAMETER');
```

Oracle XML DB Tip: Can I create an XMLIndex in one SQL to include both unstructured and structured components?

Yes, you can. In the following example, we create both components in a single SQL (*create_xmlindex_mixed.sql*):

```
CREATE INDEX contact_xidx ON contact_xsxtbl (OBJECT_VALUE)
INDEXTYPE IS XDB.XMLIndex
PARAMETERS ('PATH TABLE contact_xidx_path_table
       GROUP CONTACT_G
       XMLTABLE contact_topmeta_tbl
       XMLNamespaces(DEFAULT ''http://xmlbook.com/sample/contact.xsd''),
       ''/contact''
       COLUMNS
         id NUMBER PATH ''id'',
         first_name VARCHAR2(50) PATH ''first_name'',
         last_name VARCHAR2(50) PATH ''last_name'',
         email    VARCHAR2(50) PATH ''email''');
```

Without XMLIndex, the query execution plan is shown as follows (*structured_index_performance.sql*):

```
Set timing on
SET AUTOTRACE ON EXPLAIN
select /*+ NO_XMLINDEX_REWRITE */ csx.*
from contact_xsxtbl cs,
     xmltable(XMLNamespaces(DEFAULT 'http://xmlbook.com/sample/contact.xsd'),
       '/contact'
       passing cs.object_value
       COLUMNS
         id NUMBER PATH '@id',
         first_name VARCHAR2(50) PATH 'first_name',
         last_name VARCHAR2(50) PATH 'last_name',
         email    VARCHAR2(50) PATH 'email') csx;
```

Note that the XPaths in the XQuery should match the XPaths used in the XMLIndex. The execution plan is shown in Figure 14-1.

Oracle XML DB Tip: How do I turn off XMLIndex?

In Oracle XML DB, you can turn off XMLIndex with either of the following optimizer hits in SQL:

- `/*+ NO_XML_QUERY_REWRITE */` turns off all the XPath rewrites, including the use of XMLIndex.
- `/*+ NO_XMLINDEX_REWRITE */` turns off the use of all XMLIndex indexes.

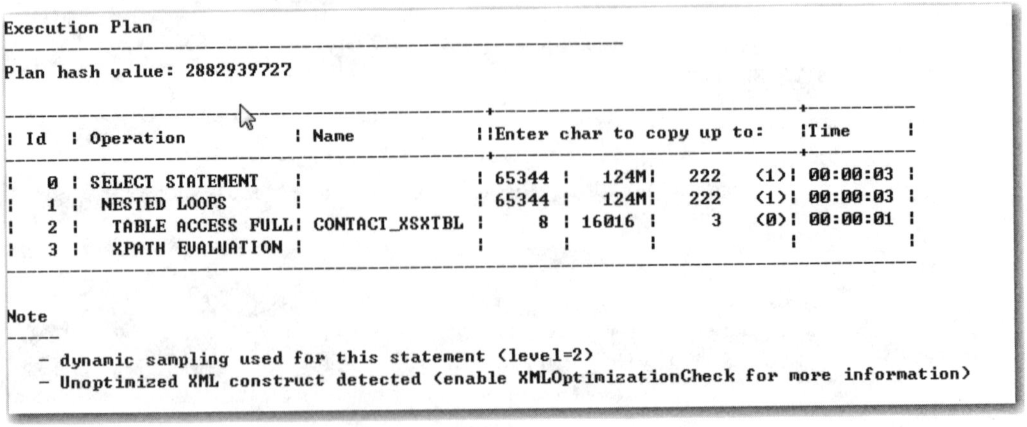

```
Execution Plan
----------------------------------------------------------
Plan hash value: 2882939727

-------------------------------------------------------+--------------------------+----------
| Id  | Operation            | Name           ||Enter char to copy up to:   |Time      |
-------------------------------------------------------+--------------------------+----------
|   0 | SELECT STATEMENT     |                | 65344 |   124M|   222   (1)| 00:00:03 |
|   1 |  NESTED LOOPS        |                | 65344 |   124M|   222   (1)| 00:00:03 |
|   2 |   TABLE ACCESS FULL| CONTACT_XSXTBL |     8 | 16016 |     3   (0)| 00:00:01 |
|   3 |   XPATH EVALUATION |                |       |       |            |          |
---------------------------------------------------------------------------------------

Note
-----
   - dynamic sampling used for this statement (level=2)
   - Unoptimized XML construct detected (enable XMLOptimizationCheck for more information)
```

FIGURE 14-1. *Structured XMLTable() query execution plan without XMLIndex*

```
Execution Plan
----------------------------------------------------------
Plan hash value: 3258046735

------------------------------------------------------------------------------------------------------------
| Id  | Operation                    | Name                     | Rows  | Bytes | Cost (%CPU)| Time     |
------------------------------------------------------------------------------------------------------------
|   0 | SELECT STATEMENT             |                          |     8 |   912 |     2   (0)| 00:00:01 |
|   1 |  NESTED LOOPS                |                          |       |       |            |          |
|   2 |   NESTED LOOPS               |                          |     8 |   912 |     2   (0)| 00:00:01 |
|   3 |    INDEX FAST FULL SCAN      | SYS_C0011153             |     8 |    80 |     2   (0)| 00:00:01 |
|*  4 |    INDEX RANGE SCAN          | SYS75060_75064_OID_IDX   |     1 |       |     0   (0)| 00:00:01 |
|   5 |   TABLE ACCESS BY INDEX ROWID| CONTACT_TOPMETA_TBL      |     1 |   104 |     0   (0)| 00:00:01 |
------------------------------------------------------------------------------------------------------------

Predicate Information (identified by operation id):
---------------------------------------------------

   4 - access("CS"."SYS_NC_OID$"="SYS_SXI_0"."OID")

Note
-----
   - dynamic sampling used for this statement (level=2)
```

FIGURE 14-2. *Structured XMLTable() query execution plan with XMLIndex*

With XMLIndex, the query is shown as follows:

```
SET AUTOTRACE ON EXPLAIN
select csx.*
from contact_xsxtbl cs,
     xmltable(XMLNamespaces(DEFAULT 'http://xmlbook.com/sample/contact.xsd'),
       '/contact'
       passing cs.object_value
       COLUMNS
         id NUMBER PATH '@id',
         first_name VARCHAR2(50) PATH 'first_name',
         last_name VARCHAR2(50) PATH 'last_name',
         email     VARCHAR2(50) PATH 'email') csx;
```

The execution plan is shown in Figure 14-2. In the execution plan, the CONTACT_TOPMETA_TBL table created by the structured XMLIndex is used.

For an unstructured index, it is useful to create *secondary indexes,* especially when XPath expressions contain scalar values. If the XPath value (stored in the VALUE column in *path table*) is in a *string* datatype, you don't need to create a secondary index, because a default secondary index is created for text (string-valued) data. However, for other scalar values such as *date* or *number,* you can create a secondary index to optimize the access. The following example creates a secondary index for the VALUE column in the XMLIndex *path table* to optimize the scalar data lookups in XQuery (*/contact/@id* in *number*) (*create_secondary_idx.sql*):

```
CALL DBMS_XMLINDEX.createNumberIndex('XMLDEMO', 'CONTACT_XIDX', 'ID_NUM_IDX');
```

Then we check the secondary indexes for XMLIndex using the following command (*check_secondary_idx.sql*):

```
SELECT c.INDEX_NAME, c.COLUMN_NAME, e.COLUMN_EXPRESSION
  FROM USER_IND_COLUMNS c LEFT OUTER JOIN USER_IND_EXPRESSIONS e
```

```
  ON (c.INDEX_NAME = e.INDEX_NAME)
  WHERE c.TABLE_NAME IN (SELECT PATH_TABLE_NAME FROM USER_XML_INDEXES
                         WHERE INDEX_NAME = 'CONTACT_XIDX')
 ORDER BY c.INDEX_NAME, c.COLUMN_NAME;
```

An example result is

```
INDEX_NAME                       COLUMN_NAME          COLUMN_EXPRESSION
------------------------------ -------------------- -------------------------
ID_NUM_IDX                       SYS_NC00007$         TO_BINARY_DOUBLE("VALUE")
SYS80177_CONTACT_XI_PIKEY_IX     ORDER_KEY
SYS80177_CONTACT_XI_PIKEY_IX     PATHID
SYS80177_CONTACT_XI_PIKEY_IX     RID
SYS80177_CONTACT_XI_VALUE_IX     SYS_NC00006$         SUBSTRB("VALUE",1,1599)
```

Let's look at the query execution plan without XMLIndex (*secondary_idx_performance.sql*):

```
SET AUTOTRACE ON EXPLAIN
select /*+ NO_XMLINDEX_REWRITE */
  XMLQuery('declare namespace ns="http://xmlbook.com/sample/contact.xsd"; /
ns:contact/ns:first_name'
  passing c.object_value RETURNING CONTENT) result
from contact_xsxtbl c
where xmlexists('declare namespace ns="http://xmlbook.com/sample/contact.xsd";
//ns:contact[@id>5] ' passing c.object_value);
```

The query execution plan result is shown in Figure 14-3.

```
Execution Plan
----------------------------------------------------------
Plan hash value: 1358022466

-------------------------------------------------------------------------------------
| Id  | Operation          | Name           | Rows  | Bytes | Cost (%CPU)| Time     |
-------------------------------------------------------------------------------------
|   0 | SELECT STATEMENT   |                |  3267 |  6393K|   223   (1)| 00:00:03 |
|   1 |  NESTED LOOPS SEMI |                |  3267 |  6393K|   223   (1)| 00:00:03 |
|   2 |   TABLE ACCESS FULL| CONTACT_XSXTBL |     8 | 16016 |     3   (0)| 00:00:01 |
|*  3 |   XPATH EVALUATION |                |       |       |            |          |
-------------------------------------------------------------------------------------

Predicate Information (identified by operation id):
---------------------------------------------------

   3 - filter(TO_BINARY_DOUBLE("P"."C_01$")>5.0E+000D)

Note
-----
   - dynamic sampling used for this statement (level=2)
```

FIGURE 14-3. *Execution plan of XQuery on Binary XMLTypes without XMLIndex*

The following is the execution plan with XMLIndex:

```
SET AUTOTRACE ON EXPLAIN
select
XMLQuery('declare namespace ns="http://xmlbook.com/sample/contact.xsd";
/ns:contact/ns:first_name'
passing c.object_value RETURNING CONTENT) result
from contact_xsxtbl c
where xmlexists(' declare namespace ns="http://xmlbook.com/sample/contact
.xsd"; //ns:contact[@id>5] ' passing c.object_value);
```

The execution plan result is shown in Figure 14-4.

```
Execution Plan
----------------------------------------------------------
Plan hash value: 734877621

---------------------------------------------------------------------------------------------------------------------
| Id  | Operation                      | Name                             | Rows  | Bytes | Cost (%CPU)| Time     |
---------------------------------------------------------------------------------------------------------------------
|   0 | SELECT STATEMENT               |                                  |     1 |    24 |     9  (12)| 00:00:01 |
|   1 |  SORT GROUP BY                 |                                  |     1 |  3524 |            |          |
|*  2 |   TABLE ACCESS BY INDEX ROWID  | CONTACT_XIDX_PATH_TABLE          |     1 |  3524 |     2   (0)| 00:00:01 |
|*  3 |    INDEX RANGE SCAN            | SYS75060_CONTACT_XI_PIKEY_IX     |     1 |       |     1   (0)| 00:00:01 |
|   4 |  NESTED LOOPS                  |                                  |     1 |    24 |     9  (12)| 00:00:01 |
|   5 |   VIEW                         | VW_SQ_1                          |     1 |    12 |     7   (0)| 00:00:01 |
|   6 |    HASH UNIQUE                 |                                  |     1 |  3076 |            |          |
|   7 |     NESTED LOOPS               |                                  |     1 |  3076 |     7   (0)| 00:00:01 |
|   8 |      NESTED LOOPS              |                                  |     1 |  3063 |     6   (0)| 00:00:01 |
|   9 |       NESTED LOOPS             |                                  |     1 |  1541 |     4   (0)| 00:00:01 |
|  10 |        TABLE ACCESS BY INDEX ROWID| X$PT6TBANBT30D9RJRG2SOI6UT4CC0 |     1 |    13 |     2   (0)| 00:00:01 |
|* 11 |         INDEX RANGE SCAN       | X$PR6TBANBT30D9RJRG2SOI6UT4CC0   |     1 |       |     1   (0)| 00:00:01 |
|* 12 |        TABLE ACCESS BY INDEX ROWID| CONTACT_XIDX_PATH_TABLE        |     1 |  1528 |     2   (0)| 00:00:01 |
|* 13 |         INDEX RANGE SCAN       | ID_NUM_IDX                       |     1 |       |     1   (0)| 00:00:01 |
|* 14 |       TABLE ACCESS BY INDEX ROWID | CONTACT_XIDX_PATH_TABLE       |     1 |  1522 |     2   (0)| 00:00:01 |
|* 15 |        INDEX RANGE SCAN        | SYS75060_CONTACT_XI_PIKEY_IX     |     1 |       |     1   (0)| 00:00:01 |
|* 16 |      TABLE ACCESS BY INDEX ROWID  | X$PT6TBANBT30D9RJRG2SOI6UT4CC0 |       |       |            |          |
|* 17 |       INDEX UNIQUE SCAN        | X+-------------------------------+|     1 |       |     0   (0)| 00:00:01 |
|  18 |   TABLE ACCESS BY USER ROWID   | C|Enter char to copy up to:     ||     1 |    12 |     1   (0)| 00:00:01 |
-------------------------------------------+--------------------------------+----------------------------------------

Predicate Information (identified by operation id):
---------------------------------------------------

   2 - filter(SYS_XMLI_LOC_ISNODE("SYS_P0"."LOCATOR")=1)
   3 - access("SYS_P0"."RID"=:B1 AND "SYS_P0"."PATHID"=HEXTORAW('7123') )
  11 - access(SYS_PATH_REVERSE("PATH")>=HEXTORAW('02580A')  AND
              SYS_PATH_REVERSE("PATH")<HEXTORAW('02580AFF') )
  12 - filter(SYS_XMLI_LOC_ISNODE("SYS_P4"."LOCATOR")=1 AND "SYS_P4"."PATHID"="ID")
  13 - access(TO_BINARY_DOUBLE("VALUE")>5.0E+000D)
  14 - filter(SYS_XMLI_LOC_ISNODE("SYS_P2"."LOCATOR")=1)
  15 - access("SYS_P4"."RID"="SYS_P2"."RID" AND "SYS_P2"."ORDER_KEY"<"SYS_P4"."ORDER_KEY")
       filter("SYS_P2"."ORDER_KEY"<"SYS_P4"."ORDER_KEY" AND
              "SYS_P4"."ORDER_KEY"<SYS_ORDERKEY_MAXCHILD("SYS_P2"."ORDER_KEY") AND
              SYS_ORDERKEY_DEPTH("SYS_P2"."ORDER_KEY")+1=SYS_ORDERKEY_DEPTH("SYS_P4"."ORDER_KEY"))
  16 - filter(SYS_PATH_REVERSE("PATH")>=HEXTORAW('0248CE')  AND
              SYS_PATH_REVERSE("PATH")<HEXTORAW('0248CEFF') )
  17 - access("SYS_P2"."PATHID"="ID")

Note
-----
   - dynamic sampling used for this statement (level=2)
```

FIGURE 14-4. *Execution plan of XQuery with unstructured XMLIndex*

The query execution plan shows that the XMLIndex CONTACT_XIDX (CONTACT_XIDX_PATH_TABLE) and its secondary index ID_NUM_IDX are used in the query execution.

Summary

In this chapter, we briefly described how to enable external network access for database users. The setup is simple and is managed by XML documents stored in XML DB Repository. Performance tuning has to be done along with the application design.

PART III

Building XML Applications

CHAPTER 15

XML DB Web Services

ative Oracle XML DB Web Services simplifies the publishing of database processes; thus, they can be integrated with SOA (Service-Oriented Architecture) applications for data exchange and business process integration. In Oracle Database 11g, we can publish Oracle database SQL queries and PL/SQL procedures as Web Services. In this chapter, let's learn how to use the native XML DB Web Services feature.

EXAMPLE SETUP

To run examples in this chapter, please first log in as SYS *(as* SYSDBA*) user to grant additional privileges to the XMLDEMO user* (grant_ws_privilege_to_xmldemo.sql)*:*

```
GRANT xdb_webservices TO xmldemo;
GRANT xdb_webservices_over_http TO xmldemo;
```

Setting Up XML DB Web Services

Native Oracle XML DB Web Services is provided in an XML DB servlet, named *orawsv,* which supports SOAP 1.1–based Web Services. In the default XML DB installation, the native database Web Services is not enabled. To check status of the native XML DB Web Services feature, we can review the status of the *orawsv* servlet deployed on the XML DB HTTP server (logging in as *SYS* or *XDB* user to run the SQL command) (*check_oraws.sql*):

Listing 15-1 *Checking Setup of the XML DB Web Service*

```
SELECT * FROM XMLTable(
         XMLNamespaces(DEFAULT 'http://xmlns.oracle.com/xdb/xdbconfig.xsd'),
                '/xdbconfig/sysconfig/protocolconfig/httpconfig/
webappconfig/servletconfig/servlet-mappings/servlet-mapping'
                passing dbms_xdb.cfg_get()
                COLUMNS
                Servlet_Name VARCHAR2(20) PATH 'servlet-name');
```

With the default installation, the result should be as follows:

```
SERVLET_NAME
--------------------
TestServlet
DBURIServlet
ReportFmwkServlet
PublishedContentServ
APEX
```

If the *orawsv* servlet is not on the list, we need to enable this feature by registering the *orawsv* servlet to the XML DB HTTP server (*enable_oraws.sql*):

Listing 15-2 *Registering XML DB Web Service to XML DB HTTP Server*

```
BEGIN
  DBMS_XDB.addServlet(NAME => 'orawsv',
                      LANGUAGE => 'C',
                      DISPNAME => 'XML DB Native Web Service',
                      DESCRIPT => 'Publish SQL, XQuery queries and PL/SQL
functions/procedures',
                      SCHEMA => 'XDB');
  DBMS_XDB.addServletSecRole(SERVNAME => 'orawsv',
                             ROLENAME => 'XDB_WEBSERVICES',
                             ROLELINK => 'XDB_WEBSERVICES');
  DBMS_XDB.addServletMapping(PATTERN => '/orawsv/*', NAME => 'orawsv');
END;
```

After this command, the *orawsv* servlet should be deployed to the Oracle XML DB HTTP server. To disable the servlet, run the following command (*disable_oraws.sql*):

Listing 15-3 *Disabling XML DB Web Service*

```
BEGIN
  DBMS_XDB.deleteServletMapping('orawsv');
  DBMS_XDB.deleteServlet('orawsv');
END;
```

After the *orawsv* servlet is deployed to the Oracle XML DB HTTP server, the following XML DB Web Services deployment description is shown in the XML DB configuration file (*/xdbconfig.xml*) (*check_oraws_config.sql*):

Listing 15-4 *Checking the XML DB Web Services' Configuration*

```
SELECT XMLSerialize(content
         XMLQuery('declare namespace ns="http://xmlns.oracle.com/xdb/
xdbconfig.xsd"; (: :)
                 $r//ns:servlet[ns:servlet-name="orawsv"]'
         passing DBMS_XDB.CFG_GET() AS "r" returning content)
         AS CLOB indent size=2) servelt_config
FROM dual;
SERVELT_CONFIG
--------------------------------------------------------
<servlet>
<servlet-name>orawsv</servlet-name>
<servlet-language>C</servlet-language>
<display-name>Oracle Query Web Service</display-name>
```

```
<description>Servlet for issuing queries as a Web Service</description>
<security-role-ref>
<role-name>XDBWEBSERVICES</role-name>
<role-link>XDBWEBSERVICES</role-link>
</security-role-ref>
</servlet>
<servlet-mapping>
<servlet-pattern>/orawsv/*</servlet-pattern>
<servlet-name>orawsv</servlet-name>
</servlet-mapping>
```

The description tells us that Oracle XML DB Web Services is written in C and grants access to the XDBWEBSERVICES role.

There are several database roles defined to access XML DB Web Services:

- **XDB_WEBSERVICES** This is the mandatory role for any database user to use XML DB Web Services. By default, this role is only granted to the *DBA* role.
- **XDB_WEBSERVICES_OVER_HTTP** This allows HTTP access of XML DB Web Services.
- **XDB_WEBSERVICES_WITH_PUBLIC** This grants the access of PUBLIC objects in the Oracle database through XML DB Web Services.

As discussed in the chapter example setup, we have granted the XMLDEMO user the XDB_WEB_SERVICES role to use the XML DB Web Services feature and the XDK_WEB_SERVICES_OVER_HTTP role to access the Web Services over HTTP.

Oracle XML DB Tip: How do I to access the public functions/procedures in Web Services?

If a PL/SQL function/procedure grants its access to PUBLIC, a database user needs to have the XDB_WEBSERVICES_WITH_PUBLIC role to access the PL/SQL function/procedure. Otherwise, you will get the PLS-00201: *Identifier must be declared* error.

The XML DB Web Services' Web Services Description Language (WSDL) file is located at *http://host_name:xdb_http_port/orawsv?wsdl*. An example URL is *http://localhost:8081/orawsv?wsdl*, with *localhost* as the XML DB HTTP server's host name and *8081* as the XML DB HTTP server's port.

When accessing the WSDL URL, you need to log in as a valid database user (e.g., XMLDEMO). Then, the successful enabling of XML DB Web Services allows you to see the WSDL:

```
<definitions name="orawsv" targetNamespace="http://xmlns.oracle.com/orawsv"
    xmlns="http://schemas.xmlsoap.org/wsdl/"
    xmlns:tns="http://xmlns.oracle.com/orawsv"
    xmlns:soap="http://schemas.xmlsoap.org/wsdl/soap/"
    xmlns:xsd="http://www.w3.org/2001/XMLSchema"
    xmlns:xsi="http://www.w3.org/2001/XMLSchema-instance"
xsi:schemaLocation="http://schemas.xmlsoap.org/wsdl/ http://schemas.xmlsoap
.org/wsdl/">
```

```
<types>
 <xsd:schema targetNamespace="http://xmlns.oracle.com/orawsv"
  elementFormDefault="qualified">
  <xsd:element name="query">
   <xsd:complexType>
    <xsd:sequence>
     <xsd:element name="DDL_text" type="xsd:string"
      minOccurs="0" maxOccurs="unbounded" />
     <xsd:element name="query_text">
      <xsd:complexType>
       <xsd:simpleContent>
        <xsd:extension base="xsd:string">
         <xsd:attribute name="type">
          <xsd:simpleType>
           <xsd:restriction base="xsd:NMTOKEN">
            <xsd:enumeration value="SQL" />
            <xsd:enumeration value="XQUERY" />
           </xsd:restriction>
          </xsd:simpleType>
         </xsd:attribute>
        </xsd:extension>
       </xsd:simpleContent>
      </xsd:complexType>
     </xsd:element>
     <xsd:choice minOccurs="0" maxOccurs="unbounded">
      <xsd:element name="bind">
       <xsd:complexType>
        <xsd:simpleContent>
         <xsd:extension base="xsd:string">
          <xsd:attribute name="name" type="xsd:string" />
         </xsd:extension>
        </xsd:simpleContent>
       </xsd:complexType>
      </xsd:element>
      <xsd:element name="bindXML">
       <xsd:complexType>
        <xsd:sequence>
         <xsd:any/>
        </xsd:sequence>
       </xsd:complexType>
      </xsd:element>
     </xsd:choice>
     <xsd:element name="null_handling" minOccurs="0">
      <xsd:simpleType>
       <xsd:restriction base="xsd:NMTOKEN">
        <xsd:enumeration value="DROP_NULLS" />
        <xsd:enumeration value="NULL_ATTR" />
        <xsd:enumeration value="EMPTY_TAG" />
       </xsd:restriction>
      </xsd:simpleType>
     </xsd:element>
```

```
      <xsd:element name="max_rows" type="xsd:positiveInteger" minOccurs="0"/>
      <xsd:element name="skip_rows" type="xsd:positiveInteger" minOccurs="0"/>
      <xsd:element name="pretty_print" type="xsd:boolean" minOccurs="0"/>
      <xsd:element name="indentation_width" type="xsd:positiveInteger"
minOccurs="0"/>
      <xsd:element name="rowset_tag" type="xsd:string" minOccurs="0"/>
      <xsd:element name="row_tag" type="xsd:string" minOccurs="0"/>
      <xsd:element name="item_tags_for_coll" type="xsd:boolean"
minOccurs="0"/>
     </xsd:sequence>
    </xsd:complexType>
   </xsd:element>
   <xsd:element name="queryOut">
    <xsd:complexType>
     <xsd:sequence>
      <xsd:any/>
     </xsd:sequence>
    </xsd:complexType>
   </xsd:element>
  </xsd:schema>
 </types>
  <message name="QueryInput">
   <part name="body" element="tns:query"/>
  </message>

  <message name="XMLOutput">
   <part name="body" element="tns:queryOut"/>
  </message>

  <portType name="ORAWSVPortType">
   <operation name="XMLFromQuery">
    <input message="tns:QueryInput"/>
    <output message="tns:XMLOutput"/>
   </operation>
  </portType>

  <binding name="ORAWSVBinding" type="tns:ORAWSVPortType">
   <soap:binding style="document" transport="http://schemas.xmlsoap.org/soap/
http"/>
   <operation name="XMLFromQuery">
    <soap:operation soapAction="http://localhost:8081/orawsv"/>
    <input> <soap:body use="literal"/> </input>
    <output> <soap:body use="literal"/> </output>
   </operation>
  </binding>

  <service name="ORAWSVService">
   <documentation>Oracle Web Service</documentation>
   <port name="ORAWSVPort" binding="tns:ORAWSVBinding">
    <soap:address location="http://localhost:8081/orawsv"/>
```

```
    </port>
  </service>
</definitions>
```

XML DB Web Services allow us to publish SQL and XQuery database queries as Web Services or publish PL/SQL functions/procedures as Web Services.

As described in the WSDL file, for the SQL query and XQuery, we can use either Data Definition Language (DDL) commands (with *DDL_text* input) or SQL/XQuery (with *query_text* input). Table 15-1 summarizes the XML DB Web Services' input parameters. The XML DB Web Services returns the XML results in SOAP messages.

Parameter	**Description**	**Values**
DDL_text: string	DDL SQL command	DDL SQL command
query_text: string	Query content	SQL or XQuery string
type: NMTOKEN	Attribute of *query_text* specifying the query types	SQL or XQuery
bind	Optional. Provides binding variable for query or DDL text.	Name(string)=content(string)
null_handling: NMTOKEN	Optional. Specifies how the null columns are handled.	DROP_NULLS NULL_ATTR EMPTY_TAG
max_rows: positiveInteger	Optional. Maximum number of rows to be retrieved.	Positive integer. By default, XML DB Web servers return all rows.
skip_rows: positiveInteger	Optional. Used with max rows for pagination, specifies the number of rows to skip before start generation.	Positive integer. Default is 0.
pretty_print: boolean	Optional. Specifies whether the document is pretty printed.	True or false. Default is *true*, which gives pretty-printed result.
indentation_width: positiveInteger	Optional. Specifies the number of characters used to indent in pretty printing.	Positive integer. Default is 1.
rowset_tag: string	Optional. ROWSET tag name.	String
row: string	Optional. ROW tag name.	String
Item_tags_for_col: boolean	Optional. Collection items are generated with element name as COLUMNAME_ITEM.	True or false. Default is *false*.

TABLE 15-1. *XML DB Web Services Binding Attributes*

Querying Oracle Database with Web Services

To learn XML DB Web Services, let's build an application that manages stock trading data.

First, we create the following tables to store the stock trading transactions and client information (*create_tables.sql*):

```
CREATE TABLE stock_trans_tbl(
    client_id   NUMBER,
    stock_id    VARCHAR2(20),
    trans_type  VARCHAR2(10),
    shares      NUMBER,
    stock_price NUMBER);
CREATE TABLE client_tbl(
    client_id NUMBER,
    username  VARCHAR2(20),
    client_pwd RAW(16));
```

Next, we add the following client data (*insert_data.sql*):

```
INSERT INTO client_tbl VALUES(1,'jsmith',
utl_raw.cast_to_raw('jsmith'||'good'));
```

To protect the client password, we use the database utl_raw.cast_to_raw() function to convert the string into RAW data. We then add the following transactions:

```
INSERT INTO stock_trans_tbl VALUES(1, 'ORCL', 'Buy', 1000,22.32);
INSERT INTO stock_trans_tbl VALUES(1, 'JBLU', 'Sell', 500,5.46);
```

To query user *jsmith*'s transaction data, we use the following query (*query_trans.sql*):

```
SELECT username, stock_id, trans_type, shares, stock_price
FROM stock_trans_tbl s, client_tbl c
WHERE s.client_id = c.client_id;
```

The SQL query result is shown as follows:

```
USERNAME             STOCK_ID             TRANS_TYPE     SHARES STOCK_PRICE
-------------------- -------------------- ---------- ---------- -----------
jsmith               ORCL                 Buy              1000        22.3
jsmith               JBLU                 Sell              500        5.46
```

Let's learn how to submit the same query via XML DB Web Services:

1. After creating an Oracle JDeveloper 11*g* workspace and project (refer to Chapter 16 if you don't know how to do this), add a copy of the XML DB Web Services WSDL to a local file in the project (*XMLDBWS.wsdl*). Make sure that you update the WSDL location based on your system setup.

2. Open Oracle JDeveloper 11*g* and click the Tools | HTTP Analyzer menu. In the HTTP Analyzer window, create a new HTTP request, as shown here:

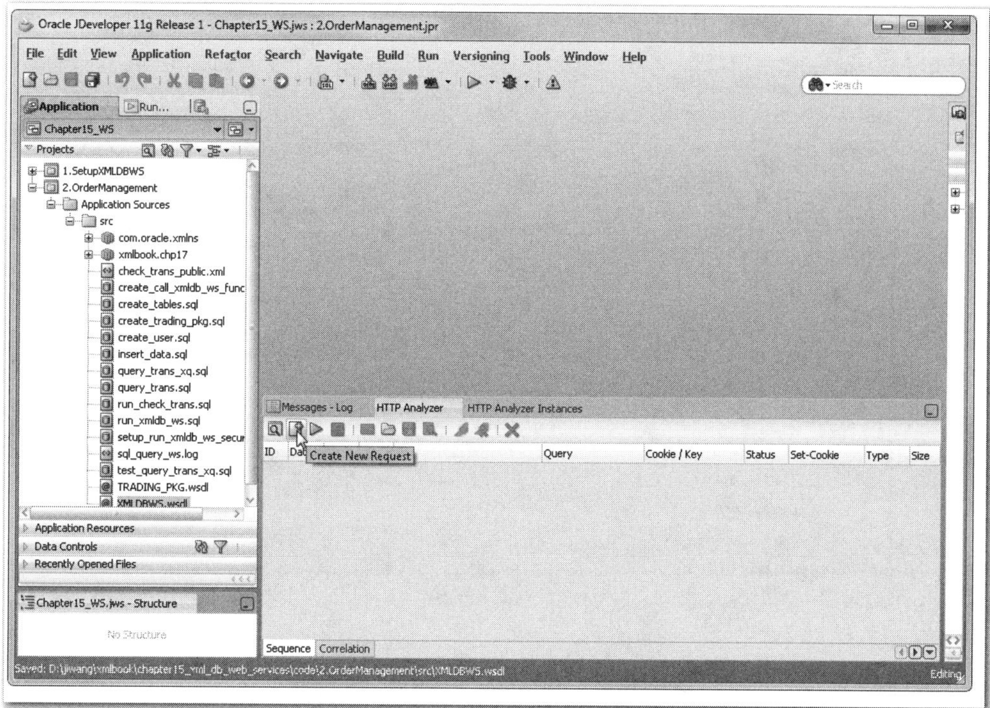

3. In the dialog window creating the HTTP request, click the Open WSDL… button, select the local XML DB Web Services WSDL file (*XMLDBWS.wsdl*), and click OK. This step leads to auto-created setup, which allows us to create the HTTP request to use the XML DB Web Services.

4. To submit a query, you need to click the Include button for *DDL_Text:Array* and then click the X (cross) icon to remove the *DDL_text:string* attribute. Click the Include button for *DDL_Text:Array* again to complete this step.

5. Then set up *query_text*. Specify the *type:NMTOKEN* attribute of *query_text* to be **SQL**. Add the following SQL command in the *content:string* attribute with the Include checkbox checked:

```
SELECT username, stock_id, trans_type, shares, stock_price
FROM stock_trans_tbl s, client_tbl c
WHERE s.client_id = c.client_id AND c.username=:e
```

6. Uncheck all other options. Include checkboxes except the pretty_print:boolean option. The value of pretty_print:boolean is set to **true** to allow indented XML output. The setup is shown here.

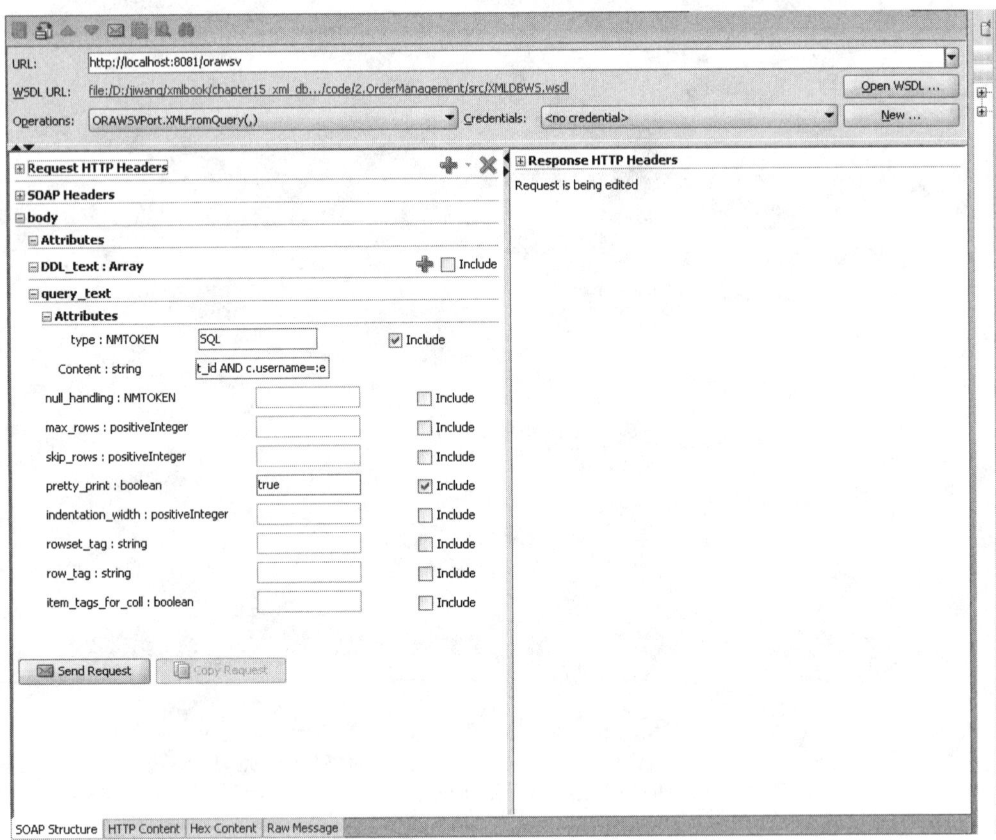

7. Click the "–" (minus sign) icon to expand the Request HTTP Headers section, then click the "+" button and choose the Authorization Basic option as shown here.

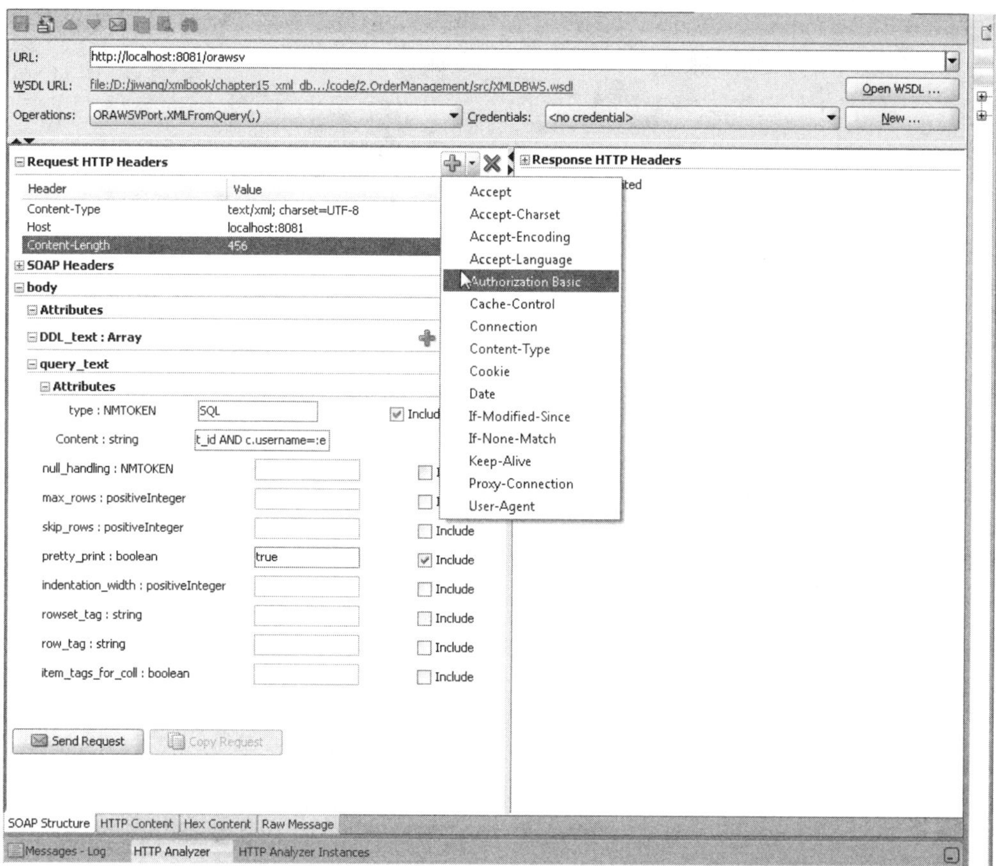

You then can set up the username and password (e.g., xmldemo/xmldemo) by typing in the Authorization option as shown here.

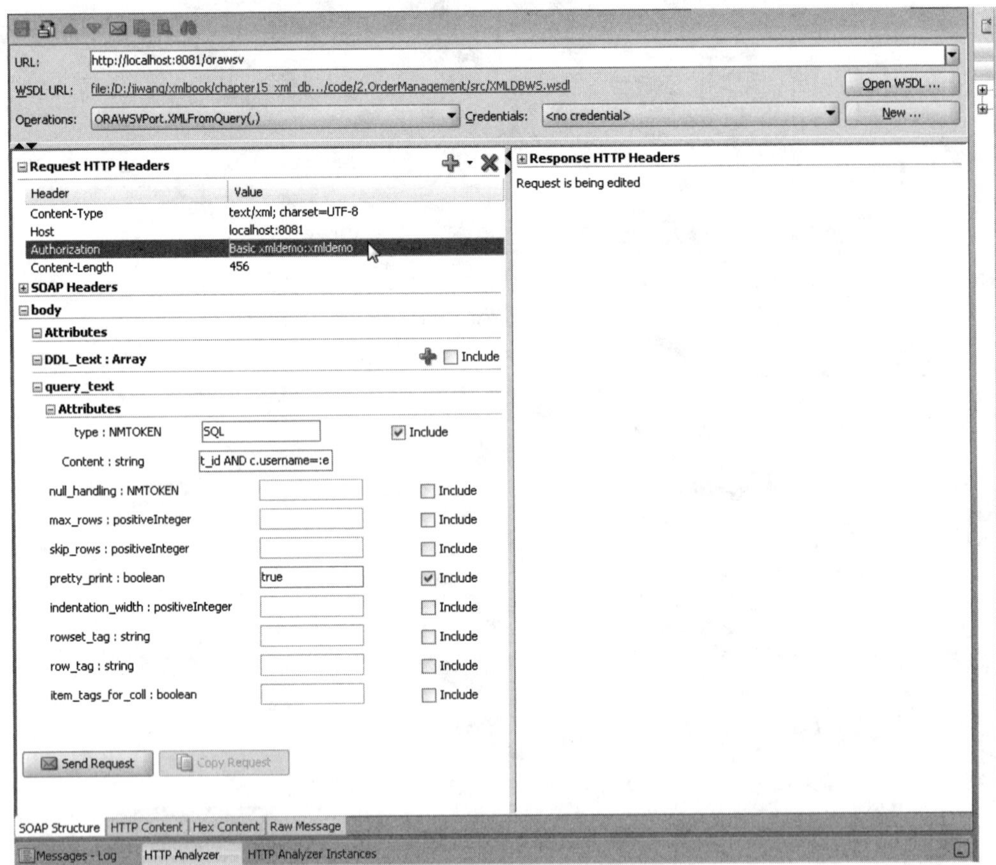

8. You can also edit the HTTP request message directly. In this example, we add the binding parameter to the SOAP request:

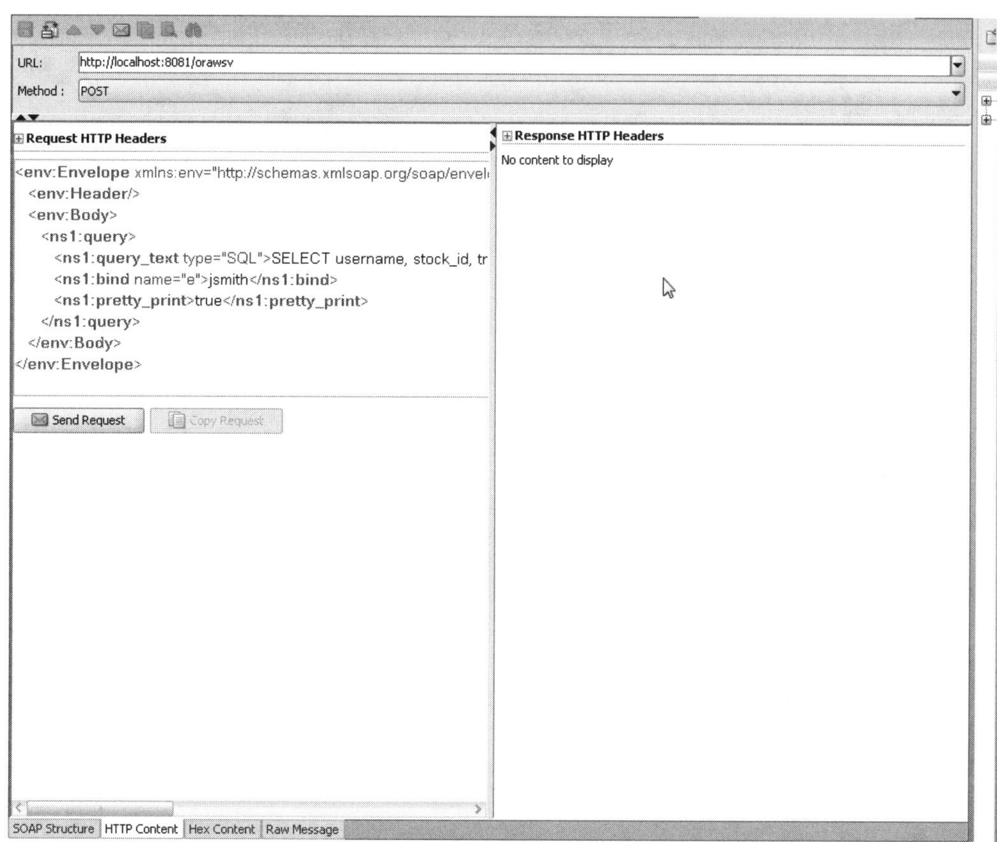

9. Click the Send Request button at the bottom of the request setup form. You can receive the responding XML message as shown here.

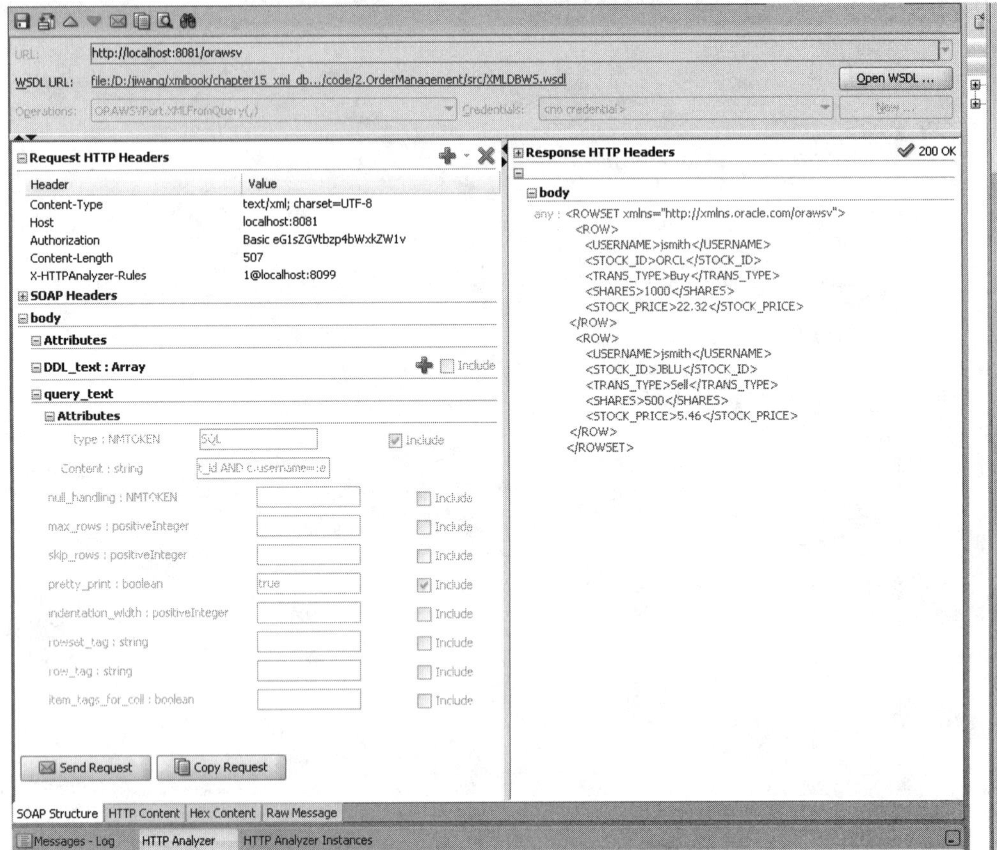

10. You can then review the SOAP messages in Oracle JDeveloper 11*g* by selecting the RAW Message view:

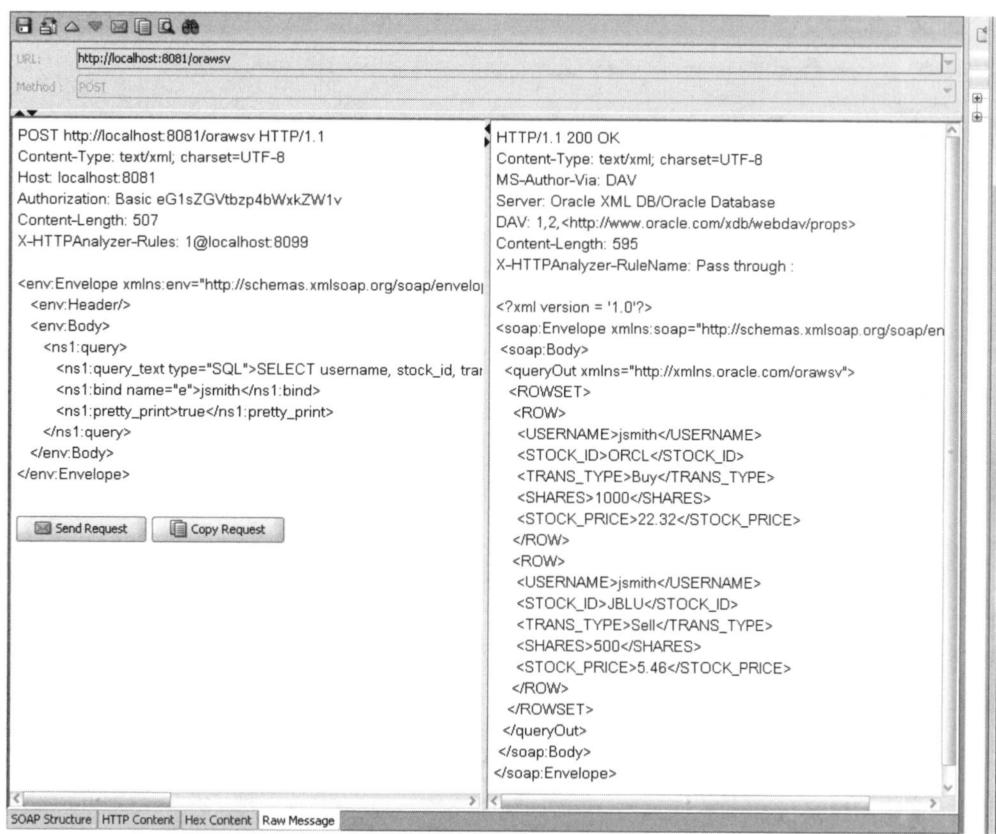

In SOAP, the request message is

```
<env:Envelope xmlns:env="http://schemas.xmlsoap.org/soap/envelope/"
xmlns:ns1="http://xmlns.oracle.com/orawsv">
   <env:Header/>
   <env:Body>
      <ns1:query>
         <ns1:query_text type="SQL">select  username, stock_id, trans_type,
shares, stock_price from stock_trans_tbl s, client_tbl c where s.client_id
= c.client_id and c.username=:e</ns1:query_text>
         <ns1:bind name="e">jsmith</ns1:bind>
         <ns1:pretty_print>true</ns1:pretty_print>
      </ns1:query>
   </env:Body>
</env:Envelope>
```

The XML DB Web Services SOAP response is

```
<?xml version = '1.0'?>
<soap:Envelope xmlns:soap="http://schemas.xmlsoap.org/soap/envelope/">
   <soap:Body>
      <queryOut xmlns="http://xmlns.oracle.com/orawsv">
         <ROWSET>
            <ROW>
               <USERNAME>jsmith</USERNAME>
               <STOCK_ID>ORCL</STOCK_ID>
               <TRANS_TYPE>Buy</TRANS_TYPE>
               <SHARES>1000</SHARES>
               <STOCK_PRICE>22.3</STOCK_PRICE>
            </ROW>
            <ROW>
               <USERNAME>jsmith</USERNAME>
               <STOCK_ID>JBLU</STOCK_ID>
               <TRANS_TYPE>Sell</TRANS_TYPE>
               <SHARES>500</SHARES>
               <STOCK_PRICE>5.46</STOCK_PRICE>
            </ROW>
         </ROWSET>
      </queryOut>
   </soap:Body>
</soap:Envelope>
```

Oracle XML DB Tip: How do I debug native XML DB Web Services?
To debug XML DB Web Services, you need to log in *SYS* as *SYSDBA* set the *"31098 trace name context forever, level 2"* event at the database level as follows:

```
alter database set event="31098 trace name context forever, level 2"
```

Then, you need to re-bounce the database instance. Look for a trace file with the name *<ora_sid>_s000_xxx.trc* in the database diagnostic USER_DUMP_DEST folder, i.e., `$ORACLE_HOME\diag\rdbms\<ora_sid>\<ora_sid>\trace folder.`

You can find the USER_DUMP_DEST directory using the following SQL:

```
SELECT name, value FROM v$parameter2  WHERE name IN ('user_dump_dest')
```

Publishing PL/SQL Functions/Procedures

Let's learn how to publish PL/SQL functions and procedures as Web Services using the Oracle XML DB Web Services.

Creating PL/SQL Packages and Functions

First, we create a PL/SQL package with the check_transactions() function that checks the transaction data (create_trading_pkg.sql):

```
CREATE OR REPLACE PACKAGE trading_pkg AS
  FUNCTION check_transactions(p_uname IN VARCHAR2,p_pwd IN VARCHAR2) RETURN
XMLType;
END trading_pkg;
/
CREATE OR REPLACE PACKAGE body trading_pkg AS
 FUNCTION check_transactions(p_uname IN VARCHAR2,p_pwd IN VARCHAR2) RETURN
XMLType
 AS
  v_out xmltype :=xmltype('<null/>');
  v_md5key raw(16);
 BEGIN
  SELECT c.client_pwd INTO v_md5key FROM client_tbl c WHERE c.username =
p_uname;

  IF (v_md5key = utl_raw.cast_to_raw(p_uname||p_pwd)) THEN
   SELECT XMLQuery('for $j in ora:view("CLIENT_TBL")
                    let $c_id:= $j/ROW/CLIENT_ID
                    return
                     <Transactions client="{$j/ROW/USERNAME}">
                     { for $i in ora:view("STOCK_TRANS_TBL")
                       where $j/ROW/CLIENT_ID = $c_id
                       return
                        <Transaction type="{$i/ROW/TRANS_TYPE}">
                         <ID>{$i/ROW/STOCK_ID/text()}</ID>
                         <PRICE>{$i/ROW/STOCK_PRICE/text()}</PRICE>
                         <SHARES>{$i/ROW/SHARES/text()}</SHARES>
                        </Transaction>}
                       </Transactions>' returning content) INTO v_out
    FROM dual;
   END IF;
  RETURN v_out;
END check_transactions;
END trading_pkg;
/
show errors;
```

We can run this PL/SQL function in the database (*run_check_trans.sql*):

```
SELECT XMLSerialize(content trading_pkg.check_transactions('jsmith','good')
       as CLOB indent size=2)
FROM DUAL;
```

The result is shown as follows:

```
<Transactions client="jsmith">
  <Transaction type="Buy">
```

```
    <ID>ORCL</ID>
    <PRICE>22.3</PRICE>
    <SHARES>1000</SHARES>
  </Transaction>
  <Transaction type="Sell">
    <ID>JBLU</ID>
    <PRICE>5.46</PRICE>
    <SHARES>500</SHARES>
  </Transaction>
</Transactions>
```

Reviewing the WSDL of the PL/SQL Function

The WSDL publishing the PL/SQL procedure is auto-created by XML DB at

```
http://localhost:8081/orawsv/XMLDEMO/TRADING_PKG/CHECK_TRANSACTIONS?wsdl
```

XMLDEMO is the user schema name. *TRADING_PKG* is the package name. *CHECK_TRANSACTIONS* is the PL/SQL function name. All of these names in the URL are capitalized. In general, the PL/SQL WSDL URL includes

```
http://[HOST_NAME]:[XMLDB_HTTP_PORT]/orawsv/[USER_SCHEMA]/[PACKAGE_NAME]/
[PROCEDURE/FUNCTION_NAME]?wsdl
```

The WSDL is shown as follows:

```
<definitions name="CHECK_TRANSACTIONS"
targetNamespace="http://xmlns.oracle.com/orawsv/XMLDEMO/TRADING_PKG/CHECK_
TRANSACTIONS"  xmlns="http://schemas.xmlsoap.org/wsdl/"
xmlns:tns="http://xmlns.oracle.com/orawsv/XMLDEMO/TRADING_PKG/CHECK_
TRANSACTIONS"
    xmlns:xsd="http://www.w3.org/2001/XMLSchema"
    xmlns:soap="http://schemas.xmlsoap.org/wsdl/soap/">
  <types>
    <xsd:schema
targetNamespace="http://xmlns.oracle.com/orawsv/XMLDEMO/TRADING_PKG/CHECK_
TRANSACTIONS"
     elementFormDefault="qualified">
      <xsd:element name="CXMLTYPE-CHECK_TRANSACTIONSInput">
        <xsd:complexType>
            <xsd:sequence>
              <xsd:element name="UNAME-VARCHAR2-IN" type="xsd:string"/>
              <xsd:element name="PWD-VARCHAR2-IN" type="xsd:string"/>
            </xsd:sequence>
          </xsd:complexType>
      </xsd:element>

      <xsd:element name="CHECK_TRANSACTIONSOutput">
        <xsd:complexType>
```

```
            <xsd:sequence>
              <xsd:element name="RETURN">
                 <xsd:complexType>
                  <xsd:sequence>
                   <xsd:any/>
                  </xsd:sequence>
                 </xsd:complexType>
                </xsd:element>
            </xsd:sequence>
          </xsd:complexType>
      </xsd:element>
   </xsd:schema>
  </types>
  <message name="CHECK_TRANSACTIONSInputMessage">
    <part name="parameters" element="tns:CXMLTYPE-CHECK_TRANSACTIONSInput"/>
  </message>
  <message name="CHECK_TRANSACTIONSOutputMessage">
    <part name="parameters" element="tns:CHECK_TRANSACTIONSOutput"/>
  </message>
  <portType name="CHECK_TRANSACTIONSPortType">
  <operation name="CHECK_TRANSACTIONS">
      <input message="tns:CHECK_TRANSACTIONSInputMessage"/>
      <output message="tns:CHECK_TRANSACTIONSOutputMessage"/>
    </operation>
  </portType>
  <binding name="CHECK_TRANSACTIONSBinding"
           type="tns:CHECK_TRANSACTIONSPortType">
    <soap:binding style="document"
transport="http://schemas.xmlsoap.org/soap/http"/>
    <operation name="CHECK_TRANSACTIONS">
      <soap:operation
 soapAction="CHECK_TRANSACTIONS"/>
      <input>
        <soap:body parts="parameters" use="literal"/>
      </input>
      <output>
        <soap:body parts="parameters" use="literal"/>
      </output>
    </operation>
  </binding>

  <service name="CHECK_TRANSACTIONSService">
    <documentation>Oracle Web Service</documentation>
    <port name="CHECK_TRANSACTIONSPort" binding="tns:CHECK_TRANSACTIONSBinding">
       <soap:address
location="http://localhost:8081/orawsv/XMLDEMO/TRADING_PKG/CHECK_TRANSACTIONS"/>
     </port>
  </service>
</definitions>
```

Calling PL/SQL XML DB Web Services in Java

To call this Web Service, let's follow these steps using Oracle JDeveloper 11*g*:

1. Open Oracle JDeveloper 11*g* project, and click File | New....
2. Click the All Technologies tab, choose Business Tier | Web Services | Web Service Proxy, and click OK.
3. Click Next in the Create Web Service Proxy dialog.
4. Choose a local copy (*TRADING_PKG.wsdl*) of the WSDL URL for the PL/SQL CHECK_TRANSACTIONS function. Click Next.
5. In the Specify Default Mapping Options dialog, you need to specify the Java package name. We can set the Package Name to **xmlbook.chp15** and then click Next. Skip the Custom Mapping and click Next.
6. In the Default Mapping dialog, Oracle JDeveloper 11*g* will detect the endpoint. Choose to run the service deployed on the Oracle XML DB HTTP server, as shown here and then click Next.

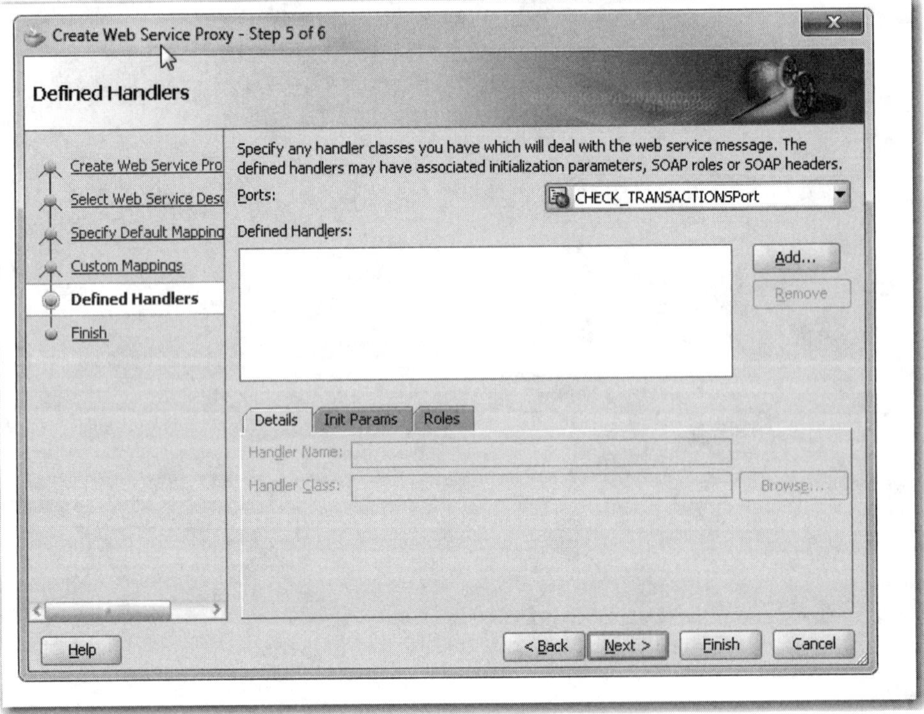

7. Leave the handler setup blank and click Next.

8. Confirm the proxy setup as shown here and click Finish. Oracle JDeveloper 11*g* will then create the proxy Java code.

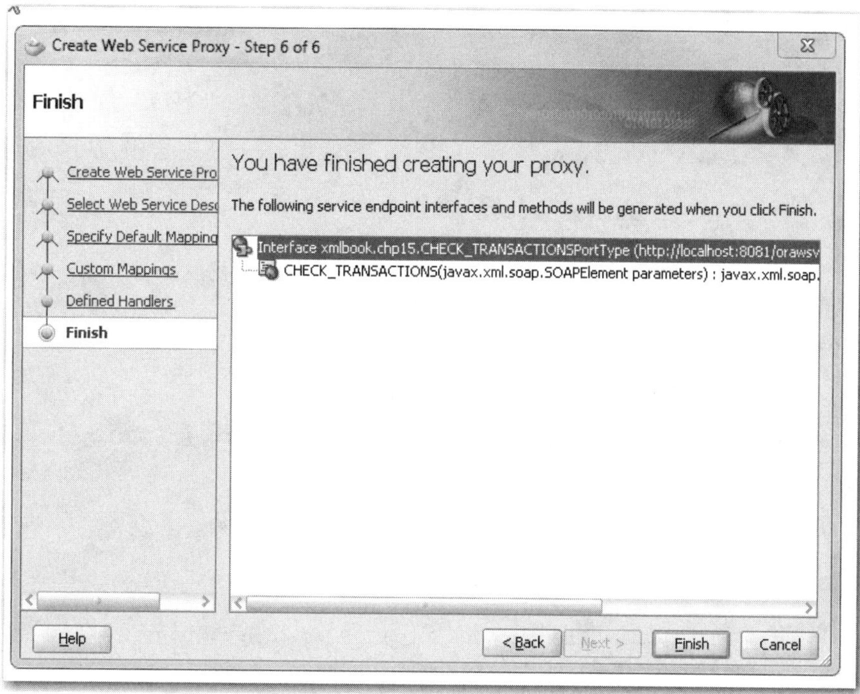

We can create a *TradingManger.java* to invoke the Web Service as follows:

Listing 15-5 *Calling PL/SQL Web Services and Serializing DOM Output*

```
package xmlbook.chp15;
import com.oracle.xmlns.orawsv.xmldemo.trading_pkg.check_transactions.CHECK_
TRANSACTIONSOutput;
import com.oracle.xmlns.orawsv.xmldemo.trading_pkg.check_transactions
.CXMLTYPECHECK_TRANSACTIONSInput;
import javax.xml.soap.SOAPElement;
import oracle.xml.parser.v2.XMLAttr;
import oracle.xml.parser.v2.XMLDocument;
import oracle.xml.parser.v2.XMLElement;
import org.w3c.dom.NamedNodeMap;
import org.w3c.dom.Node;

public class TradingManager {
    public static void main(String[] args) {
        try {
            CHECK_TRANSACTIONSService_Impl hw =
                new CHECK_TRANSACTIONSService_Impl();
```

```
            CHECK_TRANSACTIONSPortType hp =
                hw.getCHECK_TRANSACTIONSPort("xmldemo".getBytes(),
                                             "xmldemo".getBytes());
            CXMLTYPECHECK_TRANSACTIONSInput ci =
                new CXMLTYPECHECK_TRANSACTIONSInput();
            ci.setP_PWDVARCHAR2IN("good");
            ci.setP_UNAMEVARCHAR2IN("jsmith");

            CHECK_TRANSACTIONSOutput ho = hp.cHECK_TRANSACTIONS(ci);
            SOAPElement se = ho.getRETURN().get_any();
            XMLDocument m_target_doc = new XMLDocument();
            copyDOM(se.getOwnerDocument().getFirstChild(), null, m_target_doc);
            m_target_doc.print(System.out);
        } catch (Exception e) {
            e.printStackTrace();
        }
    }

    private static void copyDOM(Node start, Node target, XMLDocument doc) {
        XMLElement elem;
        XMLAttr nattr;
        Node attr;
        if (start.getNodeValue() == null) {
            elem = (XMLElement)doc.createElement(start.getNodeName());
        } else {
            elem = (XMLElement)doc.createElement(start.getNodeName());
            elem.setNodeValue(start.getNodeValue());
        }
        if (start.getNodeType() == start.ELEMENT_NODE) {
            NamedNodeMap startAttr = start.getAttributes();
            for (int i = 0; i < startAttr.getLength(); i++) {
                attr = startAttr.item(i);
                nattr = (XMLAttr)doc.createAttribute(attr.getNodeName());
                nattr.setNodeValue(attr.getNodeValue());
                elem.setAttributeNode(nattr);
            }
        }
        if (target == null) doc.appendChild(elem);
        else target.appendChild(elem);
        for (Node child = start.getFirstChild(); child != null;
              child = child.getNextSibling()) {
            if (child.getNodeType() == start.TEXT_NODE) {
                elem.addText(child.getNodeValue());
                continue;
            }
            copyDOM(child, elem, doc);
        }
    }
}
```

The program first creates *CHECK_TRANSACTIONSService_Impl* and then opens the Web Services port by providing the user name and password to access the XML DB Web Services via the basic HTTP authentication.

```
CHECK_TRANSACTIONSService_Impl hw = new CHECK_TRANSACTIONSService_Impl();
CHECK_TRANSACTIONSPortType hp =
    hw.getCHECK_TRANSACTIONSPort("xmldemo".getBytes(),"xmldemo".getBytes());
```

Then set up the inputs of the Web Service call:

```
CXMLTYPECHECK_TRANSACTIONSInput ci =
     new CXMLTYPECHECK_TRANSACTIONSInput();
ci.setP_PWDVARCHAR2IN("good");
ci.setP_UNAMEVARCHAR2IN("jsmith");
```

After setting all of the parameters, the Web Service is invoked with *CHECK_TRANSACTIONSOutput* as the output, and the XML result is printed out:

```
CHECK_TRANSACTIONSOutput ho = hp.cHECK_TRANSACTIONS(ci);
SOAPElement se = ho.getRETURN().get_any();
```

The XML content is retrieved into a *javax.xml.soap.SOAPElement* object.

To help debugging the result from the SOAP message, let's use Oracle JDeveloper 11*g* to check the actual message content. Click View | HTTP Analyzer and then click the green arrow button to start the analyzer. Then when running the Web Services client, we can check the SOAP message in the HTTP Analyzer, as shown in Figure 15-1.

In this example, the SOAP request message is

```
<env:Envelope xmlns:env="http://schemas.xmlsoap.org/soap/envelope/">
   <env:Header/>
   <env:Body>
      <chec:CXMLTYPE-CHECK_TRANSACTIONSInput xmlns:chec="http://xmlns.oracle
.com/orawsv/XMLDEMO/TRADING_PKG/CHECK_TRANSACTIONS">
         <chec:UNAME-VARCHAR2-IN>jsmith</chec:UNAME-VARCHAR2-IN>
         <chec:PWD-VARCHAR2-IN>good</chec:PWD-VARCHAR2-IN>
      </chec:CXMLTYPE-CHECK_TRANSACTIONSInput>
   </env:Body>
</env:Envelope>
```

The returned SOAP message is

```
<?xml version = '1.0'?>
<soap:Envelope xmlns:soap="http://schemas.xmlsoap.org/soap/envelope/">
   <soap:Body>
      <CHECK_TRANSACTIONSOutput xmlns="http://xmlns.oracle.com/orawsv/XMLDEMO/
TRADING_PKG/CHECK_TRANSACTIONS">
         <RETURN>
            <Transactions client="jsmith">
               <Transaction type="Buy">
                  <ID>ORCL</ID>
                  <PRICE>22.3</PRICE>
```

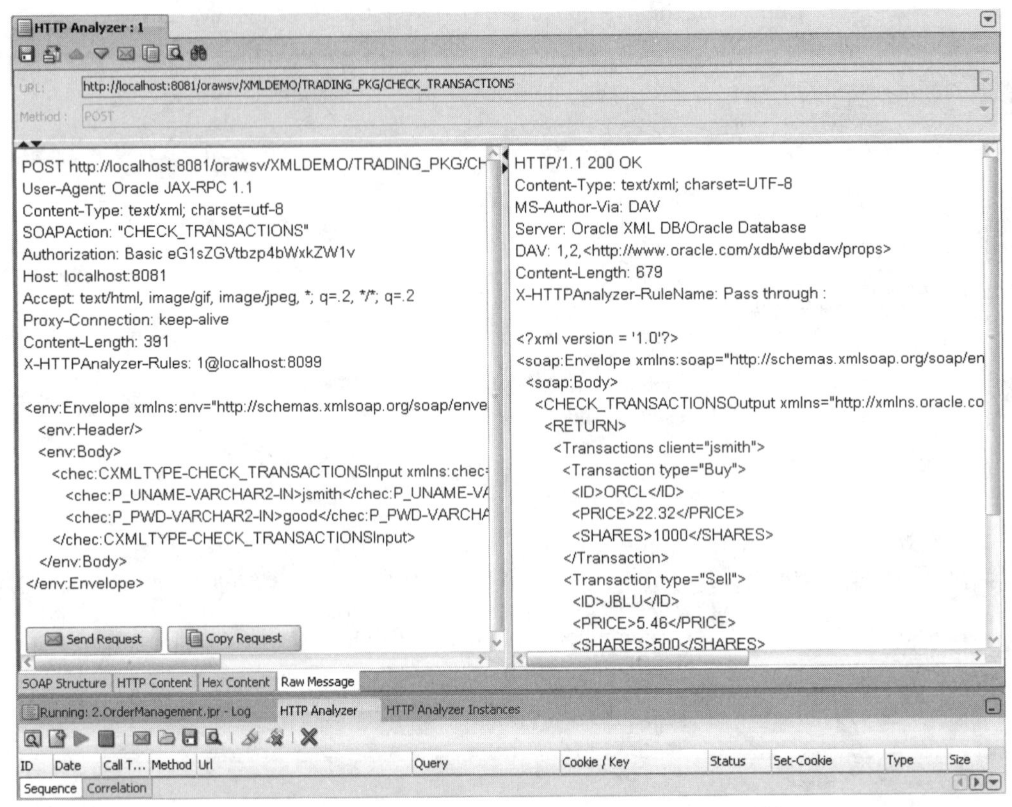

FIGURE 15-1. *Debugging Web Services in Oracle JDeveloper 11g*

```
                    <SHARES>1000</SHARES>
                 </Transaction>
                 <Transaction type="Sell">
                    <ID>JBLU</ID>
                    <PRICE>5.46</PRICE>
                    <SHARES>500</SHARES>
                 </Transaction>
              </Transactions>
           </RETURN>
        </CHECK_TRANSACTIONSOutput>
     </soap:Body>
</soap:Envelope>
```

Knowing the XML content, we then need to perform the XML operations. The *SOAPElement* object can return an *org.w3c.dom.Document*:

```
javax.xml.soap.SOAPElement.getOwnerDocument()
```

The SOAP message might not be created by the Oracle XDK parser (e.g., the Oracle WebLogic server doesn't use Oracle XDK parsers). Therefore, we can't cast the *org.w3c.dom.Document* object to *oracle.xml.parser.v2.XMLDocument* with the following command:

```
XMLDocument m_target_doc = (XMLDocument) se.getOwnerDocument();
```

We will get the following error message:

```
java.lang.ClassCastException: weblogic.xml.saaj.SaajDocument cannot be cast to
oracle.xml.parser.v2.XMLDocument
```

We create a function called copyDOM() to copy a DOM from another implementation to Oracle XDK DOM in the preceding code example. This is a function with recursive function calls to traverse the source DOM document tree and copy the DOM document content to an Oracle XDK DOM document.

Summary

Through examples, we learned the basics of the Oracle XML DB native Web Services feature. This feature reduces the amount of coding efforts needed to call the SQL/XQuery queries and PL/SQL procedures from Web Services. The Oracle XML DB native Web Services also provides better performance than publishing the Web Services using the Java programs, which call the SQL/XQuery queries and PL/SQL procedures from Java using JDBC. To fine-tune the performance of Oracle XML DB native Web Services, you can optimize the database listener/shared server processes.

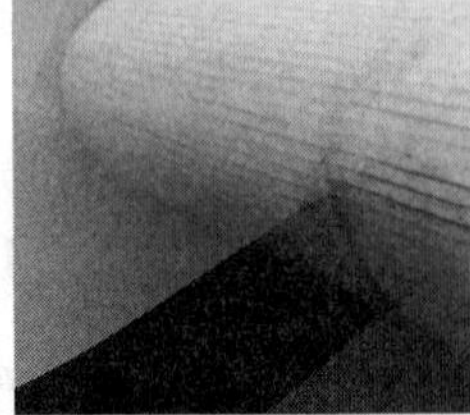

CHAPTER 16

Using Oracle JDeveloper 11*g*

Oracle JDeveloper 11*g* is an integrated Java development environment. It offers features to build, debug, and deploy applications in Java, XML, SQL, PL/SQL, and others. In this chapter, we will discuss how to use Oracle JDeveloper 11*g* and its XML features to build Oracle XML DB applications. The examples are created using Oracle JDeveloper 11.1.1.4.0.

Oracle JDeveloper Tip: What if I see a UI that differs from the examples in this chapter?
You might see UI differences if you're using an earlier version of Oracle JDeveloper 11*g*. For example, some major UI updates took place between 11.1.1.2.0 and 11.1.1.4.0. Please upgrade to the 11.1.1.4.0 version.

Creating the First XML Project

To create your first XML project in Oracle JDeveloper 11*g*, you need to create an Oracle JDeveloper *Application* by setting up an application *workspace* in Oracle JDeveloper 11*g*. The steps are described as follows:

1. Start Oracle JDeveloper 11*g*. Click the File | New... menu.
2. Choose General | Applications | Generic Application in the All Technologies tab to create a new application. Then click OK.
3. Specify the Application Name, Directory, and Application Package Prefix, as shown here, and click Next to continue.

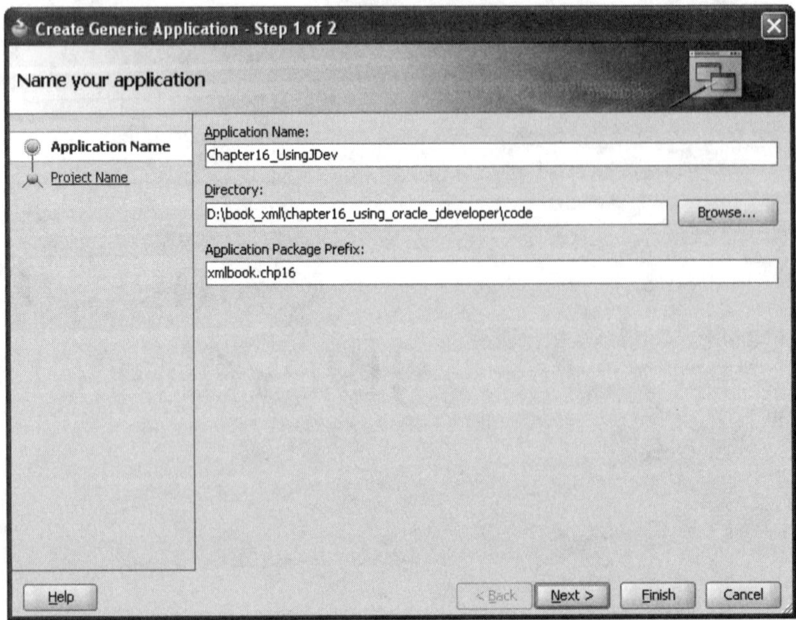

Next, you can create a project within the application workspace:

1. Click the File | New... menu in Oracle JDeveloper 11*g*.
2. Choose General | Projects | Generic Project in the All Technologies tab to create a new project. Click OK to continue.
3. Specify the project name, its directory, and the project technologies. In general, you can include Java, XML, and HTML in the Project Technologies tab. Click Finish.

The new application and new project are set up.

Creating XML Documents

To create a new XML document, you need to click the File | New... menu and select General | XML | XML Document option in the All Technologies tab. Then you need to confirm the document details, including the File Name (i.e., *john_smith.xml*) and the Directory, to store the XML document. You can then click OK to create the XML document. In the example, we create an XML document by simply copying and pasting the XML text into the created document, as shown here (*john_smith.xml*):

```
<?xml version="1.0" encoding="UTF-8"?>
<contact xmlns="http://xmlbook.com/sample/contact.xsd" id="1">
  <category>customer</category>
  <first_name>John</first_name>
  <last_name>Smith</last_name>
  <email>john.smith@hfarm.com</email>
 </contact>
```

To properly display international characters in Oracle JDeveloper 11*g*, you need to set up the Code Editor in Oracle JDeveloper 11*g* by clicking the Tools | Preferences... menu. In the pop-up Preferences dialog, choose the Code Editor | Fonts option to select a font that can display the international characters. For example, to display the XML documents with Chinese characters, the Arial Unicode MS font is selected.

Oracle JDeveloper Tip: How do I check XML syntax errors in Oracle JDeveloper 11*g*?

In Oracle JDeveloper 11*g*, the XML syntax errors are indicated by red lines under the element/attribute names. You can move your mouse to the red line to see the error messages. After correcting the errors, the red line will go away.

If you have an XML Schema predefined, you can create an XML Schema–based XML document. You then need to click the File | New... menu, and choose General | XML | XML Document from the XML Schema option. In addition to specifying the File Name (*john_smith.xml*) and Directory to store the XML document, you need to either specify an XML Schema registered to Oracle JDeveloper 11*g* or pick an XML Schema from the file system in the Schema Location setup (*contact.xsd*). The XML Schema file will be parsed by Oracle JDeveloper 11*g* before the XML document is created. In the XML Schema setup, you can then specify the XML Schema's Target Namespace, Root Element Name, and other options in the Options dialog. Then a stub XML document is created based on the XML Schema. You can update the XML document (*john_smith_with_xsd.xml*) as follows:

```
<?xml version="1.0" encoding="UTF-8" ?>
<contact xmlns:xsi="http://www.w3.org/2001/XMLSchema-instance"
         xsi:schemaLocation="http://xmlbook.com/sample/contact.xsd contact.xsd"
         xmlns="http://xmlbook.com/sample/contact.xsd" >
  <category>customer</category>
  <first_name>John</first_name>
  <last_name>Smith</last_name>
  <email>john.smith@hfarm.com</email>
 </contact>
```

During the edit of an XML Schema–based XML document, Oracle JDeveloper 11*g* will provide hints via a drop-down menu to list the valid element or attribute names. For example, after you type in the "<", Oracle JDeveloper will provide a listing of all available elements that you can add in the current document location.

Validating XML with XML Schema

For the XML document created from XML schemas, the XML Schema location attributes are added by default to the XML document (*john_smith_with_xsd.xml*). If you right-click the document name, you can select the Validate XML option to validate the document.

However, if you don't want to add the XML Schema location attributes in XML documents, you can register the XML schemas to Oracle JDeveloper 11*g* as follows:

1. Go to File | New... menu and select General | XML | XML Schema in the All Technologies tab and then click OK. Create a new XML schema document (*contact.xsd*).
2. Click the Tools | Preferences... menu. In the pop-up Preferences dialog, choose the XML Schemas category at the bottom of the list, and add an XML schema (*contact.xsd*) to the

User Schemas For XML Editing section by clicking the Add... button. You need to choose the XML Schema file (*contact.xsd*) from the file system as shown here. Click OK.

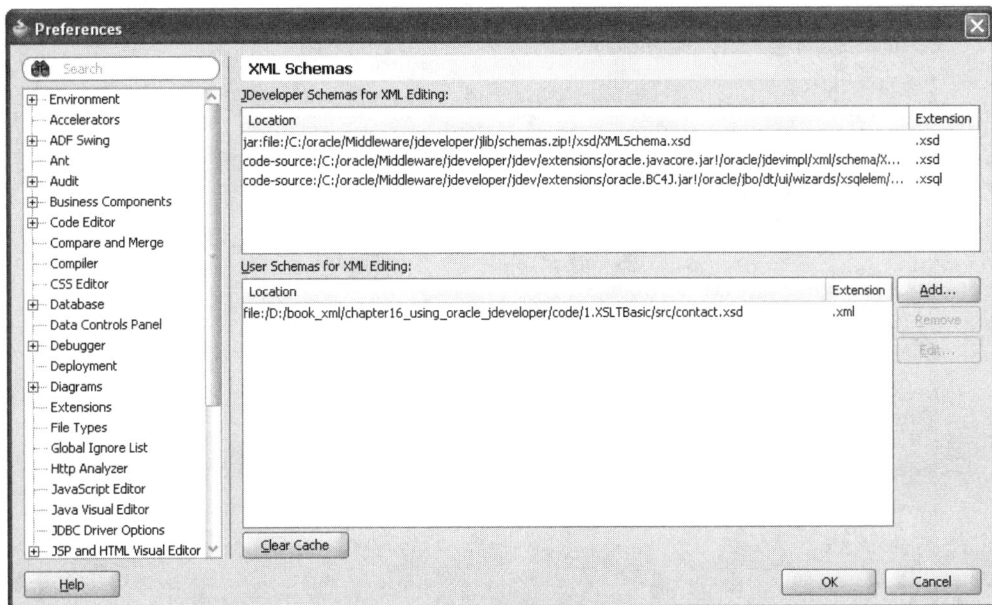

3. Right-click the XML document (*john_smith.xml*). The Validate XML option is enabled. You can click it to validate the XML document.

Transforming XML with XSLT

Before creating an XSL stylesheet, you can evaluate the XPaths in Oracle JDeveloper 11*g* using the XPath Analyzer feature. After opening an XML document (*john_smith.xml*), you can choose Search | XPath Search from the main menu. An XPath Search-Log tab will be created in the log window. In the XPath Search-Log tab, you can start by clicking the small book icon to the left of the search text box to copy XPath for the current selection. With the XML document highlighted, you can get an XPath (*/ns1:contact[1]*). Then you can edit the XPath (*/ns1:contact/ns1:first_name*) to query the XML text input and click OK. The XPath Search-Log window will show the XPath evaluation result, as shown in Figure 16-1.

Note that Oracle JDeveloper 11*g*'s XPath Analyzer only works for XML content extraction. It doesn't evaluate XPath functions.

After the XPath evaluation, you can create an XSL stylesheet by clicking the File | New... menu and selecting General | XML | XSL Style Sheet in the All Technologies tab. The following is an example XSL stylesheet (*show_contact.xsl*) displaying a contact (*john_smith.xml*) on an HTML page:

```
<xsl:stylesheet version="1.0" xmlns:xsl="http://www.w3.org/1999/XSL/Transform"
xmlns:book="http://xmlbook.com/sample/contact.xsd">
  <xsl:template match="/">
<html>
  <head>
```

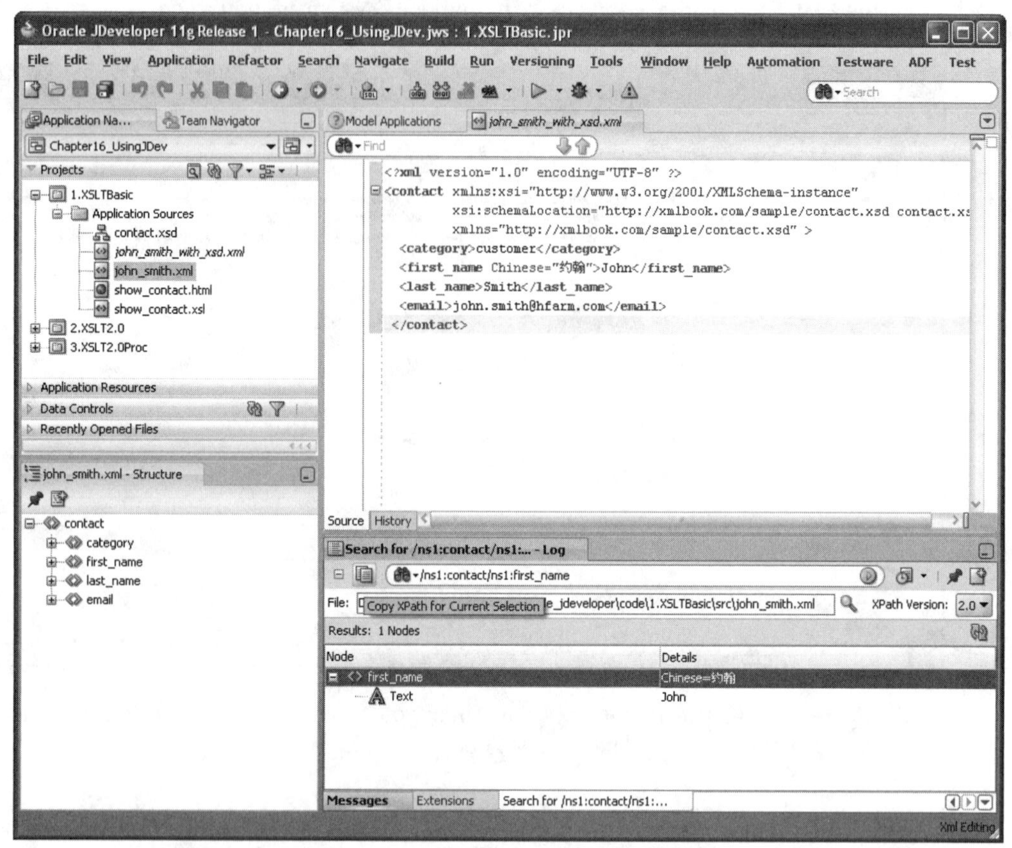

FIGURE 16-1. *XPath search in Oracle JDeveloper 11g*

```
    <meta http-equiv="Content-Type" content="text/html; charset=UTF-8"></meta>
    <title>contact_profile</title>
  </head>
  <body>
    <table cellspacing="2" cellpadding="3" border="1" width="100%">
      <tr>
        <td width="190">First Name</td>
        <td width="295">Last Name</td>
        <td width="312">Email Address</td>
      </tr>
      <tr>
        <td width="190"><xsl:value-of select="book:contact/book:first_name"/>
</td>
```

```
        <td width="295"><xsl:value-of select="book:contact/book:last_name"/>
</td>
        <td width="312"><xsl:value-of select="book:contact/book:email"/></td>
      </tr>
    </table>
  </body>
</html>
  </xsl:template>
</xsl:stylesheet>
```

Oracle JDeveloper 11*g* provides built-in XSL transformation using the Oracle XDK XSLT processing. To set up the XSL transformation, you can click the project name, go to Edit | Project Properties..., and choose Run/Debug/Profile as shown.

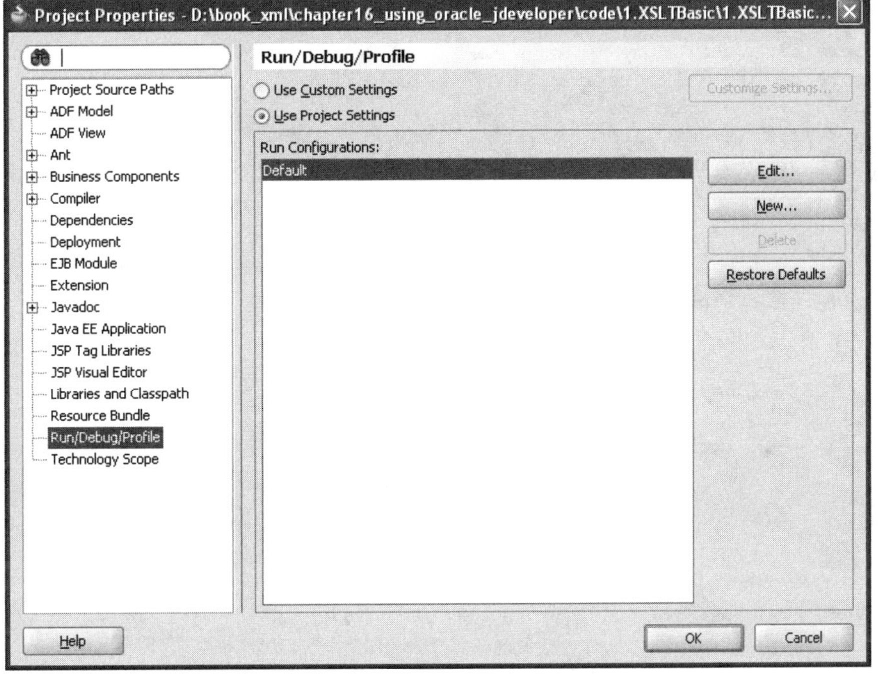

Click the Edit... button to open the Edit Run Configuration dialog. Then, after clicking the Launch Settings | XSLT option, you can choose the Input XML File (*john_smith.xml*) and specify the Output File (*show_contact.html*). After the setup, click the OK buttons to exit. Next, you can right-click the XSL stylesheet file (*show_contact.xsl*) and click the Run menu to execute the XSL transformation. The result (*show_contact.html*) will be created from the XSL transformation.

You can use the Oracle JDeveloper 11*g*'s built-in XSLT Debugger to debug XSL transformations. You can set debugging breakpoints by right-clicking a selected line in the XSL stylesheet and choosing the Run | Toggle Breakpoint menu (or press F5 key). Then, you can run the XSLT in *debug* mode by right-clicking the XSL stylesheet file and choosing the Debug menu. Oracle JDeveloper 11*g* will stop at the breakpoints and provide the XSL variable values and the current transformation result.

Now, you have learned the basics to create, validate, query, and transform XML using Oracle JDeveloper 11*g*. Next, let's learn how to build XML applications.

Running Oracle XML Java Program

In Oracle JDeveloper 11*g*, we can build Oracle XML DB applications in SQL, PL/SQL, and Java. In this section, let's use a Java application as an example.

You can open the *2.XSLT2.0.prj* project in this chapter's examples. A Java program is provided to perform XSL transformation, shown as follows (*XSLTTransform.java*):

Listing 16-1 *XSL Transformation Allowing User Inputs*

```
package xmlbook.chp07;

import java.net.URL;
import oracle.xml.parser.v2.DOMParser;
import oracle.xml.parser.v2.XMLDocument;
import oracle.xml.parser.v2.XSLStylesheet;
import oracle.xml.parser.v2.XSLProcessor;
import oracle.xml.util.XMLUtil;
import java.io.BufferedReader;
import java.io.InputStreamReader;

public class XSLTransform {
    public static void main(String[] args) throws Exception {
        DOMParser parser;
        XMLDocument xml, xsldoc;
        URL xslURL;
        URL xmlURL;
        try {
            if (args.length != 1) {
                // Must pass in the names of the XSL and XML files
                System.err.println("Usage: java XSLTransform xmlfile");
                System.exit(1);
            }
            // Parse xsl and xml documents
            parser = new DOMParser();
            parser.setPreserveWhitespace(true);
            // Parse XML document
            xmlURL = XMLUtil.createURL(args[0]);
            parser.parse(xmlURL);
            xml = parser.getDocument();
            // Read in XSL File and Apply Stylesheet
            String com;
            BufferedReader reader;
            InputStreamReader sr = new InputStreamReader(System.in);
            reader = new BufferedReader(sr);
            while (true) {
                System.out.println(" ");
```

```
                System.out.print('?');
                com = reader.readLine();
                if (com.equals("exit")) {
                    System.out.println("Bye");
                    return;
                }
                // parser input XSL file
                xslURL = XMLUtil.createURL("src/" + com + ".xsl");
                System.out.println("Transforming using " + "src/" + com +
                                   ".xsl");
                parser.parse(xslURL);
                xsldoc = parser.getDocument();

                // instantiate a stylesheet
                XSLProcessor processor = new XSLProcessor();
                processor.setBaseURL(xslURL);
                XSLStylesheet xsl = processor.newXSLStylesheet(xsldoc);

                // display any warnings that may occur
                processor.showWarnings(true);
                processor.setErrorStream(System.err);

                // Process XSL
                processor.processXSL(xsl, xml, System.out);
            }
        } catch (Exception e) {
            e.printStackTrace();
        }
    }
}
```

There are several steps to run this program.

First, you need to add XML libraries to the Oracle JDeveloper 11*g* project. To build Oracle XML Java applications, you need to add the following Java libraries ($ORACLE_HOME means the home directory of the Oracle database installation):

- **$ORACLE_HOME/LIB/xmlparserv2.jar** Oracle XDK parsers, XSL transformers, and XML schema validator.
- **$ORACLE_HOME/LIB/xml.jar** Oracle XDK XML utilities such as XML Diff, XSQL servlet, and so on.
- **$ORACLE_HOME/LIB/xsu12.jar** Oracle XDK XML SQL utility.
- **$ORACLE_HOME/RDBMS/jlib/xdb.jar** Oracle XML DB Java library, including support of XMLType objects.
- **$ORACLE_HOME/jlib/orai18n.jar** and **$ORACLE_HOME/jlib/orai18n-collation.jar** Oracle international language support.

To add these libraries, do the following:

1. Click the current project and click the Edit | Project Properties… menu.

2. Select the Libraries And Classpath category and click the Add Library… button.
3. In the Add Library dialog, click the New… button. A Create Library dialog will pop up. Because these libraries will be used in multiple projects, choose User (instead of Project) as the Library Location. Specify a unique Library Name and then click the Add Entry… button. Then, after returning to the Add Library dialog, pick up the libraries from the path created and click OK. Click the OK buttons to complete the setting. The example result is shown here.

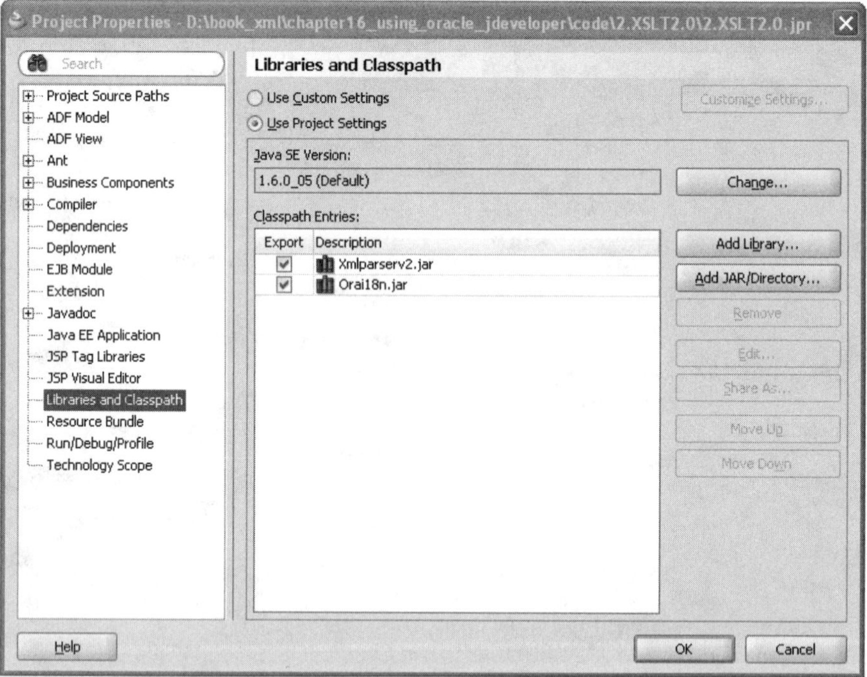

Oracle XML DB Tip: Which Java libraries should I use?

When building Oracle XML DB applications, it's a good practice to use the Java libraries provided by the Oracle database, including orai18n.jar, xmlparserv2.jar, and xdb.jar. This ensures that the library versions are in line with the Oracle database.

Highlighted in this Java program are the sections in which we allow users to specify the XSL stylesheet file name. To run this project, you need to turn on the Allow Program Input option in Oracle JDeveloper 11g.

1. Open the *XSLT 2.0* project.
2. Click the Edit | Project Properties… menu. In the pop-up dialog, choose the Run/Debug/ Profile category and edit the current Default profile. In the profile editing dialog, click the

Tool Settings option and then check the Allow Program Input option under the Additional Runner Options category. The example setup is shown here.

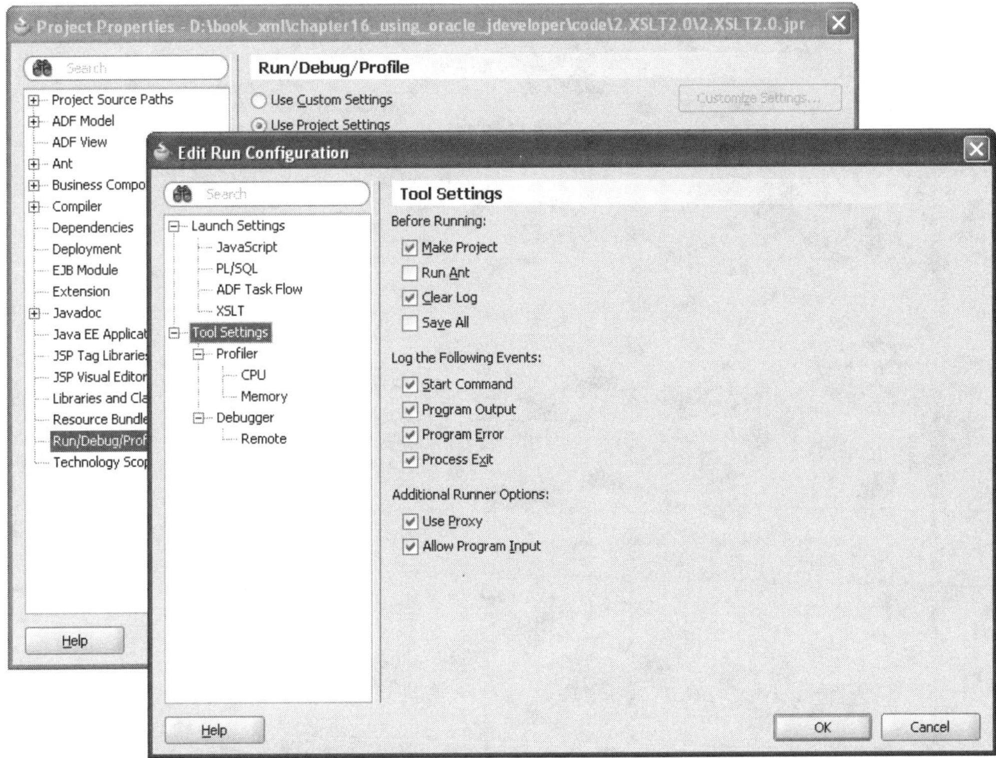

After you set this up, you can run *XSLTransform.java*. This program will pop up a "?" to ask for input. You then type in the XSLT 2.0 stylesheet names without the *.xsl* extension (**grouping**, **temptree**, **temptree_advanced**, **multioutput**, **charmapping**). These XSL stylesheets demonstrate some key XSLT 2.0 features. Figure 16-2 shows an example screenshot.

Creating Java Stored Procedures: Basics

Java Stored Procedures are useful when running Java-based XML processes inside the Oracle database. For example, to run XSLT with Java extensions or perform SAX-based XPath extractions, you can create Java Stored Procedures.

There are several steps needed to create a Java Stored Procedure. These include writing a Java program, setting up Oracle Java Virtual Machine (JVM) in the Oracle database, loading the compiled Java program to Oracle JVM, and creating a PL/SQL procedure for the loaded Java program.

Using Oracle JDeveloper 11*g*, you can easily create, debug, and deploy Java Stored Procedures. This section explains how to create and deploy a Java Stored Procedure for XML DB applications using Oracle JDeveloper 11*g*. You can start by opening *3.XSLTProc.prj* in the book examples.

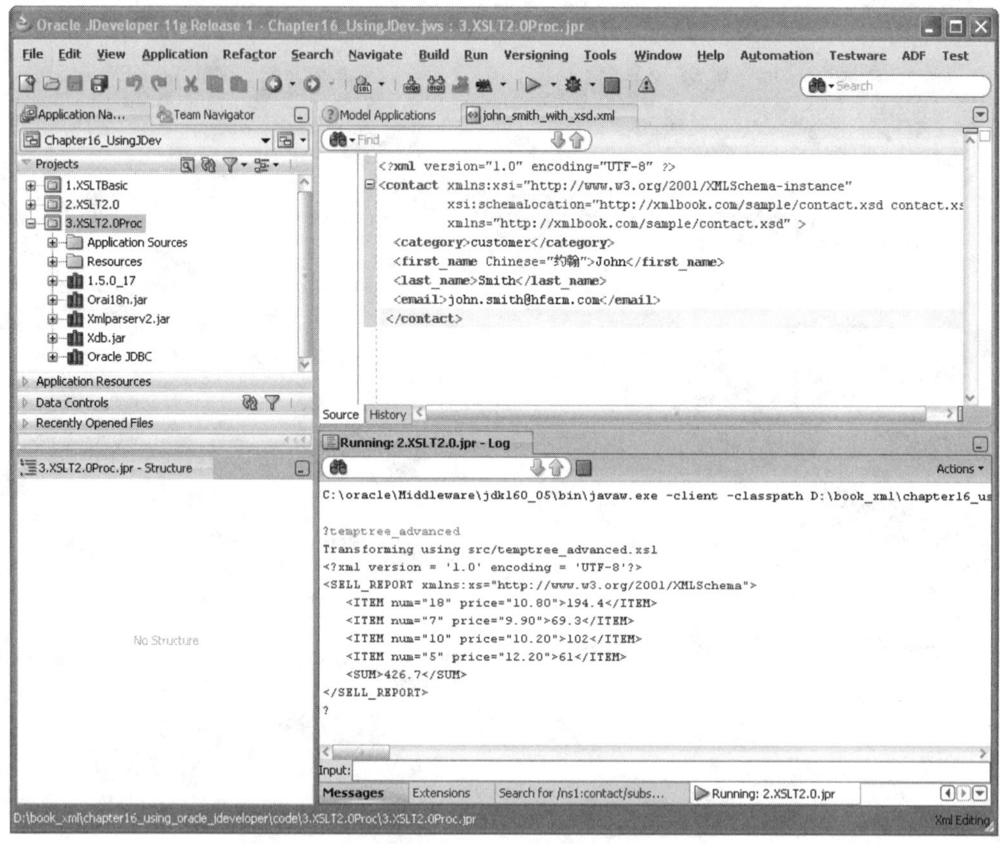

FIGURE 16-2. *Running XSLT 2.0 examples*

Oracle XML DB Tip: Which Java version should I use for Java Stored Procedures?

You need to compile the Java classes for Java Stored Procedures using the JDK shipped with the Oracle database. For example, in Oracle Database 11.2.0.2, you need to use JDK 1.5.0_17. To set the Java version in Oracle JDeveloper 11*g*, you can click the Edit | Project Properties… menu, and then select the Libraries And Classpath option. In the Java SE Version option, click the Change… button. Then you pick the Oracle database–provided Java Executable, (i.e., $ORACLE_HOME\jdk\bin\java.exe). Otherwise, you get the following error: ORA-29552: *Verification warning: java.lang.UnsupportedClassVersion.*

Setting Up Oracle Java Virtual Machine

Oracle Java Virtual Machine (Oracle JVM or JServer) has been provided by default since Oracle 8*i* (8.1.5) as a Java execution environment inside the Oracle database. With Oracle JVM, we can create Java Stored Procedures, which are PL/SQL functions/procedures running on the Java code deployed to Oracle JVM.

Before using Oracle JVM, you first need to check if it is ready for use. The following command checks whether Oracle JVM is installed by logging in as SYS user (as SYSDBA) (*check_jvm.sql*):

```
column comp_name format a30
column status format a10
column version format a10
select comp_name,status,version from dba_registry
where comp_name in ('JServer JAVA Virtual Machine');
```

With the default Oracle database installation, Oracle JVM should be ready to use:

```
COMP_NAME                      STATUS     VERSION
------------------------------ ---------- ----------
JServer JAVA Virtual Machine   VALID      11.2.0.2.0
```

If the status is not shown as VALID, you then need to install Oracle JVM. Please refer to the Oracle documentation, *Java Developer's Guide*, for installation details.

With Oracle JVM installed, you also need to check whether the required Java libraries for your applications have been uploaded to Oracle JVM. For XML applications, you need at least the Oracle XDK and Oracle XML DB libraries. By default in the Oracle database installation, Oracle XDK and XML DB libraries are loaded to Oracle JVM. You can use the following command to check the Java class status (*check_xml_lib.sql*):

```
column object_name format a50
column object_type format a15
column status format a5
SELECT object_name, object_type, status
       FROM user_objects
       WHERE object_name LIKE '%oracle/xml/xslt%';

SELECT object_name, object_type, status
       FROM user_objects
       WHERE object_name LIKE '%oracle/xdb/XMLType%';

SELECT object_name, object_type, status
       FROM user_objects
       WHERE object_name LIKE '%oracle/xml/parser/v2/DOMParser%';
```

This SQL query checks the Java classes for XSLT, DOM, and XML DB classes, which are needed to run the example application of this chapter. *oracle/xml/xslt%* includes the classes for XSL transformation. *oracle/xdb/XMLType%* includes the classes to process XMLType objects. *oracle/xml/parser/v2/DOMParser%* includes the classes in the Oracle XDK DOM parser. When all of the Java classes are shown as VALID, we're ready to build Java Stored Procedures. Otherwise, we need to reload the following Java libraries to Oracle JVM:

- **Oracle XDK libraries** $ORACLE_HOME/LIB/xmlparserv2.jar for XSLT processor and XML parser.
- **Oracle XML DB** $ORACLE_HOME/RDBMS/jlib/xdb.jar for XMLType objects management.

Creating the Java Program

Writing Java code for Java Stored Procedures is not much different from writing Java code that runs outside the Oracle database. However, the Java methods have to be *static*, and you have to process database object as inputs/outputs. The following is the Java code running XSL transformations (*XMLTransform.java*):

```
import oracle.xml.parser.v2.DOMParser;
import oracle.xml.parser.v2.XMLDocument;
import oracle.xml.parser.v2.XSLStylesheet;
import oracle.xml.parser.v2.XSLProcessor;
import java.io.PrintWriter;
import java.io.Writer;
import java.sql.Clob;
import oracle.xdb.XMLType;
...
public static String transform(XMLType xml, XMLType xsl,
                                              Clob[] result) throws Exception {
        try {
            XSLProcessor processor = new XSLProcessor();
            XMLDocument xmldoc = (XMLDocument)xml.getDocument();
            // Instantiate a stylesheet
            DOMParser parser = new DOMParser();
            parser.parse(xsl.getInputStream());
            XMLDocument xsldoc = parser.getDocument();
            XSLStylesheet xslt = processor.newXSLStylesheet(xsldoc);

            Writer out = result[0].setCharacterStream(1);
            PrintWriter pw = new PrintWriter(out);
            processor.processXSL(xslt, xmldoc, pw);
            pw.close();

            return "Transformation succeed.";
        } catch (Exception ex) {
            ex.printStackTrace();
            return "Transformation failed.";
        }
    }
```

In XSLT processing, XMLType objects are used as the inputs. The XSL transformation result is written to the passed-in CLOB (Character Large Object).

First, let's look at the XMLType input objects. You can get the DOM *Document* object directly from XMLTypes. In the example, we get the DOM *Document* object and cast it to *XMLDocument* for the Oracle XDK XSLT processor to use:

```
XMLDocument xmldoc = (XMLDocument)xml.getDocument();
```

However, the DOM *Document* object in XMLType doesn't have all of the information needed to build *XSLStylesheet*. Therefore, we re-parse the XSL input as follows:

```
DOMParser parser = new DOMParser();
parser.parse(xsl.getInputStream());
XMLDocument xsldoc = parser.getDocument();
XSLStylesheet xslt = processor.newXSLStylesheet(xsldoc);
```

Second, the passed-in CLOB is used to retrieve the XSL transformation result. CLOB is better than VARCHAR2 because it can handle large documents. To read it, you need to use the java.sql .Clob.setCharacterStream() function:

```
Writer out = result[0].setCharacterStream(1);
PrintWriter pw = new PrintWriter(out);
```

Then *PrintWriter* is passed into the XSLT processor:

```
processor.processXSL(xslt, xmldoc, pw);
```

After the Java code is compiled, it's ready to be loaded to the Oracle database.

Creating Database Connections

In Oracle JDeveloper 11*g*, before you create the deployment profile to deploy Java classes to the Oracle databases, you must set up a database connection. In Oracle JDeveloper 11*g*, the database connection can be used to run SQL commands, analyze SQL executions, and review database objects. The steps for creating a database connection are as follows:

1. Click the View | Database | Database Navigator menu to open the Database Navigator windows. In the Database Navigator windows, right-click IDE Connections and choose the New Connection option as shown:

   In this example, you need to create a database connection for the SYS user and the XMLDEMO user. The XMLDEMO user is created in the "About the Examples" instructions in the Introduction of this book. If you haven't done so, follow those instructions and run *create_xmldemo_user.sql*.

2. Set up the JDBC connection parameters as shown next, test the connection, and then click OK.

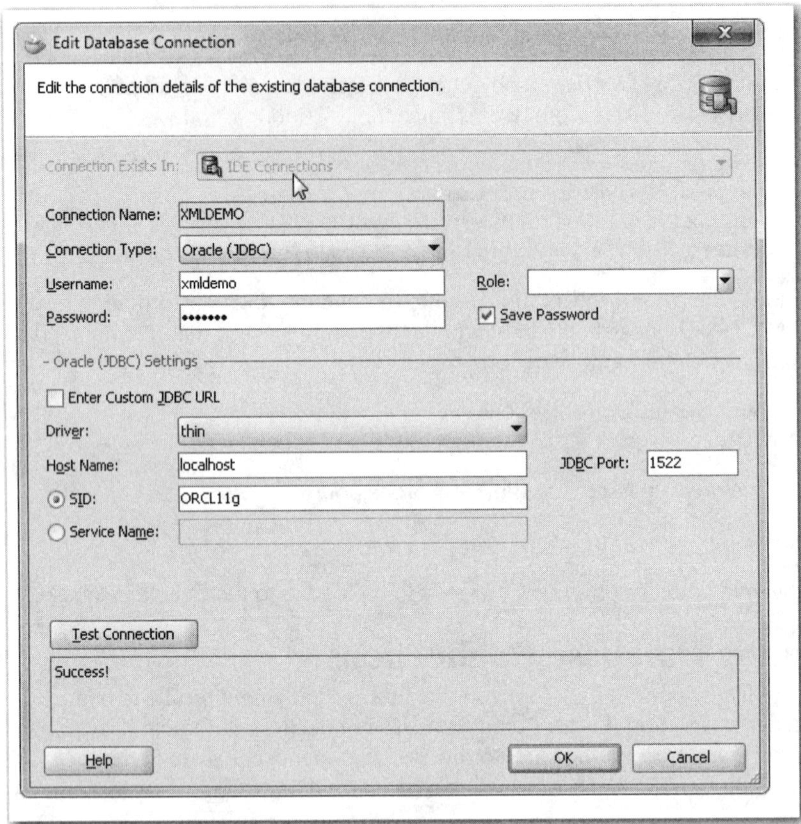

Now you can see the new database connection listed under the connection category. The database connection is ready for use.

Deploying Java Stored Procedures

The steps to create a deployment profile in Oracle JDeveloper 11*g* to deploy the Java code to the Oracle database are as follows:

1. Open the File | New... menu. Select the All Technologies tab and choose Database Tier | Database Files. Choose Loadjava And Java Stored Procedures and click OK.
2. Specify the Export File name (*xslt20.dbexport*) and the directory to store the exported file. Click OK.
3. In the Loadjava And Java Stored Procedures Database Export Properties dialog, select File Groups | Project Output | Contributors to specify the correct contributors. The default setting includes Project Output Directory, which has the compiled Java classes. Click the

File Groups | Project Output | Filters menu to select the Java class to be loaded (*xmlbook .chp07.XSLTransform.class, xmlbook.chp07.DBEntityResolver.class*), as shown here (*xslt20.dbexport*).

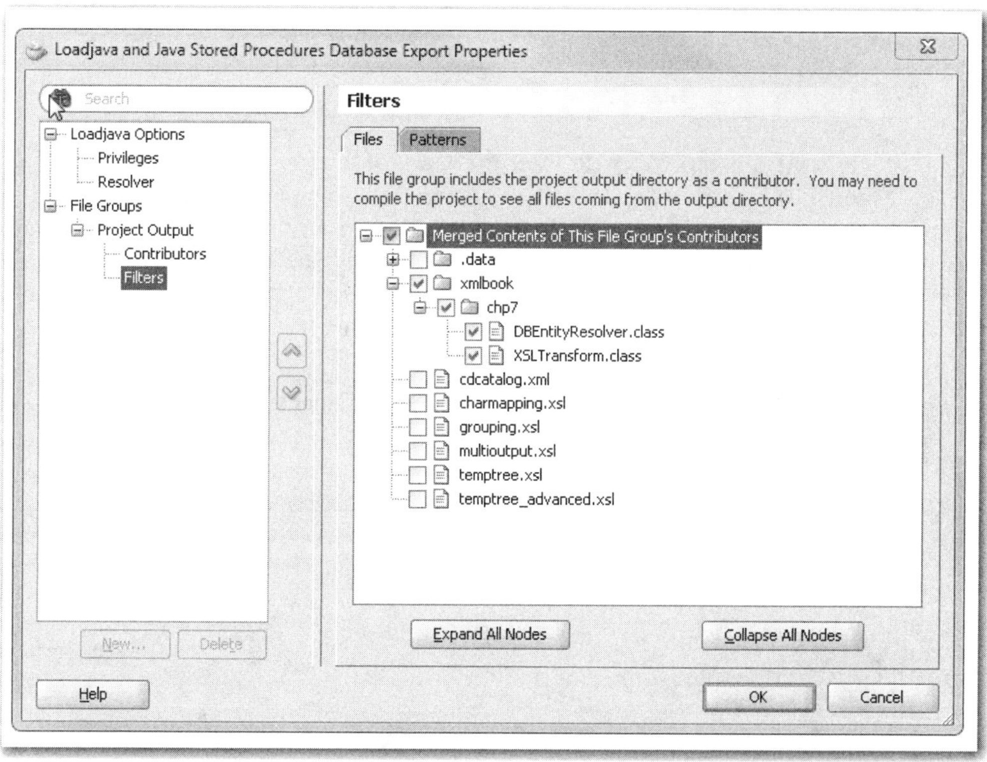

4. Click OK to complete the profile setup. Note that we include one additional class, *DBEntityResolver.class*, in the deployment file. This file will be used and discussed later in the "Creating Java Stored Procedures: Advanced Topics" section.
5. Right-click the deployment file, and then export the profile to a database connection, as shown here.

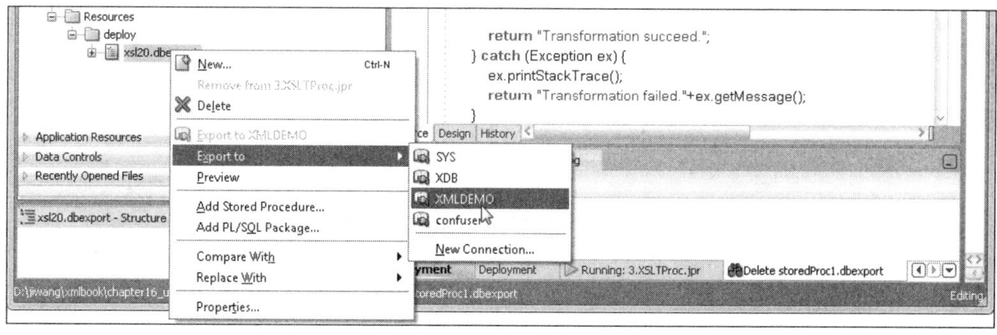

6. If deployment completes successfully, you will get the following message in the Deployment log window:

```
Invoking loadjava on connection 'orcl11g' with arguments:
-order -resolve -thin -schema xmldemo
Loadjava finished.
Publishing finished.
```

Oracle XML DB Tip: Why do I get the *Cannot access oracle.sql.OPAQUE* error?
This could be caused by the wrong JDBC library. For example, in Oracle Database 11.2.0.2, you need to choose the JDBC library provided by Oracle DB (i.e., *$ORACLE_HOME/jdbc/lib/ojdbc5.jar*).

To check if a Java class is loaded to the database, we can open SQL*Plus from Oracle JDeveloper 11*g* by right-clicking the SQL file name and choosing Run In SQL*Plus | IDE Connections | XMLDEMO. A SQL*Plus window appears. After logging in as the XMLDEMO user, the query result is shown. See Figure 16-3.

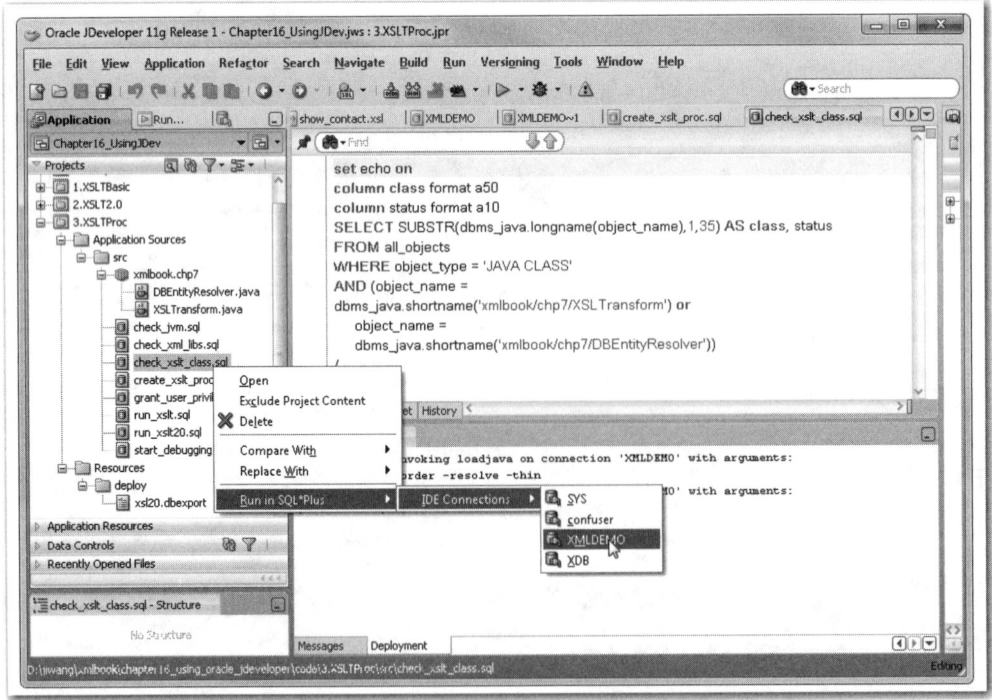

FIGURE 16-3. *Opening the SQL worksheet*

The SQL query is shown as follows (*check_xslt_class.sql*):

```
SELECT SUBSTR(dbms_java.longname(object_name),1,35) AS class, status
FROM all_objects
WHERE object_type = 'JAVA CLASS'
AND object_name =
dbms_java.shortname('xmlbook/chp07/XSLTransform') or
     object_name =
     dbms_java.shortname('xmlbook/chp07/DBEntityResolver'));
CLASS                                               STATUS
--------------------------------------------------- ----------
xmlbook/chp07/DBEntityResolver                       VALID
xmlbook/chp07/XSLTransform                           VALID
```

If the result shows the status of the class is VALID, then the deployment of the Java class into Oracle JVM is successful.

Creating PL/SQL Specifications

After the Java classes are loaded to Oracle JVM, you then can create the PL/SQL specification for the Java Stored Procedures. In the PL/SQL definition, we use the AS LANGUAGE JAVA syntax to specify the Java classes (*create_xslt_proc.sql*):

```
CREATE or replace FUNCTION xmltransform10(xml in XMLType,
xsl in XMLType, res in out nocopy CLOB) RETURN VARCHAR2
authid current_user
AS LANGUAGE JAVA
NAME 'xmlbook.chp07.XSLTransform.transform(oracle.xdb.XMLType, oracle.xdb
.XMLType, java.sql.Clob[]) return java.lang.String';
```

This is the specification for the Java method transform() in the *xmlbook.chp07.XSLTransform* class:

```
public static String transform(XMLType xml, XMLType xsl, Clob[] result)
```

Note that the Java class name and parameter names are *case-sensitive.*

Oracle Database Tip: Troubleshooting

If you write the class or parameter name incorrectly in the PL/SQL function/procedure specification, you will get the *no method found* error. For example, if you write *java.sql .clob[]* instead of *java.sql.Clob[]* in the previous example, you will get the following error:

```
ORA-29531: no method transform in class xmlbook/chp07/XSLTransform
```

By default, the current user will have the execution privileges of the created procedure. If we want other users to run the procedure, we can use AUTHID to specify the other users.

Oracle Database Tip: How do I specify CLOB inputs for Java Stored Procedures?

You might notice that we accept a CLOB array (CLOB[]) as the parameter in Java. This is because in the PL/SQL stored procedure, the CLOB is defined using the IN OUT NOCOPY modifier. It's a rule that PL/SQL parameters with OUT mode must map to an array of the object type in Java. For example, the first element of this input CLOB[] *result* array is *result[0]*.

Running Java Stored Procedures

These PL/SQL functions/procedures are no different from other PL/SQL procedures. They can be run in PL/SQL packages, triggers, or SQL commands. For example, you can run the PL/SQL procedure as follows (*run_xslt.sql*):

```
set serveroutput on
declare
  mesg varchar2(4000);
  res clob;
begin
  dbms_lob.createtemporary(lob_loc => res,cache => true, dur=>dbms_lob.session);
  mesg := xmltransform10(xmltype('<?xml version="1.0" encoding="windows-1252" ?>
<CATALOG>
  <CD>
    <TITLE>Empire Burlesque</TITLE>
    <ARTIST>Bob Dylan</ARTIST>
    <COUNTRY>USA</COUNTRY>
    <COMPANY>Columbia</COMPANY>
    <PRICE>10.80</PRICE>
    <YEAR>1985</YEAR>
  </CD>
  <CD>
    <TITLE>Hide your heart</TITLE>
    <ARTIST>Bonnie Tyler</ARTIST>
    <COUNTRY>UK</COUNTRY>
    <COMPANY>CBS Records</COMPANY>
    <PRICE>9.90</PRICE>
    <YEAR>1988</YEAR>
  </CD>
  <CD>
    <TITLE>Still got the blues</TITLE>
    <ARTIST>Gary Moore</ARTIST>
    <COUNTRY>UK</COUNTRY>
    <COMPANY>Virgin Records</COMPANY>
    <PRICE>10.20</PRICE>
    <YEAR>1990</YEAR>
  </CD>
  <CD>
```

```
    <TITLE>This is US</TITLE>
    <ARTIST>Gary Lee</ARTIST>
    <COUNTRY>UK</COUNTRY>
    <COMPANY>Virgin Records</COMPANY>
    <PRICE>12.20</PRICE>
    <YEAR>1990</YEAR>
  </CD>
</CATALOG>'),
  xmltype('<xsl:stylesheet version="2.0"
  xmlns:xsl="http://www.w3.org/1999/XSL/Transform">
  <xsl:output indent="yes"/>
  <xsl:template match="/">
    <xsl:for-each-group select="/CATALOG//CD" group-by="COUNTRY">
      <xsl:sort select="COUNTRY"/>
      <COUNTRY name="{COUNTRY}">
        <xsl:for-each-group select="current-group()" group-by="YEAR">
          <YEAR year="{YEAR}">
            <xsl:copy-of select="current-group()/TITLE"/>
          </YEAR>
        </xsl:for-each-group>
      </COUNTRY>
    </xsl:for-each-group>
  </xsl:template>
</xsl:stylesheet>
'), res);
dbms_output.put_line(res);
DBMS_LOB.FREETEMPORARY(lob_loc => res);
dbms_output.put_line(mesg);
End;
/
```

The example result is

```
<?xml version = '1.0' encoding = 'UTF-8'?>
<COUNTRY name="UK">
   <YEAR
year="1988">
      <TITLE>Hide your heart</TITLE>
   </YEAR>
   <YEAR
year="1990">
      <TITLE>Still got the blues</TITLE>
      <TITLE>This is US</TITLE>
   </YEAR>
</COUNTRY>
<COUNTRY name="USA">
   <YEAR
year="1985">
      <TITLE>Empire Burlesque</TITLE>
   </YEAR>
</COUNTRY>
Transformation succeed.
```

Because Oracle XDK Java supports XSLT 2.0, we can use the XSLT 2.0 grouping feature when running Java Stored Procedures.

Remote Debugging of Java Stored Procedures

After the deployment, we can debug the Java Stored Procedures using the Oracle JDeveloper 11*g* through the *remote debugging* feature. The steps are as follows:

1. Click the Java Project (*XSLTProc*) and then click the Edit | Project Properties… menu to open the Project Properties setup dialog. Choose Run/Debug/Profile and then pick up the current Run Configuration profile (*StoredProcedureDebug* is provided in the book example). Click the Edit… button.
2. In the Edit Run Configuration dialog, check Remote Debugging under Launch Settings, as shown here.

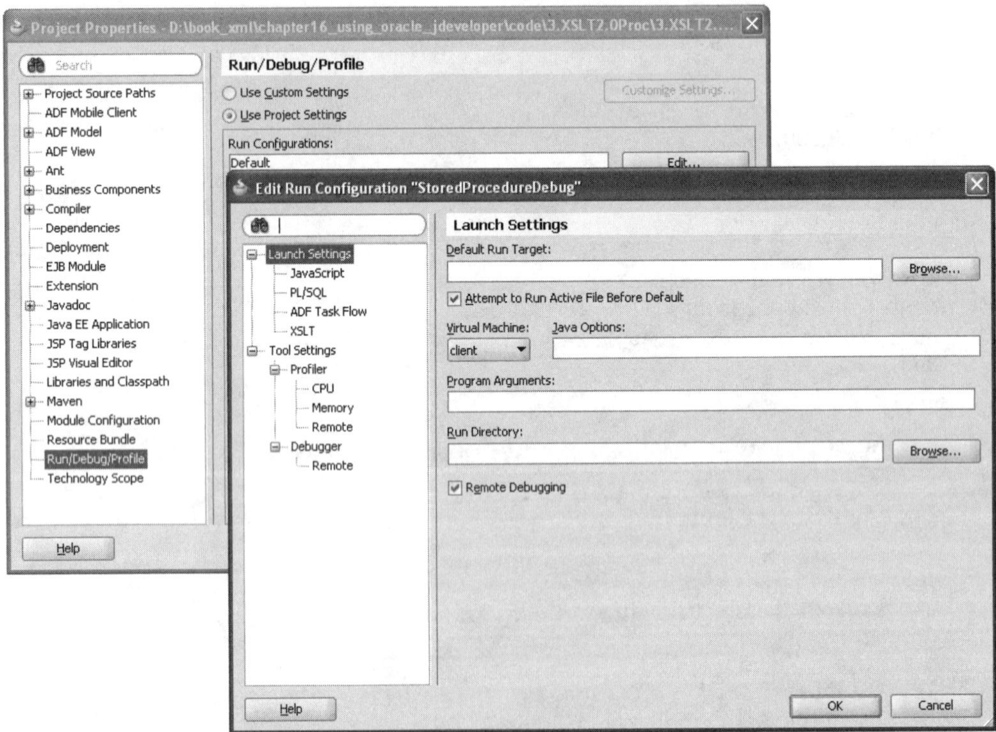

3. Choose Tool Settings | Debugger | Remote. Set the Remote debugging protocol to Listen For JPDA. Keep the rest of the default setup, as shown next.

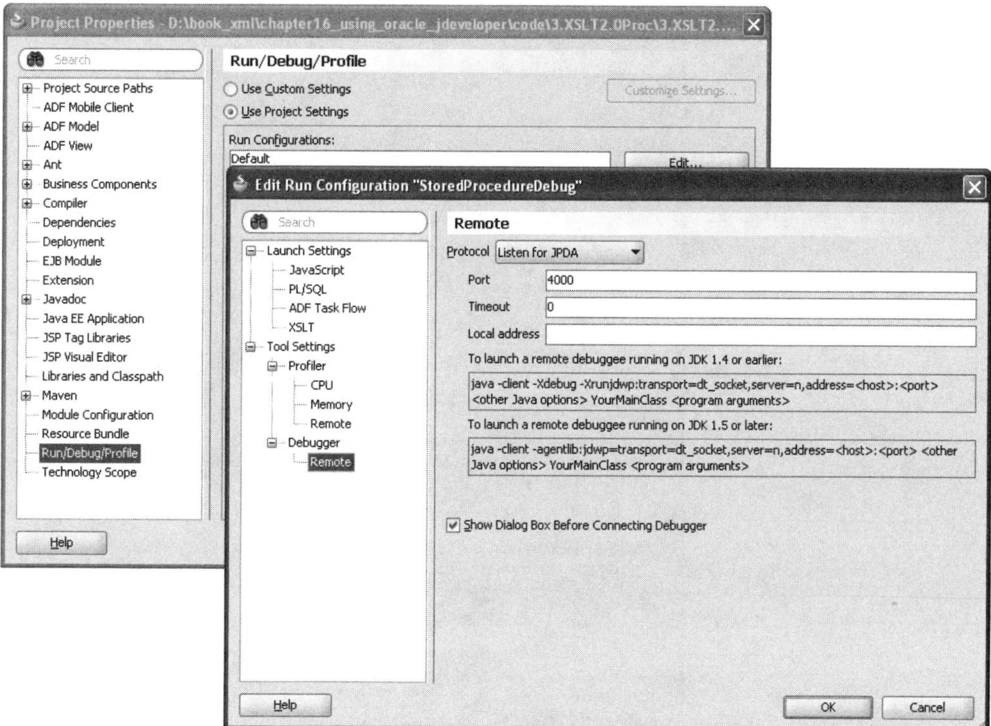

4. Click the OK buttons to close the Edit Run Configuration and Project Properties... dialogs.
5. Set breakpoints in Java code.

6. Right-click the Java code. Select Start Remote Debugger, as shown here.

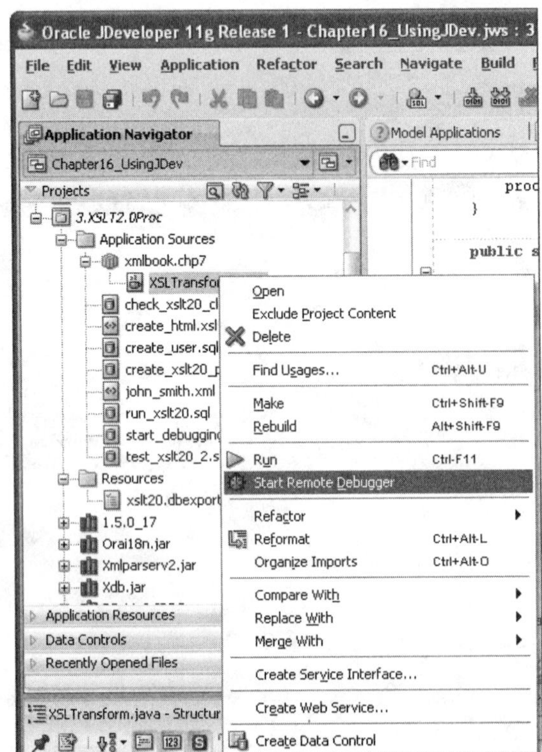

You will find the remote debugger running in the Run Manager window.

7. Open a SQL*Plus window, connect as the SYS (as SYSDBA) user and grant the XMLDEMO user the debug required privileges (*grant_debugging_privileges.sql*):

```
grant debug any procedure, debug connect session to xmldemo;
```

In order to run the Oracle JDeveloper 11*g* remote debugging feature, the SQL*Plus session must be connected to a user with *debug* privileges. Otherwise, you will get the ORA-01031: *insufficient privileges* error.

8. Then, log in as the XMLDEMO user and issue the following command (*start_debugging.sql*):

```
alter session set plsql_debug=true;
call dbms_debug_jdwp.connect_tcp('127.0.0.1', '4000');
```

The process is shown in Figure 16-4.

The address *127.0.0.1* is the IP address for the machine running Oracle JDeveloper. *4000* is the port running the remote debugger. After running this SQL command in SQL*Plus,

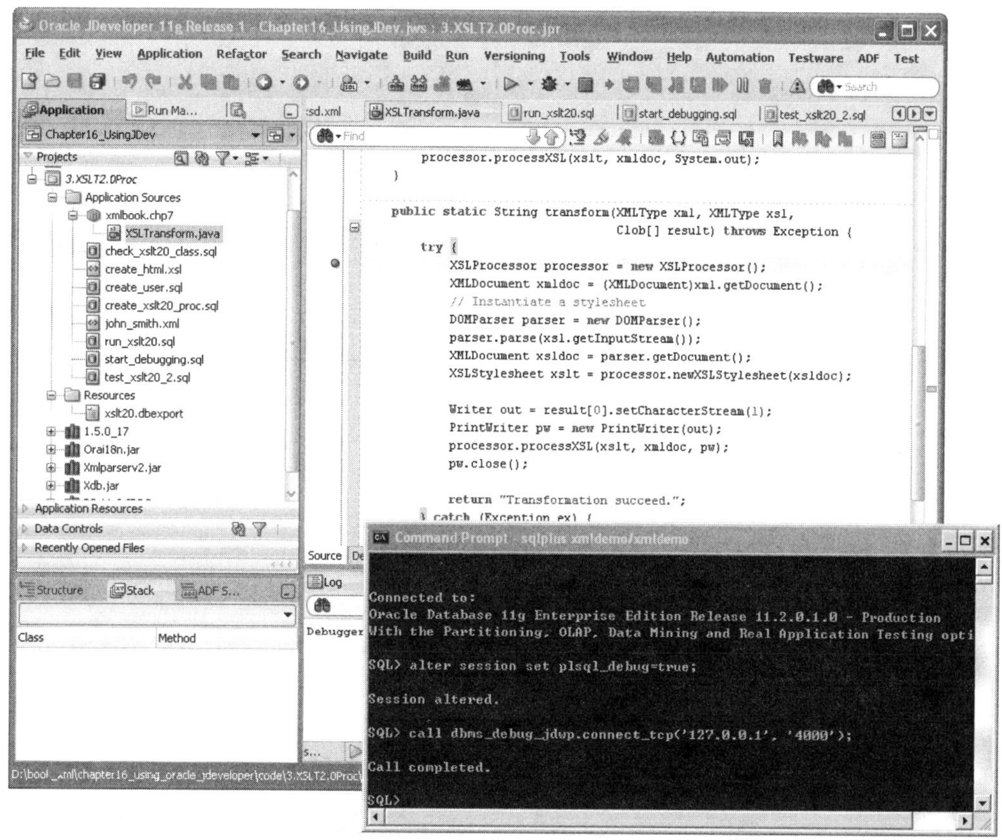

FIGURE 16-4. *Remote debugger listener in Run Manager*

the Oracle JDeveloper 11*g* debugger should accept the debugging connection; you will see a debugging process in the Run Manager. In the Oracle JDeveloper project Log window, you will receive the following message, as shown in Figure 16-5.

```
Debugger accepted connection from remote process on port 4000.
```

9. Return to SQL*Plus with the debugging session started and run the PL/SQL procedure (*run_xslt.sql*). The program will stop at the breakpoints and show all of the debugging information. Figure 16-6 shows an example debugging session running.

This feature in Oracle JDeveloper 11*g* greatly simplifies the process of creating the Java Stored Procedures.

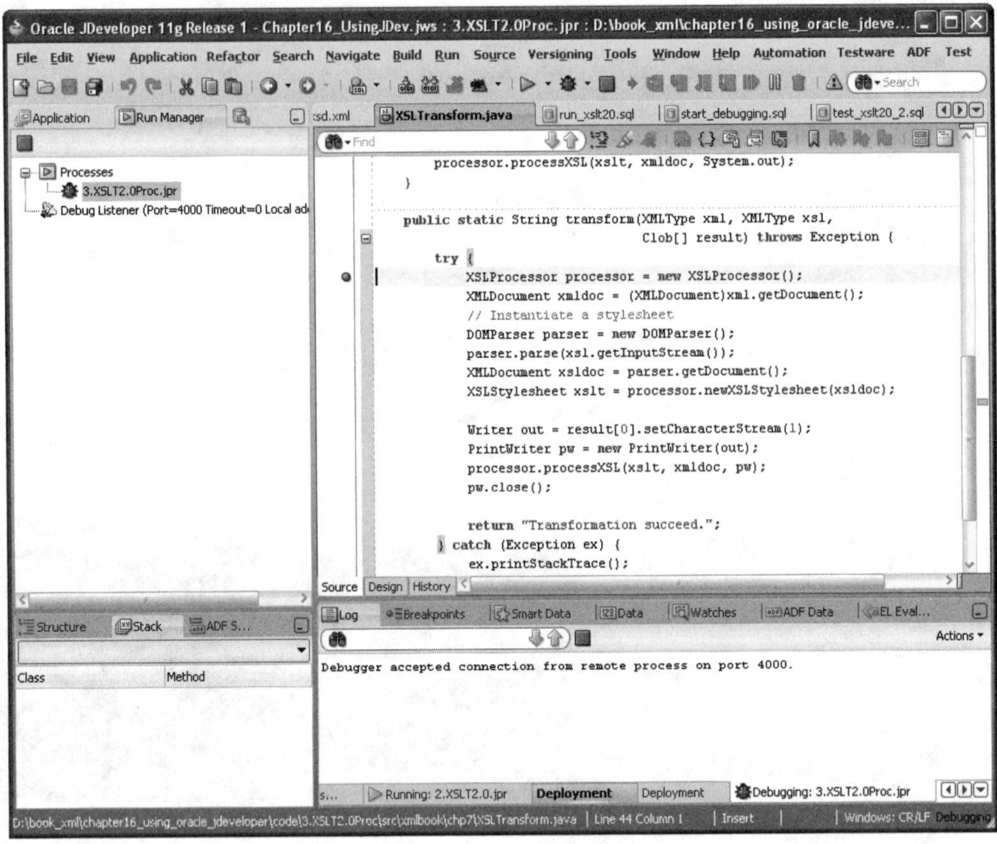

FIGURE 16-5. *Remote debugging process in Run Manager*

Creating Java Stored Procedures: Advanced Topics

In the previous section, we discussed the basic steps to set up Java Stored Procedures in the Oracle database. This section extends the discussion by adding disk I/O operations in the Java Stored Procedures. This allows running more comprehensive XSL transformations.

First, we know that an XSL stylesheet can include (*<xsl:include>*) and import (*<xsl:import>*) other XSL stylesheets. To enable this in Java Stored Procedures, we need to implement the document URL resolving process. With this process, we can then retrieve the included/imported XSL stylesheets. In Oracle XDK, this URL resolving processing is handled by *EntityResolver*. Oracle XDK allows you to overwrite the default entity resolver shown as follows (*XSLTransform.java*):

```
//Parsing XSL stylesheet
XSLProcessor processor = new XSLProcessor();
//Resolving URL References for xs:import, xs:include
```

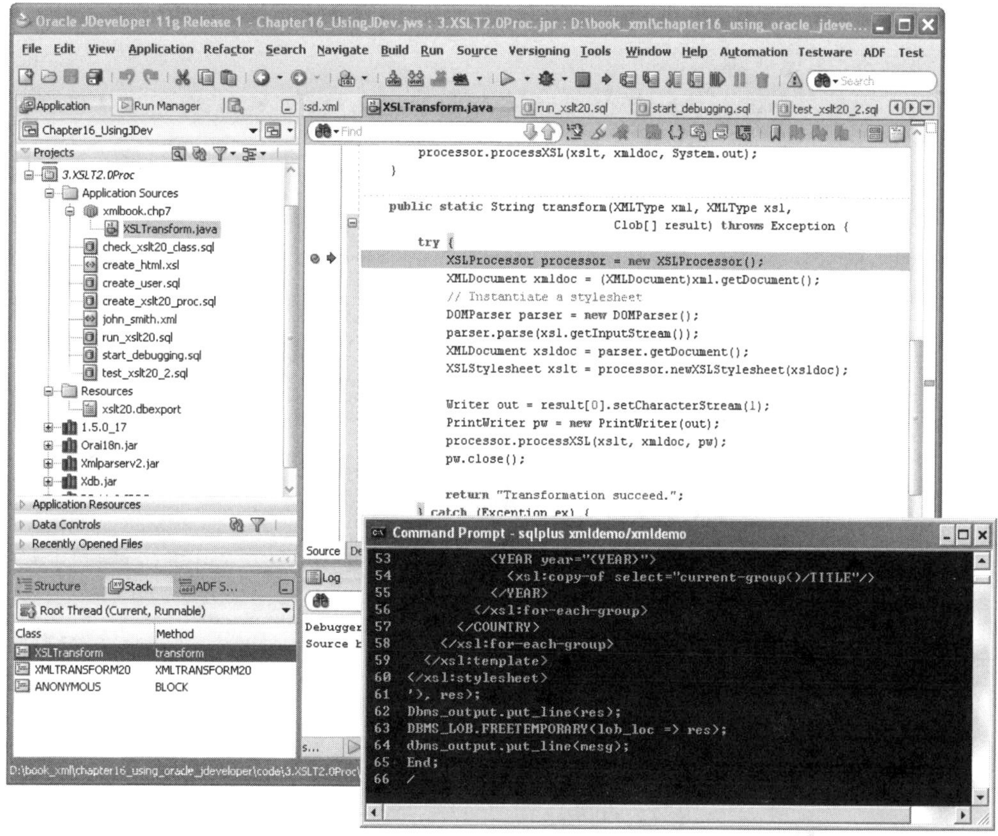

FIGURE 16-6. *Remote debugging session*

```
DBEntityResolver dber = new DBEntityResolver();
processor.setEntityResolver(dber);
```

In this example, *DBEntityResolver* extends *EntityResolver* to retrieve imported/included XSL stylesheets from the database (*DBEntityResolver.java*):

```
package xmlbook.chp07;

import java.io.IOException;
import java.io.InputStream;
import java.sql.Connection;
import java.sql.Driver;
import java.sql.DriverManager;
import java.sql.PreparedStatement;
import java.sql.ResultSet;
import oracle.jdbc.driver.OracleDriver;
```

```
import org.xml.sax.EntityResolver;
import org.xml.sax.InputSource;
import org.xml.sax.SAXException;

public class DBEntityResolver implements EntityResolver {
    // JDBC Connection
    Connection m_conn;

    // Class Construction
    DBEntityResolver(){
        try  {
            // Initialize the JDBC driver
            Driver d = new OracleDriver();
            m_conn = DriverManager.getConnection("jdbc:oracle:kprb:");
        } catch (Exception ex)  {
            ex.printStackTrace();
        } finally  {
        }
    }

    public InputSource resolveEntity(String publicId, String systemId)
    throws SAXException, IOException
    {
        InputSource dbsource = null;
        String file_location = systemId;
        InputStream file_input = null;
        try {
         PreparedStatement ps =
          m_conn.prepareStatement("select xdburitype(?).getclob() from dual");
          ps.setString(1,"/public/chp07/"+file_location);
          ResultSet rset = ps.executeQuery();
          while (rset.next()){
              file_input = rset.getBinaryStream(1);
            }
            rset.close();
        } catch (Exception ex) {
            ex.printStackTrace();
        } finally {
        }
        dbsource = new InputSource(file_input);
        return dbsource;
    }
}
```

The same entity resolving process is also used by URL references in XML parsing, such as external DTD URL references and the XML schema include (*<xsd:include>*) and import (*<xsd:import>*).

Second, an XSL stylesheet uses the document() function to read additional inputs and uses *<xsl:result-document>* to create multiple outputs. These URL resolving processes rely on the base URL setting. The user can set up *baseURL* for *XSLProcessor* (*XSLTransform.java*) as follows:

```
processor.setParam("", "base_path", "\'"+baseURL+"\'");
```

The Java program running the XSLT process should have access to the specified URLs. Within Java Stored Procedures, the database user should have the right to access the specified files and folder. The privileges are granted by the SYS user (*grant_user_pivileges.sql*):

```
exec dbms_java.grant_permission( 'XMLDEMO', 'SYS:java.io.FilePermission', 'd:\
xmlbook\data\chp07','read,write' );
exec dbms_java.grant_permission( 'XMLDEMO', 'SYS:java.io.FilePermission', 'd:\
xmlbook\data\chp07\altwords_1.xml', 'read');
exec dbms_java.grant_permission( 'XMLDEMO', 'SYS:java.io.FilePermission', 'd:\
xmlbook\data\chp07\altwords_2.xml', 'read');
exec dbms_java.grant_permission( 'XMLDEMO', 'SYS:java.io.FilePermission', 'd:\
xmlbook\data\chp07\altwords_3.xml', 'read');
exec dbms_java.grant_permission( 'XMLDEMO', 'SYS:java.io.FilePermission', 'd:\
xmlbook\data\chp07\altwords_4.xml', 'read');
exec dbms_java.grant_permission( 'XMLDEMO', 'SYS:java.io.FilePermission', 'd:\
xmlbook\data\chp07\altwords_5.xml', 'read');
exec dbms_java.grant_permission( 'XMLDEMO', 'SYS:java.io.FilePermission', 'd:\
xmlbook\data\chp07\output\altwords_merged_ses.xml', 'write');
exec dbms_java.grant_permission( 'XMLDEMO', 'SYS:java.io.FilePermission', 'd:\
xmlbook\data\chp07\output\altwords_merged.xml', 'write');
exec dbms_java.grant_permission( 'XMLDEMO', 'SYS:java.io.FilePermission', 'd:\
xmlbook\data\chp07\output', 'read,write');
```

Here, the example data file of the book is installed in the *d:\xmlbook\data* directory. All of the XSL transformation files are stored in the *d:\xmlbook\data\chp07* directory. The output is set in the *d:\xmlbook\data\chp07*\output folder. With the privileges granted, the XSLT processor, run by the Java Stored Procedure in XMLDEMO user, can then pick up those files and create output files to the specified output folder.

With this setup, you can create a new Java Stored Procedure (*create_xslt_proc.sql*):

```
CREATE or replace FUNCTION xmltransform20(xml in XMLType, xsl in XMLType,
baseurl in varchar2, res in out nocopy CLOB) RETURN VARCHAR2
AUTHID CURRENT_USER
AS LANGUAGE JAVA
NAME 'xmlbook.chp07.XSLTransform.transform(oracle.xdb.XMLType, oracle.xdb
.XMLType, java.lang.String, java.sql.Clob[]) return java.lang.String';
```

Then, you can use the created Java Stored Procedure to run the complex XSLT 2.0 transformation discussed in Chapter 7, which merges the alternative word files and creates multiple dictionary files (*run_xslt20.sql*):

```
set serveroutput on
declare
  mesg varchar2(4000);
  res clob;
begin
  dbms_lob.createtemporary( lob_loc => res , cache => true , dur => dbms_lob
.session );
  mesg := xmltransform20(
    xdburitype('/public/chp07/altwords_1.xml').getxml(),
    xdburitype('/public/chp07/gen_alterword_list.xsl').getxml(),
```

```
    'file:///d:/jiwang/xmlbook/data/chp07/',
    res);
  dbms_output.put_line(res);
  dbms_lob.freetemporary(lob_loc => res);
  dbms_output.put_line(mesg);
end;
/
```

After running the command, you can find the transformed results in the *d:\xmlbook\data\chp07* output folder.

Summary

In this chapter, we briefly discussed how to use Oracle JDeveloper 11*g* to build XML applications, including XML document creation, transformation, validation, and XPath evaluation. We also learned how to run XML applications in Java, and deploy and debug Java Stored Procedures. Oracle JDeveloper 11*g* can also generate JAXB classes (discussed in Chapter 5) and create Web Services (discussed in Chapter 15).

CHAPTER 17

Pulling It All Together

ooking back over the previous chapters, we have discussed various XML application development techniques. In this chapter, let's use the skills we've learned to build an XML application.

In this application, we allow users to create contact documents in XML and then store the XML files in a file system outside of the Oracle database. The XML files are loaded to the Oracle database by copying the files to Oracle XML DB Repository via FTP. Storing XML in Oracle XML DB provides a persistent storage of the XML documents, and allows us to validate the consistency of the XML data. We then create an APEX application to publish and manage the XML content on the Web. A simple business process is created in the APEX application to send emails to those selected contacts. XML is used to define the email template. XSLT is used to generate the personalized emails. After the email is sent, we can keep a record of the process by storing the email templates and creating links to the selected contacts in a new folder in the XML DB Repository. Let's learn this step by step.

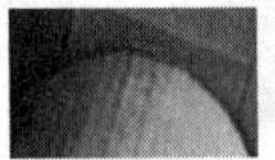

EXAMPLE SETUP
Before running the examples, please run the example setup described in the "About the Examples" section in the Introduction of this book, where the contact documents should be loaded to XML DB Repository/public/contact folder. You also should be familiar with building APEX applications. You can find APEX tutorials on the Oracle Technology Network (OTN).

Creating XML Documents

Users can manage their contacts in XML, without connecting to an Oracle database. These contact XML documents can be stored in a local file system. In practice, you would create an XML Schema file first and use it to create the XML documents. Using Oracle JDeveloper 11g, as discussed in Chapter 16, you can create an XML document from XML schemas. However, when creating the XML documents, note that the XML document format is evolving over time. For example, it's very common to introduce new XML elements into the XML documents. Therefore, it's important to review the content in your XML documents, even though they are created based on XML schemas.

In our application, we use the approach discussed in Chapter 6 to extract XPaths from the contact documents. In addition, we extend the example by allowing the recording of unique XPaths across all of the contact XML documents. The new function created is shown as follows (*RunXPathExtraction.java*):

Listing 17-1 *Extracting Unique XPaths from Multiple XML Documents*

```
public static void checkXPath(String pathRoot, PrintStream out) {
        Vector cfiles = XMLUtility.getFileList(pathRoot, "xml");
        Hashtable s_XPath = new Hashtable();
        if (cfiles != null) {
            try {
```

```
                for (int i = 0; i < cfiles.size(); i++) {
                    XPathExtraction xe = new XPathExtraction(true);
                    String fp = pathRoot + cfiles.elementAt(i).toString();
                    xe.extract(XMLUtility.createURL(fp));

                    Hashtable cs_XPath = xe.getXPathStack().getXPathValues();
                    Enumeration eKeys = cs_XPath.keys();
                    while (eKeys.hasMoreElements()) {
                        s_XPath.put(eKeys.nextElement(),"");
                    }
                }
            } catch (Exception ex) {
                ex.printStackTrace();
            }
        }
        Vector v = new Vector(s_XPath.keySet());
        Collections.sort(v);
        Iterator it = v.iterator();
        while (it.hasNext())  out.println(it.next());
    }
```

In this program, we first read a set of files from a local file system to a Vector *cfiles*:

```
Vector cfiles = XMLUtility.getFileList(pathRoot, "xml");
```

Then we create a *hashtable* to hold the XPaths:.

```
Hashtable s_XPath = new Hashtable();
```

When iterating all of the XML files, we call the streaming XPath function to extract XPath by calling the extract() function in *XPathExtraction*:

```
XPathExtraction xe = new XPathExtraction(true);
String fp = pathRoot + cfiles.elementAt(i).toString();
xe.extract(XMLUtility.createURL(fp));
```

For each file, the extracted XPaths (*cs_XPath*) are added to the hashtable *s_XPath*:

```
Hashtable cs_XPath = xe.getXPathStack().getXPathValues();
Enumeration eKeys = cs_XPath.keys();
while (eKeys.hasMoreElements()) {
s_XPath.put(eKeys.nextElement(),"");
}
```

The Java program prints out the sorted unique XPaths for all of the contacts:

```
Vector v = new Vector(s_XPath.keySet());
Collections.sort(v);
Iterator it = v.iterator();
while (it.hasNext())  out.println(it.next());
```

For example, when running this program on the example contact XML files provided with the examples for this book, we get the following set of XPaths:

```
/contact/
/contact/@id
/contact/@type
/contact/@xmlns
/contact/address/
/contact/address/city/
/contact/address/country/
/contact/address/state/
/contact/address/street1/
/contact/address/zipcode/
/contact/business/
/contact/business/company/
/contact/business/department/
/contact/business/title/
/contact/business/website/
/contact/cellphone/
/contact/email/
/contact/first_name/
/contact/first_name/@Chinese
/contact/last_name/
/contact/phone/
/contact/references/
/contact/references/reference/
/contact/references/reference/@relationship
/contact/references/reference/email/
/contact/references/reference/first_name/
/contact/references/reference/last_name/
```

This report indicates all of the possible XPaths in the contact XML documents. This is very useful when updating contact documents and preparing the XML queries (i.e., XMLTable() queries) in Oracle XML DB.

Storing XML in XML DB Repository

To load the contact documents into the Oracle database, we can use Oracle XML DB Repository's FTP protocol access.

With the XML documents stored in XML DB Repository, we manage the XML data using the Oracle XML DB functions.

Creating an SQL View

Using the XPath content analysis result, we can create an SQL view of the contacts using XMLTable() (*create_contact_vw.sql*):

Listing 17-2 *Creating Contact SQL View with XMLTable()*

```
create or replace view contact_vw as
select c.*, rv.any_path from resource_view rv,
XMLTable(XMLNamespaces(DEFAULT 'http://xmlbook.com/sample/contact.xsd',
'http://xmlns.oracle.com/xdb/XDBResource.xsd' as "ns"),
'$r/ns:Resource/ns:Contents/*' passing rv.res as "r"
COLUMNS
id number PATH '/contact/@id',
category varchar2(4000) PATH '/contact/category',
first_name varchar2(100) PATH '/contact/first_name',
last_name varchar2(100) PATH '/contact/last_name',
email varchar2(4000) PATH '/contact/email',
address XMLType path '/contact/address',
business XMLType path '/contact/business',
cellphone varchar2(4000)  path '/contact/cellphone',
references XMLType  path '/contact/references',
phone varchar2(4000)  path '/contact/phone') c
where under_path(res,'/public/contact/xml',1)>0;
```

In this SQL, we keep some of the XML content in XMLTypes, such as *references, business details,* and *address,* to avoid creating multiple tables.

Adding Contact IDs

When editing contacts in file systems, it's difficult to perform operations across multiple XML documents, such as assigning a unique ID to each contact (*check_id.sql*). However, after the data is loaded to XML DB Repository, these operations become easy; we can use *contact_vw.*

The first step is to make the *contact_vw* view content updatable. We need to create an *instead-of* trigger (*create_contact_vw_trigger.sql*):

Listing 17-3 *Creating Instead-of Trigger for Updating XMLTable() View (1)*

```
create or replace trigger contact_vw_update
instead of update on contact_vw
referencing new as new
for each row
begin
  Update RESOURCE_VIEW
  set res = updateXML(res,
      '/r:Resource/r:Contents/contact/@id',:new.id,
      'xmlns:r="http://xmlns.oracle.com/xdb/XDBResource.xsd"
       xmlns="http://xmlbook.com/sample/contact.xsd" ')
  where equals_path(res,:new.any_path)=1;
end;
/
show error;
```

This *instead-of* trigger provides update on the *id* attribute only.

Then, we can create a database SEQUENCE and open a database cursor to update all records in the *contact_vw* view (*assign_contact_vw_id.sql*):

Listing 17-4 *Assigning Unique ID to Contact with SQL SEQUENCE*

```
drop sequence contact_vw_id_seq;
create sequence contact_vw_id_seq start with 1;

set serveroutput on
declare
   cursor contact_vw_id_cur is select id, any_path from contact_vw;
begin
 for contact_rec in contact_vw_id_cur loop
     update contact_vw set id=contact_vw_id_seq.nextval
     where any_path = contact_rec.any_path;
  end loop;
end;
/
commit;
```

The IDs are from the *contact_vw_id_seq* sequence. We open the database cursor *contact_vw_id_cur* to process the rows in *contact_vw*.

Oracle Database Tip: Why do I get the ORA-29915: *Cannot select FOR UPDATE from collection operand* error?

Because the XMLTable() view uses the collection operand, we can't use the following update command:

```
declare
   cursor contact_vw_id_cur is select id from contact_vw for update;
begin
 for contact_rec in contact_vw_id_cur
  loop
     update contact_vw set id=contact_vw_id_seq.nextval
     where current of contact_vw_id_cur;
  end loop;
end;
```

You will get the error report. Instead, open the simple cursor shown in the example to avoid such errors.

After running this command, we will have a consistent contact *id*, which can serve as the primary key for our contact records (*check_id.sql*).

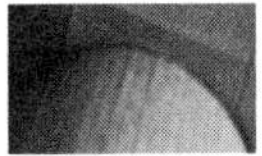

EXAMPLE SETUP
Please make sure you run the process in this section to assign unique IDs for each contact. This ID will be used to retrieve the contact record in the APEX application. Without a unique ID, you won't be able to retrieve a unique contact record for updates.

Reformatting the Data String

When you are editing XML files in the files system, the format might not be consistent over time (*check_content.sql*). For example, some contact names and emails might be in lowercase, while others might be capitalized. To make the data format consistent, we can use XQuery to update the content.

To begin, we need to extend the *contact_vw* trigger to allow updates for last_name, first_name, and email content (*cleanup_contact_vw.sql*):

Listing 17-5 *Creating Instead-of Trigger for Update XMLTable() View (2)*

```
create or replace trigger contact_vw_update
instead of update on contact_vw
referencing new as new
for each row
begin
  update RESOURCE_VIEW
  set res = updateXML(res,
      '/r:Resource/r:Contents/contact/first_name/text()',:new.first_name,
      '/r:Resource/r:Contents/contact/last_name/text()',:new.last_name,
      '/r:Resource/r:Contents/contact/email/text()',:new.email,
      'xmlns:r="http://xmlns.oracle.com/xdb/XDBResource.xsd"
       xmlns="http://xmlbook.com/sample/contact.xsd" ')
  where equals_path(res,:new.any_path)=1;
end;
/
show error;
```

Then, we can run the following command:

Listing 17-6 *Updating String Content in XMLTable() View*

```
declare
   cursor contact_vw_id_cur is select id, any_path, first_name, last_name,
email from contact_vw;
begin
 for contact_rec in contact_vw_id_cur loop
     update contact_vw set
        first_name = INITCAP(contact_rec.first_name),
        last_name = INITCAP(contact_rec.last_name),
        email = LOWER(contact_rec.email)
     where any_path = contact_rec.any_path;
```

```
    end loop;
  end;
  /
```

We use the SQL string functions to set up the data format.

Publishing XML in APEX

In Oracle Database 11*g*, Oracle APEX is installed by default and can be used to build Web applications on top of the Oracle database. After the contact documents are stored in Oracle XML DB, let's create the APEX Web application to manage the contacts and send emails.

Creating a Report

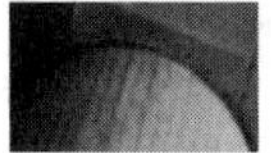

EXAMPLE SETUP

Before proceeding with this section, make sure the contact_vw *view is created in the previous section (running Project 1.* ManageData/create_contact_vw.sql*). Refer to the Appendix for the APEX setup instructions.*

First, let's log into the APEX workspace (**CONTACT_MANAGEMENT**) and then create an application with a report listing all of the contacts in the *contact_vw* view:

1. In Application Builder, click Create Application to create a new application.
2. Select the Create Application option and click Next.
3. Specify the Application Name (**Contact**) and the Application ID (**104**). Choose to create the application method (From Scratch) and the default schema (**XMLDEMO**). Click Next.
4. For Select Page Type, choose to add a Report. Set Page Source to SQL Query. Set up the Page Name (**Contact Report**). For Implementation, choose Interactive. The SQL query is as follows (*apex_contact_report.sql*):

```
SELECT APEX_ITEM.checkbox(1,id,'UNCHECKED') " ",
   id, first_name, last_name, email,
   XMLSerialize(content XMLTransform(address,
XMLType('<xsl:stylesheet version="1.0" xmlns:xsl="http://www.w3.org/1999
/XSL/Transform" xmlns:book="http://xmlbook.com/sample/contact.xsd">
  <!-- Root template -->
  <xsl:template match="/">
    <xsl:value-of select="/book:address/book:street1"/>
     <xsl:value-of select="/book:address/book:street2"/>,
     <xsl:value-of select="/book:address/book:city"/><xsl:text>,</
xsl:text><xsl:value-of select="/book:address/book:state"/><xsl:text> </
xsl:text><xsl:value-of select="/book:address/book:zipcode"/>
  </xsl:template>
</xsl:stylesheet>'))as CLOB) address, category,
phone, any_path, id as to_update, id as search_po
from contact_vw
```

This setup is shown here:

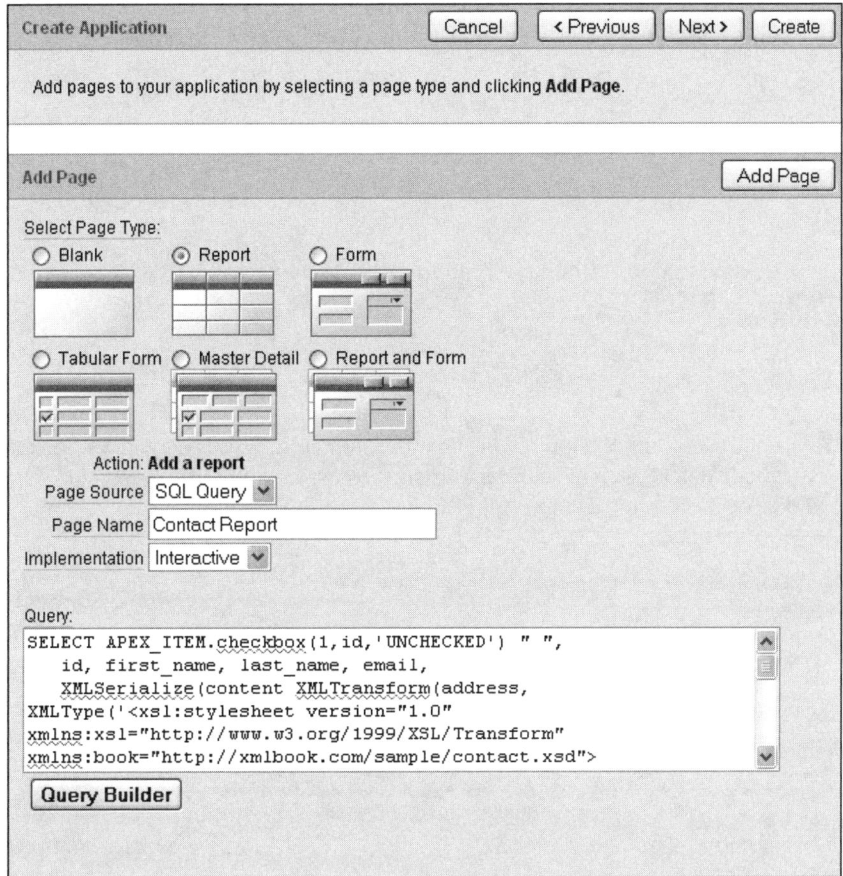

Note that, in the contact report query, we use XMLSerialize() to convert XMLTypes to CLOBs so that the XML content can be displayed by APEX in a well-indented format. In addition, an XSL transformation is applied to the *<address>* element to create a well-formatted address content for APEX display. Next, click the Add Page button and then click Next.

5. Select the Tabs setup (One Level of Tabs) and click Next.
6. Set up the Share component option (No for Copy Shared Component from Another Application). Click Next.
7. Specify the Authentication Scheme (No Authentication). Click Next.
8. Choose the application theme (Theme1). Click Next. Confirm the setup and click Create. The application is created.

Next, we need to update the created report by setting up some report attributes:

1. Click the created page (**1 - Contact Report**). Click the Interactive Report link (**Contact Report**) in the Regions section, as shown here, to edit the report.

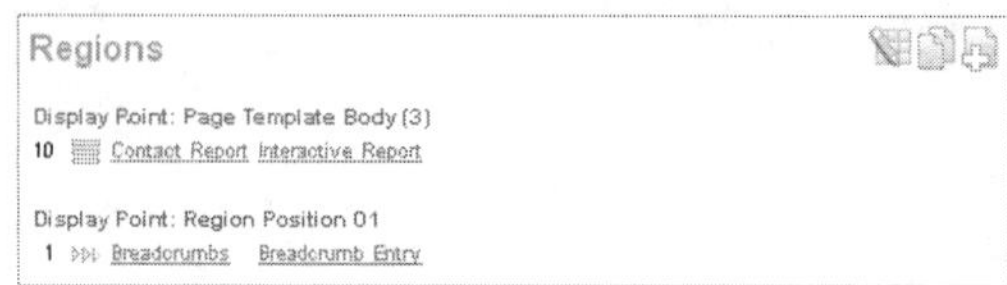

2. Click the Report Attributes tab, in the report editing page, to edit the report attributes.

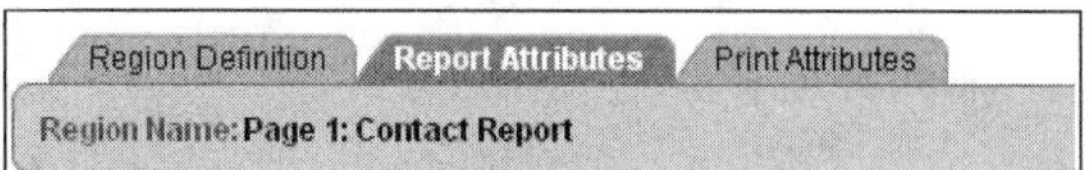

3. The first column is shown with no attribute name. This is an APEX checkbox item. We specify Select as the Heading, and change the default Display As Text setup to Standard Report Column. Click the Apply Changes button as shown here.

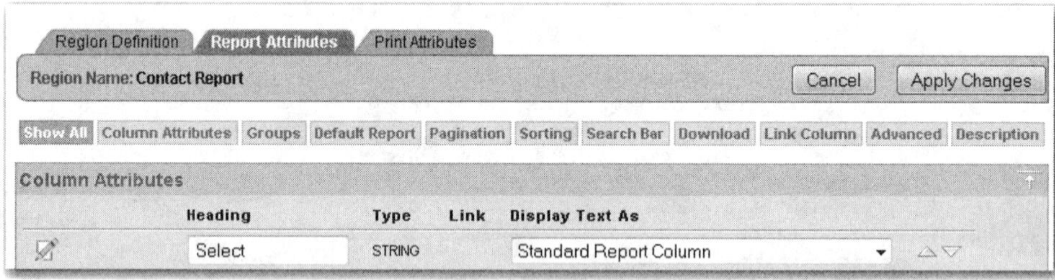

Figure 17-1 shows the created report.

Logout
Page 1: Contact Report

Page 1: Contact Report

Rows 15 Go

Select	Id	First Name	Last Name	Email	Address	Category	Phone	Any Path	To Update	Search Po
☐	1	Jennifer	Wang	jennifer.wang@acme.com	-	customer	(86) 1068739218	/public/contact /xml/jennifer_wang.xml	1	1
☐	2	John	Smith	john.smith@hfarm.com	1234 sunflower road, austin,texas 78701	customer	(512)781-9230	/public/contact /xml/john_smith.xml	2	2
☐	3	Lawrence	Liu	lawrence.liu@abcshopping.com	-	customer	-	/public/contact /xml/lawrence_liu.xml	3	3
☐	4	Mark	Richardson	mark.richardson@xmlbook.com	400 Oracle Parkway, Redwood Shores,California 94065	developement	(650)544-5044	/public/contact /xml/mark_richardson.xml	4	4
☐	5	Richard	Liu	richard.liu@xmlbook.com	-	sales, region/apac	-	/public/contact /xml/richard_liu.xml	5	5
☐	6	Robert	Tian	robert.tian@xmlbook.com	-	sales	-	/public/contact /xml/robert_tian.xml	6	6
☐	7	Tim	Robbins	tim.robbins@xmlbook.com	-	development	(650)606-5005	/public/contact /xml/tim_robbins.xml	7	7
☐	8	Vicent	Zhang	vicent.zhang@iprint.com	-	customer	-	/public/contact /xml/vicent_zhang.xml	8	8

1 - 8

ANONYMOUS

FIGURE 17-1. *Contact SQL report in APEX*

Editing XML

After creating the interactive contacts report, let's create a page to update contacts.

Enabling Update in Database

To begin, let's prepare the update operation in the database. The update has to be done on the XML document stored in Oracle XML DB Repository. This is accomplished by updating the *contact_vw* view with the following *instead-of* trigger defined (*contact_vw_trigger.sql*).

Listing 17-7 *Instead-of Trigger for XML View*

```
CREATE OR REPLACE TRIGGER contact_vw_update INSTEAD OF
  UPDATE ON contact_vw
  REFERENCING NEW AS NEW
  FOR EACH row
  declare
  var_address varchar2(4000);
  var_phone varchar2(4000);
  BEGIN
    UPDATE RESOURCE_VIEW
    SET res  = updateXML(res,
    '/r:Resource/r:Contents/contact/category/text()',:new.category,
    '/r:Resource/r:Contents/contact/first_name/text()',:new.first_name,
    '/r:Resource/r:Contents/contact/last_name/text()',:new.last_name,
    '/r:Resource/r:Contents/contact/email/text()',:new.email,
    '/r:Resource/r:Contents/contact/phone/text()',:new.phone,
    '/r:Resource/r:Contents/contact/cellphone/text()',:new.cellphone,
    'xmlns:r="http://xmlns.oracle.com/xdb/XDBResource.xsd" xmlns="
http://xmlbook.com/sample/contact.xsd">')
    WHERE equals_path(res,:new.any_path)=1;

   -- Update the Address
    SELECT XMLSerialize(content XMLQuery('declare default element namespace
"http://xmlbook.com/sample/contact.xsd"; (: :)
declare namespace ns="http://xmlns.oracle.com/xdb/XDBResource.xsd"; (: :)
      $rs/ns:Resource/ns:Contents/contact/address' passing res AS "rs"
      returning content) as varchar2(4000)) into var_address
    FROM resource_view
    WHERE equals_path(res,:new.any_path)=1;

    IF var_address is null THEN
      dbms_output.put_line('no value');
      UPDATE resource_view
      SET res  = insertchildxml(res,
      '/r:Resource/r:Contents/contact', 'address',
      :new.address,
      'xmlns:r="http://xmlns.oracle.com/xdb/XDBResource.xsd"
```

```
xmlns="http://xmlbook.com/sample/contact.xsd">')
      WHERE equals_path(res,:new.any_path)=1;
    ELSE
       dbms_output.put_line('with value');
     UPDATE RESOURCE_VIEW
      SET res = updateXML(res, '/r:Resource/r:Contents/contact/address',:new
.address,
      'xmlns:r="http://xmlns.oracle.com/xdb/XDBResource.xsd" xmlns="http://
xmlbook.com/sample/contact.xsd">')
      WHERE equals_path(res,:new.any_path)=1;
    END IF;
       -- Update the Phone
    SELECT XMLSerialize(content XMLQuery('declare default element namespace
"http://xmlbook.com/sample/contact.xsd"; (: :)
declare namespace ns="http://xmlns.oracle.com/xdb/XDBResource.xsd"; (: :)
      $rs/ns:Resource/ns:Contents/contact/phone' passing res AS "rs"
      returning content) as varchar2(4000)) INTO var_phone
    FROM resource_view
    WHERE equals_path(res,:new.any_path)=1;

    IF var_phone is null  THEN
      dbms_output.put_line('no value');
      UPDATE resource_view
      SET res  = insertchildxml(res,
      '/r:Resource/r:Contents/contact', 'phone',
      xmltype('<phone>'||:new.phone||'</phone>'),
      'xmlns:r="http://xmlns.oracle.com/xdb/XDBResource.xsd" xmlns="http://
xmlbook.com/sample/contact.xsd">')
      WHERE equals_path(res,:new.any_path)=1;
    ELSE
       dbms_output.put_line('with value');
     UPDATE RESOURCE_VIEW
      SET res = updateXML(res, '/r:Resource/r:Contents/contact/phone/
text()',:new.phone,
      'xmlns:r="http://xmlns.oracle.com/xdb/XDBResource.xsd" xmlns="http://
xmlbook.com/sample/contact.xsd">')
      WHERE equals_path(res,:new.any_path)=1;
    END IF;
  END;
  /
show errors;
```

Because the HTML page *text areas,* which will be used on our Web form, have size limitations, the XML document is retrieved in small XML fragments for updates. Note that *:new.address* is passed in as an XMLType object; therefore we need to use the XPath */r:Resource/r:Contents/*

contact/address. To check if the *<address>* element has content, we first select the <address> element content to *var_address* and check if it is NULL before updates. If there is no content, we will use the insertchildxml() function to insert the new *<address>* element. Otherwise, we use the updateXML() function to update the content. The same applies to the update of the *<phone>* element. To test the update we can run the following SQL command in the XMLDEMO (*check_content_update.sql*):

```
update contact_vw set
        first_name = INITCAP('john1'),
        last_name = INITCAP('smith1'),
        email = LOWER('jsmith1@hfarm.com'),
        cellphone = LOWER('(512)781-92301'),
        phone = LOWER('(512)781-92301'),
        address = xmltype('<address>
      <street1>1234 sunflower road1</street1>
      <city>austin</city>
      <state>texas</state>
      <zipcode>78701</zipcode>
      <country>USA</country>
  </address>')
where any_path = '/public/contact/xml/john_smith.xml';

select *
from contact_vw
where any_path = '/public/contact/xml/john_smith.xml';

rollback;
```

If the data is updated, then the update operation is ready for use. We then *roll back* the updates after the test.

Creating the Web Form

Next, we create a new Web Form page in the APEX application for contact updates. The steps are described as follows:

1. Go to the Application Home page and click the Create Page button.
2. Choose Form as the page type and click Next.
3. Select Form On A Table Or View and click Next.
4. Choose XMLDEMO as the Table/View Owner and click Next.
5. Select CONTACT_VW as the Table/View Name and click Next.

6. Specify the Page Number (**2**), Page Name (**Contact Update**), Region Title (**Contact Update Form**), and Region Template to be the Form Region. We select the Breadcrumb option to create a new entry name (**Contact Update**) and use the existing parent entry (**Contact Report**), as shown here, and then click Next.

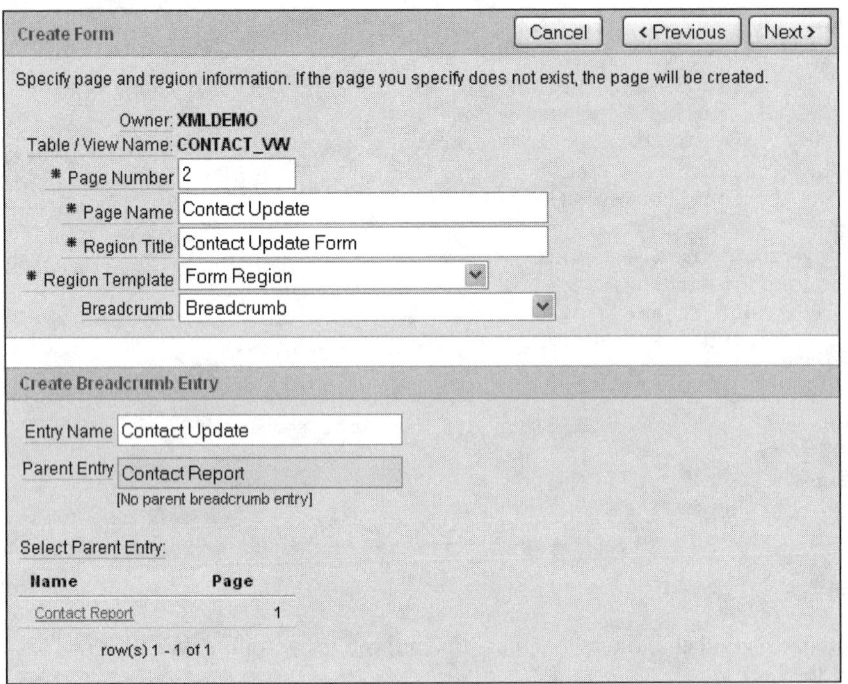

EXAMPLE SETUP

You might set different page numbers, as shown in this example. If this is the case, the APEX page item name will also be different accordingly. Please make the updates as needed.

7. Choose the Tab option (Do not use tabs) and click Next.
8. Select the Primary Key to use ANY_PATH and click Next.
9. Choose to use the Existing Trigger. Click Next.

10. Select the following columns from CONTACT_VW: ID, FIRST_NAME, LAST_NAME, EMAIL, and PHONE, as shown here, and click Next.

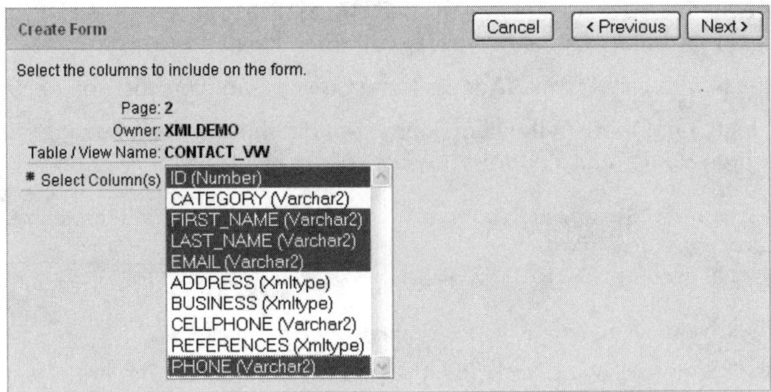

11. Choose the default form setup and click Next.
12. Specify the page to branch to after the Submit and Cancel operations. We specify Contact Report Page (1 - Contact Report) as the target page name. This means that after both operations, the APEX application will go to the contact report page. Click Next.
13. Confirm the setup and click the Finish button to create the new update page.
14. Click the new page created (2 - Contact Update). Click the P2_ANY_PATH field in the Items section as shown here.

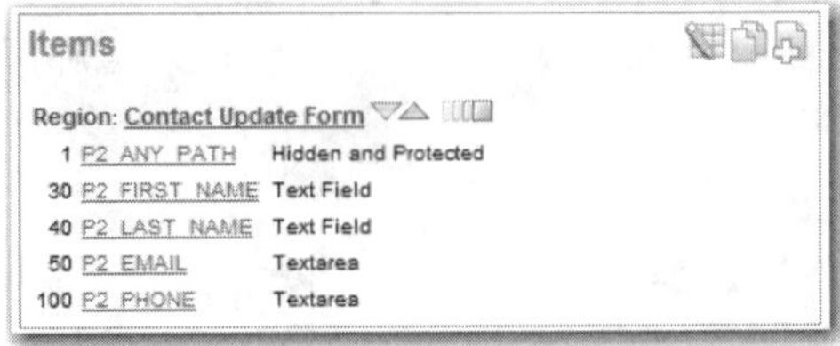

Change the Display As option to "Display as Text (escape special characters, does not save state)," and click the Apply Changes button.

Finally, we need to add the update for the XMLType columns. In the example, the *<addr* element is an XMLType column. We need to add a new page item to perform the updates. T steps are described as follows:

1. Click the create page item icon in the Items section as shown here.

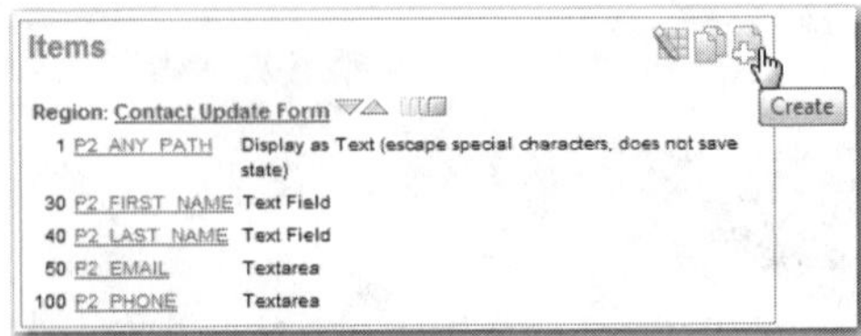

In the Create Items page, select Text Area and then click Next.

2. Choose the Type of the Text Area (Text Area with auto height), and click Next.
3. Specify the Page Item Name (**P2_ADDRESS**), Sequence Number (**110**) and then the Region (Contact Update Form (1) 10). Click Next.
4. Specify the Label name (**Address**) and other parameters (use the default). Click Next.
5. Select SQL Query in the Item Source option and use the following code for the Item Source Value (*apex_address_update.sql*):

```
select XMLSerialize(content address as CLOB indent size=2) address
from contact_vw
where any_path=:P2_ANY_PATH
```

   Click Next.
6. Use the default setup and click the Create Item button. The Address item is then created on the Web form.

Creating the Update Process for the Web Form

We need to rewrite the update process to perform the following PL/SQL process after the Apply Changes button is pressed:

1. Click the Create icon in the Processes section.
2. Select the PL/SQL category and click Next.
3. Specify the Name (**Update**), Sequence Number (**50**), and Point (on Submit after Computation and Validations). Click Next.
4. Add the following PL/SQL code (*apex_contact_update.sql*) to the PL/SQL Page Process section and click Next.

```
begin
 update contact_vw set
   first_name = INITCAP(:P2_FIRST_NAME),
   last_name = INITCAP(:P2_LAST_NAME),
   email= LOWER(:P2_EMAIL),
   phone= :P2_PHONE,
   address= :P2_ADDRESS
 where any_path like '%'||:P2_ANY_PATH||'%';
end;
```

5. Specify the Success Message (**Succeed**) and Failure Message (**Failed**) and click the Create Process button.
6. Then edit the created Update process by clicking the Edit All icon as shown here.

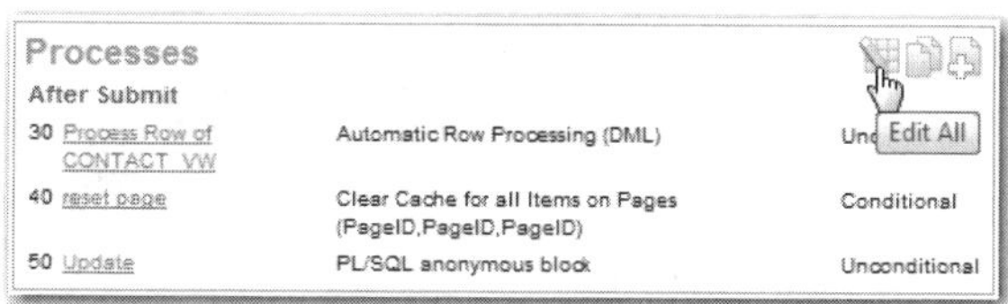

Choose Save for the When Button Pressed field (Process after Submit When this Button is Pressed) as shown here.

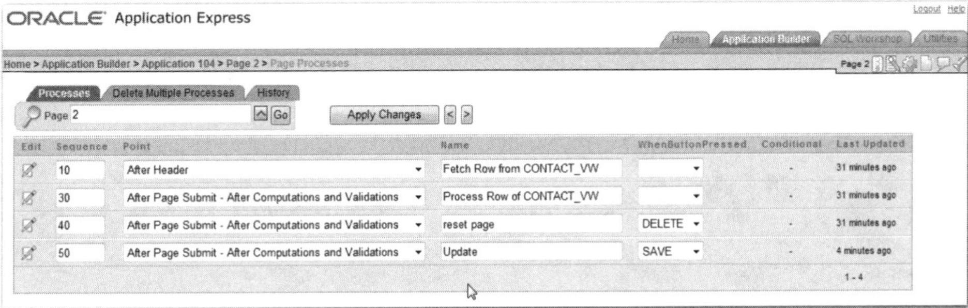

Then click the Apply Changes button.

7. Remove the process created by default (*Process Row of CONTACT_VW*). This is required. Otherwise, you will run into an exception.

Creating Links to the Updates from Report

Finally, we update the contact report page (*1 - Contact Report*) to launch the update operation from the contact report:

1. Click Contact Report in the Regions section on the Page 1 - Contact Report.
2. Click the Report Attributes tab on the report edit page.
3. Click the Edit icon of the TO_UPDATE attribute. Update the Link Text to **Update**. Set the Target option to Page In This Application, and set the Page option to Page **2** (*2 - Contact Updates*). In the request item setup, specify the **P2_ANY_PATH** parameter with the value of **#ANY_PATH#**, as shown here.

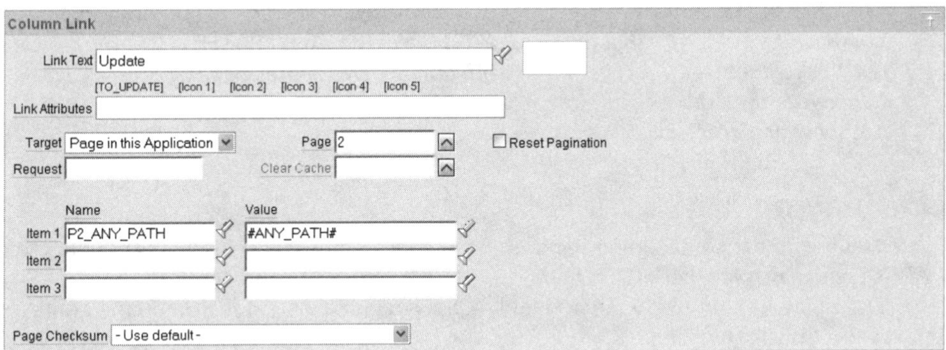

Click the Apply Changes button on the top of the page.

Running the contact report page and clicking the Update link of a contact record, you will get the update form with the Address content displayed as XML in a text area, as shown in Figure 17-2. You can use this form to update the contact records.

Contact Report > Contact Update

Contact Update Form Cancel Delete Apply Changes

Any Path /public/contact/xml/john_smith.xml

Id 2

First Name John

Last Name Smith

Email john.smith@hfarm.com

Phone (512)781-9230

Address

```
<address xmlns="http://xmlbook.com/sample/contact.xsd">
  <street1>1234 sunflower road</street1>
  <city>austin</city>
  <state>texas</state>
  <zipcode>78701</zipcode>
  <country>USA</country>
</address>
```

ANONYMOUS

FIGURE 17-2. *Editable item for XMLType*

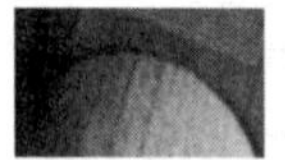

EXAMPLE SETUP

You have to make sure that the ANY_PATH item (P2_ANY_PATH) *is set using the ANY_PATH column from* contact_vw *on this page. Otherwise, the* Address *and* Contact in XML *region created later will not show any content.*

Displaying XML

After setting up the contact report and updated pages, this section discusses how to create an APEX page to display the XML content.

To display XML in APEX, we add a PL/SQL Dynamic Content region on the contact update pages (*2 - Contact Update*).

1. Click the Create icon in the Regions section, select PL/SQL Dynamic Content, and click Next.
2. Specify the region Title (**Contact in XML**), Report Region (*Report Region*), Display Point (*Page Template Region Position 3*), and other parameters. Click Next.
3. Specify the following code to the PL/SQL source (*apex_contact_display.sql*) and click the Create Region button.

Listing 17-8 *Displaying XML in APEX*

```
declare
doc clob;
begin
select replace(replace(XMLSerialize(content
XMLQuery('declare default element namespace "http://xmlbook.com/sample/
contact.xsd"; (: :)
declare namespace ns="http://xmlns.oracle.com/xdb/XDBResource.xsd"; (: :)
$r/ns:Resource/ns:Contents/contact' passing res as "r" returning content)
as CLOB indent size=2),'<','&lt;'),'>','&gt;') into doc
from resource_view
where equals_path(res,:P2_ANY_PATH)=1;

htp.p('<pre width="50">');
htp.p(doc);
htp.p('</pre>');
end;
```

In this PL/SQL code, we use XQuery on RESOURCE_VIEW to retrieve the contact data from the XML DB Repository. We then use the Page Item *:P2_ANY_PATH* to limit to the current contact record. The XMLSerialize() function serialized the contact XML into CLOB and formatted the result with indentation using *indent size=2*. We can also use *no indent* to avoid any indentation. To display XML content on an HTML page, we escape the < and > to *<* and *>* using the SQL replace() function. Then the XML CLOB content is printed out to the Web using the htp.p() function so that the XML data are included in an HTML *<pre>* formatted section:

```
htp.p('<pre width="50">');
htp.p(doc);
htp.p('</pre>');
```

Run the *Contact Update* page; the XML output is shown in Figure 17-3.

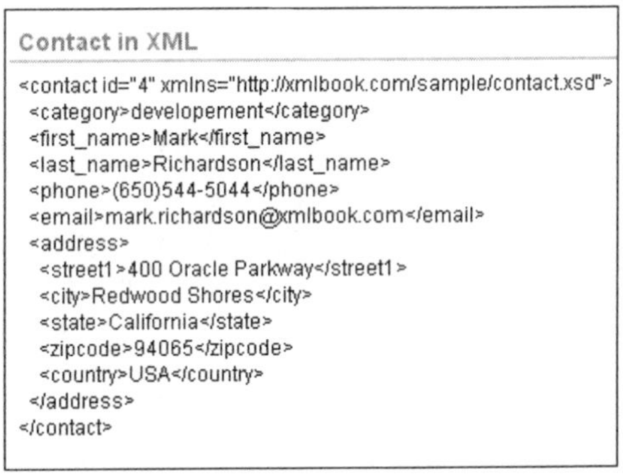

Contact in XML

```
<contact id="4" xmlns="http://xmlbook.com/sample/contact.xsd">
  <category>developement</category>
  <first_name>Mark</first_name>
  <last_name>Richardson</last_name>
  <phone>(650)544-5044</phone>
  <email>mark.richardson@xmlbook.com</email>
  <address>
    <street1>400 Oracle Parkway</street1>
    <city>Redwood Shores</city>
    <state>California</state>
    <zipcode>94065</zipcode>
    <country>USA</country>
  </address>
</contact>
```

FIGURE 17-3. *Display XML in APEX*

Exporting Contacts

After the user selects the contacts, the application allows the user to export the contact document to a new XML DB Repository folder by creating links to the existing contact documents. Let's learn how to achieve this in the APEX application.

Creating Database Table for Contact Selection

To enable exporting selected contacts, we create a temporary table *select_contact_tbl* to keep the selected contact records in the XMLDEMO user schema (*create_select_contact_tbl.sql*):

```
create table select_contact_tbl (id number);
```

We simplify the use case by allowing only a single user to access the application and select contacts. If multiple users need access in your application, you can add a *user name* column in *select_contact_tbl* to allow for different user selections.

Creating an APEX Report for Selected Contacts

Next, we enable the contact selection operations with the following steps.

Step 1: Creating an APEX report for the selected contacts To show the selected contacts, we create another SQL report (**Selected Contacts**) on the contact report page (*1 - Contact Report*).

1. Click Edit on the contact report page and then click the Create icon in Regions section.
2. Choose Report as the Region Type and click Next.
3. Select SQL Report and click Next.
4. Specify the Title (**Selected Contact**) and the Display Point (*Page Template Region Position 3*), and click Next.
5. Specify the following SQL query (*apex_selected_contact.sql*):

```
select s.id, c.first_name, c.last_name, c.email
from select_contact_tbl s, contact_vw c
where s.id=c.id
```

6. Click the Create Region button.

Step 2: Creating the Select button

1. Edit the contact report page (*1 - Contact Report*), and click the Create icon in the Buttons section. Within the Create Button page, click the Create Multiple Buttons link.
2. Create the new button (**Select**) on the Top of Region with default Button template and the set the region to Selected Contact (1) 20, as shown here.

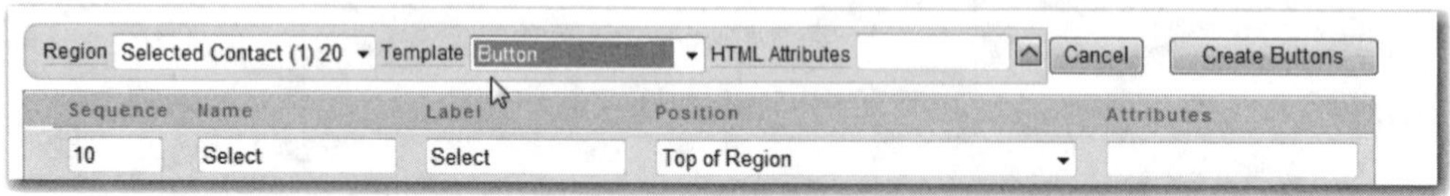

Click Create Buttons.

Step 3: Creating the selection process

1. Click the Create icon in the Processes section and choose PL/SQL as the Process Category. Click Next.
2. Specify the Process Name (Select), Sequence (10), and Point (*On Submit – After Computations and Validations*). Click Next.
3. Enter the following PL/SQL code in the Enter PL/SQL Process area (*apex_select_contacts .sql*):

```
BEGIN
FOR i in 1..APEX_APPLICATION.G_F01.COUNT LOOP
 insert into select_contact_tbl values(APEX_APPLICATION.G_F01(i));
END LOOP;
COMMIT;
END;
```

   Click Next.
4. Specify the Success Message (**Succeed**) and Failure Message (**Failed**). Click Next.
5. On the next page, select when the Select (Select) button is pressed for AFTER_SUBMIT. Leave the Conditional Type setup as is.
6. Click the Create Process button to create the process. Click Created Processing to make sure that Conditional Processing is set up to allow only the Select (Select) button to be pressed to run the process, as shown next.

Conditional Processing
Condition Type
- Select Condition Type -
[PL/SQL] [item=value] [item not null] [request=e1] [page in] [page not in] [exists] [none] [never]
Expression 1
Expression 2
When Button Pressed (Process After Submit When this Button is Pressed)
Select (Select)

Step 4: Creating the page branches To avoid the ERR-1777: *Page N provided no page to branch to* error, we need to create a branch for the button actions:

1. Select the Branches section and click the Create icon.
2. Set the Branch Point to On Submit: After Processing *(After Computation, Validation And Processing)*, and specify the Branch Type to be Branch To Page Of URL. Click Next.

3. Choose the Page In This Application and specify the contact report page (*1 - Contact Report*) as the Branch Target. In the Request, set the sequence ID as "*10*" and then click Next.
4. Specify the Branch Sequence Number (**10**) and choose When Select (Select) in the When Button Pressed option. Click Create Branch.

Step 5: Creating the Clear button Follow the same process to create a Clear button, with its process running the following PL/SQL code (*apex_clear_contact_selection.sql*):

```
begin
  delete from select_contact_tbl;
  commit;
end;
```

You also need to create a page branch for the Clear process as we did for the Select process.

After this step, a contact selection section is added in the contact report page. We select the contact using the check boxes and then click the Select button on the Report page. The contacts selected are listed, as shown in Figure 17-4.

Step 6: Creating the Export process Similar to the process to create the Select and Clear buttons, we need to create another Export button on the Bottom of Region of the Selected Contacts region. Make sure to add a branch that redirects the request to the contact report page (*1 - Contact Report*) in the Optional URL Redirect.

Then add an Export process to call the following PL/SQL procedure. Part of the code is shown here (*create_contact_export_proc.sql*):

```
-- Create export_selected_contacts() procedure
create or replace procedure export_selected_contacts(target_dir in varchar2) as
   cursor contact_cur is select c.any_path as path
         from select_contact_tbl s, contact_vw c where c.id=s.id;
   path_elements token_list_typ;
   file_name varchar2(400);
   j varchar2(400);
begin
  create_path_proc(target_dir, 2);
  for contact_rec in contact_cur loop
   select tokenize_func(contact_rec.path,'/') into path_elements from dual;
   file_name := path_elements(path_elements.last);
   dbms_output.put_line(contact_rec.path);
   dbms_xdb.link(contact_rec.path, target_dir, file_name);
```

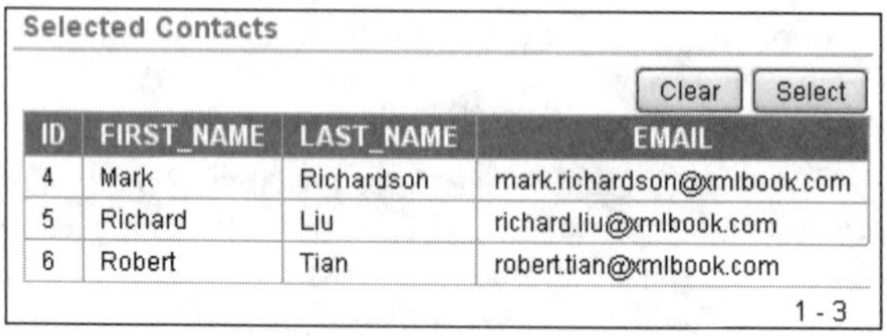

Selected Contacts

Clear | Select

ID	FIRST_NAME	LAST_NAME	EMAIL
4	Mark	Richardson	mark.richardson@xmlbook.com
5	Richard	Liu	richard.liu@xmlbook.com
6	Robert	Tian	robert.tian@xmlbook.com

1 - 3

FIGURE 17-4. *Contact Selections*

```
 end loop;
end;
/
show errors;
```

The export_selected_contacts() PL/SQL function exports the selected contacts by creating a new link to the original document in a separate directory in XML DB Repository. Please refer to Listing 3-2 for how we create the create_path_proc() function to recursively create a directory in XML DB Repository. The PL/SQL block in the APEX Export process is (*apex_export_contacts.sql*):

```
begin
export_selected_contacts(:P1_EXPORT_PATH);
end;
```

To allow users to select from the existing directory in XML DB Repository, we create a new page item as follows:

1. Click the Create icon in the Items section.
2. Choose the Popup List Of Values (LOV) and click Next.
3. Choose the Popup LOV (Fetches First Rowset) type and click Next.
4. Specify the Item Name (*P1_EXPORT_PATH*), select Select Contact(1) 20 for the Region, and use the default Sequence number. Click Next.
5. Add the following SQL code to the List Of Values Query (*apex_list_export_path.sql*):

   ```
   SELECT any_path d, any_path r
   FROM RESOURCE_VIEW
   WHERE under_path(res,'/public/chp17/event',1)=1
   ```

6. Use the default options on the reminder of the pages and click the Create Item button to create the new item.

Run the contact report page. After selecting contact, choosing the contact export path, and clicking the Export button, a new folder is created in XML DB Repository. Within the folder, there are all XML documents of the selected contacts.

Integrating with Full-Text Search

When content size is growing significantly, it's impossible for you to go over each document to look up the content that you need. Therefore, full-text search comes into the picture. Within APEX reports, basic search is provided. In addition, just like the way you use Google.com, you can create your own full-text search server using search engines, such as the Oracle search engine (Oracle Secure Enterprise Search) as we did in Chapter 10 and make it available as a search service for your applications. Because Oracle SES provides RSS feeds for its search results, we can easily retrieve its content via XML DB HTTPUriType and then create reports in APEX applications.

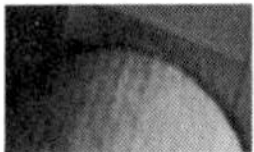

EXAMPLE SETUP
This search query depends on the Oracle SES search application setup in Chapter 10. Please make sure you have the Oracle SES application running.

Using the Oracle SES search applications created in Chapter 10, which search purchase orders, customers, and account managers, we retrieve the full-text search result for the contacts we are interested in with a simple full-text query ("*lawrence liu*"):

```
http://localhost:7777/search/query/feed.jsp?group=PO+in+XML&q=lawrence+liu
```

With XML DB HTTPUriType, the RSS feed is retrieved using the following SQL query in the Oracle database (*get_ses_rss.sql*):

```
set define off
select c.* from XMLTable('$k//item'
passing HTTPUriType('http://localhost:7777/search/query/feed.jsp?group=PO+in+
XML&q=lawrence+liu').getxml() as "k"
COLUMNS
title varchar2(400) PATH 'title/text()',
link varchar2(400) PATH 'link/text()',
description varchar2(4000) PATH 'description/text()') c;
```

In Oracle Database 11*g*, you have to grant the HTTP access to the XMLDEMO and APEX database users to run the SQL query in the APEX application (*create_apex_acl.sql* and *create_http_connect_acl.sql*). The detailed explanation is included in Chapter 14 where we discuss the ACL security in the Oracle database.

To create a report page in APEX, we need to simplify the calling process and thus control the security role setup. We create the following PL/SQL function owned by XMLDEMO to query the external content (*create_get_search_rss_func.sql*):

```
create or replace function get_search_rss( first_name in varchar2, last_name
in varchar2)
return XMLType
AUTHID CURRENT_USER as
 v_url varchar2(4000);
 email varchar2(400);
 output xmltype;
begin
v_url:= 'localhost:7777/search/query/feed.jsp?q=%22'||first_name||'%20'||last_
name||'%22&group= PO+in+XML';
 select HTTPUriType(v_url).getXML() into output from dual;
 return output;
end;
/
show errors;
```

In this PL/SQL procedure, we construct the HTTP request URL by passing the first name (*first_name*) and last name (*last_name*) of a contact to the Oracle SES search URL.

Oracle Database Tip: Why do I get the *ORA-24247* error when running the PL/SQL procedures/functions, but not in the SQL command?

The PL/SQL procedures/functions are not running with the current database user's context. You need to specify AUTHID CURRENT_USER. Otherwise, the assigned network access to the current user will not be used and thus will result in the ORA-24247 error.

Calling this PL/SQL function in XMLTable(), we can get the SQL result with the following query (*create_sql_query_for_rss.sql*):

```
select c.title, c.link, c.description from XMLTable('$k//item'
passing get_search_rss('lawrence','liu') as "k"
COLUMNS
title varchar2(400) PATH 'title/text()',
link varchar2(400) PATH 'link/text()',
description varchar2(4000) PATH 'description/text()') c;
```

In APEX, we can create a new report page based on the run-time construction of the SQL query.

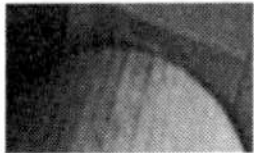

EXAMPLE SETUP
Please make sure you have this hidden item (P1_ID) created; otherwise, you can't find this item when setting up the search link to query RSS feeds from the search application.

When creating the APEX report, we first need to create a new search report page as follows:

1. Select the Created Application (*Contact - 104*) and click the Create Page button.
2. Choose Report as the page type and click Next.
3. Select SQL Report option and click Next.
4. Specify the Page Number (3), Page Name (**Search Report**), and Breadcrumb (do not use breadcrumbs on page). Click Next.
5. Select Tab options (do not use tabs) and click Next.
6. Specify the following PL/SQL block as the SQL query (*apex_search_report.sql*):

```
declare
  var_first_name varchar2(4000);
  var_last_name varchar2(4000);
  var_query varchar2(32767);
begin
  select first_name, last_name
       into var_first_name, var_last_name
  from contact_vw where id= v('P1_ID');

   var_query:='select title, link, description ';
  var_query:=var_query||'from XMLTable(''$k//item'' passing ';
  var_query:=var_query||'get_search_rss('''||
          var_first_name||''','''
          ||var_last_name||''') as "k" ';
  var_query:=var_query||'COLUMNS ';
  var_query:=var_query||'  title varchar2(400) PATH ''title/text()'',';
  var_query:=var_query||'  link varchar2(400) PATH ''link/text()'',';
  var_query:=var_query||'  description varchar2(4000) PATH';
  var_query:=var_query||' ''description/text()'')';
  return var_query;
end;
```

Oracle Database Tip: Why do I get the PLS-00103: *Encountered the symbol "end-of-file"* error?

If you select the SQL query as the identification type, the parsing of the anonymous PLSQL processing will not be successful and you will get the following error:

```
ORA-06550: line 21, column 3:
PLS-00103: Encountered the symbol "end-of-file" when expecting one of the
following: ;
The symbol ";" was substituted for "end-of-file" to continue.
```

You also need to check the Use Generic Column Name (Parse Query At Runtime Only) option during report creation. Then use the default settings for the rest of the setups and click Finish.

7. In the report attributes, we edit the first column (COL01) to be a link, with the Link Text as #COL01# (the *title* attribute), and the Target as a URL, with the value #COL02# (the *link* attribute). We hide the COL02 attribute by unchecking the *Show* attribute of the *COL02* attribute. Click on Apply Changes to complete the attribute updates.

   Then, we need to create a Hidden item called P1_ID on contact report page (*1 - Contact Report*) by clicking the Items Create icon in APEX and selecting the Hidden item type. P1_ID is used to pass the contact ID from the contact report page to the search report page.

   Now, we need to update the contact report (the interactive report *Contact Report* created on Page 1 - Contact Report) Search PO attribute by clicking the Report Attribute tab. Click the Edit icon of the Search PO attribute. In the Search PO attribute setup page, update the Column Link | Link Text to be Search POs, the Target to be Page In This Application, the Page to be the created search report page (Page 3 - Search Report), and the Items Passed In Name to be P1_ID with the value as the #ID# attribute from the contact report. Click on Apply Changes to complete the setup.

   Then running from the contact report, we can click the Search PO link and generate the report, as shown in Figure 17-5.

Report 1

TITLE	DESCRIPTION
ORDER000000000000003: Lawrence Liu order on iPhone 4G	0003 Order Date:2009-10-05 Customer Name: Lawrence Liu Phone: (86)1337459948 Email: lliu@xmlbook
ORDER000000000000002: Lawrence Liu order on iPad	0002 Order Date:2010-06-05 Customer Name: Lawrence Liu Phone: (86)1337459948 Email: lliu@xmlbook
ORDER000000000000001: Lawrence Liu order on iPhone 4G;iPad	0001 Order Date:2010-04-05 Customer Name: Lawrence Liu Phone: (86)1337459948 Email: lliu@xmlbook

1 - 3

FIGURE 17-5. *Full-text search report in APEX based on RSS feeds*

Sending Emails Using Oracle XML DB

In this section, we will enable sending customized emails to selected contacts from the APEX application.

Creating an Email Template

The email content is defined via an email template in XML. The following XML document is an example email template (*xmlbook_ann_tpl.xml*):

```
<email_template>
  <attachment>
     <imageContent baseurl="http://localhost:8081/public/chp17/event/
xmlbook_ann">
       <image id="001">book_cover.jpg</image>
       <image id="002">learnmore.gif</image>
     </imageContent>
     <attachedContent>
       <file>sample_chapter.pdf</file>
     </attachedContent>
   </attachment>
  <xsl_content>
  <xsl:stylesheet version="1.0" xmlns:xsl="http://www.w3.org/1999/XSL/
Transform"
   xmlns:book="http://xmlbook.com/sample/contact.xsd">
  <xsl:template match="/">
  <html><body>
  <table bgcolor="#ffffff" border="0" bordercolor="#ffffff"
  width="492" height="236">
  <tbody>
  <tr bgcolor="#ffffff">
  <td valign="top"><img src="cid:002"/></td>
   </tr>
   <tr bgcolor="#ffffff">
    <td valign="top">
     <p>Hi <xsl:value-of select="/book:contact/book:first_name"/>,</p>
     <p> Oracle Database 11g: Building Oracle XML DB Applications is
published.<br/>
     <img src="cid:001" href="http://community.oraclepressbooks.com/profile
.php?aid=1284"/></p>
     <table>
      <tr>
       <td>Feel free to send me your comments, suggestions and
questions . <br/>
  Sincerely,<br/>
       Jinyu</td>
      </tr>
    </table>
   </td></tr>
  </tbody>
</table> </body></html>
</xsl:template>
```

```
</xsl:stylesheet>
</xsl_content>
</email_template>
```

The template contains two sections. The first section defines the *<attachment>* element to specify email attachments. Within *<attachment>*, *<imageContent>* specifies the embedded images. Each embedded image is given a unique *id*, which then can be referred by the *src* attribute of the *<img>* tags in the email content. *<attachedContent>* includes files to be attached. The *<attachment>* element has a *baseURL* attribute to specify the XML DB Repository location where the attachment files are stored. The second section is included in the *<xsl_content>* element. The content is an XSL stylesheet, which will be used to create customized emails by transforming the contact XML documents. For example, in this template, we use *<xsl:value-of select="/contact/first_name"/>* to update the person's name from the contact document. As we learned in Chapter 7, XSLT can be used to create comprehensive content from one or more XML documents.

Selecting an Email Template

In the APEX application, we can preview the email template and the emails to be sent to our contacts. Let's learn how to do this.

First, we create a new blank page in the application by clicking the Create Page button and choosing the Blank Page option. We set the page number (**4**), the page Alias (**SendEmail**), and the Page Name (**Send Email**) without using the breadcrumbs. We create a new tab (**Send Email**) within the existing tab set (*TS1 (Contact Report)*) for this page. Then, click Finish to complete the page creation.

Then, we edit the created page by adding a new Report (**Selected Contacts**) with the following SQL query to display the selected contacts (*apex_selected_contact.sql*):

```
select s.id, c.first_name, c.last_name, c.email
from select_contact_tbl s, contact_vw c
where s.id=c.id
```

In the Selected Contacts region, we create a blank HTML region (**Create Email**) to include the Web form for creating emails.

Then, we click the Items Create icon to create an email form with the following setup:

1. In the Create Item dialog, click the Create Multiple Items Using Drag And Drop Layout option and create the Web form as shown here. Then click Next.

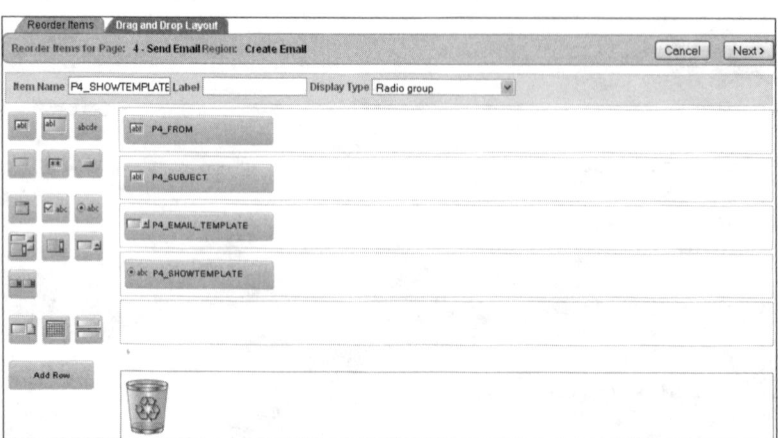

2. On the next page set up the labels and click Apply Changes.

3. Edit the radio group item (*P4_SHOWTEMPLATE*). Set the Display As to Radio Group *(With Submit)* and set the following value for the List Of Values Definition:

```
STATIC2:Hide;HIDE,Preview;SHOW
```

In this setup, the radio group has two choices: Hide (with value as HIDE) and Preview (with value as SHOW). We set HIDE as the Default Value for the radio group. To display both of them in the same line, we need to set the Number Of Columns for the List Of Values item to "*6*". Then, click Apply Changes.

4. When a selection is made in the radio group, an auto page "*submit*" is sent. We need to create a page branching for this process. Click the Create icon in the Branches section. Select On Submit: After Processing *(After Computation, Validation, and Processing)* with Branch Type to be Branch To Page Or URL. The Branch Target is Page In This Application and points to the same Send Email page (*4 - Send Email*). Click Next and then click the Create Branch button.

5. Edit the Popup LOV *(Fetches First Rowset)* item (*P4_EMAIL_TEMPLATE*) to allow the user to select templates from XML DB Repository. In this item, the LOV (*List Of Values Definition*) is set with the following SQL query (*apex_select_templates.sql*):

```
SELECT any_path d, any_path r
FROM RESOURCE_VIEW
WHERE under_path(res,'/public/chp17/event',1)=1 AND depth(1) <3
and any_path like '%tpl.xml'
```

The SQL query uses the under_path() and depth() functions to list only those files that are no more than three levels deep in the */public/chp17/event* folder. The *any_path like '%tpl.xml'* lists only XML files with **top.xml* in the file name. After the LOV item is selected in the APEX application, the P4_EMAIL_TEMPLATE parameter will be assigned the path (defined in *any_path* column of RESOURCE_VIEW) for the template, which is an XML DB Repository resource. Click Apply Changes.

6. Then, we need to create a *PL/SQL Dynamic Content Region* (**Template Preview**) by clicking the Create icon in the Regions section. The Display Point is Page Template Body *(3. Item above region content)*. The PL/SQL source for this region is shown as follows (*apex_preview_template.sql*):

Listing 17-9 *Previewing XML Document Source in APEX*

```
DECLARE
  var_doc clob;
BEGIN
  select replace(replace(XMLSerialize(content XMLQuery('declare namespace
ns="http://xmlns.oracle.com/xdb/XDBResource.xsd"; (: :)
     $r/ns:Resource/ns:Contents/*' passing res as "r" returning content)
     as CLOB indent size=2),'<','&lt;'),'>','&gt;') into var_doc
  from RESOURCE_VIEW r
  where equals_path(res,v('P4_EMAIL_TEMPLATE'))=1;
```

```
  htp.p('<pre width="50">');
  htp.p(var_doc);
  htp.p('</pre>');
END;
```

The PL/SQL code retrieves the template file from the P4_EMAIL_TEMPLATE input, serializes the content to CLOB, and then escapes the < and > characters to *<* and *>* for the HTML display. The final display content is stored in the *var_doc* variable and then printed out to the APEX web page by the htp.p() function. Because of displaying XML source code, the HTML *<pre width="50">* element is used to include the *var_doc* content. This allows us to display the code within a preformatted HTML area with line size equaling 50. Then, set the Conditions of the Template Preview region to be *Value of Item in Expression 1 = Expression 2,* with P4_SHOWTEMPLATE in the Expression 1 field and SHOW in the Expression 2 field, as shown here.

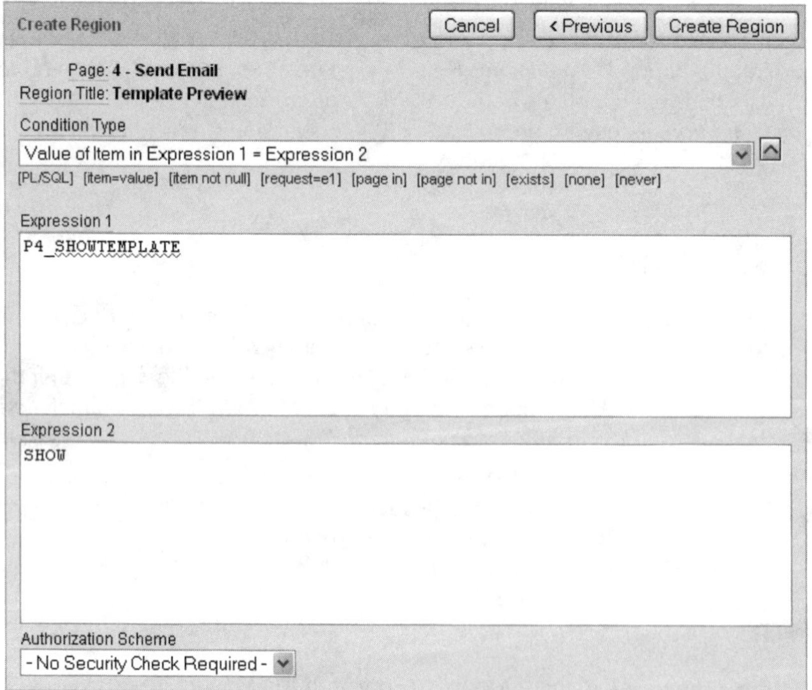

Click the Create Region button. Now, run the *4-Send Email* page and select an email template (*/public/chp17/event/xmlbook_ann/xmlbook_ann_tpl.xml*). You will get the Template Preview in XML format, as shown in Figure 17-6.

Choosing the Show Template radio group will toggle the show and hide the Template Preview content.

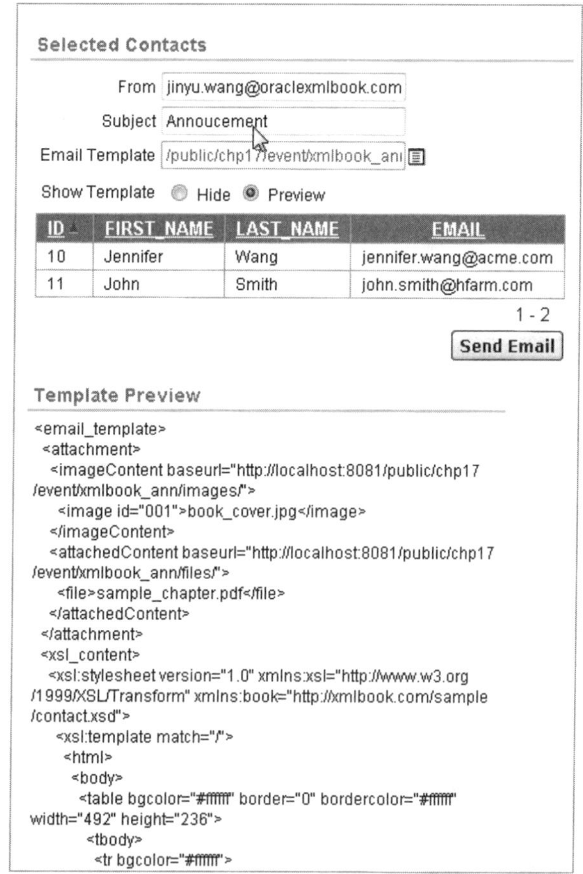

FIGURE 17-6. *Previewing Email template*

Previewing Emails

In this section, we allow users to select one of the contacts and preview the pre-rendered emails with the following steps:

1. Create a PL/SQL Dynamic Content region (**Preview Email**) by clicking the Create icon in the Regions section at Page Template Region Position 3. The region has the following PL/SQL code (*apex_preview_email_with_images.sql*):

Listing 17-10 *Previewing HTML Content Transformed by XSLT in APEX*

```
DECLARE
  var_tpl XMLType;
  var_xsl XMLType;
  var_email CLOB;
```

```
BEGIN
  select xmltransform(XDBUriType(v('P4_EMAIL_TEMPLATE')).getxml(),
  XDBUriType('/public/chp17/email_template/xsl/gen_preview_stylesheet.xsl')
.getxml())
  into var_tpl from dual;

  select XMLQuery('$r/email_template/xsl_content/*'
    passing var_tpl as "r" returning content) into var_xsl
  from dual;

  select XMLSerialize(content XMLTransform(
  XDBUriType(v('P4_CONTACT_SELECTED')).getxml(),var_xsl) as clob indent
size=2)
  into var_email from dual;

  htp.p(var_email);
END;
```

We also apply the same display condition as we set for the email template preview and click the Create Region button to create the region. Click Generate Region.

Let's understand the query used in the email preview in more detail. The first SQL query retrieves the XSL stylesheet from the email template specified by P4_EMAIL_TEMPLATE using XDBUriType(), then transformed by *gen_preview_stylesheet.xsl*. The XSL transformed result is then serialized to the *var_tpl* XMLType variable, because we want to update *<img src= "cid:<content-id">* in the template by replacing it with the *baseURL* attribute value of *<imageContent>*. We have discussed this XSL transformation in Listing 7-6.

In the second SQL query, we called the XMLQuery() functions by passing in the *var_tpl* template, extracting the XSL content using the XPath *$r/email_template/xsl_content/**, and then assigning the extracted content to the *var_xsl* XMLType variable. As discussed in Chapter 7, the *$r/email_template/xsl_content/** XPath returns the sub-elements within the *<xsl_content>* element.

In the third SQL query, the XSL is applied on the selected contact documents specified by P4_CONTACT_SELECTED using the XMLTransform() function. The transformed result is serialized into a CLOB using the XMLSerialize() call *var_email*.

Finally, the htp.p() function is called to print out *var_email* to the APEX web page.

This is different from the email template preview, because we don't show the source code, there is no character-escaping, and we don't use the HTML *<pre>* element.

2. In the Preview Emails region, we create a new APEX item in the Select List With Submit Item type called P4_CONTACT_SELECTED to pick up the contact used for the email previews. The P4_CONTACT_SELECTED item is defined with the following LOV query (*apex_select_email_preview_contact.sql*):

```
select c.first_name||' '||c.last_name||'('||c.email||')' as d, c.any_
path as r
from select_contact_tbl s, contact_vw c
where s.id = c.id
order by 1
```

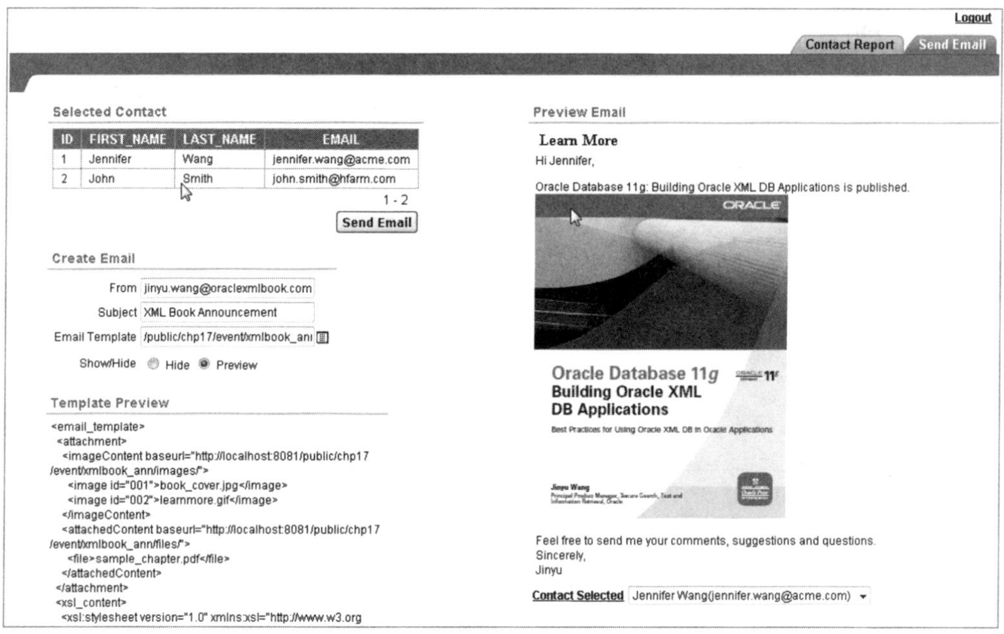

FIGURE 17-7. *APEX page preview emails*

P4_CONTACT_SELECTED uses the contact name (concatenated from the *first_name* and *last_name* columns of *contact_vw*) for display and the contact document's XML DB Repository path as the select value. When users click the Select List item, they get a drop-down menu listing all of the selected contacts.

Figure 17-7 shows the resulting APEX page for setup and preview emails and email templates.

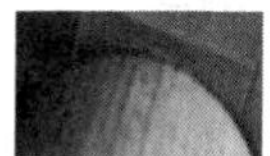

EXAMPLE SETUP

The Appendix discusses how to allow anonymous access to the XML DB Repository from APEX applications. With that setup, you should not see the pop-up dialog asking for a login when previewing emails. Otherwise, you need to provide a valid database user login when first accessing the email previews

Sending Emails

In this application, we will send HTML-formatted email with embedded images. We create a PL/SQL procedure using UTL_SMTP to open SMTP connections and write the email data to the email SMTP server.

Oracle Database Tip: When should I use APEX_MAIL?
APEX_MAIL provides comprehensive email sending and management support. However, there is no support of the MIMETYPE setups in APEX_MAIL. Therefore, we can't send email in HTML format with embedded images.

Make sure you run Listing 9-8 (*create_email_template_img_vw.sql*):

```
CREATE OR REPLACE VIEW email_template_img_vw
                                                AS
  SELECT xdburitype(a.any_path).getblob() AS photo,
    c.filename                            AS filename,
    c.mimetype                            AS mimetype,
    a.any_path
  FROM resource_view a,
    XMLTable( XMLNamespaces(DEFAULT 'http://xmlns.oracle.com/xdb/XDBResource
.xsd'),
    'for $i in . return $i/Resource'
    passing a.res columns
    filename VARCHAR2(100) path 'DisplayName',
    mimetype VARCHAR2(4000) path 'ContentType') c
  WHERE a.any_path like '/public/chp17/event/%images%' and mimetype !=
'application/octet-stream';
```

Then run the following SQL (*create_email_template_att_vw.sql*):

```
CREATE OR REPLACE VIEW email_template_att_vw
                                                AS
  SELECT xdburitype(a.any_path).getblob() AS photo,
    c.filename                            AS filename,
    c.mimetype                            AS mimetype,
    a.any_path
  FROM resource_view a,
    XMLTable( XMLNamespaces(DEFAULT 'http://xmlns.oracle.com/xdb/XDBResource
.xsd'),
    'for $i in . return $i/Resource'
    passing a.res columns
    filename VARCHAR2(100) path 'DisplayName',
    mimetype VARCHAR2(4000) path 'ContentType') c
  WHERE a.any_path like '/public/chp17/event/%files%' and mimetype !=
'application/octet-stream';
```

Then, create the following PL/SQL procedure (*create_send_email_proc.sql*):

Listing 17-11 *Sending HTML Email with Embedded Images and File Attachments in PL/SQL*

```
CREATE OR REPLACE PROCEDURE send_email_with_template_proc(
    p_from                 IN VARCHAR2,
```

```
    p_subject             IN VARCHAR2,
    p_email_template_path IN VARCHAR2) authid current_user AS
  CURSOR contact_cur
  IS
    SELECT c.any_path AS path,
           c.email    AS email
    FROM select_contact_tbl s,
      contact_vw c
    WHERE c.id=s.id;

  v_id    NUMBER;
  v_index NUMBER;
  v_vc_arr2 apex_application_global.vc_arr2;
  v_vid_arr2 apex_application_global.vc_arr2;
  v_email_body CLOB;
  v_template xmltype;
  v_xsl xmltype;
  v_attachment xmltype;
  v_contact_doc CLOB;
  v_imagelist VARCHAR2(4000):='';
  v_idlist    VARCHAR2(4000):='';
  v_mail_host VARCHAR2(100) := 'internal-mail-router.xmlbook.com';
  v_mail_conn utl_smtp.connection;
  crlf       VARCHAR2(2) := chr(13)||chr(10);
  v_boundary VARCHAR2(255) DEFAULT '__1282442766989158099abhmt016';
  v_message  VARCHAR2(32767);
  v_fname    VARCHAR2(200);
  v_img BLOB;
  v_rfile RAW(32767);
  v_offset  NUMBER;
  v_amount NUMBER;
  v_photo BLOB;
  v_mimetype VARCHAR2(100);
  v_filelist VARCHAR2(4000);
  v_file BLOB;
BEGIN
  SELECT xmlquery('declare namespace ns="http://xmlns.oracle.com/xdb/
XDBResource.xsd"; (: :)
$r/ns:Resource/ns:Contents/email_template/attachment' passing res AS "r"
returning content)
  INTO v_attachment
  FROM resource_view
  WHERE equals_path(res, p_email_template_path)=1;
  SELECT xmlquery('declare namespace ns="http://xmlns.oracle.com/xdb/
XDBResource.xsd"; (: :)
$r/ns:Resource/ns:Contents/email_template/xsl_content/*' passing res AS "r"
returning content)
  INTO v_xsl
  FROM resource_view
```

```
  WHERE equals_path(res, p_email_template_path)=1;

  v_mail_conn := utl_smtp.open_connection(v_mail_host, 25);
  utl_smtp.helo(v_mail_conn, v_mail_host);
  FOR contact_rec IN contact_cur
  LOOP
    SELECT xmlserialize(content xmlquery('declare namespace (: :)
ns="http://xmlns.oracle.com/xdb/XDBResource.xsd";
$r/ns:Resource/ns:Contents/*' passing res AS "r" returning content) AS CLOB)
    INTO v_contact_doc
    FROM resource_view
    WHERE equals_path(res, contact_rec.path)=1;
    SELECT xmlserialize(content xmltransform(xmltype(v_contact_doc), v_xsl)AS
CLOB)
    INTO v_email_body
    FROM dual;
    -- Start sending email
    utl_smtp.mail(v_mail_conn, p_from);
    utl_smtp.rcpt(v_mail_conn, contact_rec.email);
    utl_smtp.rcpt(v_mail_conn, 'jsmith@xmlbook.com');
    utl_smtp.open_data(v_mail_conn);
    v_message := 'Mime-Version: 1.0' || crlf ||
            'Date: ' || TO_CHAR(sysdate, 'dy, dd mon yyyy hh24:mi:ss') ||
crlf ||
            'From: ' || p_from || crlf ||
            'Subject: '|| p_subject || crlf ||
            'To: ' || contact_rec.email || crlf ||
            'Cc: ' || 'jsmith@xmlbook.com' || crlf ||
            'Content-Type: multipart/related; boundary="'|| v_boundary || '"'
            || crlf ||crlf;
    utl_smtp.write_data(v_mail_conn, v_message);

    -- Send HTML Content
    v_message :=  '--' || v_boundary || crlf ||
                 'Content-Type: text/html; charset=us-ascii' || crlf || crlf;
    utl_smtp.write_data(v_mail_conn, v_message);
    v_offset      := 1;
    v_amount     := 1900;
    WHILE v_offset < dbms_lob.getlength(v_email_body)
    LOOP
      utl_smtp.write_data(v_mail_conn,
                          dbms_lob.substr(v_email_body,v_amount,v_offset));
      v_offset  := v_offset + v_amount;
      v_amount := least(1900,dbms_lob.getlength(v_email_body) - v_amount);
    END LOOP;

    --Image Attachment
    SELECT rtrim(xmlserialize(content xmlquery('for $i in fn:doc($p)/email_
template/attachment/imageContent/image
```

```
return concat($i/text(),":")' passing p_email_template_path AS "p" returning
content) AS VARCHAR2(4000)),':')
    INTO v_imagelist
    FROM dual;
    SELECT rtrim(xmlserialize(content xmlquery('for $i in fn:doc($p)/email_
template/attachment/imageContent/image/@id
return concat($i,":")' passing p_email_template_path AS "p" returning content)
AS VARCHAR2(4000)),':')
    INTO v_idlist
    FROM dual;

    v_vc_arr2 := apex_util.string_to_table(v_imagelist);
    v_vid_arr2 := apex_util.string_to_table(v_idlist);
    dbms_output.put_line('Index Count:'||v_vc_arr2.count);
    v_message := crlf ||crlf;
    utl_smtp.write_data(v_mail_conn, v_message);
    FOR v_index IN 1..v_vc_arr2.count  LOOP
      dbms_output.put_line('Index loop('||v_index||'):'|| ltrim(v_vc_arr2
(v_index))||':');
      SELECT filename, photo, mimetype INTO v_fname, v_photo, v_mimetype
      FROM email_template_img_vw
      WHERE filename =ltrim(v_vc_arr2(v_index));

      dbms_output.put_line('File name:'||v_fname);
      dbms_output.put_line('File id:'||v_vid_arr2(v_index));
      dbms_output.put_line('File mimetype:'||v_mimetype);
      v_message := crlf ||'--'||v_boundary || crlf ||
      'content-type:'||v_mimetype||'; name="' || v_fname || '"' || crlf ||
      'content-disposition: inline; filename="' || v_fname || '"' || crlf ||
      'content-transfer-encoding: base64' || crlf||
      'content-id:<'||ltrim(v_vid_arr2(v_index))||'>'||crlf||crlf;
      utl_smtp.write_data(v_mail_conn, v_message);

      -- Get the image file
dbms_output.put_line(v_vc_arr2(v_index)||':('||v_index||')'||dbms_lob
.getlength(v_photo));
      v_offset      := 1;
      v_amount     := 3000;
      WHILE v_offset < dbms_lob.getlength(v_photo) LOOP
        v_rfile := utl_encode.base64_encode(
                          dbms_lob.substr(v_photo,v_amount,v_offset));
        utl_smtp.write_data(v_mail_conn, utl_raw.cast_to_varchar2(v_rfile));
        v_offset  := v_offset+ v_amount;
        v_amount := least(3000,dbms_lob.getlength(v_photo) - v_amount);
      END LOOP;
      --v_message := crlf ||crlf || '--'||v_boundary || crlf;
      --utl_smtp.write_data(v_mail_conn, v_message);
    END LOOP i_index;
```

```
    -- File Attachment
    SELECT rtrim(xmlserialize(content
     xmlquery('for $i in fn:doc($p)/email_template/attachment/attachedContent/
file
return concat($i/text(),":")'
    passing p_email_template_path AS "p" returning content)
    AS VARCHAR2(4000)),':')
    INTO v_filelist
    FROM dual;

    v_vc_arr2 := apex_util.string_to_table(v_filelist);
    dbms_output.put_line('Index Count:'||v_vc_arr2.count);
    v_message := crlf ||crlf;
    utl_smtp.write_data(v_mail_conn, v_message);
    FOR v_index IN 1..v_vc_arr2.count
    LOOP
      dbms_output.put_line('Index loop('||v_index||'):'|| ltrim(v_vc_arr2
(v_index))||':');
      SELECT filename,
        photo,
        mimetype
      INTO v_fname,
        v_file,
        v_mimetype
      FROM email_template_att_vw
      WHERE filename =ltrim(v_vc_arr2(v_index));

      dbms_output.put_line('File name:'||v_fname);
      dbms_output.put_line('File id:'||v_vid_arr2(v_index));
      dbms_output.put_line('File mimetype:'||v_mimetype);
      v_message := crlf ||'--'||v_boundary || crlf ||
      'content-type:'||v_mimetype||'; name="' || v_fname || '"' || crlf ||
      'content-disposition: inline; filename="' || v_fname || '"' || crlf ||
      'content-transfer-encoding: base64' || crlf||crlf;
      utl_smtp.write_data(v_mail_conn, v_message);
      -- Get the image file
      dbms_output.put_line(v_vc_arr2(v_index)||':('||v_index||')'||
                          dbms_lob.getlength(v_file));
      v_offset      := 1;
      v_amount      := 3000;
      WHILE v_offset < dbms_lob.getlength(v_file)
      LOOP
        v_rfile := utl_encode.base64_encode(
                       dbms_lob.substr(v_file,v_amount,v_offset));
        utl_smtp.write_data(v_mail_conn, utl_raw.cast_to_varchar2(v_rfile));
        v_offset  := v_offset                              + v_amount;
        v_amount := least(3000,dbms_lob.getlength(v_file) - v_amount);
      END LOOP;
    END LOOP i_index;
```

```
    utl_smtp.close_data(v_mail_conn);
  END LOOP;
  utl_smtp.quit(v_mail_conn);
EXCEPTION
WHEN utl_smtp.transient_error OR utl_smtp.permanent_error THEN
  dbms_output.put_line('mail sending failure');
  utl_smtp.quit(v_mail_conn);
END;
/
show errors;
```

Note that you need to change the proceeding PL/SQL procedure code with your own email account and email server setup (highlighted in bold).

Make sure you add the SMTP servers to the ACL for the XMLDEMO user, as we discussed in Chapter 14. For example, run the following command in SYS (*grant_proxy_access.sql*):

```
Begin
  dbms_network_acl_admin.assign_acl (
        acl => 'xmldemo_acl.xml',
        host => 'internal-mail-router.xmlbook.com',
        lower_port => 20,
        upper_port => 26);
end;
/
```

Let's explain the procedure in detail.

EXAMPLE SETUP

To make sure the PL/SQL procedure works, run the following command in the XMLDEMO user after the security setup (test_send_email.sql)*:*

```
set serveroutput on
begin
   send_email_with_template_proc('<your_email_
address>,'test', '/public/chp17/event/xmlbook_ann/
xmlbook_ann_tpl.xml');
end;
```

In the example code, we include the debugging information, which you can use to check the email sending process.

Sending Email with UTL_SMTP

First, let's explore how to send email using UTL_SMTP. UTL_SMTP is a PL/SQL package for sending emails over Simple Mail Transfer Protocol (SMTP). The protocol consists of a set of commands and needs to be called to properly deliver the mail messages. The following PL/SQL code lists the key steps calling UTL_SMTP in *send_email_with_template_proc*:

```
v_mail_conn := utl_smtp.open_connection(v_mail_host, 25);
utl_smtp.helo(v_mail_conn, v_mail_host);
... ...
```

```
utl_smtp.mail(v_mail_conn, p_from);
utl_smtp.rcpt(v_mail_conn, contact_rec.email);
utl_smtp.rcpt(v_mail_conn, 'jsmith@xmlbook.com');

utl_smtp.open_data(v_mail_conn);

v_message := 'Mime-Version: 1.0' || crlf ||
         'Date: ' || TO_CHAR(sysdate, 'dy, dd mon yyyy hh24:mi:ss') ||crlf ||
         'From: ' || p_from || crlf ||
         'Subject: '|| p_subject || crlf ||
         'To: ' || contact_rec.email || crlf ||
         'Cc: ' || 'jsmith@hfarm.com' || crlf ||
         'Content-Type: multipart/related; boundary="'|| v_boundary || '"' ||
          crlf ||crlf ||;
    utl_smtp.write_data(v_mail_conn, v_message);

- Send HTML Content
utl_smtp.write_data(v_mail_conn, v_message);
- Send Embedded Images
utl_smtp.write_data(v_mail_conn, v_message);
- Send File Attachments
utl_smtp.write_data(v_mail_conn, v_message);
utl_smtp.close_data(v_mail_conn);
utl_smtp.quit(v_mail_conn);
```

First, we open an SMTP connection using the utl_smtp.open_connection() function. In this function call, we need to specify the SMTP server name (passed in by the *v_mail_host* variable) and its port number (*25* by default). Then, the call of utl_smtp.helo() initializes handshaking with the SMTP server. If both of these function calls are a success, the SMTP connection is established.

Next, we need to initialize the mail transaction by calling the utl_smtp.mail() function to specify where to send the email (or the FROM field). Then, we specify the email recipients using utl_smtp.rcpt(). If there are multiple recipients to be included in the TO, CC, or BCC fields, we have to call utl_smtp.rcpt() multiple times.

Then, within the mail transaction, we call utl_smtp.open_data() to open the data session and write the data to the SMTP connection using utl_smtp.write_data(). At the beginning of the data, we specify the email header including the Date, From, To, Subject, and CC fields. We also specify the Content-Type to be *multipart/related* so that we can include multipart content in the email. The *boundary* also needs to be specified. In the PL/SQL procedure, we define the *boundary* variable as follows:

```
v_boundary VARCHAR2(255) DEFAULT '__1282442766989158099abhmt016';
```

This *boundary* must not occur in any part of the email content, but can only be placed between the parts, and at the beginning and end of the message body. We will call utl_smtp .write_data() multiple times to write different content, including HTML email body, embedded image attachments, and file attachments. Each content section needs to be separated with this *boundary*. After all of the data are written, we then close the data session by calling the utl_smtp .close_data() function.

At the end of the operation, we close the SMTP connection by calling utl_smtp.quit(). This informs the SMTP server to terminate the established SMTP connection.

Now that we understand the SMTP email sending process, let's review how each type of data is sent via SMTP data session.

Adding HTML Content

HTML email format allows us to include rich text, formatted layout, and images. To send HTML content body with rich content, we need to include the HTML content in a Multipart/Related MIME entity. Because the HTML content is created by applying the XSL stylesheet in our email template, we need to carry out the following operations.

First, the XSL stylesheet content is retrieved from the template and saved in the PL/SQL variable *v_xsl* using the following XQuery:

```
SELECT xmlquery('declare namespace ns="http://xmlns.oracle.com/xdb/
XDBResource.xsd"; (: :)
$r/ns:Resource/ns:Contents/email_template/xsl_content/*' passing res AS "r"
returning content)
  INTO v_xsl FROM resource_view
WHERE equals_path(res, p_email_template_path)=1;
```

Then, we define a CURSOR to retrieve the contact from the *selected_contact_tbl* table:

```
  CURSOR contact_cur IS
    SELECT c.any_path AS path,
           c.email    AS email
    FROM select_contact_tbl s,
      contact_vw c
    WHERE c.id=s.id;
```

Looping each contact record, we retrieve the contact document from XML DB Repository based on *contact_rec.path* in the current cursor record, and then apply the XSL transformation to create the HTML email body. The email content is stored in *v_email_body* defined as a CLOB variable.

```
FOR contact_rec IN contact_cur
LOOP
  SELECT xmlserialize(content xmlquery('declare namespace (: :)
       ns="http://xmlns.oracle.com/xdb/XDBResource.xsd";
$r/ns:Resource/ns:Contents/*' passing res AS "r" returning content) AS CLOB)
  INTO v_contact_doc FROM resource_view
  WHERE equals_path(res, contact_rec.path)=1;

  SELECT xmlserialize(content
         xmltransform(xmltype(v_contact_doc), v_xsl)AS CLOB)
  INTO v_email_body FROM dual;
... ...
END LOOP;
```

After the *v_email_body* content is retrieved, we set up the content part boundary and then create a loop to send the CLOB content in chunks (specified by *v_amount*):

```
v_message :=  '--' || v_boundary || crlf ||
              'Content-Type: text/html; charset=us-ascii' || crlf || crlf;
utl_smtp.write_data(v_mail_conn, v_message);
v_offset      := 1;
v_amount     := 1900;
WHILE v_offset < dbms_lob.getlength(v_email_body)
LOOP
   utl_smtp.write_data(v_mail_conn,
                      dbms_lob.substr(v_email_body,v_amount,v_offset));
   v_offset  := v_offset+ v_amount;
   v_amount := least(1900,dbms_lob.getlength(v_email_body) - v_amount);
END LOOP;
```

Adding Embedded Images

To add embedded images in the HTML email without further downloads, we need to add the images as a MIME part in the email by assigning a unique *Content-ID* for each image in the MIME entity header and referring to the image in the email content using *Content-ID*. The reference is in the format of *<img src="cid:[content-id]"/>*. An example is shown here. In the MIME header we set the following content:

```
--__1282442766989158099abhmt016
content-type:image/jpeg; name="oracle_view.jpg"
content-disposition: inline; filename="oracle_view.jpg"
content-transfer-encoding: base64
content-id:<001>
```

In the HTML content, we add the *<img>* tag:

```
<img src="cid:001">
```

In the PL/SQL procedure, we first retrieve the images list from the email template using the following XQuery:

```
SELECT rtrim(xmlserialize(content xmlquery('for $i in fn:doc($p)/email_
template/attachment/imageContent/image
return concat($i/text(),":")' passing p_email_template_path AS "p" returning
content) AS VARCHAR2(4000)),':') INTO v_imagelist FROM dual;

SELECT rtrim(xmlserialize(content xmlquery('for $i in fn:doc($p)/email_
template/attachment/imageContent/image/@id
return concat($i,":")' passing p_email_template_path AS "p" returning content)
AS VARCHAR2(4000)),':')
INTO v_idlist
FROM dual;
```

As we discussed in Listing 8-6, the query retrieves the image file names and IDs and then creates two colon-delimited strings. In APEX, these strings can be converted to a PL/SQL array using the apex_util.string_to _table() function. The following code is used:

```
v_vc_arr2 := apex_util.string_to_table(v_imagelist);
v_vid_arr2 := apex_util.string_to_table(v_idlist);
```

After we get the selected images and their IDs, we then iterate through the images to add them as a MIME part to the email. Before doing that, we add an empty line to separate the image MIME part from the HTML content:

```
v_message := crlf ||crlf;
utl_smtp.write_data(v_mail_conn, v_message);
```

In the iteration process shown next, we first select the image and retrieve the image data from the image index view *email_template_img_vw* created in Listing 9-8. Then, we create and write the MIMETYPE header to the data session. To send image data, we break down the CLOB image data in chucks, encode the data with Base64 by calling the utl_encode.base64_encode() function, and then write to the SMTP data session.

```
FOR v_index IN 1..v_vc_arr2.count LOOP
      SELECT filename, photo, mimetype INTO v_fname, v_photo, v_mimetype
      FROM email_template_img_vw
      WHERE filename =ltrim(v_vc_arr2(v_index));

     v_message := crlf ||'--'||v_boundary || crlf ||
      'content-type:'||v_mimetype||'; name="' || v_fname || '"' || crlf ||
      'content-disposition: inline; filename="' || v_fname || '"' || crlf ||
      'content-transfer-encoding: base64' || crlf||
      'content-id:<'||ltrim(v_vid_arr2(v_index))||'>'||crlf||crlf;
       utl_smtp.write_data(v_mail_conn, v_message);

        -- Get the image file
      v_offset      := 1;
      v_amount     := 3000;
      WHILE v_offset < dbms_lob.getlength(v_photo) LOOP
        v_rfile := utl_encode.base64_encode(
                dbms_lob.substr(v_photo,v_amount,v_offset));
        utl_smtp.write_data(v_mail_conn, utl_raw.cast_to_varchar2(v_rfile));
        v_offset  := v_offset+ v_amount;
        v_amount := least(3000,dbms_lob.getlength(v_photo) - v_amount);
      END LOOP;
END LOOP i_index;
```

Adding Attachments

Adding file attachments is similar to sending embedded images, except that we don't need to set up the Content-ID and create the ID references. We will not discuss this further.

Setting Up the APEX Component

After creating the PL/SQL procedure, we need to create a button (Send Email) at the bottom of the Select Contacts region, and then can add a PL/SQL process in the APEX application called *Send Email* to be called after the Send Email button is pressed. The steps are described as follows:

Step 1: Creating the Send Email button

1. Edit the send email page (*4 - Send Email*). Click the Create icon in the Buttons section. Within Create Button page, click the Create Multiple Buttons link.
2. Create the Send Email button on the Bottom of Region with default Button template and the region to be *Selected Contacts(1) 10*. Click Create Buttons.

Step 2: Creating the Send Email process

1. Click the Create icon in the Processes section and choose PL/SQL as the process category. Click Next.
2. Specify the process name (**Send Email**), Sequence (**10**) and Point (*On Submit – After Computations and Validations*). Click Next.
3. Enter the following PL/SQL code in the Enter PL/SQL Process area (*apex_send_email.sql*):

```
BEGIN
   send_email_with_template_proc(v('P4_FROM'),v('P4_SUBJECT'), v('P4_
EMAIL_TEMPLATE'));
END;
```

   Click Next.
4. Specify the Success Message (**Succeed**) and Failure Message (**Failed**). Click Next.
5. In next page, select When The Send Email (**Send Email**) Button Is Pressed for the AFTER_SUBMIT option. Leave the Conditional Type setup as is.
6. Click the Create Process button to create the process.

Step 3: Creating the page branches We need to create a branch for the Send Email action.

1. Select the Branches section and click the Create icon.
2. Specify the Branch Point to be On Submit: After Processing *(After Computation, Validation and Processing)*, the Branch Type to be Branch to Page of URL. Click Next.
3. Choose the Page In This Application option and specify the contact report page (*4 - Send Email*) as the branch target. In the Request field, set the sequence ID to **10** and then click Next.
4. Specify the branch sequence number (**10**) and choose Send Email (**Send Email**) in the When Button Pressed option. Click Create Branch.

When the Send Email button is pressed, the send_email_with_template_proc() PL/SQL procedure is called to send the email. An example email is shown in Figure 17-8.

Now, we have completed our application.

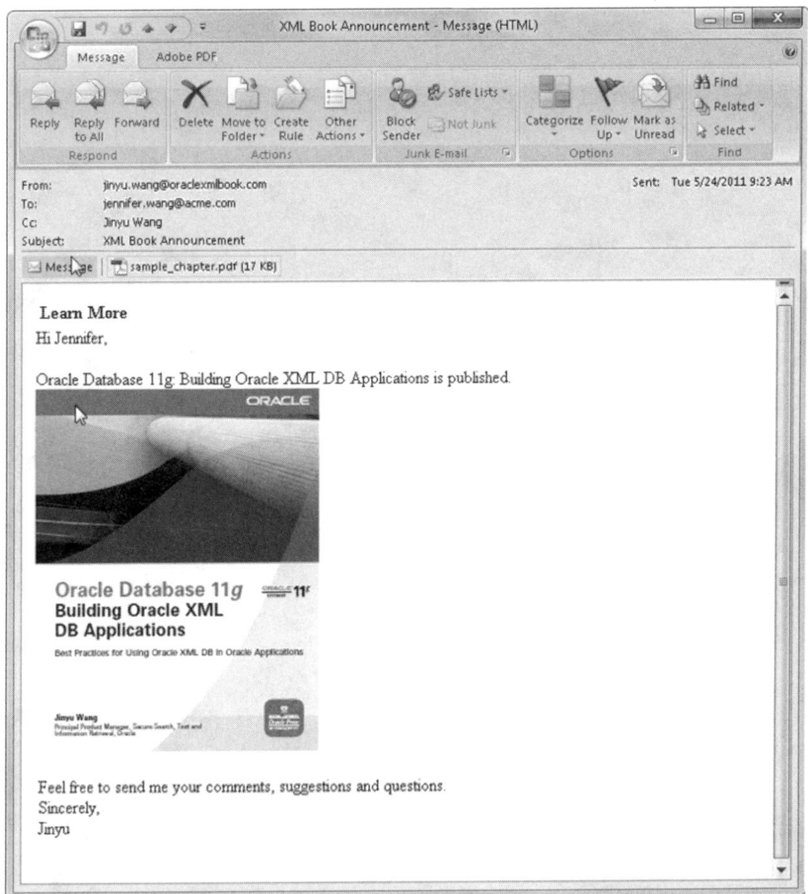

FIGURE 17-8. *Email sent from the APEX application*

Summary

In this chapter, we have demonstrated how to build an Oracle XML DB application:

- The XML data format, and the flexibility of the XQuery and XSLT process, allow us to fully perform powerful actions.
- XML DB storage provides easy access to XML documents in SQL and Internet protocols. The integration of SQL and XML access provides extensive data management functionality.
- APEX simplifies Web application development on top of Oracle XML DB.
- With the current XML technology in the Oracle database, storage of XML is more reliable and XML processing and application development is much simpler.

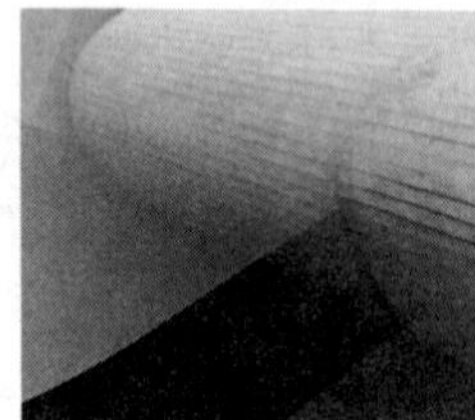

APPENDIX

Installing Oracle Application Express in Oracle Database 11*g*

This appendix explains how to set up Oracle Application Express (APEX) in Oracle Database 11*g*. With Oracle APEX, we can build Web applications using XML DB.

Configuring Oracle APEX

In Oracle Database 11gR2, Oracle Application Express 3.2.1 is installed by default. APEX files are located at the *$ORACLE_HOME/apex* directory, where $ORACLE_HOME refers to the Oracle database home directory. The following steps will guide you in setting up APEX. You need to log in as SYS user (as SYSDBA) to run the setup.

Step 1: Check APEX Installation in Oracle Database 11*g*

To check the APEX installation, run the following command (*check_apex_registry.sql*):

```
column comp_name format a30
column status format a10
column version format a15
SELECT comp_name,status,version
FROM DBA_REGISTRY
WHERE comp_name in ('Oracle Application Express');
```

An example output is

```
COMP_NAME                      STATUS     VERSION
------------------------------ ---------- ---------------
Oracle Application Express     VALID    3.2.1.00.11
```

By default, APEX is installed with a VALID status shown in DBA_REGISTRY. If the status is INVALID or LOADING, you then need to refer to the "Uninstalling Oracle APEX" and "Reinstalling Oracle APEX" sections later in this chapter to do a fresh APEX install. Otherwise, continue to Step 2.

Step 2: Check DAD Setup

With APEX installed, we then need to set up DAD (Database Access Descriptor). DAD contains a set of instructions for the Oracle HTTP server, used by APEX, to connect to the Oracle database. The following command checks the DAD status (*check_dad.sql*):

```
@?/rdbms/admin/epgstat.sql
```

Here is an example correct APEX DAD setup:

```
+---------------------------------------+
| XDB protocol ports:                   |
|  XDB is listening for the protocol    |
|  when the protocol port is non-zero.  |
+---------------------------------------+
HTTP Port FTP Port
--------- --------
     8081     2121
1 row selected.
```

```
+--------------------------+
| DAD virtual-path mappings |
+--------------------------+
Virtual Path                      DAD Name
--------------------------------  --------------------------------
/apex/*                           APEX
1 row selected.
+----------------+
| DAD attributes |
+----------------+
DAD Name   DAD Param                     DAD Value
---------- ----------------------------  --------------------------------
APEX       database-username             ANONYMOUS
           default-page                  apex
           document-table-name           wwv_flow_file_objects$
           request-validation-function   wwv_flow_epg_include_modules.authorize
           document-procedure            wwv_flow_file_mgr.process_download
           nls-language                  american_america.al32utf8
           document-path                 docs
7 rows selected.
+---------------------------------------------------+
| DAD authorization:                                |
|  To use static authentication of a user in a DAD, |
|  the DAD must be authorized for the user.         |
+---------------------------------------------------+
no rows selected
+----------------------------+
| DAD authentication schemes |
+----------------------------+
DAD Name             User Name                         Auth Scheme
-------------------- --------------------------------  --------------
APEX                 ANONYMOUS                         Anonymous
1 row selected.
+----------------------------------------------------------+
| ANONYMOUS user status:                                   |
|  To use static or anonymous authentication in any DAD,  |
|  the ANONYMOUS account must be unlocked.                 |
+----------------------------------------------------------+
Database User   Status
--------------- --------------------
ANONYMOUS       EXPIRED & LOCKED
1 row selected.
+--------------------------------------------------------------------+
| ANONYMOUS access to XDB repository:                                |
|  To allow public access to XDB repository without authentication, |
|  ANONYMOUS access to the repository must be allowed.               |
+--------------------------------------------------------------------+
Allow repository anonymous access?
----------------------------------
false
1 row selected.
```

If you don't see the correct DAD setup as shown, you need to run *apex_epg_config.sql* to set up DAD. Because the DAD setup needs to load the APEX-related files to XML DB Repository, we need to copy the files from the *$ORACLE_HOME\apex\images* folder to a local directory (e.g. *d:\temp*) first (running on Windows) and then give the valid path when running *apex_epg_config .sql*:

```
SQL>@?/apex/@apex_epg_config.sql d:\temp
```

Oracle Database Tip: Why does a user login dialog pop up when I'm accessing the APEX websites?

This is normally because you don't have the correct DAD setup for the APEX installation. First, the Oracle Application Express (APEX) DAD setup relies on Oracle XML DB. If you reinstalled Oracle XML DB but haven't reinstalled DAD, you will get this error. To resolve this, first run *epgstat.sql* to check the DAD configuration and then run *apex_epg_config.sql* to perform the DAD setup as described. Another reason for the dialog could be that the ANONYMOUS account is not enabled. If the user account is shown as EXPIRED & LOCKED, you need to unlock the ANONYMOUS user, as described in Step 4.

Step 3: Configure Oracle APEX in Oracle Database 11g

After the DAD setup, you then need to run *apxconf.sql* to configure Oracle APEX. The following is the configuration command (*config_apex.sql*):

```
SQL> @?/apex/apxconf.sql
      PORT
----------
      8081
Enter values below for the XDB HTTP listener port and the password for the
Application Express ADMIN user.
Default values are in brackets [ ].
Press Enter to accept the default value

Enter a password for the ADMIN user              []
Enter a port for the XDB HTTP listener [       8081]
...changing HTTP Port
PL/SQL procedure successfully completed.
PL/SQL procedure successfully completed.
Session altered.
...changing password for ADMIN
PL/SQL procedure successfully completed.
Commit complete.
```

When prompted to *Enter a password for the ADMIN user*, you can type in the ADMIN user password (i.e., *apex*). This is a temporary password. You will need to update it when first logging in to the APEX administration UI. You can also update the XML DB HTTP server port if it's not *8081*.

Step 4: Unlock the ANONYMOUS User

Oracle APEX connects to Oracle XML DB via the ANONYMOUS user. Therefore, this user needs to be unlocked to run APEX applications. To check the ANONYMOUS user account status, run the following command (*check_anonymous_user.sql*):

```
COLUMN username FORMAT a25
COLUMN account_status FORMAT a30
SELECT username, account_status
FROM DBA_USERS
WHERE username='ANONYMOUS';
```

If the account is not shown as OPEN, such as when it is showing as EXPIRED & LOCKED, unlock the ANONYMOUS user using the following command:

```
SQL> alter user anonymous account unlock;
```

After you unlock the ANONYMOUS account, if the account is still showing as EXPIRED, then run the following command to activate the account:

```
alter user anonymous identified by <new_password>;
```

For example, the following command activates the ANONYMOUS account using *apex* as its password:

```
ALTER USER anonymous IDENTIFIED BY apex;
```

Then run the SQL command:

```
SELECT username, account_status
FROM DBA_USERS
WHERE username='ANONYMOUS';
```

You should get the following output:

```
Database User   Status
--------------- --------------------
ANONYMOUS       OPEN
1 row selected.
```

In APEX applications, when showing a page which includes URLs pointing to files stored in XML DB repository, a login is required by default to access the files in XML DB repository. To avoid the login pop-ups when showing such APEX pages, you can enable the anonymous access from APEX to the XML DB repository. The SQL script is shown as follows (*enable_anonymous_access.sql*):

```
DECLARE
l_cfgxml XMLTYPE;
BEGIN
   l_cfgxml := DBMS_XDB.cfg_get();
   IF l_cfgxml.existsNode('/xdbconfig/sysconfig/protocolconfig/httpconfig/
allow-repository-anonymous-access') = 0
   THEN
     -- Add the missing element.
```

```
      SELECT insertChildXML(DBMS_XDB.cfg_get(),
        '/xdbconfig/sysconfig/protocolconfig/httpconfig',
        'allow-repository-anonymous-access',
        XMLType('<allow-repository-anonymous-access
xmlns="http://xmlns.oracle.com/xdb/xdbconfig.xsd">true</allow-repository-
anonymous-access>'),
        'xmlns="http://xmlns.oracle.com/xdb/xdbconfig.xsd"') INTO l_cfgxml
      FROM dual;
    ELSE
      -- Update existing element.
      SELECT updateXML( DBMS_XDB.cfg_get(),
       '/xdbconfig/sysconfig/protocolconfig/httpconfig/allow-repository-
anonymous-access/text()',
      'true',
      'xmlns="http://xmlns.oracle.com/xdb/xdbconfig.xsd"') INTO l_cfgxml
      FROM dual;
    END IF;
    DBMS_XDB.cfg_update(l_cfgxml);
    DBMS_XDB.cfg_refresh;
END;
/
```

With successful running of the script in SYS, you should see that the anonymous access to XML DB repository is enabled. If you check the DAD configuration again (*check_dad.sql*), you will get the following output:

```
+-----------------------------------------------------------------+
| ANONYMOUS access to XDB repository:                              |
|   To allow public access to XDB repository without authentication, |
|   ANONYMOUS access to the repository must be allowed.            |
+-----------------------------------------------------------------+
Allow repository anonymous access?
----------------------------------
true
1 row selected.
```

Step 5: Set Up Oracle Database HTTP Server

Set up the Oracle DB HTTP server port based on the APEX configuration:

```
SQL>exec dbms_xdb.sethttpport (8081);
SQL> commit;
```

Please refer to Chapter 11 for instructions on how to validate XML DB HTTP server status.

Step 6: Set Up ACL Security

In Oracle Database 11g, the access to external sources via Internet protocols such as HTTP and SMTP are managed by ACLs (Access Control Lists). Please refer to Chapter 14 for a detailed discussion. Here, we set up an ACL to access external websites/servers. The following script gives the APEX power users access to the network (*setup_apex_acl.sql*).

```
DECLARE
  ACL_PATH  VARCHAR2(4000);
  ACL_ID    RAW(16);
BEGIN
  SELECT ACL INTO ACL_PATH
  FROM DBA_NETWORK_ACLS
  WHERE HOST = '*'
    AND LOWER_PORT IS NULL
    AND UPPER_PORT IS NULL;

  SELECT SYS_OP_R2O(extractValue(P.RES, '/Resource/XMLRef'))
  INTO ACL_ID
  FROM
    XDB.XDB$ACL A,
    PATH_VIEW P
  WHERE extractValue(P.RES, '/Resource/XMLRef') = REF(A)
    AND EQUALS_PATH(P.RES, ACL_PATH) = 1;

  DBMS_XDBZ.ValidateACL(ACL_ID);
  IF DBMS_NETWORK_ACL_ADMIN.CHECK_PRIVILEGE(ACL_PATH, 'APEX_030200',
     'connect') IS NULL
  THEN
    DBMS_NETWORK_ACL_ADMIN.ADD_PRIVILEGE(ACL_PATH,
    'APEX_030200', TRUE, 'connect');
  END IF;

EXCEPTION
  WHEN NO_DATA_FOUND THEN
    DBMS_NETWORK_ACL_ADMIN.CREATE_ACL
      ( 'power_users.xml',
        'ACL that lets power users to connect to everywhere',
        'APEX_030200',
        TRUE,
        'connect' );
  DBMS_NETWORK_ACL_ADMIN.ASSIGN_ACL('power_users.xml','*');
END;
/
COMMIT;
```

Step 7: Validate APEX Access

After the setup, the APEX websites are ready to be accessed. The URLs are listed as follows:

- http://localhost:8081/apex for development access
- http://localhost:8081/apex/apex_admin for administration access.

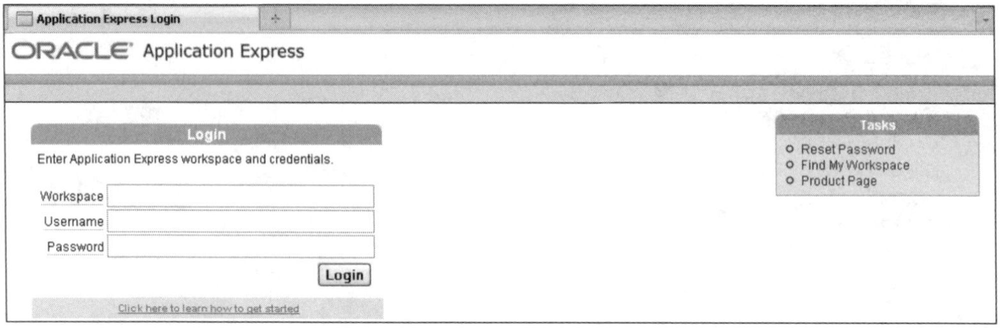

FIGURE A-1. *Oracle APEX Homepage*

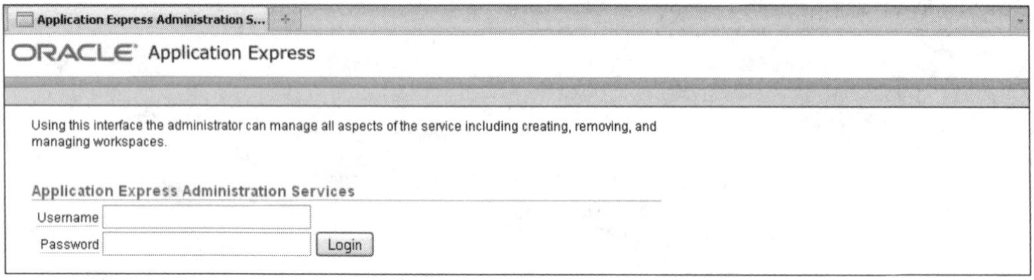

FIGURE A-2. *Oracle APEX Administration Homepage*

The host name might be different; *localhost* can be changed to your machine's host name and *8081* to the DB HTTP Server port on your server. You should see the web pages shown in Figure A-1 and Figure A-2.

Uninstalling Oracle APEX

You normally need to check the APEX-related database schemas before uninstalling Oracle APEX using the following command (*check_apex_schema.sql*):

```
COLUMN username FORMAT a25
COLUMN account_status FORMAT a30
SELECT username, account_status
FROM dba_users
WHERE username in('APEX_PUBLIC_USER', 'FLOWS_FILES')
      or username like'APEX_%' or username like 'FLOWS_%';
```

An example output is

```
USERNAME                       ACCOUNT_STATUS
------------------------------ --------------------------------
APEX_PUBLIC_USER               OPEN
FLOWS_FILES                    LOCKED
APEX_030200                    LOCKED
```

Export all the workspaces and applications created by Oracle APEX as a backup. Then drop the APEX-related database schemas. For example, the following command drops the listed schemas (*drop_apex.sql*):

```
DROP USER flows_files CASCADE;
DROP USER apex_public_user CASCADE;
DROP USER apex_030200 CASCADE;
```

Then we need to remove APEX-created packages, synonyms, directories, and so on:

```
@?/apex/apxremov.sql
```

Reinstalling Oracle APEX

If you have APEX installed but it is not running correctly, you need to uninstall APEX before taking the following steps.

Step 1: Install Oracle APEX and Set Up DAD

Log in as SYS user and run the following command in the *$ORACLE_HOME/apex* directory (*install_apex.sql*):

```
@?/apex/apexins SYSAUX SYSAUX TEMP /i/
```

The installation will take a few minutes. After running the script, you can follow the steps described in Step 1 in the "Configuring Oracle APEX" section earlier in the chapter to check the APEX installation status.

Steps 2–7: Set Up DAD, Configure APEX in DB, and More

Please refer to Steps 2–7 in the "Configuring Oracle APEX" section to set up DAD, configure APEX in DB, unlock the ANONYMOUS user, set up the HTTP server, and validate APEX access by visiting the administration and development websites.

Setting Up APEX Development Environment

After APEX is installed, we need to log in to the APEX admin UI to create the APEX application workspace. Log in to the APEX admin UI (*http://localhost:8081/apex/apex_admin*) and update the ADMIN user password as shown in Figure A-3.

After you receive confirmation of the updated password, click the *Return* button to return to the login page.

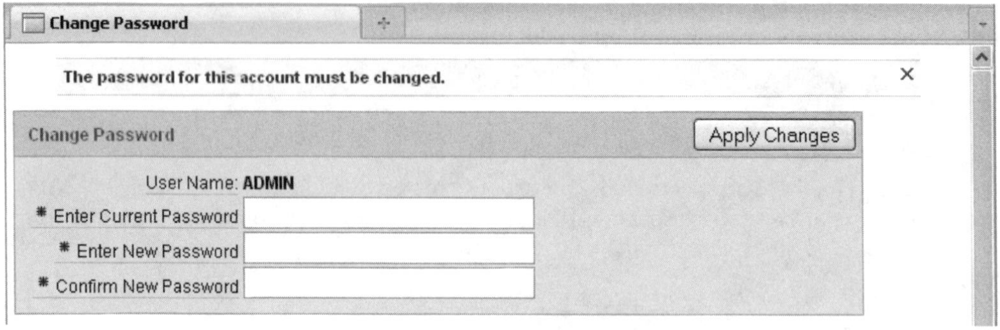

FIGURE A-3. *Changing the APEX Administration Password*

Creating a Workspace

After logging in to the APEX admin page, we can create the new workspace by choosing Manage Workspace | Manage Workspaces | Create Workspace shown in Figure A-4.

You need to specify the workspace name (**CONTACT_MANAGEMENT**) and its database schema (**XMLDEMO**) as shown in Figures A-5 to A-6.

Specify the workspace administrator's user name, password, and other information as shown in Figure A-7 and then click Next.

Confirm the setup as shown in Figure A-8 and click Create.

You will see the Workspace Created message as shown in Figure A-9.

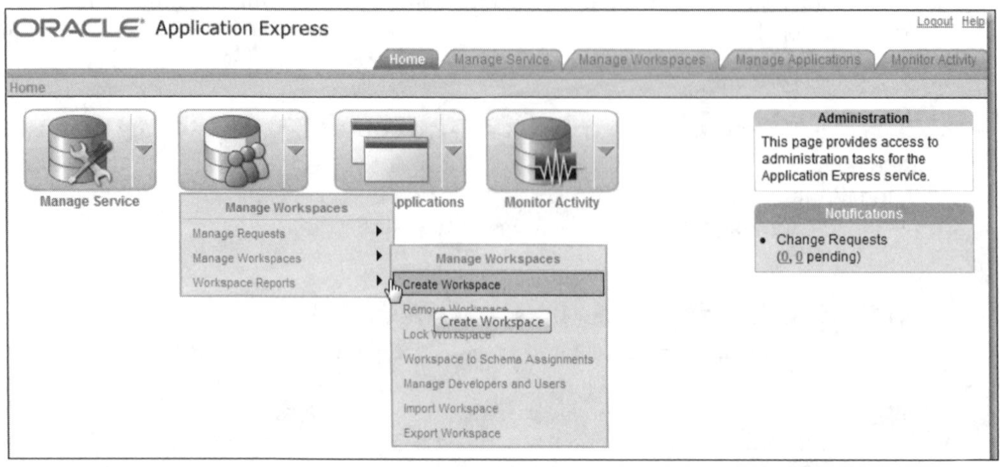

FIGURE A-4. *Creating an APEX Workspace*

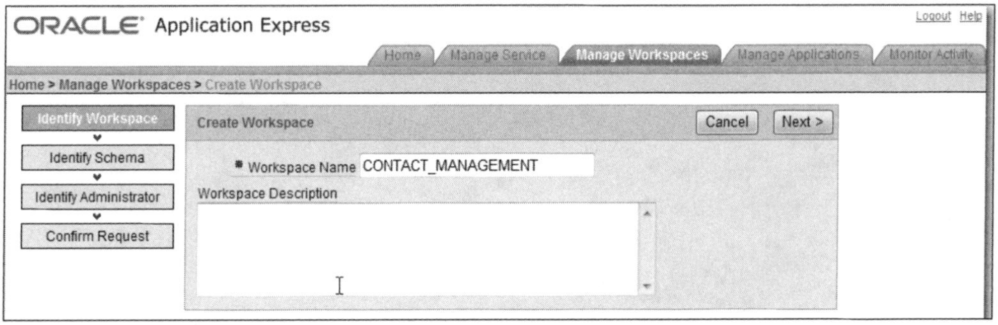

FIGURE A-5. *Specifying APEX Workspace Name*

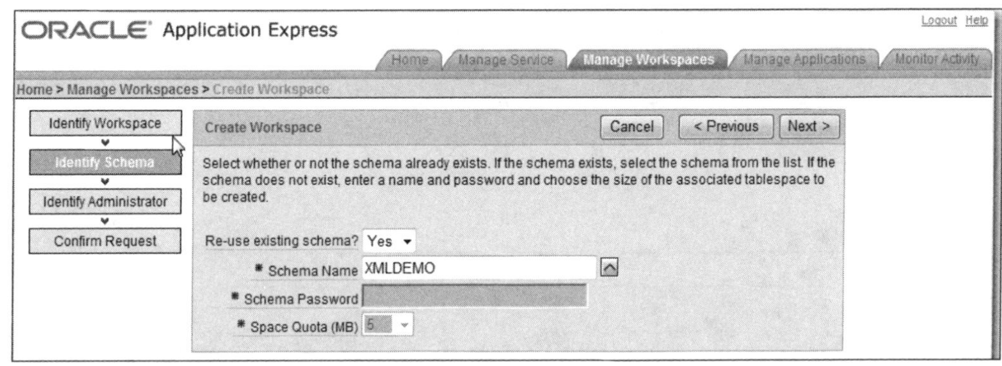

FIGURE A-6. *Specifying APEX Workspace Database Schema*

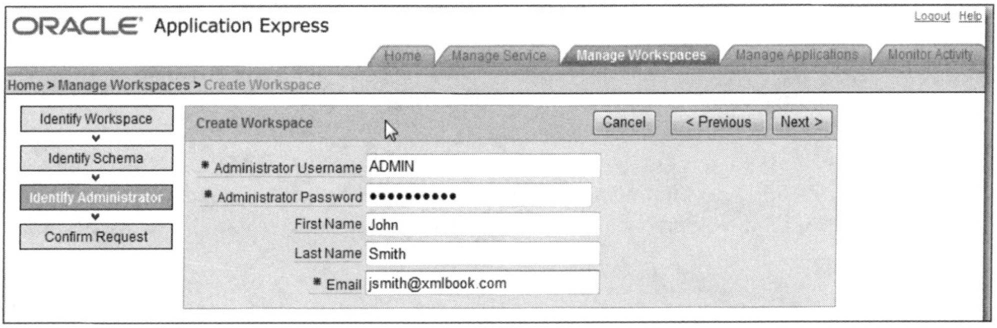

FIGURE A-7. *Creating Workspace ADMIN*

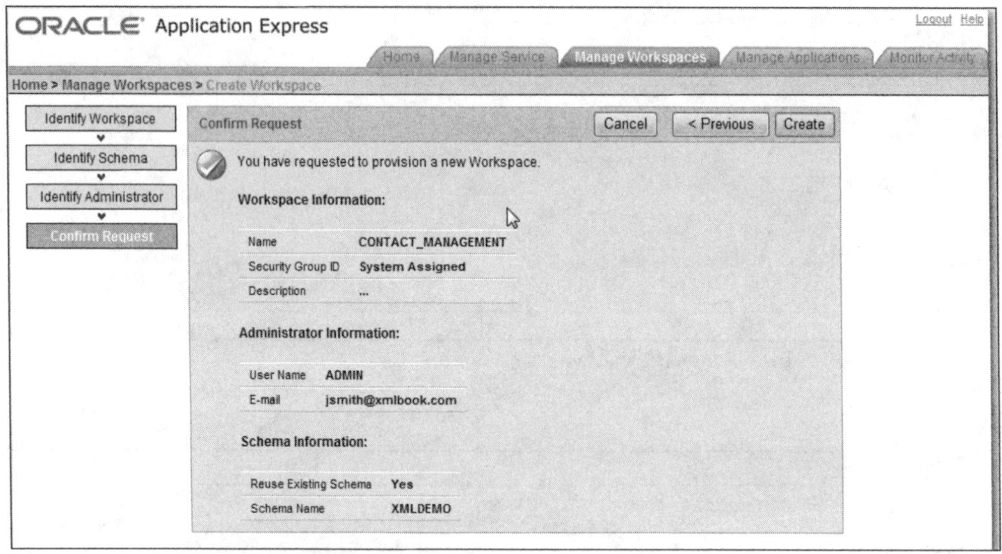

FIGURE A-8. *Confirming the request*

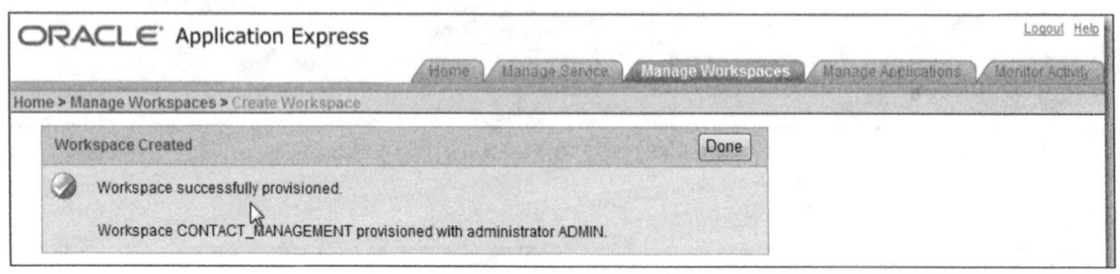

FIGURE A-9. *Workspace successfully created*

After the workspace is created, you can log out of the APEX admin UI. Now, the APEX is ready for application development. To start using the created APEX workspace, you just need to log in to the APEX development site (*http://localhost:8081/apex*) using the workspace admin user.

Index

B

C

D

E

F

G

H

I

J

O

P

Q

R

S

V

W

X

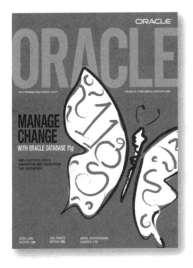

Want your own FREE subscription?

To receive a free subscription to *Oracle Magazine*, you must fill out the entire card, sign it, and date it (incomplete cards cannot be processed or acknowledged). You can also fax your application to +1.847.763.9638. **Or subscribe at our Web site at oracle.com/oraclemagazine**

○ **Yes, please send me a FREE subscription *Oracle Magazine*.** ○ No.

○ From time to time, Oracle Publishing allows our partners exclusive access to our e-mail addresses for special promotions and announcements. To be included in this program, please check this circle. If you do not wish to be included, you will only receive notices about your subscription via e-mail.

○ Oracle Publishing allows sharing of our postal mailing list with selected third parties. If you prefer your mailing address not to be included in this program, please check this circle.

If at any time you would like to be removed from either mailing list, please contact Customer Service at +1.847.763.9635 or send an e-mail to oracle@halldata.com. If you opt in to the sharing of information, Oracle may also provide you with e-mail related to Oracle products, services, and events. If you want to completely unsubscribe from any e-mail communication from Oracle, please send an e-mail to: unsubscribe@oracle-mail.com with the following in the subject line: REMOVE [your e-mail address]. For complete information on Oracle Publishing's privacy practices, please visit oracle.com/html/privacy/html

X

signature (required) date

name title

company e-mail address

street/p.o. box

city/state/zip or postal code telephone

country fax

Would you like to receive your free subscription in digital format instead of print if it becomes available? ○ Yes ○ No

YOU MUST ANSWER ALL 10 QUESTIONS BELOW.

① WHAT IS THE PRIMARY BUSINESS ACTIVITY OF YOUR FIRM AT THIS LOCATION? (check one only)

- □ 01 Aerospace and Defense Manufacturing
- □ 02 Application Service Provider
- □ 03 Automotive Manufacturing
- □ 04 Chemicals
- □ 05 Media and Entertainment
- □ 06 Construction/Engineering
- □ 07 Consumer Sector/Consumer Packaged Goods
- □ 08 Education
- □ 09 Financial Services/Insurance
- □ 10 Health Care
- □ 11 High Technology Manufacturing, OEM
- □ 12 Industrial Manufacturing
- □ 13 Independent Software Vendor
- □ 14 Life Sciences (biotech, pharmaceuticals)
- □ 15 Natural Resources
- □ 16 Oil and Gas
- □ 17 Professional Services
- □ 18 Public Sector (government)
- □ 19 Research
- □ 20 Retail/Wholesale/Distribution
- □ 21 Systems Integrator, VAR/VAD
- □ 22 Telecommunications
- □ 23 Travel and Transportation
- □ 24 Utilities (electric, gas, sanitation, water)
- □ 98 Other Business and Services ________

② WHICH OF THE FOLLOWING BEST DESCRIBES YOUR PRIMARY JOB FUNCTION? (check one only)

CORPORATE MANAGEMENT/STAFF

- □ 01 Executive Management (President, Chair, CEO, CFO, Owner, Partner, Principal)
- □ 02 Finance/Administrative Management (VP/Director/ Manager/Controller, Purchasing, Administration)
- □ 03 Sales/Marketing Management (VP/Director/Manager)
- □ 04 Computer Systems/Operations Management (CIO/VP/Director/Manager MIS/IS/IT, Ops)

IS/IT STAFF

- □ 05 Application Development/Programming Management
- □ 06 Application Development/Programming Staff
- □ 07 Consulting
- □ 08 DBA/Systems Administrator
- □ 09 Education/Training
- □ 10 Technical Support Director/Manager
- □ 11 Other Technical Management/Staff
- □ 98 Other

③ WHAT IS YOUR CURRENT PRIMARY OPERATING PLATFORM (check all that apply)

- □ 01 Digital Equipment Corp UNIX/VAX/VMS
- □ 02 HP UNIX
- □ 03 IBM AIX
- □ 04 IBM UNIX
- □ 05 Linux (Red Hat)
- □ 06 Linux (SUSE)
- □ 07 Linux (Oracle Enterprise)
- □ 08 Linux (other)
- □ 09 Macintosh
- □ 10 MVS
- □ 11 Netware
- □ 12 Network Computing
- □ 13 SCO UNIX
- □ 14 Sun Solaris/SunOS
- □ 15 Windows
- □ 16 Other UNIX
- □ 98 Other
- 99 □ None of the Above

④ DO YOU EVALUATE, SPECIFY, RECOMMEND, OR AUTHORIZE THE PURCHASE OF ANY OF THE FOLLOWING? (check all that apply)

- □ 01 Hardware
- □ 02 Business Applications (ERP, CRM, etc.)
- □ 03 Application Development Tools
- □ 04 Database Products
- □ 05 Internet or Intranet Products
- □ 06 Other Software
- □ 07 Middleware Products
- 99 □ None of the Above

⑤ IN YOUR JOB, DO YOU USE OR PLAN TO PURCHASE ANY OF THE FOLLOWING PRODUCTS? (check all that apply)

SOFTWARE

- □ 01 CAD/CAE/CAM
- □ 02 Collaboration Software
- □ 03 Communications
- □ 04 Database Management
- □ 05 File Management
- □ 06 Finance
- □ 07 Java
- □ 08 Multimedia Authoring
- □ 09 Networking
- □ 10 Programming
- □ 11 Project Management
- □ 12 Scientific and Engineering
- □ 13 Systems Management
- □ 14 Workflow

HARDWARE

- □ 15 Macintosh
- □ 16 Mainframe
- □ 17 Massively Parallel Processing
- □ 18 Minicomputer
- □ 19 Intel x86(32)
- □ 20 Intel x86(64)
- □ 21 Network Computer
- □ 22 Symmetric Multiprocessing
- □ 23 Workstation Services

SERVICES

- □ 24 Consulting
- □ 25 Education/Training
- □ 26 Maintenance
- □ 27 Online Database
- □ 28 Support
- □ 29 Technology-Based Training
- □ 30 Other
- 99 □ None of the Above

⑥ WHAT IS YOUR COMPANY'S SIZE? (check one only)

- □ 01 More than 25,000 Employees
- □ 02 10,001 to 25,000 Employees
- □ 03 5,001 to 10,000 Employees
- □ 04 1,001 to 5,000 Employees
- □ 05 101 to 1,000 Employees
- □ 06 Fewer than 100 Employees

⑦ DURING THE NEXT 12 MONTHS, HOW MUCH DO YOU ANTICIPATE YOUR ORGANIZATION WILL SPEND ON COMPUTER HARDWARE, SOFTWARE, PERIPHERALS, AND SERVICES FOR YOUR LOCATION? (check one only)

- □ 01 Less than $10,000
- □ 02 $10,000 to $49,999
- □ 03 $50,000 to $99,999
- □ 04 $100,000 to $499,999
- □ 05 $500,000 to $999,999
- □ 06 $1,000,000 and Over

⑧ WHAT IS YOUR COMPANY'S YEARLY SALES REVENUE? (check one only)

- □ 01 $500, 000, 000 and above
- □ 02 $100, 000, 000 to $500, 000, 000
- □ 03 $50, 000, 000 to $100, 000, 000
- □ 04 $5, 000, 000 to $50, 000, 000
- □ 05 $1, 000, 000 to $5, 000, 000

⑨ WHAT LANGUAGES AND FRAMEWORKS DO YOU USE? (check all that apply)

- □ 01 Ajax
- □ 02 C
- □ 03 C++
- □ 04 C#
- □ 05 Hibernate
- □ 06 J++/J#
- □ 07 Java
- □ 08 JSP
- □ 09 .NET
- □ 10 Perl
- □ 11 PHP
- □ 12 PL/SQL
- □ 13 Python
- □ 14 Ruby/Rails
- □ 15 Spring
- □ 16 Struts
- □ 17 SQL
- □ 18 Visual Basic
- □ 98 Other

⑩ WHAT ORACLE PRODUCTS ARE IN USE AT YOUR SITE? (check all that apply)

ORACLE DATABASE

- □ 01 Oracle Database 11*g*
- □ 02 Oracle Database 10*g*
- □ 03 Oracle9*i* Database
- □ 04 Oracle Embedded Database (Oracle Lite, Times Ten, Berkeley DB)
- □ 05 Other Oracle Database Release

ORACLE FUSION MIDDLEWARE

- □ 06 Oracle Application Server
- □ 07 Oracle Portal
- □ 08 Oracle Enterprise Manager
- □ 09 Oracle BPEL Process Manager
- □ 10 Oracle Identity Management
- □ 11 Oracle SOA Suite
- □ 12 Oracle Data Hubs

ORACLE DEVELOPMENT TOOLS

- □ 13 Oracle JDeveloper
- □ 14 Oracle Forms
- □ 15 Oracle Reports
- □ 16 Oracle Designer
- □ 17 Oracle Discoverer
- □ 18 Oracle BI Beans
- □ 19 Oracle Warehouse Builder
- □ 20 Oracle WebCenter
- □ 21 Oracle Application Express

ORACLE APPLICATIONS

- □ 22 Oracle E-Business Suite
- □ 23 PeopleSoft Enterprise
- □ 24 JD Edwards EnterpriseOne
- □ 25 JD Edwards World
- □ 26 Oracle Fusion
- □ 27 Hyperion
- □ 28 Siebel CRM

ORACLE SERVICES

- □ 28 Oracle E-Business Suite On Demand
- □ 29 Oracle Technology On Demand
- □ 30 Siebel CRM On Demand
- □ 31 Oracle Consulting
- □ 32 Oracle Education
- □ 33 Oracle Support
- □ 98 Other
- 99 □ None of the Above

08014004